Library of New Testament Studies

631

formerly the Journal for the Study of the New Testament Supplement series

Editor
Chris Keith

Editorial Board
Dale C. Allison, John M. G. Barclay, Lynn H. Cohick, R. Alan Culpepper,
Craig A. Evans, Robert Fowler, Simon J. Gathercole, Juan Hernandez Jr., John
S. Kloppenborg, Michael Labahn, Matthew Noveson, Love L. Sechrest, Robert Wall,
Catrin H. Williams, Britanny Wilson

The Divine Builder in Psalm 68

Jewish and Pauline Tradition

Todd A. Scacewater

LONDON • NEW YORK • OXFORD • NEW DELHI • SYDNEY

T&T CLARK
Bloomsbury Publishing Plc
50 Bedford Square, London, WC1B 3DP, UK
1385 Broadway, New York, NY 10018, USA
29 Earlsfort Terrace, Dublin 2, Ireland

BLOOMSBURY, T&T CLARK and the T&T Clark logo are trademarks of
Bloomsbury Publishing Plc

First published in Great Britain 2020
This paperback edition published in 2022

Copyright © Todd Scacewater, 2020

Todd Scacewater has asserted his right under the Copyright, Designs and Patents Act, 1988, to be identified as Author of this work.

All rights reserved. No part of this publication may be reproduced or transmitted in any form or by any means, electronic or mechanical, including photocopying, recording, or any information storage or retrieval system, without prior permission in writing from the publishers.

Bloomsbury Publishing Plc does not have any control over, or responsibility for, any third-party websites referred to or in this book. All internet addresses given in this book were correct at the time of going to press. The author and publisher regret any inconvenience caused if addresses have changed or sites have ceased to exist, but can accept no responsibility for any such changes.

A catalogue record for this book is available from the British Library.

A catalog record for this book is available from the Library of Congress.

ISBN: HB: 978-0-5676-9422-5
PB: 978-0-5677-0522-8
ePDF: 978-0-5676-9423-2
ePUB: 978-0-5676-9425-6

Series: Library of New Testament Studies, volume 631
ISSN 2513–8790

Typeset by Newgen KnowledgeWorks Pvt. Ltd., Chennai, India

To find out more about our authors and books visit www.bloomsbury.com and sign up for our newsletters.

Contents

List of Tables		viii
List of Abbreviations		ix
Introduction		1
1	Ephesians 4:8 in Context	9
	Authorship of Ephesians	9
	Pseudepigraphy in the Ancient World	10
	Objections to Paul's Authorship of Ephesians	12
	Summary on Authorship	14
	Destination of Ephesians	15
	The Literary Context of Ephesians 4:8	17
	The Discourse Function of Ephesians 4:8	18
	Gifts for Building the Temple in Ephesians 4:7–16	24
	The Temple Theme in Colossians	26
2	Gifts for Building the Temple in Psalm 68:19	31
	Hermeneutical Approaches to the Psalter	31
	The Narratival Structure of Psalm 68	36
	War Spoils as Gifts to God for Building the Temple	46
	Conclusion	49
3	The Divine Builder Literary Topos	51
	The Divine Builder	52
	Egyptian Texts	52
	Assyrian Texts	53
	Ugaritic *Baal Cycle*	55
	Babylonian *Enuma Eliš*	58
	Aramean Texts	59
	Summarizing the Traditions	60
	Distinctives in the Traditions	61

	Yahweh as Baal?	62
	Who Is Riding on What?	62
	Words and Ideas Possibly Reminiscent of Baal	67
	Similarity of the Divine Builder Motif	68
	Conclusion on Psalm 68 and Baal Traditions	69
	Conclusion	69
4	**Old Testament Scripture in Psalm 68**	**71**
	Three Victory Songs	72
	Characteristics of Victory Songs	72
	Exodus 15, Judges 5, and Psalm 68 as Songs of Victory	73
	Dating Ancient Poetry	75
	Characteristics of Ancient Poetry	75
	Dating Exodus 15	75
	Dating Judges 5	78
	Dating Psalm 68	80
	Conclusions to Dating	83
	Deborah's Use of the Song of the Sea	83
	Psalm 68's Use of Judges 5 and Exodus 15	84
	Psalm 68's Vision of the Latter Days	87
5	**Psalm 68 in Early and Late Judaism**	**91**
	Mosaic Interpretation of Psalm 68	91
	Evidence of the Mosaic Interpretation of Psalm 68	91
	Pushing the Mosaic Tradition Back	97
	Eschatological Interpretation of Psalm 68	102
	The Editors of the Hebrew Psalter	102
	Psalm 68 in the Septuagint	104
	The Dead Sea Scrolls	105
	Summary of the Eschatological Interpretation	115
	Conclusion	117
6	**Psalm 68 in Ephesians 4:8–10**	**119**
	Previous Views of the Use of Psalm 68:19 in Ephesians 4:8	119
	Psalm 68:19 as Directly Prophetic of Christ	120
	Borrowing from an Alternative Text Form	123
	Contextual Solutions to Paul's Use of Psalm 68:19	126

Paul's Use of Psalm 68:19 in Ephesians 4:8	129
Paul's Change from "Received" to "Gave"	134
Christ's Descent in Ephesians 4:9–10	135
Ephesians 4:9–10 as a Descent to Hades	136
Ephesians 4:9–10 as the Incarnation	138
Ephesians 4:9–10 as the Descent of the Spirit at Pentecost	140
Evaluating the Three Views of Ephesians 4:9–10	141
Conclusions on Ephesians 4:9–10	147
Paul's Theological Use of Psalm 68:19	148
Paul's Rhetorical Use of Psalm 68:19	151
Conclusion	152
Conclusion	155
Bibliography	159
Scripture Index	175
Subject Index	185

Tables

1.1	The Church as the Temple in Ephesians 4:11–16	25
3.1	"Rider" Passages in Psalm 68 as Allusions to Deuteronomy 33	66
4.1	Allusions to Judges 5 in Psalm 68	85
5.1	1QM XII, 7–16's Use of OT Traditions Used by Psalm 68	116
5.2	Psalm 68's Use of Genesis 49, Numbers 23–24, and Deuteronomy 32–33	117

Abbreviations

AB	Anchor Bible
AEL	Lichtheim, Miriam. *Ancient Egyptian Literature: A Book of Readings.* 3 vols. Berkeley: University of California Press, 2006.
AIL	Ancient Israel and its Literature
AJSLL	*American Journal of Semitic Languages and Literature*
ANE	Ancient Near East
ANET	J. B. Pritchard, ed. *Ancient Near Eastern Texts Relating to the Old Testament.* 3rd ed. Princeton, NJ: Princeton University Press, 1969.
ANF	Coxe, A. Cleveland, Alexander Roberts, and James Donaldson, eds. *The Ante-Nicene Fathers.* American reprint of the Edinburgh Edition. New York: Charles Scribner's Sons, 1918.
AOAT	Alter Orient and Altes Testament
ArBib	The Aramaic Bible
ARI	Assyrian Royal Inscriptions
ATR	Anglican Theological Review
AUGGSE	Acta Universitatis Gothoburgensis: Gothenburg Studies in English
AUSDDS	Andrew University Seminary Doctoral Dissertation Series
AV	Authorized Version (King James Version [1611])
BBR	*Bulletin for Biblical Research*
BDAG	Bauer, Walter. *A Greek-English Lexicon of the New Testament and Other Early Christian Literature.* Edited by Frederick W. Danker, William Arndt, and F. W. Gingrich. 3rd ed. Chicago, IL: University of Chicago Press, 2000.
BECNT	Baker Exegetical Commentary on the New Testament
BHGNT	Baylor Handbook on the Greek New Testament
BHT	Beiträge zur historischen Theologie
BIBALDS	BIBAL Dissertation Series
BIS	Biblical Interpretation Series
BJS	Biblical and Judaic Studies
BO	*Bibliotheca Orientalis*
BibOr	Biblica et Orientalia
BRS	The Biblical Resource Series
BS	*Bibliotheca Sacra*
BSL	Biblical Studies Library
BTS	Biblisch-Theologische Studien
BWANT	Beiträge zur Wissenschaft vom Alten und Neuen Testament
BZAW	Beihefte zur Zeitschrift für die alttestamentliche Wissenschaft
CAG	Commentaria in Aristotelem Graeca

CBQ	*Catholic Bible Quarterly*
CJB	Complete Jewish Bible
COQG	Christian Origins and the Question of God
COS	William W. Hallo, ed. *The Context of Scripture: Canonical Compositions, Monumental Inscriptions, and Archival Documents from the Biblical World.* 3 vols. Leiden: Brill, 1997–2002.
CSB	Christian Standard Bible
CTL	Cambridge Textbooks in Linguistics
CTR	*Criswell Theological Review*
DPL	Hawthorne, Gerald F., Ralph P. Martin, and Daniel G. Reid, eds. *Dictionary of Paul and His Letters.* Downers Grove, IL: InterVarsity Press, 1993.
EB	Études Bibliques
EBS	Encountering Biblical Studies
ECC	The Eerdmans Critical Commentary
EKKNT	Evangelisch-Katholischer Kommentar zum Neuen Testament
ESV	English Standard Version
FAT	Forschungen zum Alten Testament
FB	Forschung zur Bibel
FC	Halton, Thomas P., ed. *The Fathers of the Church: A New Translation.* Washington, DC: Catholic University of America, 1947–.
FOTL	The Forms of the Old Testament Literature
FRLANT	Forschungen zur Religion und Literatur des Alten und Neuen Testaments
GBS	Gorgias Biblical Studies
GDBS	Gorgias Dissertations in Biblical Studies
HALOT	Koehler, Ludwig, Walter Baumgartner, and Johann J. Stramm. *The Hebrew and Aramaic Lexicon of the Old Testament.* Translated and edited under the supervision of Mervin E. J. Richardson. 4 vols. Leiden: Brill, 1994–99.
HAT	Handkommentar zum alten Testament
HBAT	Handbuch zum Alten Testament
HBI	A History of Biblical Interpretation
HCSB	Holman's Christian Standard Bible
HNT	Handbuch zum Neuen Testament
HR	*History of Religions*
HUCA	*Hebrew Union College Annual*
HUT	Hermeneutische Untersuchungen zur Theologie
HTKNT	Herders theologischer Kommentar zum Neuen Testament
ICC	The International Critical Commentary
JAOS	*Journal of the American Oriental Society*
JBL	*Journal of Biblical Literature*
JCS	*Journal of Cuneiform Studies*
JETS	*Journal of the Evangelical Theological Society*
JHS	*Journal of Hebrew Scriptures*
JPSTC	The JPS Torah Commentary

JSJPHRP	*Journal for the Study of Judaism in the Persian, Hellenistic, and Roman Period*
JSNT	*Journal for the Study of the New Testament*
JSNTSS	Journal for the Study of the New Testament Supplement Series
JSOT	*Journal for the Study of the Old Testament*
JSOTSS	Journal for the Study of the Old Testament Supplement Series
JSS	*Journal of Semitic Studies*
KEHAT	Kurzgefasstes exegetisches Handbuch zum Alten Testament
KHCAT	Kurzer Hand-Commentar zum Alten Testament
KTU	Dietrich, M., O. Loretz, and J. Sanmartin, eds. *Die Keilalphabetischen Texte aus Ugarit, einschliesslich der keilalphabetischen Texte ausserhalf Ugarits. Teil I: Transkription*. AOAT 24,1. Kevelaer: Butzon & Bercker, 1976.
LCL	Loeb Classical Library
LNTS	Library of New Testament Studies
LXX	Septuagint
MLALP	Mathematical Linguistics and Automatic Language Processing
MLBS	Mercer Library of Biblical Studies
MT	Masoretic Text
NAB	New American Bible
NAC	New American Commentary
NASB	New American Standard Bible
NET	New English Translation
NICNT	New International Commentary on the New Testament
NICOT	New International Commentary on the Old Testament
NIV	New International Version
NJB	New Jerusalem Bible
NLT	New Living Translation
NPNF	Schaff, Philip, and Henry Wace, eds. *The Nicene and Post-Nicene Fathers*. New York: Charles Scribner's Sons, 1908.
NRSV	New Revised Standard Version
NSBT	New Studies in Biblical Theology
NT	New Testament
NTD	Das Neue Testament Deutsch
NTS	*New Testament Studies*
NVBS	New Voices in Biblical Studies
NovT	*Novum Testamentum*
NovTSup	Supplements to Novum Testamentum
OBO	Orbis Biblicus et orientalis
ÖBSB	Österreichische Biblische Studien
OILS	Oxford Introductions to Language Study
OS	Oudtestamentische Studiën
OT	Old Testament
OTL	The Old Testament Library
OTM	Oxford Theological Monographs
PAST	Pauline Studies

ProEccl	*Pro Ecclesia*
PNTC	Pillar New Testament Commentaries
PPS	Popular Patristics Series
RevQ	*Revue de Qumran*
RevScRel	Revue des Sciences Religieuses
RINAP	The Royal Inscriptions of the Neo-Assyrian Period
SB	Subsidia Biblica
SBL	Studies in Biblical Literature
SBLDS	Society of Biblical Literature Dissertation Series
SBLMS	Society of Biblical Literature Monograph Series
SBLSS	Society of Biblical Literature Semeia Studies
SBLHBS	Society of Biblical Literature History of Biblical Studies
SBLRBS	Society of Biblical Literature Resources for Biblical Study
SBT	Studies in Biblical Theology
SC	Scripture in Context
SDSSRL	Studies in the Dead Sea Scrolls and Related Literature
SSN	Studia Semitica Neerlandica
SOTBT	Studies in Old Testament Biblical Theology
STDJ	Studies on the Texts of the Desert of Judah
SUNT	Studien zur Umwelt des Neuen Testaments
SNT	Studien zum Neuen Testament
SNTSMS	Society for New Testament Studies Monograph Series
SVT	Supplements to Vetus Testamentum
TAB	The Aramaic Bible
TDNT	*Theological Dictionary of the New Testament*. Edited by Gerhard Kittel and Gerhard Friedrich. Translated by Geoffrey W. Bromiley. 10 vols. Grand Rapids, MI: Eerdmans, 1964–76.
THNT	Theologischer Handkommentar zum Neuen Testament
TLZ	*Theologische Literaturzeitung*
TNTC	Tyndale New Testament Commentaries
TOTC	Tyndale Old Testament Commentaries
TSSI	Textbook of Syrian Semitic Inscriptions
TT	Text and Translations
TynBul	*Tyndale Bulletin*
UBL	Ugaritisch-Biblische Literatur
UCOP	University of Cambridge Oriental Publications
VT	Vetus Testamentum
WAW	Writings from the Ancient World
WBC	Word Biblical Commentary
WMANT	Wissenschaftliche Monographien zum Alten und Neuen Testament
WTJ	*Westminster Theological Journal*
WUNT	Wissenschaftliche Untersuchungen zum Neuen Testament
ZAW	*Zeitschrift für die alttestamentliche Wissenschaft*
ZBK	Zürich Bibelkommentare

Introduction

Therefore it says, "ascending on high, he took captive captives, he gave gifts to men."
—Eph 4:8

We would be hard-pressed to find a more difficult case study for the NT's use of the OT than Ps 68:19 in Eph 4:8.[1] In his letter to the Ephesians, the author adapted a text from a most ancient psalm, Ps 68, to describe a historical moment bound up with the crucifixion and resurrection of Jesus Christ. At first glance, there is little problem with the text. That Christ ascended to the right hand of God was a firm conviction for early Christians, based on Christian applications of Ps 110:1, "sit at my right hand until I make your enemies your footstool."[2] That he took captives is somewhat more ambiguous, but it was easily understood by the Fathers as Christ taking us captive from the grips of the devil. Finally, that Christ has gifted the church is beyond dispute and is made immediately clear by the surrounding context: "grace was given to each one of us" (Eph 4:7). The surface meaning of this text is therefore coherent within early Christianity.

However, when one attends to the context from which the author drew these words, the waters become murkier. Who ascended in the psalm? The immediate context (Ps 68:16–19) does not obviously answer this question. Who were the captives in the psalm, and are they the same in the context of Ephesians? What did "gifts" refer to in Ps 68:19? The quotation begins with "therefore it says," which is a far cry from, for example, the fulfillment formulas in Matthew's Gospel (ἵνα πληρωθῇ).[3] So does Eph 4:8 declare that the psalm has been fulfilled somehow, or is he simply illustrating a point with OT language, or something else? These problems are compounded by the fact that most commentators begin their exposition of Ps 68 by declaring it the most

---

[1] Throughout this study, I use MT versification for the Psalter, unless otherwise specified. Psalm 68 is labeled Ps 67 in the LXX, and its versification follows the MT by considering the superscription the first verse. The English versions do not label the superscription as a verse. Thus, Ps 68:2 in the MT is Ps 67:2 in the LXX and Ps 68:1 in English versions.

[2] Cited or alluded to in Matt 22:44; 26:64; Mark 12:36; 14:62; Luke 20:42; 22:69; Acts 2:34; Rom 8:34; 1 Cor 15:25; Eph 1:20; Col 3:1; Heb 1:3, 13; 8:1; 10:12; 12:2. See further, David M. Hay, *Glory at the Right Hand: Psalm 110 in Early Christianity*, SBLMS 18 (Nashville, TN: Abingdon Press, 1973).

[3] Matt 1:22, 2:15, 4:14, 12:17, 21:4, and 26:56.

difficult psalm in the entire Psalter to translate and interpret.[4] The biggest problem, of course, is that Ephesians does not retain the same language. The author altered the quotation in several ways, the most significant being his change from "you received" (Ps 68:19) to "he gave" (Eph 4:8).

This quotation has garnered considerable attention, as early as Justin Martyr, who employed it as a proof text without any indication of its hermeneutical difficulties.[5] Later Fathers, though, began considering these problems, especially the verbal change. Discussion advanced with early modern commentators, who debated mainly whether or not Ps 68:19 was a direct prophecy of Christ. But in the nineteenth century, critical scholarship began scrutinizing the NT's use of the OT in a rather negative light. One commentator could say of Eph 4:8 that it used Ps 68:19 "arbitrarily."[6] During the twentieth century, commentators renewed the Patristic search for a convincing hermeneutical explanation of the verbal change in the quotation. From the 1950s until today, the quotation has been analyzed in multifarious ways in dozens of articles, commentaries, and monograph sections. The most comprehensive analysis to date is H. Harris's dissertation, published in 1998 as *The Descent of Christ: Ephesians 4:7-11 and Traditional Hebrew Imagery*.[7] Harris tried to interpret Ps 68:19 primarily in light of a certain strand of Jewish interpretation of the verse without much consideration of the context of Ps 68 itself. Harris did not have the definitive word. Several scholars have advanced the conversation in the last two decades, and most have taken a different direction than Harris. The questions posed above, and attendant questions not yet raised, have yet to receive definitive answers. Indeed, answers to date may not even be deemed satisfactory to a majority of those who have studied the quotation. Another full investigation like Harris's is therefore warranted, especially if it uses a vastly different approach than Harris's.

This investigation of Ps 68:19 in Eph 4:8 fits into the wider topic of the NT's use of the OT. The bibliography for this topic is now enormous, but we can briefly survey the major points of contention. First, from where did the NT authors pull their quotations? Did they cite them from their own study through their own interpretive ingenuity, or were there collections of proof texts (*testimonia*) from which they harvested citations? R. J. Harris wrote the definitive work arguing for the use of *testimonia* by the apostolic writers.[8] But while such collections are extant in Patristic writings, positing that the NT authors used them requires abductive logic (reasoning to the best explanation of the available evidence). C. H. Dodd in the 1950s provided a serious alternative to Harris's *testimonia* thesis by suggesting that the early church had an unofficial "Bible of the

---

[4] E.g., Mitchell J. Dahood, *Psalms*, AB (Garden City, NY: Doubleday, 1966), 2:133; Sigmund Mowinckel, *The Psalms in Israel's Worship* (1962; repr. Grand Rapids, MI: Eerdmans 2004), 1:5; Artur Weiser, *The Psalms: A Commentary*, OTL (Philadelphia, PA: Westminster Press, 1962), 481; Hans-Joachim Kraus, *Psalms 60-150: A Commentary*, trans. Hilton C. Oswald (Minneapolis, MN: Fortress Press, 1993), 47.

[5] *Dial.* 39, 87.

[6] H. J. Holtzmann, *Kritik der Epheser- und Kolosserbriefe: Auf Grund einer Analyse ihres Verwandtschaftsverhältnisses* (Leipzig: Wilhelm Engelmann, 1872), 6.

[7] W. Hall. Harris, *The Descent of Christ: Ephesians 4:7-11 and Traditional Hebrew Imagery*, BSL (Grand Rapids, MI: Baker Books, 1998).

[8] R. J. Harris, *Testimonies*, 2 vols. (Cambridge: Cambridge University Press, 1916-1920).

early church."[9] He noticed that OT sections such as Isa 40–66, Dan 7–12, Gen 1–3 and 12–22, Deut 28–32, as well as other lesser cited passages such as Zech 9–14, Joel 2–3, and Pss 22 and 69 were significant for multiple authors of the NT. Thus, it was not only select verses that the authors were attracted to but also larger contexts, which happened to revolve around a plotline resembling Jesus's life, death, and vindication. A. C. Sundberg Jr. suggested that Dodd's early Bible thesis fails for the same reason the *testimonia* thesis fails, namely, that if it existed, it surely would have survived in some form.[10] Perhaps because of Sundberg's critique, Dodd later clarified that he was not suggesting a physical book but an unofficial set of texts that were significant for early Christians as they wrestled with how a dying and rising Messiah fit with their expectations formed from the OT.[11] David Lincicum has brought this discussion up to date by considering the evidence from Qumran for various collections of OT excerpts, and he argues that, at least with respect to Paul, he probably employed multiple means of engaging with Scripture, not ruling out excerpted collections, but not totally relying upon them either.[12]

Dodd provided a plausible alternative to the *testimonia* theory, but the most lasting contribution from his *According to the Scriptures* was his argumentation throughout the book that, when the NT authors cite the OT, they to greater and lesser extents have the wider context in mind. For example, Matthew, Mark, John, and the author of Acts all appeal to different verses of Ps 69, which points to the conclusion that the psalm *in its entirety* was significant for the early church as a witness to Jesus.[13] He concluded that this NT hermeneutic, which sought out broader contexts to illuminate the work of Christ, originated with "Jesus Christ Himself who first directed the minds of His followers to certain parts of the scriptures as those in which they might find illumination upon the meaning of His mission and destiny."[14]

Influential works such as B. Lindars's *New Testament Apologetic* in 1961 and R. Longenecker's *Biblical Exegesis in the Apostolic Period* in 1974 challenged the notion that NT authors used the OT contextually.[15] Lindars argued that NT authors used the OT apologetically, using proof texts ripped from their contexts to undergird Christological doctrine. Longenecker argued that the NT authors used contemporary Jewish hermeneutical methods so that, while their results are inspired and authoritative, their methodology is not normative. Influential works supporting Dodd's contextual notion were E. E. Ellis's *Paul's Use of the Old Testament* in 1957 and R. T. France's *Jesus*

---

[9] C. H. Dodd, *According to the Scriptures: The Sub-Structure of New Testament Theology* (London: Nisbet, 1952).

[10] Albert C. Sundberg Jr., "On Testimonies," *NovT* 3 (1959): 280.

[11] C. H. Dodd, "The Old Testament in the New," in *The Right Doctrine from the Wrong Texts: Essays on the Old Testament in the New*, ed. G. K. Beale (Grand Rapids, MI: Baker Books, 1994), 171–72.

[12] David Lincicum, "Paul and the Testimonia: quo vademus?" *JETS* 51, no. 2 (2008): 297–308.

[13] Dodd, *According to the Scriptures*, 57–59.

[14] Ibid., 110.

[15] Barnabas Lindars, *New Testament Apologetic: The Doctrinal Significance of the Old Testament Quotations* (London: SCM Press, 1961); Richard N. Longenecker, *Biblical Exegesis in the Apostolic Period* (Grand Rapids, MI: Eerdmans, 1974).

and the Old Testament in 1971.¹⁶ While neither work focused solely on the contextual issue, their analysis of OT quotations and allusions from the pen of Paul and the lips of Jesus suggested a more or less contextual approach. R. Hays in 1989 advanced the field with a study on Paul's use of the OT that analyzed not only explicit quotations but also "allusions" and "echoes."[17] He demonstrated that Paul's letters are more saturated with Israel's Scriptures than it appears at first sight and that Paul quoted more or less contextually, although always with a transformation of meaning. One might consider the culmination of the history of this field to be the publication in 2007 of the *Commentary on the New Testament Use of the Old Testament*, which analyzes every quotation, every clear allusion, and many purported echoes of the OT in the NT.[18] The contextual question is not yet settled convincingly. Some believe the NT authors were always (or almost always) contextual; some believe they were sometimes contextual; others believe they were rarely, if ever, contextual.[19] We may be approaching the point of diminishing returns in our investigation of the contextual question, but on a text as problematic as Ps 68:19 in Eph 4:8, a full investigation can still contribute significantly to the discussion.

Another issue involved in the NT's use of the OT is the extent to which Christ may be found, read into, or foreshadowed in the OT. Patristic hermeneutics tended to find Christ everywhere in the OT, whether through typology, allegory, direct prophecy, prosopological exegesis, or some other means.[20] Modern critical OT scholarship has emphasized the ancient Near Eastern context of Israel's Scriptures, which has resulted in a loss of Messianism, Christophanies, and other forms of the presence of Christ in the OT.[21] Christ has become more the climax of Israel's long narrative, or the conclusion to an unfinished story, rather than one who sporadically appears throughout Israel's history in various forms.[22] Various works, however, still emphasize reading the OT Christocentrically by various means. G. Hasel, for example, has given seven ways the NT and OT can be read together to facilitate reading the OT Christocentrically, and many of these are still used widely.[23] This debate currently has no end in sight. Ephesians 4:8 is wrapped up in the debate, though, since the language of Ps 68:19 is applied to Christ. So here again we have another test case for trying to understand how

---

[16] R. T. France, *Jesus and the Old Testament: His Application of Old Testament Passages to Himself and His Mission* (1971; repr., Vancouver, B.C.: Regent College, 1998); E. Earle Ellis, *Paul's Use of the Old Testament* (1957; repr., Eugene, OR: Wipf & Stock, 1981).

[17] Richard B. Hays, *Echoes of Scripture in the Letters of Paul* (New Haven, CT: Yale University Press, 1989).

[18] G. K. Beale and D. A. Carson, eds, *Commentary on the New Testament Use of the Old Testament* (Grand Rapids, MI: Baker Academic, 2007).

[19] E.g., Christopher D. Stanley's *Arguing with Scripture: The Rhetoric of Quotations in the Letters of Paul* (New York: T&T Clark International, 2004), argues from a new methodology (rhetorical criticism) that Paul generally cites non-contextually as a move of power to coerce his audience into obedience.

[20] E.g., Ignatius, *Magn.* 8:2; *Phld.* 2; Barn. 10:2; 8:6–7; Justin, *Dial.* 91, 114, 131; Irenaeus, *Dem.* 6, 46, 49; Origen, *De Prin.* 11–17; Augustine, *Civ.* 15.2; 16.43. Examples could be multiplied.

[21] E.g., the last thorough positive investigation of Christology in the OT might be considered Ernst Wilhelm Hengstenberg, *Christology of the Old Testament and a Commentary on the Messianic Predictions*, trans. Theodore Meyer and James Martin, 4 vols. (1872–1878; repr., Grand Rapids, MI: Kregel, 1956).

[22] E.g., N. T. Wright, *The New Testament and the People of God* (Minneapolis, MN: Fortress Press, 1992).

[23] Gerhard F. Hasel, *New Testament Theology: Basic Issues in the Current Debate* (Grand Rapids, MI: Eerdmans, 1978), 186–96.

Christ relates to and fulfills Israel's Scriptures. This case is complicated, though, by the verbal change in the quotation, so a simple answer is not forthcoming.

A thorough study of Ps 68:19 in Eph 4:8 will be useful for other reasons not yet mentioned. Ephesians 4:9–10 is an interpretation of the quotation in 4:8 and refers to the descent of Christ to the "lower regions of the earth." When the Apostle's Creed says "κατελθόντα εἰς τὰ κατώτατα" ("having descended into the lowest parts"), it surely borrowed its language from Eph 4:9 (κατέβη εἰς τὰ κατώτερα τῆς γῆς, "he descended into the lower regions of the earth"). There are in fact three mainline interpretations of Eph 4:9's "lower regions of the earth," but early Christians clearly understood it to refer to Christ's descent into the underworld (known as the *descensus ad inferos*). Since Eph 4:9–10 is the author's own interpretation of the quotation in Eph 4:8, a full investigation of the quotation will better equip us to understand what the descent is and why the author brings it up here.

Those interested in Ephesians will also benefit from further study of this quotation. Ephesians 4:8–10 is significant for the study of the epistle because so many themes coalesce in these three verses, such as divine warfare, spiritual powers, Christ's fullness, the use of the OT, Christology, pneumatology, atonement, the ascension and the heavenly places, and corporate theological structures. One of these corporate structures in Eph 4:7–16—the temple of God—has remained unnoticed by almost all those who have written on this issue, and yet it is the largest of several keys that help us understand how the author is using Ps 68.

Finally, Ps 68, as noted above, is fraught with interpretive difficulties. Most studies of Ps 68:19 in Eph 4:8 provide some analysis of the psalm, but nothing extensive.[24] Two monographs have been written on Ps 68 itself, but neither have been received as definitive solutions for its many problems.[25] Scholars continue to publish articles on various issues throughout the psalm, but there appears to be no growing consensus on its structure, meaning, tradition-historical background, or theology. In Chapters 2, 3, and 4, I argue for a narratival structure in Ps 68 that coheres with a common ancient Near Eastern literary topos. I also tackle the many proposed Ugaritic parallels in the psalm since they could affect my narratival argument. Thus, while I hope my main contribution will be in understanding the quotation of the psalm in Ephesians, I do also hope my chapters on the psalm will be useful to OT scholars as they continue to wrestle with its difficulties.

That I devoted half of this study to the OT context of the quotation is an indication of the methodology I employ. One author has recently suggested that the OT context is not the key to understanding the use of the psalm in Eph 4:8 but rather the LXX and its use of κύριος.[26] This author had plausible reasons for coming to this conclusion, but my methodology begins by searching first for contextual reasons why an author might

---

[24] Perhaps the most comprehensive exegesis of the psalm in a study of Eph 4:8 is the approximately ten pages in Rainer Schwindt, *Das Weltbild des Epheserbriefes: Eine religionsgeschichtlich-exegetische Studie*, WUNT 148 (Tübingen: Mohr Siebeck, 2002), 399–409.

[25] Sigmund Mowinckel, *Der achtundsechzigste Psalm* (Oslo: I kommisjon hos J. Dybwad, 1953); J. P. LePeau, "Psalm 68: An Exegetical and Theological Study" (PhD diss., University of Iowa, 1981).

[26] Seth Ehorn, "The Use of Psalm 68(67).19 in Ephesians 4.8: A History of Research," *CBR* 12, no. 1 (2013): 96–120.

have employed Scripture from any specific context. There are indeed some problematic NT texts that are difficult to explain as contextual uses of the OT, but they are few and far between and are therefore not representative of a NT hermeneutic.[27] The fact that the NT authors were drawn to certain contexts more than others (e.g., Isa 40–66) suggests they were not simply proof-texting but rather reading the broader contexts of the story of their forefathers and attempting to understand them fully in light of what happened in Christ's death and resurrection. This conviction is the reason I spend three chapters analyzing the psalm's structure, meaning, and theology, as well as v. 19's function in the psalm.

Also important is that we analyze the psalm within its ancient Near Eastern milieu. Often, the analysis of a quotation's OT context focuses on literary features to the exclusion of the historical and social context of the text's composition. Probably canonical criticism, which focuses on the final form of the text as the faithful community read it, is largely responsible for this imbalance in reading OT texts. Given the complexity of critical methodologies in OT studies, canonical criticism has offered a way for NT scholars to read the text "as it is" and to look for clues as to why the NT author would be drawn to such a passage. The genuine complexities of OT passages—the interpretations of which involve comparative philology, history of religions, ancient Oriental religious and literary motifs, archaeology, geography, and other areas of OT specialty—are generally beyond the competency of NT scholars, or else the time required to investigate an OT passage in this manner would be prohibitive for research projects. One attempt to improve the methodology of a contextual approach to NT quotations would be to analyze Ps 68 thoroughly in its ancient Near Eastern milieu without skimping on historical investigation, as I attempt to do in this study.

This approach to studying the OT context of a citation has implications for the "contextual question." The NT authors did not possess the modern tools we have for studying the OT contextually.[28] We therefore have the potential to draw more meaning out of a text than the NT authors did with respect to the historical dimension of a text's meaning.[29] This fact suggests that there are really two contextual questions. First, is

---

[27] E.g., Gal 3:19; 1 Cor 10:1–4; Rom 10:6–8; Gal 3:16; 1 Cor 9:9; Gal 4:24; Melchizedek in Heb 7; 1 Pet 1:24–25.

[28] E.g., ancient texts from Israel's neighbors, comparative philology, modern textual criticism, and comparative religions are all tools that we possess that the NT authors did not, or at least did not to the same extent. For various takes on the contextual method, see William W. Hallo, "Compare and Contrast: The Contextual Approach to Biblical Literature," in *The Bible in the Light of Cuneiform Literature*, ed. William W. Hallo, B. W. Janes, and G. L. Mattingly, SC 3 (Lampeter: Edwin Mellen, 1990), 1–30; Brent A. Strawn, "Comparative Approaches: History, Theory and the Image of God," in *Method Matters: Essays on the Interpretation of the Hebrew Bible in Honor of David L. Petersen*, ed. Joel M. LeMon and Kent H. Richards, SBLRBS 56 (Atlanta, GA: Society of Biblical Literature, 2009), 129–35; K. Lawson Younger, "The Figurative Aspect and the Contextual Method in the Evaluation of the Solomonic Empire (1 Kings 1–11)," in *The Bible in Three Dimensions: Essays in Celebration of Forty Years of Biblical Studies in the University of Sheffield*, ed. D. J. A. Clines, et al., JSOTSS 87 (Sheffield: Sheffield University Press, 1990), 157–75; Roberto Ouro, "Similarities and Differences between the Old Testament and the Ancient Near Eastern Texts," *Andrews University Seminary Studies* 49, no. 1 (2011): 5–32.

[29] Several scholars have recently emphasized three dimensions to a text's meaning: historical, theological, and literary. E.g., see Wright, *The New Testament and the People of God*, 47–144; Andreas Köstenberger and Richard Patterson, *Invitation to Biblical Interpretation: Exploring the*

the NT author's interpretation or application of a text—however incomprehensive it may be—faithful to the original meaning of the OT text? The author may only grasp a small amount of the total import of an OT text, but if his understanding is in line with the original meaning, then he has used the text "contextually."[30] If this first contextual question ("did the author interpret the OT text contextually?") were the only question, it would be unfair to interpret the OT text with tools unavailable to the NT authors and then use that interpretation as the standard by which to judge theirs. Thus, for this question, contextual study of the OT text with attention to its ancient Near Eastern milieu is less important.

The second contextual question, however, requires that we use all the tools available to us to discover as much meaning in the OT text as possible. This second question is, "how has the meaning of the OT text been transformed by its use in a new context?"[31] In order to answer this question, we cannot limit ourselves to the way the NT authors would have interpreted a text, or else we would only be comparing their understanding of a text with its meaning in its new context. Nor should we believe that the meaning of an OT text completely "filters" through an author's mind, so that only the meaning he consciously comprehends can transfer into its new context. Even though an author might not grasp some aspects of an OT text's meaning, some of that meaning might still carry over subconsciously. To determine how much meaning has transferred (continuity), and to see how the meaning has been transformed (discontinuity), we must search for as much meaning of the text as possible in its original and new context and then compare these two meanings. Those concerned with God as the "divine author" will be interested in this question since he is the only being who could know the full import of a text in its old and new contexts, and since he has an intention in authoring the text in both contexts. Answering these contextual questions helps us get at the divine intent in the original text and the way it has been transferred into and transformed in the NT.

As an example of meaning subconsciously transferring from an old to a new context, I argue in Chapter 3 that the psalmist uses a distinct literary topos from the ancient Near East. This topos is a key for recognizing significant thematic coherence between the psalm and Eph 4:7–16. But we cannot know whether the author of Ephesians would have been aware of such an ancient literary topos. He seems to have discerned some themes of the topos (e.g., divine warfare, temple building, and reception of gifts) and may have chosen to cite the text for that reason, but we know he could not have grasped the full meaning of the text (as no one can). In light of the preceding discussion, we face two questions. First, does the author's interpretation of Ps 68 accurately represent at least part of the original meaning of Ps 68? Second, how much of the original meaning of Ps 68:19 transferred to its new context in Ephesians? Since—as we will see—elements of the ancient topos pervade Ephesians, it may be

---

Hermeneutical Triad of History, Literature, and Theology (Grand Rapids, MI: Kregel Academic, 2011). Note that the NT authors may well draw more meaning out of an OT text than modern readers do with regard to the literary and theological dimension.

[30] Answering this first "contextual question" is complicated by the margin of error that exists because of the subjective elements of our own interpretation of both the OT text and the NT author's use of it.

[31] This second question is the one pursued more by Hays in his *Echoes of Scripture*, cited above.

that some meaning from Ps 68:19 has transferred subconsciously to its new context in Ephesians through the influence of the entire psalm on the author's thought. While the elements of Ps 68:19's meaning that fall outside of the author's awareness are irrelevant for judging whether he used the text contextually, they are relevant for the task of comparing Ps 68:19's original meaning with its transformed meaning in Eph 4:8.

This study divides into six chapters and a conclusion. The first chapter situates Eph 4:8 within its wider context, Eph 4:1–16, and argues for the presence of a motif that is significant for understanding the quotation of the psalm. Evidence for this same motif is also found throughout Ephesians and also Colossians, which corroborates my suggestion that the motif is present in Eph 4:1–16. Since some subsidiary matters in this study are affected by who authored Ephesians and the destination to which it was sent, the chapter opens with brief consideration of the evidence for both matters. After explaining the function of Eph 4:8 in its wider context in the first chapter, we turn to three chapters on the psalm, using the methodology described above. Chapter 2 predominantly argues for a narratival flow to the psalm with v. 19 as the narrative's climax. I also suggest that the "divine builder" literary topos is utilized in this psalm, so Chapter 3 presents evidence for the pervasive use of this topos throughout the ancient Near East. Chapter 4 then analyzes the psalm's use of prior OT traditions, which provides further corroborative evidence for my narratival reading of the psalm and which is essential for understanding the latter half of the psalm.

Chapter 5 analyzes Jewish uses of Ps 68, which are significant for two reasons. First, many NT scholars, including H. Harris in his influential monograph, have suggested that the author of Ephesians relied on Jewish traditions for his interpretation of Ps 68:19. I review the evidence for whether certain Jewish traditions were available in the first century and whether it is likely that the author of Ephesians would have known them, relied on them, or both. Even more important is the use of Ps 68 in the Dead Sea Scrolls. No one discussing Eph 4:8 has made much of the fact that a pesher was written on Ps 68, and no one has caught (what I argue is) the subtle use of Ps 68 in the War Scroll (1QM). The use of Ps 68 in the Dead Sea Scrolls is significant because it demonstrates an interpretive stream that is in line with the original meaning of the psalm for which I argue, and it provides precedent for the manner in which Ephesians applies the psalm to Christ.

The final chapter brings the previous five chapters to bear on the central question of how Eph 4:8 used the psalm. I provide a comprehensive history of interpretation of Ps 68:19 in Eph 4:8, demonstrating the lack of consensus on how the author used the psalm. I then provide my own understanding of how the author used the psalm and what I believe was the rationale for the verbal change in the quotation. Since Eph 4:9–10 is an explicit interpretation of Eph 4:8, I then provide an exegesis of Eph 4:9–10 and explain what the author meant by saying Christ descended "to the lower regions of the earth" and how this descent was inferred (or not) from the context of Ps 68. The chapter concludes with suggestions on the rhetorical effect the author might have intended with Eph 4:8–10 and on the contribution the citation makes theologically to broader Pauline theology.

Now we begin by turning briefly to introductory matters of the authorship and destination of Ephesians before we turn to the literary context of Eph 4:7–16.

1

Ephesians 4:8 in Context

In order to understand how an author is using a text, one must first understand the context in which that use occurs. The immediate context of the citation of Ps 68:19 in Eph 4:8 is the wider section 4:1–16. The purpose of this chapter is to analyze Eph 4:1–16 as a discourse unit and to discern the function of v. 8 in that context. Subsequently, I will make two arguments regarding the author's representation of the "gifts" that are given by Christ and the purpose for which they are given. These two arguments are integral for my understanding of how the author is using the psalm. Finally, I will add some corroborative evidence for these arguments by surveying similar ideas throughout Ephesians and Colossians. However, before this analysis, I must discuss some introductory matters relating to Ephesians. Authorship matters because the various NT authors have tendencies in the way that they use the OT and vary in the degree to which and the manner in which they are influenced by early Jewish traditions. The destination of Ephesians matters because the social milieu of the audience is an important component of investigating what the author would have meant in any specific utterance. For this study, the destination plays a large factor in interpreting Eph 4:9–10 and in the rhetorical effect of the author's use of Ps 68. And so we begin with a discussion of the authorship of Ephesians, followed by its destination, and finally on to the proper subject of this chapter, an analysis of Eph 4:1–16.

Authorship of Ephesians

Christians unanimously believed Paul wrote Ephesians until the modern period.[1] E. Evanson first objected to Pauline authorship in 1792 because the author of Ephesians did not know his readers (Eph 1:15–16; 3:2), while Paul knew the Ephesians well

---

[1] The earliest support comes from Irenaeus, *Ad. Haer.* 5.2.3; Clement of Alexandria, *Strom.* 4.8; *Paedagogus* 1.5; Marcion (cited in Tertullian, *Adv. Marc.* 5.17); Tertullian, *De Monogomia* 5; *De Praescriptionibus* 36; the gnostic writings *Exegesis of the Soul* (2.6.131), c. AD 200, and *Hypostasis of the Archons* (11.86.20–25), dated second or third century AD. For a thorough discussion of this early evidence, see Harold Hoehner, *Ephesians: An Exegetical Commentary* (Grand Rapids, MI: Baker Academic, 2002), 2–6. On the two Gnostic writings, see Clinton Arnold, "Ephesians, Letter to the," *DPL*, 241.

(Acts 19:1–21; 20:17–38).² In 1824, L. Usteri objected due to Ephesians' similarity to Colossians.³ W. M. L. De Wette followed suit in 1847, employing Evanson's and Usteri's arguments and adding arguments from style.⁴ Since these initial challenges, scholars have been divided. H. Hoehner surveyed scholars who have accepted, rejected, or have been uncertain of Pauline authorship from 1519 to 2001.⁵ In only five decades since 1851 have the majority of scholars surveyed by Hoehner denied Pauline authorship. The main arguments of this study do not hinge on Pauline authorship, although some of the more subsidiary arguments and the proposed rhetorical effects of Eph 4:8–10 on the audience are more plausible if Paul did author Ephesians. A survey of the evidence for authorship is therefore not irrelevant. Since Pauline authorship fits into the wider discussion about pseudepigraphy in the ancient world, and since some argue that the authorship issue is irrelevant because pseudepigraphy was an ethically acceptable practice in the early church, it is also worthwhile to briefly survey the discussions about pseudepigraphy first.

Pseudepigraphy in the Ancient World

Pseudepigraphy was a common Jewish practice that continued in the Christian tradition.⁶ The three major questions are whether pseudepigraphy was a standard and accepted literary practice, whether pseudepigraphers intended to deceive their readers, and what the early church's attitude was toward pseudepigraphs. These questions are tied up with the likelihood that Ephesians could be pseudepigraphal and the implications of viewing it as such.

Scholars now commonly claim that some or all pseudepigraphers did not intend to deceive their readers and that there are no ethical dilemmas with the practice.⁷

---

² Edward Evanson, *The Dissonance of the Four Generally Received Evangelists and the Evidence of their Respective Authenticity, Examined; With That of Some Other Scriptures Deemed Canonical*, 2nd ed. (Gloucester: D. Walker, 1805), 312–14. The first edition was published in 1792. Evanson argued that the majority of the NT documents were forgeries, including all the Gospels save Luke.
³ Leonhard Usteri, *Entwickelung des paulinischen Lehrbegriffes mit Hinsicht auf die übrigen Schriften des Neuen Testamentes: Ein exegetisch-dogmatischer Versuch* (Zürich: Orell, Füssli, und Compagnie, 1824), 1–8.
⁴ Wilhelm Martin Leberecht De Wette, *Kurze Erklärung der Briefe an die Colosser, an Philemon, an die Ephesier und Philipper* (Leipzig: Weidmann'sche Buchhandlung, 1847), 86–93.
⁵ Authors and their date of publication are listed in the chart on Hoehner, *Ephesians*, 9–18. Results with percentages are included in the charts on pp. 19–20. The survey includes only those who have published on the issue.
⁶ The standard collection of Jewish pseudepigrapha is *The Old Testament Pseudepigrapha*, ed. James H. Charlesworth, 2 vols. (Peabody, MA: Hendrickson, 2011). Most relevant for Ephesians are Christian pseudepigraphal epistles, e.g., *3 Corinthians, Epistle to the Laodiceans, Letters of Paul and Seneca, Letters of Jesus and Abgar, Letter of Lentulus*, and *Epistle of Titus*.
⁷ Andrew T. Lincoln, *Ephesians*, WBC 42 (Dallas: Word Books, 1990), lxx; C. Leslie Mitton, *The Epistle to the Ephesians: Its Authorship, Origin, and Purpose* (Oxford: Clarendon Press, 1951), 222; D. E. Nineham, "The Case against the Pauline Authorship," in *Studies in Ephesians*, ed. F. L. Cross (London: A. R. Mowbray, 1956), 22; Larry J. Kreitzer, *Hierapolis in the Heavens: Studies in the Letter to the Ephesians*, LNTS 368 (London: T&T Clark, 2007), 7; Karl Fischer, "Anmerkungen zur Pseudepigraphie im Neuen Testament," *NTS* 23 (1977): 76–81; W. J. Dalton, "Pseudepigraphy in the New Testament," *CTR* 5 (1983): 29–35; David Meade, *Pseudonymity and Canon: An Investigation into the Relationship of Authorship and Authority in Jewish and Early Christian Tradition*, WUNT 39 (Tübingen: J.C.B. Mohr, 1986), 103–61, esp. 103–5.

But these claims are substantiated by little evidence. The OT is no source for accepted pseudepigraphy because there are no authorial claims in the OT.[8] In Jewish pseudepigrapha, writers attempted to legitimate their authorial claims to bolster their authority, which suggests that known pseudepigrapha were not accepted as authoritative, inspired, or "canonical."[9] Concern for genuine authorship is explicit later in Josephus (*Ag. Ap.* 1.37–42) and the Talmud (*b. Bat.* 14b–15a). Pseudepigraphy was similarly condemned in the Greco-Roman world.[10] Some believe Porphyry and Iamblichus provide definitive evidence that it was acceptable for Pythagoras's disciples to publish in his name. But Porphyry distinguished between Pythagoras's genuine writings, those of his school, and pseudepigraphal works by "shameful people," while Iamblichus referred to students' compilations of Pythagoras's lecture notes.[11] Thus, in the ancient world, pseudepigraphy was common but was disparaged by those who did not practice it.[12]

There is also no evidence of which I am aware that pseudepigraphal *epistles* were morally acceptable. Greco-Roman pseudepigraphers never took pains to make their epistles appear authentic.[13] But the disputed Pauline letters in many places claim to be written by Paul, sometimes even warning against pseudepigraphers.[14] These passages are either blatant attempts at ancient identity theft or they are penned by Paul himself.

The early church shared the same negative attitude toward pseudepigraphy.[15] Pseudepigraphal epistles were not acceptable and were rejected outright by the church

---

[8] Daniel I. Block, "Recovering the Voice of Moses: The Genesis of Deuteronomy," *JETS* 44, no. 3 (2001): 386–87. Writings or prophecies are said to be of a specific person (e.g., "the vision of Isaiah, which he saw" [Isa 1:1]), but such clauses do not tell us who authored the final literary work.

[9] Compare 1 En. 1:1–2 with Deut 33:1; Num 24:15–16 (Armin D. Baum, "Authorship and Pseudepigraphy in Early Christian Literature: A Translation of the Most Important Source Texts and an Annotated Bibliography," in *Paul and Pseudepigraphy*, ed. Stanley E. Porter and Gregory P. Fewster, PAST 8 [Leiden: Brill, 2013], 24). See also 1 En. 82:1; 2 En. 47:1–2; Mart. Isa. 11:36–39.

[10] Herodotus, *Hist.* 2.117; Vitruvius, *De architectura* 7 pr. 3–11; Pliny the Elder, *Naturalis historia* pr. 21–23; Diogenes Laertius, *Lives* 8.54; 10.3; Galen, *In Hippocratis epidemiarum II commentarium*; Galen, *In Hippocratis de natura hominis commentarium* 1.44; Galen, *Libr. propr. pr*; Lucian, *Pseudol.* 30; Pausanias, *Descr.* 6.18.5.

[11] See Bart Ehrman, *Forgery and Counterforgery: The Use of Literary Deceit in Early Christian Polemics* (Oxford: Oxford University Press, 2014), 109; G. L. Archer, *Jerome's Commentary on Daniel* (Grand Rapids, MI: Baker, 1977), 15–16, 142, in which Jerome says that Porphyry condemned pseudepigraphy; Leonid Zhmud, *Wissenschaft, Philosophie und Religion im frühen Pythagoreismus* (Berlin: Akademie Verlag, 1997), 91; Iamblichus, *De Vita Pythagorica* 158, 198.

[12] Similar conclusions are reached by Jeremy Duff, "A Reconsideration of Pseudepigraphy in Early Christianity" (DPhil thesis, University of Oxford, 1998); Ehrman, *Forgery and Counterforgery*, 11–145; Baum, *Pseudepigraphie*, 149–77, although he allows for the legitimacy of the practice if the message, but not the exact wording, comes from the author; Lewis R. Donelson, *Pseudepigraphy and Ethical Argument in the Pastoral Epistles*, HUT 22 (Tübingen: J.C.B. Mohr, 1986), 9–23.

[13] Wilder, *Pseudepigraphy*, 217–43. Regarding the disputed Paulines, if they were in fact deutero-Pauline, then "the authors of these NT documents expended great effort to create verisimilitude for their works, sometimes going well out of their way to do so." If the disputed Paulines are pseudepigraphal, then they "give clear indication that they were written to deceive their readers" (236).

[14] E.g., Col 4:7–14 (cf. Phlm 23–24), 18; Eph 3:2–13; 6:19–23; 1 Tim 1:1–2; 3:14–15; Titus 1:4–5; 3:8, 12–14; 2 Tim 1:2; 4:9–18; 2 Thess 2:2 (!); 2 Thess 3:17 (!). His commendation of Tychichus in Ephesians matches nearly word-for-word the corresponding commendation in Col 4:7–8.

[15] Mur. Can. 64–65; Eusebius, *Hist. eccl.* 3.3.1–3; 3.25.4–7; 6.12.3; 6.25.13; cf. 2.25.4–7; Tertullian, *Bapt.* 17; *Cult. fem.* 1.3; *Marc.* 4.2; Epiphanius, *Pan.* 30.15.1–3; 38.2.5; Augustine, *Civ.* 15.23; *Tract. Ev. Jo.* 98.8; *Doctr. Chr.* 2.8.13; *Faust.* 33.6; see his unusual acceptance of Wisdom of Solomon and Sirach in *Civ.* 17.20, but he rules out all pseudepigrapha as authoritative in *Civ.* 18.38; Jerome *Vir. ill.* 4; *Epist.*

if known to be forged. If Ephesians is pseudepigraphal, it is deceptive in its many authorial claims and its personal and historical details, and the early church would have rejected it had they discovered that it was pseudepigraphal. Even so, many scholars still find linguistic, theological, and historical evidence to claim that Ephesians could not have been authored by Paul.

Objections to Paul's Authorship of Ephesians

Four arguments are generally adduced to argue against Paul's authorship of Ephesians. First, many claim that Ephesians has a significant amount of unique vocabulary—some of which occurs more frequently in post-apostolic literature than in the NT—and that its style is overly pleonastic.[16] But these objections are all reasonably countered. Much of the vocabulary is not as odd as is claimed and the relative proportion of *hapax legomena* is lower than in some of the undisputed epistles.[17] It is not rare for Paul's language to influence the Fathers.[18] Finally, Paul uses a pleonastic style many times elsewhere.[19] It should also be noted that many arguments ignore the role of amanuenses, coauthors, and preformed traditions,[20] and that advances in

---

107.12; *Prologus in libris Salomonis de hebraeo translates*; Salvian of Marseille's letter to Salonius, the bishop of Geneva, in A. E. Haefner, "A Unique Source for the Study of Ancient Pseudonymity," *ATR* 16 (1934): 11–15. As Wilder concludes, "the early church did not *knowingly* allow either pseudo-apostolic or heretical works to be read publicly in the churches along with apostolic writings. . . evidence is lacking for a convention of pseudonymity which existed amongst orthodox Christians" (Wilder, *Pseudepigraphy*, 147). See also Ehrman, *Forgery and Counterforgery*, 149–548; Baum, *Pseudepigraphie*, 31–148.

[16] Ephesians has forty *hapax legomena* and fifty-one words not found in the undisputed Paulines (Lincoln, *Ephesians*, lxv). For pleonastic style, see 1:3–14, 15–23; 3:1–7; 4:11–16; 5:7–13; 6:14–20. Examples of unique vocabulary include ἐπουρανίοις; ὁ ἠγαπημένος; χαριτόω; δίδωμι; διὸ λέγει; ὁ διάβολος. See further, Werner G. Kümmel and Paul Feine, *Introduction to the New Testament*, trans. Howard C. Kee (Nashville, TN: Abingdon Press, 1975), 252–53; Rudolf Schnackenburg, *Der Brief an die Epheser*, EKKNT (Zürich: Benziger, 1982), 22–23; Mitton, *Ephesians*, 8–10; Jürgen Becker and Ulrich Luz, *Die Briefe an die Galater, Epheser, und Kolosser*, NTD 8 (Güttingen: Vandenhoeck & Ruprecht, 1998), 110; Nils Alstrup Dahl, "Einleitungsfragen zum Epheserbrief," in *Studies in Ephesians: Introductory Questions, Text- & Edition-Critical Issues, Interpretation of Texts and Themes*, ed. David Hellholm, Vemund Blomkvist, and Tord Fornberg (Tübingen: Mohr Siebeck, 2000), 48.

[17] E.g., on διὸ λέγει, see 2 Cor 6:2; Gal 3:16; Rom 15:10; Paul alternates ἐπουρανίοις with οὐρανοῖς; διάβολος is only one of several synonyms Paul uses (1 Thess 3:5; 1 Cor 10:10; 2 Thess 3:1); see further the comprehensive study, A. van Roon, *The Authenticity of Ephesians*, SNT 39 (Leiden: Brill, 1975). On the *hapax legomena* in Ephesians, see P. N. Harris, *The Problem of the Pastoral Epistles* (London: Oxford University Press, 1921), 20.

[18] E.g., ἐπουράνιος according to *Thesaurus Linguae Graecae* is extant only thirty times prior to Paul. It is then used twelve times by Paul and seven times elsewhere in the NT, after which it occurs hundreds of times in the Fathers in ways that accord with Paul's use (e.g., 1 Clem. 61:2; 2 Clem. 20:5; Ign. *Eph.* 13:2; *Trall.* 5:1–2; 9:1; *Smyrn.* 6:1; Mart. Pol. 14:3; 23:5; Pol. *Phil.* 2:1). It seems clear that Paul, and Ephesians in particular, was the source of the proliferation of this word among the Fathers.

[19] For pleonastic sentences in the accepted Paulines, see Rom 3:21–26; 8:28–39; 11:33–36; 1 Cor 1:4–7; 1:26–29; 2:6–9; 1 Cor 12:8–11; Phil 1:3–8; 1 Thess 1:2–5; 2 Thess 1:3–10; Phil 1:27–2:11 (Peter T. O'Brien, *The Letter to the Ephesians*, PNTC [Grand Rapids, MI: Eerdmans, 1999], 7). A. van Roon provides fifty sentences in the accepted Paulines that correspond to the length of the pleonastic sentences in Ephesians (*The Authenticity of Ephesians*, 108).

[20] Amanuenses and coauthors: Rom 16:22; 1 Cor 16:21; Col 4:18; Phlm 19; 2 Thess 3:17; Gal 6:11. E. Earle Ellis, *History and Interpretation in New Testament Perspective*, BIS 54 (Atlanta,

stylometrics and register demonstrate problems with arguments from language and style.[21]

Second, many claim that the theology expressed in Ephesians differs from the undisputed Paulines or, more strongly, "makes the Pauline composition of the Epistle completely impossible."[22] Examples include revealed mysteries, ascension mysticism, religious cosmology, the nature of the law, the supposed lack of the cross and Christ's death, Christ's cosmic lordship, realized eschatology, and the status of Israel.[23] Some of these examples rest on debatable exegetical positions of various passages, while others assume hypothetical religio-historical backgrounds. A few themes could represent developments in Paul's thought.[24] Themes such as realized eschatology and Christ's cosmic lordship are carried over from Colossians. The value of theological themes for discussing Pauline authorship is limited since each theme is developed via debatable exegesis.

Third, parts of Ephesians may suggest that it was written from a time later than Paul's ministry. Ephesians 3:4–8 could reveal a pseudepigrapher feigning authority (3:5).[25] But it is reasonable to see Paul's self-presentation in Ephesians as coherent with his self-presentation in the undisputed Paulines.[26] Ephesians 4:7–16 could suggest a post-Pauline period when a multiplicity of teachings had developed.[27] But the exhortation to unity alludes back to the "one new man" of 2:13–18, not to contemporary heresies.[28] The ecclesiastical structure of the church in Ephesians does

---

GA: Society of Biblical Literature, 2001), 13; E. Randolph Richards, *Paul and First-Century Letter Writing: Secretaries, Composition, and Collection* (Downers Grove, IL: InterVarsity Press, 2004); Jerome Murphy-O'Connor, *Paul the Letter-Writer: His World, His Options, His Skills* (Collegeville, MN: Liturgical Press, 1995); Dalton, "Pseudepigraphy in the New Testament," 32.

Preformed traditions: see, e.g., Col 1:15–20; Phil 2:5–11; 1 Tim 3:16; E. Earle Ellis estimates (perhaps overzealously) that preformed pieces take up anywhere from 7% (Philippians) to 54% (Ephesians) to 72% (Jude) of NT writings (*The Making of the New Testament Documents*, BIS 39 [Leiden: Brill, 1999], 53–142).

[21] For stylometrics, see Anthony Kenny, *A Stylometric Study of the New Testament* (Oxford: Oxford University Press, 1986); Matthew Brook O'Donnell, "Linguistic Fingerprints or Style by Numbers? The Use of Statistics in the Discussion of Authorship of New Testament Documents," in *Linguistics and the New Testament: Critical Junctures*, ed. Stanley Porter and D. A. Carson, JSNTSS (Sheffield: Sheffield Academic Press, 1999), 206–62. For register, the seminal study is Douglas Biber, *Variation across Speech and Writing* (Cambridge: Cambridge University Press, 1988). For the application of register to the Pauline corpus, see Andrew W. Pitts, "Style and Pseudonymity in Pauline Authorship: A Register Based Confirguration," in *Paul and Pseudepigraphy*, 113–52.

[22] Kümmel and Feine, *Introduction to the New Testament*, 254.

[23] Nils Alstrup Dahl, "The Letter to the Ephesians: Its Fictional and Real Setting," in *Studies in Ephesians*, 456; Schnackenburg, *Epheser*, 23; Lincoln, *Ephesians*, lxiii–lxv.

[24] E.g., see Sigurd Grindheim, "A Deutero-Pauline Mystery? Ecclesiology in Colossians and Ephesians," in *Paul and Pseudepigraphy*, 173–95; Gregory MaGee, *Portrait of an Apostle: A Case for Paul's Authorship of Colossians and Ephesians* (Eugene, OR: Wipf & Stock, 2013), 28–37.

[25] As argued by Lincoln, *Ephesians*, lxiii; cf. Schnackenburg, *Epheser*, 23–25.

[26] As argued in MaGee, *Portrait of an Apostle*.

[27] Dahl, "The Letter to the Ephesians," 454. Schnackenberg also takes the mention of "apostles and prophets" as evidence of a later historical situation because Eph 2:20 makes them the foundation of the church (*Epheser*, 185).

[28] Similarly, Petr Pokorný, *Der Brief des Paulus an die Epheser*, THNT (Leipzig: Evangelische Verlagsanstalt, 1992), 160; Jean-Noël Aletti, *Saint Paul, Épître aux Éphésiens: Introduction, Traduction et Commentaire*, EB 42 (Paris: J. Gabalda, 2001), 207.

not necessitate a late date, since Paul mentions ecclesiastical leaders in his accepted letters (Phil 1:1; 1 Thess 5:12; 1 Cor 12:28; Phlm 2).[29] Nor must Eph 2:11–22 suggest a unified, second-century Catholic church, since 2:11–22 is more theological (or ideal) than historical. In sum, nothing in Ephesians must have been written in a post-Pauline era.

Fourth, Ephesians' relationship with the Pastorals and Colossians creates questions. P. Pokorný believes the portrayal of the church in Ephesians and the Pastorals is late, but he also stresses the different eschatologies, which makes a conflicted argument that the epistles are too similar *and* too different.[30] Ephesians' similarity to Colossians for many suggests a "changed perspective" in Ephesians, which "requires for its explanation a lapse of time."[31] But the literary similarities between Ephesians and Colossians are too overblown.[32] And if a pseudepigrapher were copying historical details from Colossians, why was Timothy not included as a coauthor, and why are all the names in Col 4 except Tychicus omitted? "No theory of imitation offers a suitable explanation of this inconcinnity."[33] Even the notion of Colossians's priority has been challenged in recent years by A. van Roon and E. Best, so that one cannot even be certain that Colossians could have been the *Vorlage* of Ephesians.[34]

Summary on Authorship

In summary, pseudepigraphy was common in the ancient world but generally was not accepted by those who did not practice it. Approaches to Ephesians as deutero-Pauline should not, then, shirk the ethical and canonical implications of such claims. While many arguments have been made for deutero-Pauline authorship, it is certainly not a foregone conclusion. This sketch of the evidence and arguments has been necessarily brief and I do not pretend to have solved any problems. For the purposes of this study, I will refer to the author as "Paul," which is more convenient than "the author of Ephesians" or some other designation. While I personally take Paul to be the author, I do not believe the central arguments of this work depend on that position. Pauline authorship is relevant to some of the details of my ancillary arguments, and the reader is free to decide whether those details hold true under a deutero-Pauline theory of authorship and to what extent my thesis would be affected in either case.

---

[29] See further, Roger W. Gehring, *House Church and Mission: The Importance of Household Structures in Early Christianity* (Peabody, MA: Hendrickson, 2004), 196–210.

[30] The relationship includes liturgical formulas (Eph 6:23; 1 Tim 1:14), concepts ("mystery" in Eph 5:32; 1 Tim 3:16; "word of truth" in Eph 1:13; 2 Tim 2:15), paraenetic forms (household codes) and "theological accents" (e.g., baptism as a bath of regeneration in Eph 5:26; Titus 3:5; "works" in Eph 2:10; 1 Tim 2:10; 6:18; 2 Tim 3:17; Titus 3:8). Pokorný, *Epheser*, 40.

[31] Lincoln, *Ephesians*, lxvii; cf. Pokorný, *Epheser*, 37.

[32] Similarly, Mitton, *Ephesians*, 55–75. In only four places in Ephesians do the verbal parallels extend beyond seven words; in two places, five words are parallel (O'Brien, *The Letter to the Ephesians*, 9).

[33] Bo Reicke, *Re-examining Paul's Letters: The History of the Pauline Correspondence*, ed. David P. Moessner and Ingalisa Reicke (Harrisburg, PA: Trinity Press International, 2001), 79.

[34] Roon, *Authenticity*, 413–37; Ernest Best, "Who Used Whom? The Relationship of Ephesians and Colossians," *NTS* 43 (1997): 72–96.

Destination of Ephesians

The destination of the letter we know as Ephesians is uncertain. The destination ἐν Ἐφέσῳ is missing from the earliest extant manuscripts (𝔓⁴⁶, B, ℵ) and the manuscripts used by Origen, Basil, and Tertullian, while Marcion called it "the epistle to the Laodiceans."[35] Πρὸς Ἐφεσίους was included as the title of the epistle as early as 𝔓⁴⁶ (c. AD 200), and several early sources indicate that the letter was sent to Ephesus.[36] Although Marcion in the mid-second century entitled it "the epistle to the Laodiceans," Tertullian says Marcion "was very desirous of giving it the *new* title (of Laodicean)," so both may have known the title πρὸς Ἐφεσίους.[37] The title πρὸς Ἐφεσίους was therefore definitely affixed by AD 200 and may have been affixed by the mid-second century. Yet ἐν Ἐφέσῳ did not enter Eph 1:1 of our extant manuscripts until the fifth century in Alexandrinus. There can be little doubt that the original text of Eph 1:1 lacked ἐν Ἐφέσῳ.[38]

Because most scholars take ἐν Ἐφέσῳ as a later addition, Ephesians has been understood as a general or circular letter. This theory fits Paul's seeming lack of personal knowledge of the audience (1:15–16; 3:2; 4:21), which contrasts with his intimate knowledge of the Ephesians (Acts 19:9–10; 20:17–38). Paul also excluded all the names from Colossians except the letter carrier Tychicus, perhaps because, as a general or circular letter, he could not know which churches would know his other coworkers. The lack of personal touches throughout the letter and the general nature of the exhortations also suggest a general audience.

Ephesians may have been a general or circular letter, but much depends on the original reading, especially whether a geographical destination was included.

The earliest extant readings are as follows:[39]

1. 𝔓⁴⁶: τοις αγιοις ουσιν και πιστοις εν Χριστω Ιησου
2. B: τοις αγιοις τοις ουσιν (εν Εφεσω) και πιστοις εν Χριστω Ιησου
3. ℵ: τοις αγιοις (πασι) τοις ουσι (εν Εφεσω) και πιστοις εν Χριστω Ιησου
4. A: τοις αγιοις πασιν τοις ουσιν εν Εφεσω και πιστοις εν Χριστω Ιησου

The three earliest readings are grammatically awkward because of the ουσιν. Some interpreters have accepted the reading of 1:1 in the manuscript available to them by

---

[35] Tertullian, *Marc.* 5.11, 17; Basil, *Eunom.* 2.19; for Origen's text, which is no longer extant, see J. A. F. Gregg, "The Commentary of Origen upon the Epistle to the Ephesians," *JTS* (1902): 235.
[36] Irenaeus, *Haer.* 5.2.3; Clement of Alexandria, *Paed.* 1.5.18; Tertullian, *Marc.* 5.17; Muratorian Canon.
[37] Translation from *ANF* 3.465.
[38] T. Zahn, *Introduction to the New Testament* (Edinburgh: T&T Clark, 1909), 1:482, had "no doubt" that ἐν Ἐφέσῳ is not original. It is possible that the phrase ἐν Ἐφέσῳ was original and was preserved in other text types, while 𝔓⁴⁶ and the Alexandrian text-types dropped the phrase, but we unfortunately have no evidence one way or another.
[39] Words in parentheses are included in the margins of the manuscript by a second hand.

providing an interpretation of the difficult grammar. Origen interpreted the phrase ontologically as "the saints who are" (cf. Exod 3:14; 1 Cor 1:28–29).[40] Alternatively, one could translate "to the saints who are also faithful," but such a construction is unparalleled. Pokorný suggests three further interpretations: (1) it is purposefully redundant; (2) it means that there are some saints who are not so through Jesus Christ (i.e., the saints of the OT); or (3) it means that some saints only superficially believe.[41] These interpretations are somewhat forced, and smoother solutions should be preferred, especially solutions that alleviate the grammatical awkwardness.[42] H. Lake and R. J. Cadbury interpreted οὖσιν adjectivally meaning "local" (cf. Acts 13:2; 28:17; Rom 13:1), but οὖσιν must be followed by an explanatory phrase to be used as a technical term meaning "local."[43] Their theory also fails to explain the καί, and E. Best asks why "only the ἅγιοι and not also the πιστοί are described as 'local.'"[44] Most problematic is that when Paul includes τοῖς οὖσιν in the destination line of his other epistles, the phrase is always followed by ἐν plus a geographical location (Rom 1:7; 2 Cor 1:1; Phil 1:1).[45]

Alternative solutions have been more speculative. A popular solution traced back to Theodore Beza is that Paul wrote it as a circular letter and left a blank after τοῖς οὖσιν for Tychicus to fill in the city name upon delivery.[46] But we might expect to find ἐν, with only the city name to be filled in.[47] A blank also would not actually save any time since copies are handwritten as a whole, and no examples of such a blank in an address have been found in other ancient letters.[48] Other NT circular or general letters specify their recipients, including one by Paul (Gal 1:1; 1 Pet 1:1). Best proposed a conjectural original reading, τοῖς ἁγίοις καὶ πιστοῖς ἐν Χριστῷ Ἰησοῦ.[49] But his theory about how οὖσιν entered the text is problematic, requiring overly blatant scribal blunders and much conjecture about the letter's title. His attempt to explain the generation of the earliest texts also seems to confuse their dates.

Other speculative solutions have conjectured an original text with geographical locations. A. van Roon and A. Lincoln argued for τοῖς ἁγίοις τοῖς οὖσιν ἐν Ἱεραπόλει

---

[40] Gregg, "Commentary of Origen," 235. P. Pokorný rightfully calls this interpretation "reine Spekulation" (*Der Brief des Paulus an die Epheser*, 36).
[41] Ibid., 37.
[42] Similarly, E. Best, "Ephesians 1.1," in *Essays on Ephesians* (Edinburgh: T&T Clark, 1997), 5.
[43] Van Roon, *The Authenticity of Ephesians*, 2.
[44] Best, "Ephesians 1.1," 6.
[45] See also the same formula in Ignatius's letters, *Eph.* 1.1; *Smyrn.* 1.1; *Phld.* 1.1; *Trall.* 1.1.
[46] Ernst Percy, *Die Probleme der Kolosser- und Epheserbriefe* (Lund: C. W. K. Gleerup, 1946), 458–66; tentatively suggested as possible by E. K. Simpson and F. F. Bruce, *Commentary on the Epistles to the Ephesians and the Colossians*, NICNT (Grand Rapids, MI: Eerdmans, 1957), 250; still followed by Hanna Stettler, *Heiligung bei Paulus: Ein Beitrag aus biblisch-theologischer Sicht*, WUNT 2/368 (Tübingen: Mohr Siebeck, 2014), 568, and the NET Bible in the notes on Eph 1:1.
[47] T. Zahn, *Introduction to the New Testament* (Edinburgh: T&T Clark, 1909), 1:483; Lincoln, *Ephesians*, 3; Pokorný, *Epheser*, 35.
[48] On the lack of blanks in ancient letters, see Otto Roller, *Das Formular der Paulinischen Briefe: Ein Beitrag zur Lehre vom antike Briefe*, BWANT (Stuttgart: W. Kohlhammer, 1933), 199–212, 520–25; followed by Kümmel and Feine, *Introduction to the New Testament*, 355; Lincoln, *Ephesians*, 3; Best, "Ephesians 1.1," 10.
[49] Best, "Ephesians 1.1 Again," in *Essays on Ephesians*, 17–24. This original reading is also assumed without argumentation by John C. Kirby, *Ephesians, Baptism and Pentecost: An Inquiry into the Structure and Purpose of the Epistle to the Ephesians* (London: SPCK, 1968), 170.

καὶ ἐν Λαοδικείᾳ, πιστοῖς ἐν Χριστῷ Ἰησοῦ, which explains the καί left in the manuscripts.[50] The mention of Laodicea in Col 4:13 supposedly supports this reading, but Col 4:13 mentions a letter "from Laodicea" rather than "to Laodicea." It is also a rather blatant error for the scribe who omitted ἐν Ἱεραπόλει and ἐν Λαοδικείᾳ to retain καί. Best judges the rest of the required scribal blunders to be "very doubtful."[51] At least two scholars have suggested either that τῆς Ἀσίας (Zahn) or τοῖς Ἀσίας (Batey) was lost from the original.[52] While this destination fits with the circular letter hypothesis, Zahn fails to explain the generation of the earliest readings, and Batey's explanation relies on the ungrammatical dative form τοῖς Ἀσίας.[53] Neither author explains the presence of the καί left in the manuscripts.

In light of the available evidence and the problems with solutions proposed thus far, we cannot be certain what Eph 1:1 read in its original manuscript. Since the majority of commentators believe Ephesians was a circular or general letter to the churches in Asia Minor, Zahn's suggestion that a τῆς Ἀσίας dropped out might be the most compelling proposal, but one would still need to reconstruct the original reading and account for the subsequent extant readings in the earliest manuscripts. For the purposes of this work, I conclude that Ephesians was most likely written to churches in Asia Minor and was delivered from Rome through the port at Ephesus. The letter became associated with Ephesians (1) because it was the first city in which the letter was read, (2) because it was likely copied by the elders who know Paul so intimately, and (3) because Ephesus was a major city in Asia Minor.

The Literary Context of Ephesians 4:8

In Eph 4:8, Paul quotes Ps 68:19 as an inference (διό) based on the claim that Jesus has given gifts for the building up of the body of Christ: "therefore it says, 'When he ascended on high he led a host of captives, and he gave gifts to men.'" Commentators assume the introductory formula proper is διὸ λέγει ("therefore it says"), which causes some to question whether Paul was quoting Scripture or perhaps quoting a hymn as many believe he did in Eph 5:14, which has the same introductory formula. If διὸ λέγει is the introductory formula, it is unique to Paul in Ephesians but is used elsewhere to introduce Scriptural quotations (Heb 3:7; Jas 4:6; cf. Heb 10:5). But more important is that Paul commonly uses λέγει to introduce OT citations, with either Scripture or God as the implied subject (e.g., 2 Cor 6:2; Gal 3:16; Rom 15:10). Thus, διό in Eph 4:8 should not be considered a part of the introductory formula proper but rather a discourse marker expressing the relationship between v. 7 and the citation of Ps 68:19.

---

[50] Lincoln, *Ephesians*, 2–4; van Roon, *The Authenticity of Ephesians*, 80–85.
[51] O'Brien, *The Letter to the Ephesians*, 86. Further objections in Best, "Ephesians 1.1," 14.
[52] Zahn, *Introduction to the New Testament*, 1:489; Richard Batey, "Destination of Ephesians," *JBL* 82, no. 1 (1963): 101.
[53] E.g., Ignatius, *Eph.* 1.1; Josephus, *Ant.* 1.122, 171; 9.214; 10.74; 11.133, 334; Philo, *Leg.* 1.281; 1 Cor 16:19. There are no instances of τοῖς Ἀσίας in the Apocrypha, pseudepigrapha, Josephus, Philo, the LXX, the NT, the Apostolic Fathers, Greek literature in Thesaurus Linguae Graecae, or extant papyri searchable online.

The citation itself is too similar to Ps 68:19 [67:19 LXX] to be considered anything but a quotation. The quotation has a long history of debate, most notoriously over why Paul changes the verb "received" to "gave," and still today no consensus exists for how Paul's quotation should be understood. The first step to understanding Paul's citation of Ps 68:19, and the object of the rest of this chapter, is to explore the function and meaning of Eph 4:8 within its immediate context, Eph 4:1–16. To accomplish this goal, I will first determine the precise discourse function of Eph 4:8 in this context. I will then explore an implicit idea in Eph 4:7–16 that is crucial for understanding Paul's use Ps 68 but which no commentators have fully noticed and utilized when studying this quotation. Lastly, I will argue that the same idea implicit in Eph 4:7–16 is also abundant throughout Colossians, lending support to my reading of Eph 4:7–16.

The Discourse Function of Ephesians 4:8

In order to understand Paul's use of Ps 68:19 in Eph 4:8, one must first understand the role of Eph 4:8 in its immediate context. To locate the function of v. 8 within its wider context (4:1–16) is not easy. Andrew Lincoln says, "4:1–16 as a whole does not have a clearly defined form," and he takes 4:4–6, 7–16 as two expansions on the theme of unity expressed in the hortatory appeal in 4:1.[54] Similarly, of 4:7–16 Andreas Lindemann says, "Eine klare Gliederung läßt sich hier nicht erkennen."[55] Some commentators even believe 4:8–10 could be omitted from this section without depreciating the section's meaning.[56] But not all commentators agree. Hübner states "läßt sich als gegliederte inhaltliche Einheit verstehen."[57] Part of the difficulty arises because Paul begins the hortatory section of the letter in 4:1–3, only to resume expository prose until verse 17, where he again picks up the imperative mood. But close attention to discourse markers, boundary markers, semantic fields, and logical relationships may indeed demonstrate that Eph 4:1–16 is a cohesive passage that lends itself to a coherent reading.[58]

Verses 1–16 exhibit a high level of cohesion, which suggests it should be taken as a distinct literary unit. There are multiple words with a semantic domain of "unity" or "oneness," such as ἑνότητα (4:3, 13), ἕν, εἷς, and μία (4:4–6), συναρμολογέω and συμβιβάζω (4:16), and σῶμα (which is corporate in this context; 4:16 [x2]). The phrase

---

[54] Lincoln, *Ephesians*, 224.
[55] Andreas Lindemann, *Der Epheserbrief*, ZBK 8 (Zürich: Theologischer Verlag, 1985), 75.
[56] E.g., Lincoln, *Ephesians*, 225; Heinrich Schlier, *Christus und die Kirche im Epheserbrief*, BHT 6 (Tübingen: Mohr Siebeck, 1930), 2; J. C. Kirby, *Ephesians, Baptism and Pentecost: An Inquiry into the Structure and Purpose of the Epistle to the Ephesians* (London: SPCK, 1968), 145.
[57] Hans Hübner, *An Philemon, an die Kolosser, an die Epheser*, HNT 12 (Tübingen: Mohr Siebeck, 1997), 200.
[58] Coherence is a phenomenon whereby the reader or listener is able to fit the different elements of a discourse into a "single overall mental representation" (Robert A. Dooley and Stephen H. Levinsohn, *Analyzing Discourse: A Manual of Basic Concepts* [Dallas, TX: SIL International, 2001], 27). Cohesion from the author's point of view is the use of linguistic means to signal intended coherence. From the audience's perspective, cohesion is the linguistic means by which one discerns coherence (Gillian Brown and George Yule, *Discourse Analysis*, CTL [New York: Cambridge University Press, 1983], 224–25). For a full discourse analysis of Ephesians, see my forthcoming "Ephesians" in *Discourse Analysis of the New Testament Writings*, ed. Todd A. Scacewater (Dallas, TX: Fontes Press).

ἐν ἀγάπῃ occurs in 4:2, 15, and is the last phrase in 4:16, forming an inclusio for the section. Moreover, co-referential terms referring to Christ abound throughout. These include κύριος (4:1, 5), Χριστός (4:7, 12, 13, 15), τοῦ υἱοῦ τοῦ θεοῦ (4:13), αὐτός (4:10, 11, 15), ὅς (4:15, 16), and κεφαλή (4:15). Ephesians 4:1–16 is therefore an appropriate literary section in which to discuss the function of Eph 4:8.

Ephesians 4:1 begins not only a new section of the letter but also a new division.[59] It makes a clear break from the preceding section (3:1–21), which includes a prayer for the audience (although with an explanation in vv. 2–13 of Paul's statement that he is a prisoner *for the sake of* the Gentiles [3:1]) and concludes with a doxology in 3:21. Paul then opens 4:1 with a programmatic οὖν + first person imperative to state his main purpose in the epistle (cf. Rom 12:1; Col 3:1).[60]

The section 4:1–16 divides into two paragraphs (4:1–6, 7–16), which in turn divide into two subparagraphs each (4:1–3, 4–6, 7–10, 11–16). Verses 1–3 state the imperatival concern of the epistle. Technically, his exhortation is "I urge you to live a life worthy of your calling," but he immediately qualifies this worthy walk with two prepositional phrases and two adverbial participial phrases: "with all humility and gentleness, with long-suffering, by enduring one another in love, by striving to keep the unity that comes from the Spirit through the uniting bond, namely, peace" (4:2–3).

For multiple reasons, Paul's main concern in 4:1–3 is not the worthy walk per se but rather the focus of the worthy walk, to maintain the unity created by the Spirit.[61] First, this unity was the main theme of 2:11–22. There, Paul focused on the union of Jew and Gentile in Christ as a "new man," whose incorporation into the covenant no longer relies on ethnicity or rites such as circumcision but on faith in the Messiah. This unity is created through and fueled by the Spirit (2:18, 22). Second, as already noted, the dominant semantic domain in 4:1–16 is "unity" or "oneness." Third, 4:4–6 functions as the grounds for this participial phrase, not for the actual exhortation.[62] By referring to the oneness of each person of the Godhead, of faith, of baptism, and of the body, Paul provides a reason for his call to unity in the church. Since the unity of the church is grounded in God's nature, each exhibition of the virtues in 4:1–3 is an instance of participation in God's attributes.[63] Thus, taking into account these considerations,

---

[59] I divide the letter into two main divisions (1:3–3:21; 4:1–6:20), constituted by seven sections (1:3–23; 2:1–22; 3:1–21; 4:1–16; 4:17–5:21; 5:22–6:9; 6:10–20), each of which is composed of two or more paragraphs.

[60] On this lexico-syntactic construction as a signal of new paragraphs, see John R. Werner, "Discourse Analysis of the Greek New Testament," in *The New Testament Student and His Field*, ed. John H. Skilton (Phillipsburg, NJ: Presbyterian and Reformed, 1982), 214. For others, see John Beekman, John Callow, and Michael Kopesec, *The Semantic Structure of Written Communication*, 5th rev. ed. (Dallas, TX: Summer Institute of Linguistics, 1981), 116.

[61] Taking σπουδάζοντες as conveying means and taking the genitive τοῦ πνεύματος as conveying source.

[62] W. Hall Harris, "The Ascent and Descent of Christ in Ephesians 4:9–10," BS 151, no. 2 (1994): 204; William J. Larkin, *Ephesians: A Handbook on the Greek Text* (Waco, TX: Baylor University Press, 2009), 70; Stettler, *Heiligung bei Paulus*, 598; Becker and Luz, *Epheser*, 154. Similarly, others explain the function of vv. 4–6 as motivation for obeying the exhortation in 4:1–3, e.g., Pokorný, *Epheser*, 163; Aletti, *Éphésiens*, 211; Abbott, *A Critical and Exegetical Commentary on the Epistles to the Ephesians and to the Colossians*, ICC 34 (New York: C. Scribner's Sons, 1909), 107; O'Brien, *The Letter to the Ephesians*, 274.

[63] Becker and Luz, *Epheser*, 154.

Paul's hortatory concern in 4:1-6 is that his audience live a life worthy of their calling by striving for unity, which they should do because God himself is unified.

Verse 7 begins with a post-positive δέ, which could be either transitional ("now") or adversative ("but").[64] While it certainly is transitional by signaling a new paragraph and topic, it more importantly signals an adversative force between the corporate dimension of unity in 4:1-6 and the individual dimension of unity in 4:7-16. That is, while on the one hand the church must be unified (4:1-6), on the other hand the church need not be uniform (4:7-16). "Paul ajoute maintenant que cette unicité n'a rien d'une *uniformité*, car le tissu ecclésial est organique et diversifié – d'une 'diversité structurée.'"[65] This section emphasizing diversity among unity extends to v. 16, which is evident from the inclusio with v. 7: Ἑνὶ δὲ ἑκάστῳ ἡμῶν (4:7); ἑνὸς ἑκάστου (4:16). The paragraph as a whole therefore serves as a clarifying contrast to 4:1-6, reinforcing and strengthening the initial exhortation by ensuring a balanced response from his audience. Since the purpose of 4:7-16 is to support and balance the exhortation in 4:1-6, the exhortation to walk worthily and strive for unity remains the central concern of the entire section (4:1-16).

But the second paragraph (4:7-16) is still important in its clarifying role. These verses split into two subparagraphs. Verses 7-10 speak of the gifts Christ gave to the church, while vv. 11-16 speak of the result of these gifts: "we will all grow up in every way into Christ" (v. 15). Paul introduces the new topic in v. 7 by stating, "but to each one of us grace was given." From here, he draws an inference (διό): "Therefore, it says . . .," quoting Ps 68:19. Generally, scriptural quotations function as grounds (γάρ) for assertions or doctrines.[66] However, διό signals an inference and should be taken as such here. In other words, Christ's gift of grace (χάρις) in 4:7 is the grounds or reason for what is written in Ps 68:19.[67] Since grounds are semantically less emphatic than the inference deduced from the grounds, Paul emphasizes here the quotation.[68] Within the quotation, Paul has altered the aorist ἀνέβης from the LXX to a temporal adverbial participle ἀναβάς, which relegates the ascension clause subordinate to the two indicative clauses of the quotation, "he led captive captives, he gave gifts to men." Despite the asyndeton between the two clauses, we can see a narrative progression from taking captives to the climax of the end goal of giving gifts to men.

---

[64] Transitional: Larkin, *Ephesians*, 73-74; CJB; ESV; KJV; NAB; NASB; NET; NIV; NRSV. Adversative: CSB; Eadie calls it a "transitional contrast" (*Commentary on the Epistle to the Ephesians* [1883; repr. Minneapolis, MN: James & Klock, 1977], 279).
[65] Aletti, *Éphésiens*, 214; similarly, Eadie, *Ephesians*, 279; Anni Hentschel, *Gemeinde, Ämter, Dienste: Perspektiven zur neutestamentlichen Ekklesiologie*, BTS 136 (Neukirchen-Vluyn: Neukirchener Verlag, 2013), 143; Schnackenburg, *Epheser*, 177.
[66] Perhaps this is why CSB translates "for." Larkin seems to feel the difficulty of the conjunction, since he says it is inferential, but then defines this as meaning "grounds/proof," which is contradictory (*Ephesians*, 74).
[67] This obviously seems backwards, so I will discuss this problem later when explaining how Paul used the psalm.
[68] I am assuming that "every semantic unit of whatever type has natural prominence, what might be termed the organizational or relational center of the unit [of discourse]" (Beekman, Callow, and Kopesec, *The Semantic Structure of Written Communication*, 25). In the absence of any pragmatic marker, reasons or grounds are always less semantically prominent than the head proposition (in this case, the inference; ibid., 10).

Verses 9–10 provide an extensive commentary on the quotation in v. 8: "Now, this 'he ascended,' what does is it mean . . ." (τὸ δὲ ἀνέβη τί ἐστιν). Given the use of ἀνέβη, it seems he is inquiring only into the phrase "he ascended." However, this is probably an idiomatic use of the neuter article that asks not for the meaning of "he ascended," but for the meaning of the entire quotation.[69] Similarly, P. O'Brien says that Paul now "expounds its meaning," that is, the meaning of the quotation of Psalm 68:19.[70] Thus, vv. 9–10 expound the meaning of the entire quotation of Ps 68:19 in v. 8. Since vv. 9–10 are unpacking the meaning inherent within v. 8, the latter retains the focus of prominence in this first subparagraph (4:7–10).

In the second subparagraph, vv. 11–16 communicate that these gifts have a purpose or goal. Verse 7 had begun, "grace was given (δίδωμι) to each one of us according to the measure of Christ's gift (χάρις)." After the quotation and interpretation in vv. 8–10, v. 11 now begins with a καί that resumes the thought from v. 7: "And (καί) he gave (δίδωμι) the apostles, the prophets . . ." The use of δίδωμι in vv. 7, 8, and 11 brings coherence to the paragraph as it focuses on the church's diversity through Christ's gifts and also strengthens the resumption of the idea of Christ giving gifts.

But there is an exegetical problem here: what are the "gifts," and to whom are they given? In v. 7, the gift is χάρις and it is given to "each of us" (Ἑνὶ δὲ ἑκάστῳ ἡμῶν). While the first plural may sometimes refer only to Paul and his coworkers, such a meaning is unnatural in this context speaking of the entire church (4:1–6) and its diversity among unity (4:7–16). "Each of us" must refer to each individual believer, just as each individual believer is involved in causing the growth of the body (4:15–16). So in v. 7, all individual believers are the recipients of χάρις. In v. 11, it is the ministers of the church that are given, and it does not say to whom these ministers were given. To resolve this exegetical problem, we must first understand what is meant here by "gifts."

There are two possible identifications of the gifts. First, the classes listed in v. 11 might be a complete set of church officials who are synonymous with χάρις in v. 7. In this case, χάρις refers to people, whose identity we discover in v. 11. The five church offices are gifts given to all individuals believers for the purpose of equipping them (v. 12).[71] The problem with this view is that there is no evidence from early church literature that the five offices of Eph 4:11 are a comprehensive ecclesiastical polity.[72] The closest parallel to Eph 4:11 is 1 Cor 12:28: "And God has appointed in the church first apostles, second prophets, third teachers, then miracles, then gifts of healing, helping, administrating, and various kinds of tongues." There is no mention of evangelists or shepherds, and after the first three classes of ministers, Paul fluidly shifts to spiritual giftings. Moreover, the interpretation of χάρις in v. 7 as referring literally to the people listed in v. 11 conflicts with Paul's use of the χάρις word group in Rom 12:6 to refer to spiritual gifts given to individual believers: χαρίσματα κατὰ τὴν χάριν τὴν δοθεῖσαν ἡμῖν διάφορα.

---

[69] Cf. Mark 9:23; Luke 9:46; Rom 13:9. Wallace, *Greek Grammar beyond the Basics*, 238; so also, Abbott, *Ephesians and to the Colossians*, 114.
[70] O'Brien, *The Letter to the Ephesians*, 293.
[71] So Schnackenburg, *Epheser*, 182–85.
[72] Similarly, Hentschel, *Gemeinde, Ämter, Dienste*, 146; Becker and Luz, *Epheser*, 156–57.

The second interpretation of the "gifts" in Eph 4:7, 11 coheres with these two parallel Pauline passages (Rom 12:6; 1 Cor 12:28).[73] The difference in the list of people between Eph 4:11 and 1 Cor 12:28 suggests that neither list is comprehensive. Also, the fluidity between classes of people and spiritual gifts given to people in 1 Cor 12:28 suggests we should not view the classes listed in Eph 4:11 as offices to be occupied by different individuals at different times but rather as spiritual giftings that empower individuals for service. The repetition of δίδωμι in 4:7, 11 and the resumptive καί in 4:11 thus tie together the χάρις in v. 7 and the spiritual giftings in 4:11, with "apostles, prophets, etc." being specific examples of the χαρίσματα. So in both v. 7 and v. 11, the gifts given by Christ are spiritual gifts that empower the recipients to carry out specific functions within the church. These spiritual gifts are given to "each of us" (4:7), that is, to all individual believers, but the specific examples in 4:11, which are a subset of all spiritual giftings, are given only to some. These specific giftings, which all involve proclamation or teaching, are given for the purpose of equipping the saints (4:12). Paul chooses these specific examples to enable him to discuss further the need for maturity to withstand human cunning and "every wind of doctrine" in the following context (4:12–16).

The subparagraph (4:11–16) now continues in v. 12 to say that Christ gave these Spirit-empowered individuals for a purpose, although it is difficult to decide how to take the string of prepositional phrases that abound in vv. 12–13:

> for (πρός) the purpose of equipping of the saints
> unto (εἰς) the work of ministry
> unto (εἰς) the building up of the body of Christ,
> until we all attain
> unto (εἰς) the unity of the faith and the knowledge of the Son of God,
> unto (εἰς) the complete man,
> unto (εἰς) the measure of the maturity of the fullness of Christ.

The agents of "toward the equipping of the saints" are clearly the gifted ministers in v. 11, but the following prepositional phrase "for the work of ministry" is notoriously difficult: is it in parallel to the previous clause, so that the ministers equip and do the work of ministry, or is it subordinate to the noun equipping, so the ministers equip the saints, who in turn do the work of ministry? Since the second and third prepositional phrases use the same preposition εἰς, they most likely have the same agent who performs the actions of "work" and "building up." The third prepositional phrase refers to the building up of the body of Christ, and in 4:16 it is the "working according to the proper measure of each individual part [of the body]" that "causes the growth of the body unto the building up of itself in love" (κατ' ἐνέργειαν ἐν μέτρῳ ἑνὸς ἑκάστου μέρους τὴν αὔξησιν τοῦ σώματος ποιεῖται εἰς οἰκοδομὴν ἑαυτοῦ ἐν ἀγάπῃ). In other words, 4:16 says the proper exercise of each individual's gifts causes the body to grow.

---

[73] Even if Paul did not write Ephesians, some commentators assume these passages are so similar that the author of Ephesians had a copy of 1 Corinthians before him (Schnackenburg, *Epheser*, 175–76; Becker and Luz, *Epheser*, 156). So we have good reason to interpret Rom 12 and 1 Cor 12 mutually with Eph 4.

Thus, the most likely agent of "unto the building up of the body of Christ" in 4:12 is the saints; and if the agent of that phrase is the same as the agent of the second prepositional phrase, then the saints are also the agent of "for the work of ministry." Thus, the proclamation class of gifted believers equips the saints, the goal of which is that the saints do the work of ministry and build up the body of Christ by proper exercising of their God-given gifts.[74]

In v. 13, there are three telic εἰς clauses in series that explain the goal of the three actions in v. 12. The purpose of ministers equipping the saints to perform ministry and build up the body of Christ (4:12) is the attainment of (1) unity, (2) mature manhood, and (3) the measure of the full stature of Christ (4:13).[75] Going one step further, the purpose of the attainments expressed in v. 13 is revealed in vv. 14–15. Negatively, the purpose of these attainments is that we will no longer be deceived by false teaching (v. 14). Positively, the purpose of these attainments is that "we will grow up in every way into him," that is, into Christ (v. 15). Thus, v. 11 leads to v. 12, which leads to v. 13, which leads to vv. 14–15. The negative purpose in v. 14 serves to highlight or emphasize the more prominent, positive purpose in v. 15. After the mention of Christ in v. 15, Paul adds two descriptions of Christ: he is the head (v. 15) and he is the source of growth of the church (v. 16). The church grows when every individual member is operating properly, according to their unique giftings; each individual member "makes the body grow" so that the body builds itself up in love (v. 16). Since vv. 15–16 only serve to further clarify the identity of Christ, they are tangential to the main discourse and we can view the logical climax of 4:11–16 as the goal that "we will all grow up in every way into Christ" (4:15).

In summary, the stress of this entire section (4:1–16) falls at the very beginning, that believers should live a life worthy of their calling by striving for unity (4:1–3). The appeal to unity is grounded in the oneness of God, of faith, of baptism, and of the body in 4:4–6. This entire paragraph (4:1–6) is then clarified in a contrastive manner in the following paragraph, 4:7–16. While it is only clarifying the main exhortation to unity, it is still integral to the section. Although they should be united, he reminds them that Christ has given gifts to each of them (4:7–10). These gifts are the important means by which the church grows up in every way into Christ (4:11–16), especially through the ministers' equipping of the saints, who in turn do the work of ministry and build up the body.

How then does 4:8 function within the context of 4:1–16? The idea of Christ giving gifts, which takes the fore in 4:7–10, provides the means by which the church may "grow up in every way into Christ" (4:15). It is therefore an integral part of the section. While Paul calls for unity in the church, he notes that it is by the diversity of gifts that the church will mature, and Christ's distribution of gifts is the crucial means to achieve

---

[74] Although the literature analyzing these prepositional phrases is vast, there is no need here to discuss the issue further since it does not bear significantly on my thesis.

[75] Strictly speaking, v. 13 begins with a temporal marker (μέχρι), but the εἰς clauses communicate a goal or purpose—albeit one achieved through time. Also, in v. 13 I see both clauses "of the faith" and "of the knowledge of the Son of God" as modifying ἑνότητα. Thus, as CJB similarly has it, "until we all arrive at the unity implied by trusting and knowing the Son of God." The result is three coordinate εἰς clauses.

that end. Moreover, Eph 4:8 is the only OT reference in the entire section, which marks it as especially prominent because of the authoritative nature of the Scriptures for the early church. Paul notes some sort of connection between the ascent and the reception of gifts in Ps 68:19, on the one hand, and Christ's ascent and distribution of gifts, on the other. Thus, Eph 4:8 plays an integral role in the section as a whole and draws attention due to its reference to Scripture.

Gifts for Building the Temple in Ephesians 4:7–16

Now that we understand the context of Paul's quotation, I will make an argument that is indispensable for my thesis, that in Eph 4:7–16 Paul portrays the church not only as a body, but also as a temple. This observation to my knowledge has been hinted at by only a couple commentators, and none flesh out the idea fully or apply it to the question of how Paul used Ps 68:19.[76] So in this section, I argue that in Eph 4:7–16, Paul portrays Christ as giving various Spirit-empowered believers as his "gifts" for the purpose of building up the church through the Spirit as the temple of God. I offer supporting evidence from the rest of Ephesians that the temple was a prominent theme, even if veiled behind allusive language. As further supporting evidence, I provide a brief sketch of temple allusions throughout Colossians, which has a close literary relationship with Ephesians and, on some theories, was even the *Vorlage* for Ephesians. In either case, the presence of temple allusions in either letter strengthens the contention for finding similar allusions in the other letter.

As we have just seen, Christ's gifts include spiritual giftings (χαρίσματα and χάρις) that empower individual believers to carry out specific functions within the church toward the ultimate goal that the body would grow up in every way into Christ. While v. 7 refers to the spiritual gift given to believers, v. 11 resumes speaking about the gifts but uses synecdoche to refer to the individual (the whole) in place of the gifts themselves (the part). Because the individuals who make up the teaching class of ministers have been given gifts intended to equip the saints, these ministers themselves can be spoken of as gifts.[77] So from the perspective of v. 11, Christ's gifts are individual believers who are gifted for Spirit-empowered ministry. But why are these individuals given?

As we saw, the ultimate purpose of Christ's gifts is the growing up in every way into Christ. The body language is obvious: "body of Christ" (4:12), "the head, Christ" (4:15), "ligament" (ἁφή, 4:15), and "growth of the body" (4:16). But more allusive is the resonance of the language of this section with the idea of a temple. In fact, 4:11–16 shares five lexemes with 2:21–22, which explicitly describes the church as a temple (see Table 1.1): "in whom the whole (πᾶς) structure (οἰκοδομή), being joined together (συναρμολογέω), grows (αὐξάνω) into a holy temple (ναός) in the Lord, in whom

---

[76] Stettler observes that the author of Ephesians mixes the body and temple metaphor in Eph 4:12–16, and for her the two images belong together (*Heiligung bei Paulus*, 598). However, she makes no application toward understanding how Paul uses Ps 68:19. Schnackenburg comes close by comparing the language of 4:16 with 2:21–22, but he does not draw the conclusion that the church is being described as a temple in 4:16 (*Epheser*, 186).

[77] Alternatively, Paul could be using metonymy of cause for effect, whereby the spiritual giftings are the cause for the effect of a spiritually empowered individual.

Table 1.1 The Church as the Temple in Ephesians 4:11–16.

Ephesians 2:21–22	4:11–12, 15–16
ἐν ᾧ <u>**πᾶσα**</u> <u>οἰκοδομὴ</u> <u>συναρμολογουμένη</u> αὔξει εἰς ναὸν ἅγιον ἐν κυρίῳ, ἐν ᾧ καὶ ὑμεῖς <u>συνοικοδομεῖσθε</u> εἰς κατοικητήριον τοῦ θεοῦ ἐν πνεύματι.	Καὶ αὐτὸς ἔδωκεν . . . εἰς <u>οἰκοδομὴν</u> τοῦ σώματος τοῦ Χριστοῦ . . . ἀληθεύοντες δὲ ἐν ἀγάπῃ <u>αὐξήσωμεν</u> εἰς αὐτὸν τὰ πάντα, ὅς ἐστιν ἡ κεφαλή, Χριστός, ἐξ οὗ <u>**πᾶν**</u> τὸ σῶμα <u>συναρμολογούμενον</u> καὶ συμβιβαζόμενον διὰ πάσης ἁφῆς τῆς ἐπιχορηγίας κατ' ἐνέργειαν ἐν μέτρῳ ἑνὸς ἑκάστου μέρους τὴν αὔξησιν τοῦ σώματος ποιεῖται εἰς <u>οἰκοδομὴν</u> ἑαυτοῦ ἐν ἀγάπῃ.

Note: The various types of underlining correspond to similar words or word groups used in both passages.

you also are being built together (συνοικοδομέω) into the dwelling place of God by the Spirit (ἐν πνεύματι)" (Eph 2:21–22). Similar vocabulary and use of the building metaphor in both passages is evidence that Paul was still using the temple imagery in 4:12–16.

Further support for this claim is that the οἰκοδομή word group, which is used to describe the church in 4:12–16, is used throughout the Septuagint and the NT to refer to the building up of the temple or to the temple as a building. For example, 1 Chr 26:27 says that all the holy things which were won in war were given for τὴν οἰκοδομὴν τοῦ οἴκου τοῦ θεοῦ ("the construction of the house of God"). In 1 Esd 4:45, Zerubbabel tells King Darius to remember his promise "to build up the temple" (οἰκοδομῆσαι τὸν ναόν). Darius then writes a letter, part of the instructions of which are that twenty talents a year are to be given (δίδωμι) for the building up of the temple (εἰς τὴν οἰκοδομὴν τοῦ ἱεροῦ, 4:51).[78] One more link between 2:21–22 and 4:12–16 is that the Spirit is involved in both passages. In 2:22, it is "by the Spirit" that the church is being built up as a temple. The Spirit is mentioned in 4:3–4 and Paul elsewhere explains gifts as that which come from God through the Spirit (1 Cor 12:11 with 12:28). Thus, it is through the Spirit that the church is built as the temple, both in 2:21–22 and in 4:12–16.

The temple arises allusively elsewhere in Ephesians as well. In 1:23, the church is Christ's body, which is described as the "fullness" (πλήρωμα) of him who fills all in all. The semantic field of "filling" (πληρόω, πίμπλημι, ἐμπίμπλημι, and πλήρης) is used throughout the LXX to express God's habitation in the tabernacle or temple.[79] So although the idea is not yet explicit in Eph 1:23, Paul hints at the idea of the church as God's temple. After the church is explicitly identified as the temple of God in 2:21, the verb πληρόω is again used to describe the corporate church as the place of God's

---

[78] Other references to the temple with the οἰκοδομή word group, although not exhaustive, include 1 Esd 5:60, 70, 71; 6:6; 6:21; Tob 14:5; Ezek 40:2 (speaking of the end-time temple?); Mark 14:58; Acts 7:47, 49 (quoting Isa 66:1); 1 Pet 2:5; cf. Matt 24:1.

[79] See Exod 40:34–35; 1 Kgs 8:10–11; 2 Chr 5:13–14; 7:1–2; Isa 6:3–4; Ezek 10:3–4; 43:5; 44:4; Sir 36:13 [ET 36:19] (Christopher A. Beetham, *Echoes of Scripture in the Letter of Paul to the Colossians*, BIS 96 [Leiden: Brill, 2008], 153n41).

fullness (3:19), that is, as his temple. Similarly, in 5:18, believers should not be filled with wine, but filled with God's Spirit.

The reference to Christ as "head" (κεφαλή) in 1:22 and 4:15 may allude to Christ as the cornerstone of the temple. Psalm 117:22 LXX refers metaphorically to the cornerstone of the temple as the κεφαλὴν γωνίας. Isaiah 28:16 also uses the cornerstone of the temple metaphorically but refers to it as the ἀκρογωνιαῖος. In Eph 2:20, Paul uses the term ἀκρογωνιαῖος for cornerstone, drawing from Isa 28:16. One might wonder if Paul actually uses κεφαλή, then, to refer to Christ as the cornerstone of the temple. Paul may have linked Isa 28:16 and Ps 117:22 LXX via *gezerah shewa*, since ἀκρογωνιαῖος from Isaiah contains within it the lexeme γωνία, which constitutes part of "cornerstone" in Ps 117 (κεφαλὴν γωνίας).[80] Since the "cornerstone" language was so prominent for the NT writers, it is conceivable that Paul was familiar with both passages and that he could refer to Christ as the cornerstone using either ἀκρογωνιαῖος or simply κεφαλὴν as an abbreviated form of κεφαλὴν γωνίας.[81] In this case, κεφαλή in 1:22 and 4:15 would refer to Christ as the head (of the corner) of the temple. There are a few other possible allusions to the temple in Ephesians, but they are too allusive for our purposes.[82]

In sum, we see that the church is portrayed at points in Ephesians as God's temple. After Christ's ascension to heaven, he gave Spirit-empowered individuals so that the church might be built up through the Spirit as the temple of God. The gifts are the believers, who constitute the very building blocks of the temple, just as Paul has already said in Ephesians that the apostles and prophets are the "foundation" of this temple (Eph 2:20). Paul makes the same identification of the church as God's temple explicitly in 1 Cor 3:16 and 2 Cor 6:16. This same idea is found elsewhere in early Judaism, the NT, and the church fathers.[83] Most explicit is 1 Pet 2:5: "you yourselves as living stones are being built up as a spiritual house." The idea is therefore familiar to the apostles that they, as well as other individuals in the church, are given to constitute the very building blocks of the church as a temple.[84] This observation will shed light on the reason Paul chose to cite Ps 68:19 in conjunction with Christ's giving of gifts.

The Temple Theme in Colossians

I have argued so far that the gifts in Eph 4:7–11 are spiritually empowered individuals given to build up the body of Christ, which itself is the temple of God, so that it grows

---

[80] Grant Macaskill, *Union with Christ in the New Testament* (Oxford: Oxford University Press, 2013), 152n15. This could explain the difference between Paul's terminology in Eph 2:20 and Col 2:10.

[81] For the use of the cornerstone passages in the NT, see Mark 12:10–12; Matt 21:42–46; Luke 20:17–19; 1 Pet 2:6–10; Acts 4:8–12; Eph 2:19–22. The cornerstone passages also received much attention in early and late Jewish texts: 4Q84; 1QS VIII, 5–14; CD IV, 19; VIII, 12; Sif. Deut. 32:9; Tg. Ps. 118:22–23; Exod. Rab. 3.6; 8.10; 37.1; T. Sol. 22:7; 23:4; b. Pesaḥ 38a; 119a–b; *Mid. Teh.* 118:22–23; Pirqe R. El. XXIV. With so much attention given to these passages, it is likely Paul knew both passages well and could employ both terms for "cornerstone" in Ephesians.

[82] See Macaskill, *Union with Christ in the New Testament*, 149–54, 163–71.

[83] E.g., 1QSb IV, 28; 4Q511, fr. 35, 1–4; John 14:17; *Barn.* 6.15; 16:8–10.

[84] Cf. 1QSb IV, 28: "And may he make you a diadem of the holy of holies, because [you shall be made ho]ly for him and you shall glorify his name and his holy things." Translation from Florentino

up in every way into his fullness. The idea that the believers as gifts constitute the building blocks of the temple is foundational for my thesis, so I want to provide some more corroborating evidence that such an idea actually exists in Eph 4:7-16.[85] The relationship between Ephesians and Colossians is such that Paul either wrote them both from the same imprisoned situation around the same time period, or Paul wrote one (usually considered Colossians) and a later pseudepigrapher based Ephesians on Colossians.[86] In either case, if a certain theme is prevalent in one, it makes it more likely that the same theme may legitimately be found in the other. Recent research has found many allusions to the same theme in Colossians of Christians being built up as the eschatological temple. There is even an allusion to Ps 68:17, with which I will begin, after which I will survey the other temple allusions. There is actually more evidence of temple allusions in Colossians than there is in Ephesians, but since this is only corroborative evidence, I will survey it more quickly than I could otherwise have done.

Although somewhat implicit, an allusion to the temple is clear in Col 1:19. Christ is preeminent (1:18) ὅτι ἐν αὐτῷ εὐδόκησεν πᾶν τὸ πλήρωμα κατοικῆσαι (1:19), "because in him all the fullness was pleased to dwell." The referent of τὸ πλήρωμα is clear from the fuller expression in 2:9: the Colossians should hold to the teaching of Christ (2:8), ὅτι ἐν αὐτῷ κατοικεῖ πᾶν τὸ πλήρωμα τῆς θεότητος σωματικῶς (2:9), "because in him all the fullness of deity is dwelling bodily." So the fullness described in 1:19, which dwells in Christ, is the fullness of God. And the fullness of God, as we already saw above, is what filled the tabernacle and temple in the OT. Thus, Christ has become the new temple, the place of God's dwelling on earth, and this is the reason (ὅτι) that Christ is preeminent over the new creation (Col 1:18-20).

Significantly, the phrase ἐν αὐτῷ εὐδόκησεν πᾶν τὸ πλήρωμα κατοικῆσαι is nearly identical with Ps 67:17 LXX [68:16 ET], τὸ ὄρος ὃ εὐδόκησεν ὁ θεὸς κατοικεῖν ἐν αὐτῷ, "the mountain on which God was pleased to dwell."[87] In the psalm, Mount Bashan looks enviously on Mount Zion, the mountain on which God was pleased to dwell in the Jerusalem temple. Paul in Colossians implies that the temple is no longer located in Jerusalem but in Christ. This allusion to the temple in Ps 68 corroborates the argument

---

García Martínez and Eibert J. C. Tigchelaar, eds., *The Dead Sea Scrolls Study Edition* (Leiden: Brill, 2000), 1:107.

[85] Much of the information in this section is based on or inspired by G. K. Beale's *Colossians and Philemon*, BECNT (Grand Rapids, MI: Baker Academic, 2019), which at the time of my research was still forthcoming. I consulted all primary and secondary sources and have produced my own account of the evidence, which largely agrees with Beale's analysis.

[86] See, e.g., Mitton, *Ephesians*, 75-81. Although, Mitton demands Ephesians was written the same day or the day after Colossians, otherwise Paul would have forgotten much of his wording. This may downplay the stronger role of memory in Paul's oral culture, so it is conceivable he wrote Ephesians days or even weeks later. It also unnecessarily rules out that Paul may have kept a copy of his letter to the Colossians, which was standard practice in his day. The only reason he might not have kept a copy is because his imprisoned status may not have allowed him. See Richards, *Paul and First-Century Letter Writing*, 158-61; Murphy-O'Connor, *Paul the Letter Writer*, 118.

[87] Those who see an allusion to or echo of Ps 67:17 LXX include Beetham, *Echoes*, 143-56; N. T. Wright, *The Climax of the Covenant: Christ and the Law in Pauline Theology* (Minneapolis, MN: Fortress Press, 1992), 117; Abbott, *Ephesians and to the Colossians*, 219; G. K. Beale, "Colossians," in *Commentary on the New Testament Use of the Old Testament*, ed. G. K. Beale and D. A. Carson (Grand Rapids, MI: Baker Academic, 2007), 855-57.

that Eph 4:11–16 also draws on the temple theme in Ps 68 to present the church as the new dwelling place of God.[88]

Just as Christ is filled with the fullness (πλήρωμα) of God, so also are believers "filled" (πληρόω) with wisdom and knowledge (σοφίᾳ καὶ συνέσει [1:9]) for every good work (ἐν παντὶ ἔργῳ ἀγαθῷ [1:10]). Possibly, Paul alludes to the Bezalel narrative, where Bezalel is said to be filled (ἐμπίμπλημι) with wisdom and knowledge (σοφίας καὶ συνέσεως [Exod 31:3; cf. 36:1]) for all work (ἐν παντὶ ἔργῳ [31:3; cf. ποιεῖν πάντα τὰ ἔργα in 36:1]).[89] If so, then Paul depicts the believers as spiritually endowed to construct the latter day temple, just as he says believers build themselves up as God's dwelling place (Eph 2:21; 4:16). Otherwise, the "filling" may refer simply to God's presence and to the church as his temple. In 1:19 and 2:9, Christ's being filled with the fullness of God develops this earlier idea in 1:9 of fullness. It becomes apparent in Col 2:10 how the two concepts of Christ's fullness and the believers' fullness are related: believers are filled "in Christ"—that is, by virtue of union with Christ—with God's tabernacling presence. That which is true of the head is true also of its body, which becomes an appropriate dwelling place for God through the sanctification of the Spirit that occurs through their union with Christ.

The reference to Christ as "head" (κεφαλή) in 2:10, as in Eph 4:15 (cf. Eph 2:20), may allude to Christ as the cornerstone of the temple. Note here that Christ's victory over the spiritual powers is connected with the construction of the temple in honor of his victory, just as in Eph 4:7–16. Further allusions to believers as the temple may arise in 1:22–23; 2:7, where they are said to be "holy and blameless" (ἁγίους καὶ ἀμώμους)— terms applied to sacrifices made at the temple and to the temple itself[90]—and "founded" (θεμελιόω) and "built up" (ἐποικοδομέω), both proper terms for a temple edifice.

Colossians 2:16–23 is the heart of the epistle and the most polemical, so it is significant that the notion of the temple comes so aggressively to the fore. The false teachers in Colossae were advocating the continuance of food and drink purity laws. There were many purposes of the food purity laws, but the main reason was likely the necessity for purity in order to enter the temple for worship.[91] They also seem to have been insisting on keeping Jewish feasts, new moons, and Sabbaths (2:16), a triadic formula in the LXX always tied up with or held at the temple.[92]

---

[88] Regarding the phenomenon whereby what is true of Christ is elsewhere true of the church generally, C. H. Dodd called this "transference of attributes" via corporate representation (*According to the Scriptures: The Sub-Structure of New Testament Theology* [Eugene, OR: Wipf & Stock, 1953], 105).

[89] Beetham, *Echoes of Scripture*, 61–79; Beale, "Colossians," 846–47; Gordon D. Fee, *God's Empowering Presence: The Holy Spirit in the Letters of Paul* (Peabody, MA: Hendrickson, 1994), 642n30. There may also be an allusion to Isa 11:2, 9, as Betham argues and as Beale discusses. But the fact that the phrase "in every work" is shared by Col 1:9–10 and Exod 31:3, while it does not appear in Isa 11:2, 9, favors an allusion to Exod 31:3.

[90] Lev 1:3, 10; 2:3; 3:1; 5:15; 10:12; Ezek 42:13; 45:18; Sir 7:31; etc; Philo, *Agr.* 130; *Som.* 1.62. Of course, anything within the temple must be ἄμωμος, even the high priests (Philo, *Som.* 2.185).

[91] See, e.g., 1QH III, 20–23; Philo, *Plant.* 163; *Ebr.* 127, 131, 138; *Spec.* 1.150; *Moys.* 2.21–24, 66–78; Jos. *Ap.* 2.102–8; 11Q19 (= 11QT) XLVII, 3–4; and 4Q400 fr. 1 I, 14; Heb 9:8–14.

[92] 1 Chr 23:31; 2 Chr 2:3; 8:13; 31:3; 2 Esd 5:51–53; Neh 10:33; Isa 1:13–14; Ezek 45:17; Josephus, *Ant.* 11.77; *J.W.* 5.230; Philo, *Spec.* 1.168. Cf. also Ezek 44:24; 46:3; 1 Macc 1:39; 1:45; Philo, *Spec.* 1.182; 2.140, 144–45; m. Šebu. 1:4–5; 1QS X, 3–7; Hos 2:11; Jdt 8:6; 1 Macc 10:34. For these references and further argumentation, see Beale, *Colossians and Philemon*, 215–21.

The use of ἐμβατεύω in 2:18 likely refers to entering into the heavenly sanctuaries, where they have seen such things as asceticism and the worship of angels. M. Dibelius in 1917 argued that the verb referred to entering into visions during initiation rites for mystery cults. He based his argument on the evidence of newly found inscriptions from the Sanctuary of Apollo at Claros, dated to the second century AD.[93] Dibelius was criticized for inferring visions as the direct object of ἐμβατεύων, but his argument was improved by C. Arnold, who has demonstrated that the word ἐμβατεύω was used in the initiation rites of contemporary mystery religions to speak of initiates entering the inner sanctuary of the god after preliminary rites.[94] W. Carr before Arnold had also demonstrated the use of the verb to refer to a human or deity stepping into a temple or sacred space.[95] The truncated nature of the phrase also suggests a fixed expression for a known rite.[96] Thus, we may infer that the "heavenly temple" is the implied object of ἐμβατεύων.

This heavenly temple is where the false teachers have seen "these things" (ἅ), namely, worship by angels and asceticism.[97] Notwithstanding ongoing resistance to this reading, it is currently the interpretation with the most textual and historical evidence to support it, and it is currently the most popular interpretation among commentators.[98] Further evidence that this context refers to entering a heavenly temple is that the term θρησκεία, which is one of the things the visionaries have seen by "entering in," refers to worship in temples in many Jewish and Greco-Roman contexts.[99] Colossians 2:19 parallels closely the wording of Eph 4:11–16, which I have argued presents the church as a temple, so the idea may indeed be implicit in Col 2:19. The prohibitions not to

---

[93] Martin Dibelius, *Die Isisweihe bei Apuleius und verwandte Initiations-Riten* (Heidelberg: Carl Winters, 1917), 30–39.
[94] Clinton Arnold, *The Colossian Syncretism: The Interface between Christianity and Folk Belief at Colossae*, WUNT II/77 (Tübingen: Mohr Siebeck, 1995), 104–57.
[95] Wesley Carr, "Two Notes on Colossians," *JTS* 23 (1973): 499–500.
[96] Eduard Schweizer, *Der Brief an die Kolosser*, EKKNT 12 (Benziger: Neukirchener, 1994), 124.
[97] Taking ἀγγέλων as a subjective genitive since the worship of angels by men is rare in Jewish literature. By contrast, the Qumran liturgy *Songs of the Sabbath Sacrifice* demonstrates a lively belief, at least among that sect, of worship by angels in a heavenly court.
[98] On the prevalence of the interpretation, see Pokorný, *Der Brief des Paulus an die Kolosser*, 122–24; Peter T. O'Brien, *Colossians, Philemon*, WBC 44 (Dallas, TX: Word, 1991), 144. The second most likely meaning for ἐμβατεύω is its meaning in six of its seven occurrences in the LXX, "to march into" or "to take possession of by entering" (Josh 19:49, 51; 1 Macc 12:25; 13:20; 14:31; 15:40). In the Colossians context, ἐμβατεύω would refer to entering into their inheritance. This use would fit with the emphasis on future hope and inheritance elsewhere in Colossians (e.g., 1:12–14; 3:1–4) and is argued for extensively by Beetham (*Echoes of Scripture*, 206–8). But this view does not make much sense of the grammar; the text would mean that the false teachers have seen asceticism and the worship of angels "by entering into [their inheritance]" (Beetham's explanation of the meaning of the clause on p. 208 does not clarify this problem). Supplying "the heavenly sanctuary" as the implied direct object of ἐμβατεύων makes more sense as a location in which they would see asceticism and the worship of angels. For ongoing resistance to the temple interpretation, see Richard E. DeMaris, *The Colossian Controversy: Wisdom in Dispute at Colossae*, JSNTSS 96 (Sheffield: JSOT Press, 1994), 63–68; O'Brien, *Colossians*, 144–45.
[99] Philo, *Legat.* 298, 232; Sib. Or. 8:380; Clementine Homilies, Homily 10, chap. 22; Dionysius of Haicarnassus, *Roman Antiquities* 2.63; Dio Cassius, *Roman History* 26.87; 49.22; Sextus Empiricus, *Outlines of Pyrrhonism* (= *Pyrrhoniae hypotyposes*) III.220; Herodian, *Hist., Ab excess divi Marci*, 5.6.2; Chaeremon Frag. 10 (3x).

touch (ἅπτω) or taste (γεύομαι) were likely intended to keep the visionaries clean so they could enter the heavenly temple.[100]

While there are no explicit citations of the OT in Colossians, we do see the significant allusion to Ps 67:17 LXX [68:16 ET] that is used to present Christ as the new Zion, the new holy abode of the divine presence. Believers, by virtue of their union with Christ, are also filled by the divine presence (2:10), thereby establishing them as the present earthly temple of God. Paul may have been emphasizing this eschatological temple because the syncretistic teachers were claiming to have entered into the heavenly sanctuary, where they saw asceticism and the worship of angels (2:18). Paul wishes that they not be taken captive by this empty deceit but that they instead be filled with the tradition "according to Christ" (κατὰ Χριστόν [2:8]). Part of this tradition is that Christ is the true locus of the divine presence, as are those who are "in him," so they need not be taken in by claims to a rival heavenly temple where mystics gain spiritual superiority. That the temple is so prevalent in Colossians, which has such a close literary relationship with Ephesians, and that Col 1:19 alludes to Ps 67:17 LXX supports my reading of Eph 4:7–16 that Christ gave gifted believers as the very building blocks of the eschatological temple.

From here, in order to see how Paul was using Ps 68:19 in Eph 4:8, we must spend a significant portion of this study examining the psalm itself. The following three chapters will attempt to clarify the textual obscurities and the literary structure of the psalm (Chapter 2), situate it among similar ANE war songs as a means of supporting my proposed exegesis and literary structure (Chapter 3), and explore Ps 68's use of prior OT traditions to expand its meaning both backward and forward in time (Chapter 4).

---

[100] These terms are used to refer to ritual purity or impurity in Lev 5:2 and likewise nineteen other times in Leviticus; so also Num 19:11, 16, 21–22; 31:19; Deut 14:8; Hag 2:13; Let. Aris. 142, 162; 2 Macc 6:18–20.

2

Gifts for Building the Temple in Psalm 68:19

Study of the psalms has changed drastically over the last century in three main movements. While the first two are organically related, the third movement took a different hermeneutical approach. Any study of an NT author's use of the psalms must now wrestle with how to approach the psalms hermeneutically while also discerning the hermeneutical approach of the NT author to the psalm cited. Therefore, before studying Ps 68, we must determine what hermeneutical approach will drive the analysis.

Hermeneutical Approaches to the Psalter

Prior to the 1920s, scholars treated the psalms as autonomous songs that essentially functioned as the hymnbook of the second temple. Some scholars allowed many of the psalms to be dated to the time of David and the first temple, while others tended to date them late, composed either during the exile or after the exile (some even into the time of Alexander Jannaeus).[1] Their main function was for individual or communal use, within or without the temple or on other occasions of Israelite worship, whether in the first or second temple. In this approach to the psalms, each psalm was an autonomous composition composed for worship or devotion. Although commentaries were written on the Psalter, it was relatively ignored.[2]

The first major movement of the last century began with H. Gunkel's work on the psalms. He systematically applied form criticism to the Psalter, which sought to find the *Sitz im Leben* of each psalm by classifying it according to its genre (*Gattung*). These forms included community hymns, lament psalms, oracles, and so forth.[3] The

---

[1] For dates into the period of Jannaeus, see, e.g., D. Bernhard Duhm, *Die Psalmen*, KHCAT (Leipzig: J. C. B. Mohr, 1899).

[2] David M. Howard, "Recent Trends in Psalms Studies," in *The Face of Old Testament Studies*, ed. David W. Baker and Bill T. Arnold (Grand Rapids, MI: Baker, 1999), 330–31. For a general history of the psalms written before the third movement that I will describe, see R. E. Clements, *One Hundred Years of Old Testament Interpretation* (Philadelphia: Westminster Press, 1976), 76–98.

[3] For a full list of Gunkel's forms, see Hermann Gunkel, *The Psalms: A Form-Critical Introduction*, trans. Thomas M. Horner (Philadelphia, PA: Fortress Press, 1967), 40–41. The following short essay summarizes his lengthy exposition of the features of each *Gattung* in his introduction to the psalms: Hermann Gunkel and Joachim Begrich, *Introduction to Psalms: The Genres of the Religious Lyric of Israel*, trans. James D. Nogalski, MLBS (Macon, GA: Mercer University Press, 1998). Most of

true meaning of the psalm is that of the pristine form before the literary additions and later editing. Thus, the meaning of the psalm lies primarily in the origins of its original composition rather than its literary use in the Psalter. While he believed the earliest psalms were cultic in nature, he believed that many of these were later used by individuals and communities as spiritual songs and prayers. Gunkel's form criticism has altered the nature of psalms studies for the last century by emphasizing the original *Sitz im Leben* of the psalms and by providing some more objective means by which to interpret them.

Gunkel's most influential student was Sigmund Mowinckel, who launched the second main movement in psalms studies. While Gunkel held that the earliest psalms were related to Israel's cult, Mowinckel took this to a new extreme, arguing that virtually all of the psalms were earlier than many scholars believed and were composed as cultic material. While the psalms were originally cultic, "learned traditionalists" began gathering psalms into small collections (those now found within the Psalter) because they desired to preserve what they believed to be ancient poetry used in the cult ever since the days of David. These learned traditionalists phased out the cultic significance and framed them as products of the life of an individual.[4] Mowinckel's project essentially reversed what he believed the learned traditionalists had done by interpreting each psalm in light of Israel's ancient cult. Mowinckel thus differed from Gunkel in that he dated most of the psalms early and held that their use was always cultic, even though some elite traditionalists later tried to frame them as stemming from the *Sitze im Leben* of individuals.

By cult, Mowinckel meant the drama by which individuals experience God in all his powers and become one with the divine through festivals. This power diminishes over time, so festivals must be repeated.[5] Although the festivals in the OT are cast as opportunities to remember, Mowinckel believes Israel's early, naive cult also actualized their religious experience. The priests had systematized and elaborated the details of the cult and killed its old spirit, leaving only "overdeveloped external forms" in the P source.[6]

Tied up with the cult is Mowinckel's argument that Israel held a New Year's "Enthronement of Yahweh" festival as part of its festival of tabernacles, similar to the enthronement festivals in Babylon and Assyria.[7] He reconstructs this hypothetical festival based on scattered references throughout the psalms to what could be rituals and myths that were recited and reenacted during the festival. He fills in the gaps by comparative study of the Babylonian and Assyrian festivals, from which Israel purportedly borrowed.[8] It existed in preexilic times, according to Mowinckel, since he believes it more likely that Deutero-Isaiah uses the Enthronement psalms rather

---

his categories are still used today, although the idea of imposing modern genre titles on ancient texts has been consistently criticized.

[4] Sigmund Mowinckel, *The Psalms in Israel's Worship* (1962; repr. Grand Rapids, MI: Eerdmans 2004), 2:203–5.
[5] Sigmund Mowinckel, "The Enthronement Psalms and the Festival of YHWH's Enthronement," in *Psalm Studies*, trans. Mark E. Biddle, SBLHBS (Atlanta, GA: SBL Press, 2014), 1:197–211.
[6] Ibid., 212.
[7] In his original formulation he provided ten pieces of evidence for the festival's existence in Israel, concluding that the festival's existence "cannot justifiably be doubted" (ibid.).
[8] Ibid., 215–20, 223–364; Mowinckel, *The Psalms in Israel's Worship*, 1:123, 130, 136.

than vice versa.⁹ In his earlier work, the enthronement psalms proper were Pss 47, 93, and 95–100, while others are connected to the genre by their content (Pss 20, 24, 29, 33, 48, 84, 114, and 149; Exod 15).¹⁰ In his later work, he added Pss 68 and 118 to the enthronement psalms proper and added Pss 46, 75, 76, and 81 to those connected to the genre.¹¹ In sum, Mowinckel's approach to the psalter is to look at the psalms as composed for and used by the community in the cult as he defined it. This required a heavy use of history of religions to compare practices in other ancient Near Eastern cults in order to understand aspects of the cultic drama unfolding in each of the psalms.

Mowinckel's work has had the greatest influence on psalms studies from the founding of Gunkel's form criticism until the end of the twentieth century when the third movement in psalm studies arose. While scholars had almost always treated the psalms as autonomous, or at best as parts of smaller collections, a few scholars had begun noting signs of a larger organizational scheme in the psalter during the Gunkel–Mowinckel era.¹² In the 1970s and 1980s, Brennan, Childs, Sheppard, and Reindl focused on the canonical arrangement of the Psalter and emphasized "(1) a literary rationale as responsible for the final form of the Psalter, (2) that this rationale reflects a non-liturgical *Sitz im Leben*, (3) that an individualizing tendency can be seen in the use of the psalms and (4) that wisdom motifs play some part in the scheme."¹³ These scholars, and especially Childs's chapter on the psalms in his *Introduction to the Old Testament as Scripture*, set up Childs's student Gerald Wilson to publish the monograph that would drastically impact psalms studies, perhaps as much as Mowinckel.

Wilson was the first to propose a systematic view of a Davidic-historical shaping of the psalter created by intentional editorial positioning of the psalms. In his *Editing of the Hebrew Psalter* (1985), he first laid a careful foundation for his thesis by examining editorial evidence of hymnic collections in ancient Near Eastern collections and at Qumran.¹⁴ Chapter 6 presented evidence for editorial shaping of the MT Psalter, while chapter 7 laid out his basic thesis. Book I of the Psalter presents the Davidic covenant and David's assurance of God's continued preservation of it. Book II portrays the transmission of the covenant to David's son, portrayed in the seam Ps 72. David petitions for his son, that he would rule justly, have dominion, be blessed, and thus secure for himself the blessing of the covenant. In Ps 89, the end of Book III, the covenant comes into view as established in the remote past, seems threatened, and is viewed as failed. Yet the psalm expresses hope that Yahweh will remember his covenant.

---

⁹ Mowinckel, "Enthronement Psalms," 365–85; Mowinckel, *The Psalms in Israel's Worship*, 1:117–18.
¹⁰ Mowinckel, "Enthronement Psalms," 183–84.
¹¹ Mowinckel, *The Psalms in Israel's Worship*, 1:142.
¹² This includes scholars such as F. Delitzsch, P. A. de Lagarde, J. Forbes, E. G. King, A. F. Kirkpatrick, J. Dahse, N. H. Snaith, L. Rabinowitz, A. Guilding, A. Arens, and three Jewish scholars: A. Cohen, S. R. Hirsch, U. Cassuto. See David M. Howard Jr., "Editorial Activity in the Psalter: A State-of-the-Field Survey," in *The Shape and Shaping of the Psalter*, ed. J. Clinton McCann, JSOTSS 159 (Sheffield: JSOT Press, 1993), 54–56; David C. Mitchell, *The Message of the Psalter: An Eschatological Programme in the Books of Psalms*, JSOTSS 252 (Sheffield: Sheffield Academic Press, 1997), 46–60.
¹³ David M. Howard Jr., *The Structure of Psalms 93–100*, BJS 5 (Winona Lake, IN: Eisenbrauns, 1997), 9.
¹⁴ Gerald Henry Wilson, *The Editing of the Hebrew Psalter*, SBLDS (Chico, CA: Scholars Press, 1985), chs. 2–5.

Thus, the covenant majestically proclaimed in Ps 2 is viewed as in dire jeopardy in Ps 89. In Book IV, Pss 90–106 respond to the problem in Ps 89: (1) Yahweh is king (even if a Davidide is not); (2) he has been Israel's refuge in the past and will continue to be; and (3) those who trust in him are blessed. After Ps 116:47 calls for Yahweh to redeem Israel from exile, Ps 117 praises God for answering their plea. Two groups of Davidic psalms at the beginning and end of Book V (108–110; 138–145) provide a paradigm for trusting in God. The Hallelujah psalms (111–117) provide the theme of trusting in Yahweh. The central section focuses on Torah and acts as a guide to life for the exiles. Psalms 120–134 then break into an "almost unbroken song of reliance on YHWH alone."[15] Psalm 145 is the climax of Book V and ends with a call from David: "My mouth will speak the praise of YHWH, and let all flesh bless his holy name forever and ever." Psalms 146–150 answer this call to praise Yahweh. Thus, Book V stands as "an answer to the plea of the exiles to be gathered from the *diaspora*."[16]

The favorable reception of Wilson's monograph was evident in a 1993 collection of essays.[17] Although not all agreed with Wilson's scheme in all its details, many were convinced that there is an editorial agenda to the final form of the Psalter.[18] Since Wilson's monograph, the study of the "shape and shaping" of the Psalter has become so specialized that monographs have analyzed each Book of the Psalter, smaller collections within those books, and many articles and some monographs have studied individual psalms within their canonical context.[19] There is disagreement over whether there is a wisdom, eschatological, Messianic, or Torah shaping to the Psalter, but many agree with Wilson at least in that the editorial agenda is to mirror the history of Israel throughout the Psalter. Thus, the meaning of any individual psalm is the relation of the surface level of the psalm's language to events during the period of Israel's history reflected in the book of the Psalter in which that psalm is found. While this approach can still identify the *Gattung* of a psalm to aid interpretation, one is primarily concerned with the final form of the psalm and its meaning within its canonical context as intended

---

[15] Ibid., 224.
[16] Ibid., 227.
[17] J. Clinton McCann, ed., *The Shape and Shaping of the Psalter*, JSOTSS 159 (Sheffield: JSOT Press, 1993).
[18] Wilson later amended his heavily criticized view of Book V as one of a failed Davidic covenant. He came to agree that Book V envisioned the coming of an eschatological Davidic servant who would "establish God's direct rule over all humanity in the Kingdom of God" (Gerald Henry Wilson, "King, Messiah, and the Reign of God," in *The Book of Psalms: Composition and Reception*, ed. Peter W. Flint and Patrick D. Miller Jr., SVT 99 [Boston, MA: Brill, 2005], 396–405, quote on p. 405).
[19] To mention only a few representative and influential studies, Gianni Barbiero, *Das erste Psalmenbuch als Einheit: Eine synchrone Analyse von Psalm 1–41*, ÖBSB 16 (Frankfurt am Main: Peter Lang, 1999); Robert Luther Cole, *The Shape and Message of Book III: Psalms 73–89*, JSOTSS 307 (Sheffield: Sheffield Academic Press, 2000); Howard, *The Structure of Psalms 93–100*; Michael G. McKelvey, *Moses, David, and the High Kingship of Yahweh: A Canonical Study of Book IV of the Psalter*, GDBS 55 (Piscataway, NJ: Gorgias Press, 2010). Articles such as the following are common, although enough research has been done that articles are now much more focused: J. Clinton McCann, "Books I–III and the Editorial Purpose of the Hebrew Psalter," in *The Shape and Shaping of the Psalter*, ed. McCann; Erich Zenger, "The Composition and Theology of the Fifth Book of Psalms, Psalms 107–145," *JSOT* 80 (1998): 77–102. A recent book that is supposed to function as a summary of the state of the field is Nancy L. DeClaissé-Walford, ed., *The Shape and Shaping of the Book of Psalms: The Current State of Scholarship*, AIL 20 (Atlanta, GA: Society of Biblical Literature, 2014).

by the Psalter editor(s), not the context of its original composition.[20] The psalms are also released from their cultic context to be interpreted in light of Israel's history and applied to the church today in accord with the editorial intent, whether it be in the direction of wisdom, eschatology, Torah, or something else.

There are benefits to all three approaches to the Psalter just surveyed. Gunkel's form criticism allows interpreters to eliminate some subjectivity by understanding psalms in relation to others within the same genre. But one must be careful not to impose on the psalms a foreign and modern concept of genre that rules out deviations from the "norm" and proposes to fix these deviations by eliminating portions or considering them later redactions without any supporting evidence. Mowinckel's emphasis on the use of the psalms in the cult helps to make better sense of many psalms and corrects those scholars who saw many of the psalms as late as the second century BC. However, one cannot suppose that every psalm was only used in the cult, and one should allow some flexibility when proposing the *Sitz im Leben* of a psalm. His Enthronement Festival proposal has also become less popular today because of the lack of direct evidence and the somewhat circular nature of his argumentation.[21] So some psalms were probably composed solely for communal use in the cult, but one need not limit all the psalms to this origin. Surely they had use for individuals, groups, and even kings and their court.

While the canonical approach to the Psalter is popular and promising, it has problems when investigating the NT's use of the psalms. First, meaning is derived from the final form of the Psalter, which is ultimately the work of several editors. We cannot know if their editorial intention was the same or conflicting or perhaps even contradictory. Second, we know very little if anything about the Psalter's editors and cannot therefore convincingly seek their intentions. We have textual clues to be sure, but how to interpret those clues is not at all straightforward. Third, there is little if any evidence, according to some preliminary investigation of my own, that the NT authors interpreted the psalms in this manner.[22] There are some ancient authors who showed awareness of the concept of the canonical shape, but until arguments are made otherwise, NT authors seem to have interpreted the psalms as autonomous units, often composed by those to whom they are ascribed in the superscription.[23]

Thus, in my investigation of Ps 68, since my task is to understand the psalm's meaning and use in its original ancient Near Eastern context according to its original

---

[20] The issue of the "editor(s)" is complicated because the Psalter has many smaller collections, which other editors brought together, and the identity and number of these editors is unclear. But given the history of the composition of the Psalter (as much as we can be sure of), later editors worked to a large extent with what was edited together before them. So "editorial intent" includes multiple levels of intent spread across multiple editors, and whether later editors understood and agreed with prior editorial intent is also unclear.

[21] Yet some scholars do still believe Mowinckel was correct, even if he overstated his case or drew too many psalms into the orbit of his theory. See J. J. M. Roberts, "Mowinckel's Enthronement Festival: A Review," in *The Book of Psalms: Composition and Reception*, ed. Flint and Miller, 97–115.

[22] This is an area that needs to be explored, given the heavy use of the Psalter throughout the NT.

[23] E.g., Matt 23:43; Acts 1:16; 2:25, 34; 4:25 (although Ps 2 has no authorial attribution); Rom 4:6–7; 11:9; Heb 4:7. For evidence of ancient authors who showed awareness of the canonical shape of psalms, see Mitchell, *Message of the Psalter*, 15–65.

author(s), and to compare this meaning with how Paul interprets and uses it, the shape and shaping of the Psalter will not play much of a role in my exegesis of the psalm. However, since the canonical shape of the Psalter does inform us about the intentions, hopes, and even the theology of the second temple Jewish editors of the Psalter, it provides us a window into the earliest interpretations of the psalms alongside those of the authors of the Septuagint. The canonical approach will therefore be useful in my fourth chapter on the reception history of the psalm in early and late Judaism.

The Narratival Structure of Psalm 68

Psalm 68 is generally acknowledged as the most difficult psalm to translate and interpret: it is "widely admitted as textually and exegetically the most difficult and obscure of all the psalms."[24] Many factors contribute to its difficulty. First is the antiquity of the language and the uncertainty about some of its lexemes. Second is the attempt by modern commentators to find redactional layers within the psalm and give different parts of the psalm various cultic *Sitze im Leben*. Third is the difficulty of interpreting vv. 16–19, particularly which mountains are being referred to and what the psalmist is getting at. Fourth is the debate over its literary structure and whether the psalm contains a narrative or only a collection of hymnic lines. The last major issue is how to interpret the second half of the psalm: as eschatology, as enthronement festival, or something else.

My goal in this chapter is to argue for a narratival reading of the psalm, particularly vv. 1–19. Since my interpretation of the second half of the psalm depends largely on how the psalmist uses prior OT traditions, I will save my analysis of vv. 20–36 for the next chapter. But as I will argue, even those verses can be considered part of the narrative, since they are projecting into the future. The narrative in vv. 1–19 includes an initial hymnic opening followed by an account of God's might as he leads Israel from Egypt, through the wilderness, into Canaan, and finally to the heights of Mount Zion in Jerusalem. The last century of scholarship has not been favorable to such a reading. John Gray stated in 1977, "[I]t is now generally agreed that it is impossible to read the psalm as a well-integrated unit like most psalms."[25] H.-J. Kraus called the psalm corrupt and incoherent.[26] Because of such weighty opinion, I will discuss in turn the six sections of vv. 1–19 in order to argue that each section contributes to this progressive narrative that climaxes at v. 19. The amount of scholarship that has suggested readings antithetical to a narratival reading of the psalm is sufficient enough that the next two chapters offer corroborative evidence of my narratival reading, first

---

[24] Mitchell J. Dahood, *Psalms*, AB (Garden City, NY: Doubleday, 1966), 2:133. Similarly, Mowinckel, *The Psalms in Israel's Worship*, 1:5; Artur Weiser, *The Psalms: A Commentary*, OTL (Philadelphia, PA: Westminster Press, 1962), 481; Hans-Joachim Kraus, *Psalms 60–150: A Commentary*, trans. Hilton C. Oswald (Minneapolis, MN: Fortress Press, 1993), 47.

[25] John R. Gray, "Cantata of the Autumn Festival: Psalm 68," *JSS* 22, no. 1 (1977): 2.

[26] Kraus, *Psalms 60–150*, 47.

from the psalmist's use of other OT songs with a similar structure, and secondly from ancient Near Eastern writings with a similar literary topos.[27]

After the superscription in v. 1 ascribing the psalm to David, the psalm begins with the ambiguous form יָקוּם אֱלֹהִים, with יָקוּם being either jussive ("let God arise") or imperfect ("God will arise"). Since the rest of the psalm is not a call to present action, an imperfect rendering is most likely here. The same holds for the following three equally ambiguous imperfect/jussive forms: "his enemies shall be scattered," "those who hate him shall flee from before him," and in v. 3, "as wax melts before the fire, the wicked will perish before God." The one form that is certainly an imperfect reiterates the fate of the wicked: "as smoke is driven away, you will drive away [the wicked]" (v. 3).[28] By contrast, "the righteous will rejoice; they will exult before God and will rejoice with joy" (v. 4). These three opening verses of the psalm (excluding the superscription) frame its contents as something already done for which God should be praised.

Verse 2 is a clear allusion to Num 10:35, where Moses exhorted God, קוּמָה יְהוָה וְיָפֻצוּ אֹיְבֶיךָ וְיָנֻסוּ מְשַׂנְאֶיךָ מִפָּנֶיךָ, "arise, YHWH, and let your enemies be scattered before you, and let those who hate you flee from before you." Moses uttered these words in the wilderness whenever they would take up the ark of the covenant to relocate. Significantly, Numbers tells us that this was Moses's habit immediately after telling us that Israel set out from Mount Sinai and journeyed three days into the desert, being led by the ark of YHWH "to seek out a resting place for them" (Num 10:33). The psalmist's allusion to this passage is appropriate if indeed his narrative is the story of Israel moving from Egypt, to Sinai, and finally to their resting place in Zion.

This hymnic opening is matched by an equally hymnic conclusion in vv. 33–36, which is immediately evident from סֶלָה in v. 33 and בָּרוּךְ אֱלֹהִים in v. 36:

> Kingdoms of the earth, sing to God! Praise the Lord—Selah— to the one who rides in the heavens, the ancient heavens; behold, he sends out his voice, a voice of strength. Give strength to God; his majesty is on Israel and his strength is in the clouds. God is feared from his sanctuary; he is the God of Israel. He gives strength and might to the people. Blessed be God.

Thus, the psalm is framed by corresponding hymnic sections that praise God for his might that he had displayed on behalf of Israel. Between these hymnic sections falls the prose of the psalm, which is quite balanced. Verses 4–19 contain a progressive narrative, extolling God for his guidance of Israel from Egypt to the heights of Zion. Verses 20–33 constitute the second major division of prose, which I will discuss in the next chapter.

---

[27] The claim to Ps 68's incoherence began with a bang when E. Reuss provided some four hundred different interpretations of parts of the psalm in his *Der acht-und-sechzigste Psalm, Ein Denkmal exegetischer Noth und Kunst zu Ehren unsrer ganzen Zunft* (Jena: Friedrich Mauke, 1851).

[28] Or alternatively, A. Jirku suggests the first verb should be revocalized as a niphal infinitive construct, while the second verb should be revocalized as a niphal, imperfect, 3mp. The *tau* prefix on תנדף is an Ugaritic and Canaanite feature known from the Amarna letters. The resultant translation is "as smoke is blown away, so they should be blown" (Anton Jirku, "Zu Psalm 68:3a," *VT* 5, no. 2 [1955]: 204).

The first section of the first division of the narrative, vv. 5–7, refers to God's deliverance of Israel from Egypt. Israel is told to sing to God, to praise his name, to exult the "Rider over the deserts." This epithet is repeated in v. 34 as "Rider on the heavens," which itself comes from Deut 33:26, where Yahweh is described as one who rides on the heavens to Israel's help in Egypt and the wilderness. So this first epithet is drawn from a context that evokes the Exodus.[29] The epithet Yah (יָהּ, Ps 68:5) also first appears (canonically and historically) in the ancient Song of the Sea (Exod 15:2), which celebrates the Exodus.[30] The description of God as a "father of orphans" and "a judge for widows" (v. 6) is reminiscent of Lamentation's description of Israel in bondage in Babylon: the Israelites are "orphans, fatherless; our mothers are like widows" (Lam 5:3). Lamentations possibly borrowed the imagery from the psalm to portray Babylon as a new Egypt, which would give us the earliest interpretation of Ps 68:6 as referring to God as the redeemer from Egypt.[31] Verse 7 is even more obviously a reference to the Exodus: "God causes the lonely to dwell in a home; he brings out the prisoners with prosperity." The Psalms Targum identifies the "lonely" as the "house of Israel, who were bound in Egypt."[32] It also identifies "the stubborn" in v. 7 (those who "dwell in scorched land") as Pharaoh and his armies. The phrase "to dwell in a home" refers elsewhere to bringing the Israelites into Canaan to dwell in homes (Jer 12:7; Hos 8:1; 9:15; 11:11).[33]

Not many commentators see references to the Exodus here. A. Weiser interprets the passage as pertaining to God's theophanic presence in a cultic context because of the allusion to the ark in v. 2 and the mention of God's cloud-chariot.[34] However, he follows Mowinckel by imposing a cultic *Sitz im Leben* on the psalm that is not obvious. Other commentators interpret the commands to praise as general commands, with some connection to God's presence among his people.[35] But these commentators

---

[29] Scholars and English versions typically translate the epithet "Rider over the Desert [lit. 'steppes, plains']" (רֹכֵב בָּעֲרָבוֹת) as "Rider on the Clouds," because it so closely resembles Baal's epithet "Rider on the Clouds" (*rkb b ʿrpwt*, e.g., KTU 1.2 iv 8, 29; 1.3 ii 40), and because there are "numerous interchanges" of the bilabial consonants *b* and *p* in Northwest Semitic" (Dahood, *Psalms*, 2:136; see also Kraus, *Psalms 60–150*, 46nf; HALOT, s.v. עֲרָבָה II). This would mean the Hebrew *rkb b ʿrbwt* is borrowed from Ugaritic and the Ugaritic *p* and Hebrew *b* are interchanged. There are several other instances of potential Ugaritic borrowing throughout the psalm but often only via emendation of the text to align it with Ugaritic mythology. I will discuss in detail the psalmist's potential borrowing from Ugaritic mythology in Chapter 4. There, I will argue that in Ps 68:5 the psalmist has adapted an original "Rider" epithet to the Exodus context of Ps 68:5–7 by altering it to "Rider over the Desert." Thus, the epithet as it stands emphasizes God's action of redeeming Israel from Egypt and leading them into the desert.

[30] E. Hengstenberg said there is "no doubt" that Exod 15:2 is the foundation for all other passages that use *Yah* (*Commentary on the Psalms* [Cherry Hill, NJ: Mack, 1975], 2:341). This shortened form of the divine name occurs forty-nine times total in the OT—forty-three times in the psalms, and only six times outside (Exod 15:2; 17:6; Isa 12:2; 26:4; 38:11[x2]). For the date of Exod 15 and Ps 68, see Chapter 4.

[31] Further possible allusions with Lamentations are "we are weary; we are given no rest" (Lam 5:5; cf. Ps 68:10, "when your inheritance was weary, you revived it") and the mention of Egypt and Assyria (Lam 5:6; cf. Ps 68:32–33).

[32] The Targum text and translation used is from David M. Stec, *The Targum of Psalms: Translated, with a Critical Introduction, Apparatus, and Notes*, ArBib 16 (Collegeville, MN: Liturgical Press, 2004).

[33] Dahood, *Psalms*, 2:137.

[34] Weiser, *Psalms*, 484.

[35] E.g., Marvin E. Tate, *Psalms 51–100*, WBC 20 (Dallas, TX: Word Books, 1990), 176; John Goldingay, *Psalms* (Grand Rapids, MI: Baker Academic, 2006), 2:316–17.

miss the Exodus language noted above. Scholars who have noted the Exodus language have failed to see all of it as laid out above, but their observations do support my contention.[36] So vv. 5–7 praise God for his defeat of Pharaoh and his forces for the purpose of bringing them out of Egypt and settling them in the promised land (cf. Exod 15:17–18).

The next section (vv. 8–11) speaks of God leading Israel in the wilderness to Sinai, where he gave them the law (vv. 8–9), followed by Israel's conquest of the land (vv. 10–11). The interpretation of vv. 8–9 as recounting God's gift of the law at Sinai is evident as early as the Targum (". . . when you gave the Torah to your people") and 4 Ezra 3:17–18 as it comments on Ps 68:8–9 (". . . you brought them to Mount Sinai . . . to give the Law to the descendants of Jacob . . ."). The journey toward Sinai started when God went out before his people and "marched in the desert" (v. 8). The term for desert here is יְשִׁימוֹן, which elsewhere refers to the wilderness in which Israel wandered and in which God cared for them.[37] Verse 9 continues recounting God's theophanic presence in the wilderness when they finally arrived at Sinai: "The earth quaked, indeed, the heavens dripped before God." The quaking of the earth is said to accompany God's presence elsewhere (e.g., Pss 18:7; 77:19 [MT]; Isa 13:13), and the language here is reminiscent of other theophanic accounts.[38] Rain is not explicitly recorded in the Exodus account of God's theophany at Sinai, but it does record lightning and dark clouds (Exod 19:16), which we may presume indicates rain just as lightning and dark clouds in Ps 18:8–12 are explained to be full of rain (v. 12).

The historical reference to God's theophany at Sinai is solidified as Ps 68:9 continues, "the heavens dripped before God, זֶה סִינַי." W. Gesenius and Briggs thought this phrase was likely a corrupt text, being carried over from an early gloss in Judges 5:5.[39] P. Joüon and T. Muraoka suggest that זה could be functioning adjectivally, "this Sinai," or it could be standing in the construct state, "the One of Sinai."[40] The difficult construction has been clarified by the discovery of the use of demonstrative pronouns in Ugaritic, Mari, and Arabic epithets.[41] זֶה סִינַי is therefore a title, used here because the

---

[36] Dahood, *Psalms*, 2:137; Charles A. Briggs and Emilie Grace Briggs, *A Critical and Exegetical Commentary on the Book of Psalms*, ICC (Edinburgh: T&T Clark, 1906-1907), 2:98; Kraus, *Psalms 60–150*, 52; Nancy L. DeClaissé-Walford, Rolf A. Jacobson, and Beth LaNeel Tanner, *The Book of Psalms*, NICOT (Grand Rapids, MI: Eerdmans, 2014), 548n39.

[37] Deut 32:10; Ps 78:40; 106:14; 107:4; cf. Isa 43:19–20.

[38] E.g., Exod 19:16–18; 20:18; 1 Kgs 19:11–13; Hab 3:3–12; Mic 1:3–4; Nah 1:3–5; Ps 97:1–5 (Tate, *Psalms 51–100*, 177).

[39] Wilhelm Gesenius, E. Kautzsch, and A. E. Cowley, *Gesenius' Hebrew Grammar*, 2nd English ed. (Oxford: Clarendon Press, 1909), 442n2; Briggs, *Psalms*, 2:98.

[40] Paul Joüon and T. Muraoka, *A Grammar of Biblical Hebrew*, SB (Roma: Pontificio intituto biblico, 2006), 500.

[41] E.g., the Ugaritic epithet *il dpid*, "El the merciful one," literally "El the one of heart"; cf. Pss 75:8; 104:25. See Alexander Globe, "Literary Structure and Unity of the Song of Deborah," *JBL* 93, no. 4 (1974): 493; Dahood, *Psalms*, 2:139. Robert D. Holmstedt has recently argued that this use of comparative Semitic grammar is applied inappropriately to the demonstrative זֶה in Hebrew. He argues that זֶה, when standing before a nominal phrase or a numerical phrase, functions in every OT case as either the pronominal subject of a null copula clause or as a pronominal demonstrative in apposition to the following noun phrase (see examples of this construction in Exod 32:1; Josh 14:10; Deut 8:2; Gen 27:36; Zech 1:12, and further examples on pp. 20–26 of his essay, "Analyzing זֶה Grammar and Reading זֶה Texts of Ps 68:9 and Judg 5:5," *JHS* 14 [2014]: 1–26). If he is correct, then זֶה סִינַי in Judg 5:5 and Ps 68:9 means either "this mountain [lit. 'this one'], Sinai," or "this *is* Sinai." It

context recalls his theophany at Sinai. This verse is drawn directly from Judg 5:4–5 but with deliberate alteration: the psalmist has erased Seir as the location from which God comes (cf. Deut 33:2) in order to fit the theophanic language into the context of the narrative he is constructing. God now comes from Egypt after liberating his people to Mount Sinai, where he manifests his presence and gives his law. The same theophanic language is connected explicitly with the giving of the law in Deut 33:2, which speaks of God coming with "tens of thousands of his holy ones" to give "a fiery law."[42]

Verses 10–11 narrate the initial conquest of Canaan when God began to give the land to Israel. "Abundant rain you caused to fall, O God; when your inheritance was weary, you revived it" (v. 10). "Inheritance" may here refer to Canaan, as נַחֲלָה often does (e.g., Deut 4:21, 38; Josh 13:18).[43] However, the psalm refers not to Israel's inheritance, but to God's, which throughout the OT is Israel (e.g., Deut 4:20; Pss 28:9; 33:12; 74:2).[44] Even so, the psalmist must still be using נַחֲלָה to refer to Canaan, because v. 11 says God's creatures "dwelled in it," using a third singular feminine suffix to refer anaphorically to נַחֲלָה. Thus, God sent rain on Canaan to restore it, as all ancient Near Eastern people praised their gods for so doing, and he also allowed his creatures to dwell in that fertile land.

Verses 12–15 still give commentators trouble, as is evident from the following translation:

> The Lord gave a message: the [female] bearers of good news were a great army. Kings of armies flee, they flee! The [female] dweller of the house divides the spoil— when you lie between the sheepfolds – the wings of a dove covered in silver and its pinions with yellowish green gold. When the Almighty scattered kings in it, it snowed on Zalmon.

Perhaps no other section in the psalm has given more rise to theories that Ps 68 was a collection of song titles or incipits (the first line of ancient Near Eastern poems or liturgies).[45] My argument here is that Ps 68 does have coherence based on its narrative structure, but vv. 12–15 are so seemingly incoherent that they do not appear to be simple prose. Since it begins with, "The Lord gave a message: the [female] bearers of good news were a great army," it may be that this part of the psalm is recounting a victory during which the Lord sent a message of victory through female singers. It was common in Israel for women to meet the male warriors after a battle to sing victory

---

would then not be clarifying who is אֱלֹהִים (Ps 68:9) or יְהוָה (Judg 5:5) but standing in parallel to the "mountains" (Judg 5:5) and the "earth" (Ps 68:9) that quaked in response to God's theophany. If his argument is correct, then my argument here still holds (and is perhaps strengthened) that Ps 68:9 depicts God's theophany at Sinai.

[42] The text of Deut 33:2 is uncertain. Most versions translate either "a flame of fire" or "a fiery law," but the context is certainly referring to the giving of the law on Sinai (33:3–4).

[43] So, Franz Delitzsch, *Biblical Commentary on The Psalms*, trans. Rev. Francis Bolton, 2nd rev. ed. (Edinburgh: T&T Clark, 1880–1881), 2:251; Dahood, *Psalms 51–100*; Kraus, *Psalms 60–150*, 52.

[44] So also Hengstenberg, *Psalms*, 346; Louis Jacquet, *Les Psaumes et le Cœur de l'Homme: Étude Textuelle, Littéraire et Doctrinale* (Gembloux: Duculot, 1977), 354.

[45] E.g., W. O. E. Oesterley, *The Psalms* (London: Society for Promoting Christian Knowledge, 1939), 2:320–21; Hans Schmidt, *Die Psalmen*, HBAT I 15 (Tübingen: Mohr Siebeck, 1934), 127–28; William F. Albright, "A Catalogue of Early Hebrew Lyric Poems (Psalm LXVIII)," *HUCA* 23 (1951): 1–39.

songs (Exod 15:20–21; Judg 11:34; 1 Sam 18:6–8). Verses 13–15 may be the content of what was sung on the occasion being recounted here in the psalm. If so, then vv. 13–15 would either be a broken or ancient form of poetic expression, or they could possibly be the names of the songs that were sung on these occasions.[46] Whatever the case may be, the important matter here for my argument regarding the psalm's narrative structure is what occasion of military victory is being recounted.

The historical occasion being remembered in vv. 12–15 is clearly the defeat of Deborah and Barak over Sisera (Judg 4–5). This is evident when one notices the several allusions to Judg 5 packed within these verses.[47] The reference to dividing the spoil ("the [female] dweller of the house divides the spoil," v. 12) alludes to the dividing of spoil in Judg 5:30 ("have they not found and divided the spoil?").[48] The phrase "when you lie among the sheepfolds" in Ps 68:14 alludes to Judg 5:16, "why did you sit among the sheepfolds?"[49] The "great army" in v. 11 likely refers to the armies of Deborah or Sisera or both. There may also be a connection between the (female) dweller of the house in Ps 68:13 and Jael, the "most blessed of tent-dwelling women" in Judg 5:24, who killed Sisera. Finally, the "wings of a dove covered in silver and its pinions with yellowish green gold" may evoke the spoil of silver that was not taken by the kings of Canaan but presumably by Israel (Judg 5:19). If some of these allusions are less than convincing, the cumulative case is strongly in favor of this language evoking the battle in Judg 4–5. Indeed, the allusions may be less than obvious if these lines were in fact incipits or titles of songs used to celebrate the victory over Sisera and Jabin. Additionally, there are several other allusions to Judg 5 throughout Ps 68, which provide corroborative evidence that vv. 12–15 are recounting the military victory over Sisera.[50] Thus, while the details of Ps 68:12–15 are obscure, it seems clear enough that it recounts the deliverance that God gave Israel through the hands of Deborah and Barak.

Verses 16–19 constitute the final section of the first division of the psalm and also result in the historical climax of God's past working for Israel (i.e., the second division

---

[46] So, John P. Peters, "Notes on Some Difficult Passages in the Old Testament," *JBL* 11, no. 1 (1892): 50–52. Some commentators believe this section begins a victory song, but many see it stretching beyond v. 15, e.g., Oesterley, *The Psalms*, 2:324; DeClaissé-Walford, Jacobson, and Tanner, *The Book of Psalms*, 549. However, since v. 16 begins the section regarding the dispute between mountains, it is unlikely the victory song or songs in vv. 12–15 extend beyond that section. Tate similarly takes the song to end at v. 15, with the main message that YHWH is the victor over kings and their armies (*Psalms 51–100*, 178).

[47] See similar explications of these allusions to Judg 5 in Duhm, *Die Psalmen*, 176; Briggs, *Psalms*, 2:99–100; Jacquet, *Psaumes*, 354–58. Tate disagrees that Judg 4–5 is the occasion in mind because the language drawn from there is generalized by the psalmist and used differently. It is possible that Judg 4–5 is only one occasion in mind and that the psalmist poetically intermingles memories of other similar military victories, but the majority of the language evokes Deborah's battle.

[48] The word שָׁלָל occurs four times in Judg 5:30. The collocation of חלק and שָׁלָל occurs ten times in the OT (Gen 49:27; Exod 15:9; Josh 22:8; Judg 5:30; Ps 68:13; Prov 16:19; Isa 9:2; 33:23; 53:12; Zech 14:1). Although it is possible the psalmist had Gen 49:27 or Josh 22:8 in mind (or others, if the psalm is dated late), the multitude of allusions to Judg 5 in this context suggests the psalmist had Judg 5:30 in mind when referring to dividing the spoil. Alternatively, the psalmist could have simply had the concept of spoil division in mind, which he expressed with this common collocation, but the event that would have brought this collocation to mind is the defeat of Sisera.

[49] This language itself goes back to the prophecy about Issachar in Gen 49:14.

[50] Compare Ps 68:3 with Judg 5:31; Ps 68:8–9 with Judg 5:4–5; Ps 68:19 with Judg 5:12; Ps 68:22 with Judg 5:26; and Ps 68:28 with Judg 5:14, 18.

of the psalm does not recount past history). However, there is some debate about the identification of the mountains and various exegetical points. The biggest problems are: (1) the description of Mount Bashan; (2) which mountain is in mind in v. 19; and (3) the identification of the gifts in v. 19 (this third issue is not much debated by commentators but is a central issue for my overall thesis about how Paul uses the psalm).

The first difficulty is the identification of the mountains. Verse 16 reads הַר־אֱלֹהִים הַר־בָּשָׁן הַר גַּבְנֻנִּים הַר־בָּשָׁן. Several interpreters have wrestled with the problem that the psalmist seems to identify Mount Bashan as the Mountain of God. Briggs believed the mountain described here and in v. 17 can be none other than Mount Zion, so he claimed an original reading of הר יהוה הר דשן, "Mountain of YHWH, fertile mountain." A redactor changed יהוה to אלהים, which then allowed a later copyist to think of a grandiose mountain (taking אלהים as a superlative) and thus to insert בשן for דשן.[51] It is possible that the MT has been corrupted here as Briggs suggests, since the LXX omits Bashan and reads "the mountain of God is a rich mountain, a curdling (τυρόω) mountain, a rich mountain." Moreover, the Targum explicitly identifies this mountain of God as Mount Moriah, noting that Mount Mathnan, Mount Tabor, and Mount Carmel were disqualified.[52] This opens the possibility that the Targum author did not have Bashan in v. 16 of his text as Briggs suggests. However, the LXX consistently misunderstands the ancient Hebrew in the psalm, and the Targum itself is inconsistent. While it sees Mount Zion in v. 16, it continues in vv. 17–19 to speak of the mountain of God as the one on which he chose to give the law, not to dwell as the MT says. The Targum reinterprets this section of the psalm in a Mosaic direction (replacing God with Moses in v. 19), which explains its identification of the "mountain of God" in v. 16 as Sinai, ignoring Mount Bashan. So while an emendation such as what Briggs suggests is possible and the ancient versions could possibly suggest a corrupted MT, it is not certain, and other solutions are possible and to be preferred.

A second possible interpretation is that the phrases in v. 16 are indicatives and represent (in anthropomorphic fashion) the mountain's voice laying claim to the honor of being God's dwelling place. "The mountain of God is the mountain of Bashan. A many-peaked mountain is the mountain of Bashan." The poet in v. 17 then denies Bashan its claim, asking why it looks with envy on the mountain that God has desired for his abode (implying Mount Zion).[53] This interpretation makes good sense of the fact that v. 17 repeats "many-peaked mountain," which makes Mount Bashan to be the envious mountain that looks at the other mountain that God has chosen. It is a possible interpretation, but not one that many commentators have followed, because there are simpler solutions that avoid a forced anthropomorphic interpretation. Similarly forced is the AV, which translates "The hill of God *is as* the hill of Bashan; an high hill *as* the hill of Bashan." Even aside from the baseless comparatives, it would

---

[51] Briggs and Briggs, *Psalms*, 2:96, 101.
[52] The Targum is followed by Midr. Teh. 68:9.
[53] Samuel Horsley, *The Book of Psalms: Translated from the Hebrew with Notes, Explanatory and Critical*, 2nd ed. (Edinburgh: C. Stewart, 1815), 2:179–80.

be strange for the psalmist only to equate Zion with Bashan, setting them on equal footing.⁵⁴

A third possible interpretation is to take אלהים here as "gods," suggesting perhaps demons, in contrast to Yahweh in the next verse. M. D. Cassuto first argued for this interpretation, followed by J. Day's formidable argumentation.⁵⁵ Day points to Babylonian evidence and to 1 En. 6:6 to suggest Mount Hermon (to which he believes Bashan refers) was the locale of the Canaanite gods. The same Bashan is in view in v. 22, where it stands in contrast to the depths of the sea, the full expression referring to the highest and lowest regions of the earth.⁵⁶ Under this view, both the mountain and the sea function as enemies of God. This interpretation requires no emendation of the text, makes sense historically, fits the context, and is therefore plausible. But it is hard to believe אלהים could be used in two radically different senses from v. 16 to v. 17, first of demons and then of YHWH.⁵⁷ One might reply that if Mount Bashan was already believed to be associated with gods or demons, then the psalmist could have assumed the ambiguity would be immediately resolved by the הַר־בָּשָׁן following the second הַר־אֱלֹהִים. But I find this too speculative and rather far-fetched.

Mowinckel similarly attempted to interpret Bashan through the matrix of ancient Near Eastern mythology. Bashan is a region in the north whose northern border is Mount Hermon (Deut 3:1–10; 4:47–48; Josh 12:4–5). This has led some scholars to equate Mount Bashan with Mount Hermon, which is supported by the fact that Mount Hermon has many peaks, as the psalm says twice of Mount Bashan.⁵⁸ Since Ps 89:13 presents Mounts Hermon and Tabor together, this allowed Mowinckel to take Mount Bashan with Mount Tabor, where he supposed there was formerly a sanctuary for whose liturgy Ps 68 was written. He understood Mount Bashan to be a mythological name meaning "snake," which presented Mount Tabor as the mountain of the gods, similar to Mount Olympus.⁵⁹ J. A. Emerton rightly criticized Mowinckel for overuse of comparative data and for believing Mount Tabor could be called Bashan in the mythological sense of "snake" when the real region of Bashan was so nearby.⁶⁰

A fourth interpretation is to take v. 16 as a reference to a period in the time of the judges when the ark settled on Mount Bashan for a time. Verse 16 would not then be making a claim that Mount Bashan was still the mountain of God. Rather, the psalm poetically records the sense of envy that Bashan felt when God

---

⁵⁴ John Adney Emerton, "The 'Mountain of God' in Psalm 68:16," in *History and Traditions of Early Israel: Studies Presented to Eduard Nielsen*, ed. André Lemaire and Benedikt Otzen, SVT 50 (Leiden: Brill, 1993), 30.

⁵⁵ U. (M. D.) Cassuto, תהלים סח, *Tarbiz* 12 (1940), 15–18; English translation: "Psalm LXVIII," *Biblical and Oriental Studies I* (Jerusalem, 1973), 264–69; John Day, *God's Conflict with the Dragon and the Sea: Echoes of a Canaanite Myth in the Old Testament*, UCOP 34 (Cambridge: Cambridge University Press, 1985), 115–19.

⁵⁶ So also Kraus, *Psalms 60–150*, 55.

⁵⁷ Emerton, "Mountain of God," 34.

⁵⁸ Israel Knohl, "Psalm 68: Structure, Composition and Geography," *JHS* 12 (2012): 13.

⁵⁹ Sigmund Mowinckel, *Der achtundsechzigste Psalm* (Oslo: I kommisjon hos J. Dybwad, 1953), 43. Mowinckel's translation of Bashan as "snake" relies on the typical northwest Semitic interchange of *ṯ* for *š* (e.g., Ugaritic *ṯlṯ* ["three"] evolved into Hebrew *šlš*). Thus, Hebrew *bšn* would be equivalent to Ugaritic *bṯn*, "snake."

⁶⁰ Emerton, "Mountain of God," 31.

chose another mountain in its stead. Emerton believes the psalm in its original form (before implied redactions) may have referred to a sacred mountain in Bashan in v. 16, but he is concerned with the present form of the psalm, which states later that God's dwelling is in Jerusalem on Mount Zion (v. 30).[61] He concludes that both verses constitute a question: "Is Mount Bashan a mountain of God, Many-peaked mountain, Mount Bashan?"[62] This solution is viable, but the interrogative interpretation is still forced, at least more so than the following simple and straightforward solution that I prefer.

The best explanation is simply to take אלהים as a superlative adjective, "mighty mountain," and to take both halves of the verse as vocatives to setup the question in v. 17.[63] The same lexeme (אלהים) is used in a superlative sense in Gen 23:6; 30:8; 1 Sam 14:15; Jonah 3:3. Other divine names also occur as superlative adjectives: גן־יהוה ("mighty garden") in Isa 51:3 and, importantly, הררי־אל ("mighty mountains") in Ps 36:7, which serves as a plausible parallel to Ps 68:16.[64] The superlative adjective was recognized here as early as 1772 by D. Durell and is translated as such by the CJB, NAB, NET, NIV, NLT, and NRSV.[65] This interpretation has been challenged by a few, who rely too easily on the conclusion of D. W. Thomas that the use of אלהים as a superlative cannot escape religious significance and function simply as an "intensifying epithet."[66] But that is exactly the case in Jonah 3:3 where "the great city" does not have religious significance with reference to YHWH, so Thomas's conclusion cannot stand. So I contend that this is the most straightforward reading of the language, that it is possible linguistically, and that it fits the narrative flow of the psalm. One might object, as I did earlier, that this takes אלהים in two different senses in v. 15 and v. 16. But the proposal of Cassuto and Day requires אלהים to be read in *radically opposite* ways (demons, then YHWH), while the superlative adjective is simply attributing divine or grandiose status to the head noun and is therefore semantically related to the person of God.[67]

In summary, v. 16 transitions from the defeat of Canaanite kings in vv. 12–15 to the search for God's elect mountain (as prophesied in Exod 15:17–18). Bashan is a mighty mountain but is overlooked as the permanent place of God's dwelling. The psalmist inquires of the mighty mountain Bashan, "Why do you look enviously, O mountain of peaks, at the mountain that God desired for his dwelling? Surely the LORD will dwell

---

[61] Ibid., 33.
[62] Ibid., 37. Cf. the Jerusalem Bible.
[63] CJB; NAB; NRSV; Dahood, *Psalms*, 2:131; Jacquet, *Psaumes*, 358; Tate, *Psalms 51–100*, 166. Some other versions translate with a superlative adjective in the indicative (NLT, NIV; NAU footnote).
[64] Bruce K. Waltke and Michael Patrick O'Connor, *An Introduction to Biblical Hebrew Syntax* (Winona Lake, IN: Eisenbrauns, 1990), 268. These examples all suggest the inherent quality of the head noun (David Durell, *Critical Remarks on the Books of Job, Proverbs, Psalms, Ecclesiastes, and Canticles* [Oxford: Clarendon, 1772], 148).
[65] Durell, *Critical Remarks*, 148.
[66] Emerton, "Mountain of God," 29; Day, *God's Conflict*, 116; Knohl, "Psalm 68," 14.
[67] In other words, in the case of Jonah 3:3, the adjective "great" might be considered a semantic extension of the core meaning of "God," who himself is great, grandiose, and divine. Jonah 3:3 does not attribute religious significance to Nineveh, but it is so great a city that one may properly use a lexeme to describe it that otherwise refers to the divine.

forever" (Ps 68:17).[68] The mention of dwelling forever surely refers to Mount Zion, so v. 17 refers to God choosing to dwell on Zion and remaining there "forever." The psalm has therefore moved from the Exodus, to Sinai, to the conquering of Canaan, to his deliverance from Sisera, to a mention of Mount Zion as God's eternal dwelling place.

Verse 18 is nearly as puzzling as v. 17: רֶכֶב אֱלֹהִים רִבֹּתַיִם אַלְפֵי שִׁנְאָן אֲדֹנָי בָם סִינַי בַּקֹּדֶשׁ. The first clause is simple enough: "the chariots of God are ten thousand thousands multiplied."[69] With the second clause arise many interpretive possibilities. The NASB inserts a comparative phrase, "the Lord is among them *as at* Sinai, in holiness [or 'in the holy place']," comparing God's theophanic presence at Sinai to his presence elsewhere (specifically at his "holy place," if that is how one would translate בַּקֹּדֶשׁ). However, there is no basis for inserting the comparative clause and it also breaks the poetic structure. One could translate woodenly without an implied copulative: "the Lord is among them, Sinai in holiness," but this would make little sense of the second clause. A third and popular option is to emend the text to אדני בא מסיני, "the Lord came from Sinai."[70] The suggestion is tempting, since it makes for a smooth translation, but for that very reason it is unlikely to be original (why should *this* part of the psalm be so clear?). It is also unnecessary, given the other viable translations. A final option is to supply a copulative, "the Lord is among them; Sinai is in the holy place" (cf. ESV, "Sinai is now in the holy place"). In this case, Sinai is a metonym for God's theophanic presence at Sinai, which is stated to be manifested "in the holy place," that is, his sanctuary on Zion. Such use of metonymy is supported by the epithet זֶה סִינַי (v. 9), which identifies YHWH very closely with Sinai.[71]

So the best translation is the straightforward one, with a supplied copulative: "the Lord is among them; Sinai *is* in the holy place." After rejecting Mount Bashan as the place of his eternal dwelling, God has moved on to find his elect mountain. Verse 18 telescopes the entire journey from Sinai to this elect mountain to recapitulate the narrative thus far. He came *from Sinai* and now has come to his chosen mountain, which is described in v. 19. Sinai is a metonymy for God's theophanic presence (cf. v. 9); it has now manifested itself on his elect mountain just as it did at Sinai.[72]

---

[68] Bashan's envy is understandable, since Mount Hermon reaches 2,795 meters in elevation, while Zion reaches only 700 meters and is immediately dwarfed by the 808 meters of the Mount of Olives (Jacquet, *Psaumes*, 358–59).

[69] The word שִׁנְאָן is a hapax legomenon. It may either mean "repetition" (thus meaning "ten thousand thousands multiplied infinitely") or it may be cognate with Ugaritic *ṯnn*, "warrior," whose Akkadian cognate is *šanannu*, "archer" (HALOT s.v. שִׁנְאָן; Dahood, *Psalms*, 2:142–43). There are other possibilities, but these two are favored by most commentators. The precise meaning need not detain us here.

[70] Suggested by BHS, adopted by Kraus, *Psalms 60–150*, 44nv and the NET Bible.

[71] Somewhat similarly, Tate takes "Sinai" here as a divine epithet, similar to that in v. 9 (*Psalms 51–100*, 181). In this case, סִינַי is a shortened form of the epithet in v. 9 (זֶה סִינַי), although I prefer metonymy as an explanation.

[72] Thus Sinai acted as one of God's earlier temples, prior to Zion. See Jeffrey Jay Niehaus, *God at Sinai: Covenant and Theophany in the Bible and Ancient Near East*, SOTBT (Grand Rapids, MI: Zondervan, 1995). I must mention here also Jon Douglas Levenson's provocative *Sinai and Zion: An Entry into the Jewish Bible*, NVBS (Minneapolis, MN: Winston Press, 1985). One of his main points is that Zion traditions absorbed Sinai traditions. While many of his arguments are based on shaky diachronic suppositions, Ps 68:18–19 provides an illustration of his thesis. Traditions that once celebrated Sinai as God's special location of revelation eventually gave way to traditions that celebrated Zion as God's elect mountain.

Verse 19 concludes the first narratival division of the psalm with a climactic crescendo: "You ascended to the height; you took captive captives; you received gifts among men and indeed, among the stubborn, in order to dwell, O Yah, God." Dahood believes the verb עלה must evoke God's ascension to the height of Sinai, pointing to Ps 47:6 as his support. He also cites the mention of Sinai in v. 18 as support and believes the "stubborn" must refer to Israel in the wilderness at Sinai.[73] But we just saw that Sinai is not mentioned as God's current locale in this part of the psalm, and Ps 47:6 seems in no way to refer to God at Sinai. God is king of the world (47:3, 8), reigning over the nations from his holy throne (49:9), language fitting of God's reign on Mount Zion. Moreover, the mention of taking captive captives could not refer to any event at Sinai but fits rather well the taking of Jerusalem from the Canaanites in war.[74] The reception of gifts, to be discussed momentarily, also fits the context of Zion, not Sinai. So v. 19 concludes the past narratival division of the psalm with God's climactic taking of Jerusalem, his taking captive his enemies, his reception of gifts, and his ascension to the height of Mount Zion where he would dwell "forever" (v. 17).

War Spoils as Gifts to God for Building the Temple

The phrase "you received gifts" (לָקַחְתָּ מַתָּנוֹת) is typically understood as referring to victory spoils which Yahweh received from his defeated foes, whom he took captive—foes throughout the narrative but specifically those in Jerusalem (68:19).[75] Similarly, v. 30 says kings bear gifts to God because of his temple in Jerusalem. However, I will argue that the gifts in v. 19 are not necessarily (or at the very least, not *only*) gifts given from defeated kings. Rather, the gifts are *at least* gifts given by the Israelites to God for building up the temple. This claim is crucial for my thesis regarding Paul's use of Ps 68:19. I will present ancient Near Eastern data and similar data from the OT to argue that this is the best understanding of Ps 68:19.

That the context of vv. 18–19 is not only that of war but more importantly that of God's climactic inhabitation of his holy temple gives us reason to suspect that the gifts might not simply be war spoil. Moreover, we already saw that the context of Eph 4:7–16 is that of an organic growth of the temple, which occurs by means of the gifts given to individual believers. In other words, Christ supplies the materials for the construction of the temple. Without reading Paul's interpretation back into Ps 68, it does give us a reason to look for an association between the gifts and the Jerusalem temple rather than simply assuming that the gifts are war spoil.[76]

---

[73] Dahood, *Psalms*, 2:143.

[74] The word שְׁבִי can mean either captivity or captives. The cognate accusative phrase used here (שבה + שְׁבִי) occurs elsewhere in the OT only six times (Num 21:1; Deut 21:10; Judg 5:12; 2 Chr 6:37, 38; 28:17). The Pentateuchal references are general in nature, and the 2 Chronicles references are later than the psalm (the date of the psalm will be discussed in the next chapter). So the psalmist is likely alluding to or at least drawing the captive language from Judg 5:12, where Deborah tells Barak, "Arise, Barak, take captive your captives." Since שְׁבִי in Judg 5:12 means "captives," not "captivity," it carries the same meaning in Ps 68:19.

[75] E.g., Jacquet, *Psaumes*, 360; Goldingay, *Psalms*, 2:326.

[76] In fact, this line of reasoning was true to my actual process of researching the issue. The gifts seem to have transformed from war spoil to spiritual gifts to build up the temple. Paul, as a later interpreter,

The reception of gifts from the Israelites for the construction of God's dwelling place occurred in the narratives of the tabernacle and temple construction. The idea is therefore a key detail of both construction narratives. In Exod 25:1–2, God tells Moses to "tell the sons of Israel to take a contribution" for the construction of the tabernacle. In 1 Chr 29:2–5, David speaks of the lavish gifts for the construction of the temple which he has freely given, while 29:6–9 speaks of the Israelites' contributions. These contributions were "in order to build for you a house for your holy name" (29:16). Both occasions demonstrated the generosity of the Israelites, who brought an abundance of material for the construction of God's dwelling place (Exod 35:21–29; 1 Chr 29:9, 14, 16). Moses even had to restrain the people from bringing more gifts because of their abundant generosity (Exod 36:6). Similarly with the construction of the second temple, King Artaxerxes offered freely (נדב) silver and gold for Ezra to use in building it up (Ezra 7:15–16; cf. 1 Chr 29:5–17). Israel also set aside dedicated portions of war spoil for repairs on the temple (1 Chr 26:27), which demonstrates that Israel's gifts continued to be used not only for the construction of the temple but also for its maintenance.

The idea that a god's adherents would give gifts to construct a temple is not foreign to ancient Near Eastern records. In the Babylonian *Enuma Eliš*, the Anunnaki determine to build Marduk a temple for freeing them from the duties imposed on them by Ea (VI 17–54). They made bricks for a full year to devote to the construction of Marduk's temple, which they completed in the second year. In the Ugaritic *Baal Cycle*, the gods petition El until he allows a temple to be built for victorious Baal. It is somewhat unclear whether those who gather the materials are only Kothar-wa-Hasis or also Baal's adherents, but the ornate materials are brought to Baal and used by Kothar-wa-Hasis to construct his temple.[77] In *Marduk Prophecy*, Marduk calls out, "Bring your tribute, O you lands, to Babylon!" The purpose is that "a king of Babylon will arise" and "he will renew the house of announcement, the Ekur-sagil."[78] In Tiglath-pileser I's (1114–1076 BC) lengthy annals, he notes a couple times that he either donated war spoil to his gods or used the war spoil to adorn a temple.[79] In some cases, it is ambiguous whether those bringing building material bring it as gifts or tax, but in these cases friendly gifts seems more likely, since otherwise the king would emphasize their subjugation to tout his grandeur.[80]

---

caused me to reread the psalm to investigate whether the gifts really were war spoil, or perhaps something more related to the temple.

[77] See the ambiguous plural forms in KTU 1.4 vi 15–35. They may only refer to Kothar-wa-Hasis since the drama occurs in the mythological realm, but the materials are still brought to Baal for the construction of his temple.

[78] "The Marduk Prophecy," trans. Tremper Longman III (*COS* 1:480–81). However, there is a slight lacuna after "Bring your tribute, O you lands, to Babylon . . .," while the following section begins "A king of Babylon will arise . . ." It seems a fair inference that the tribute will be used to rebuild the house.

[79] I, 15, 18 in Albert Kirk Grayson, *From Tiglath-pileser I to Ashur-nasir-apli II*, ARI 2 (Wiesbaden: Otto Harrassowitz, 1976), 8, 11.

[80] E.g., in the cases of the temples built by Gudea and Darius, on which see Victor Hurowitz, *I Have Built You an Exalted House: Temple Building in the Bible in Light of Mesopotamian and Northwest Semitic Writings*, JSOTSS 115 (Sheffield: JSOT Press, 1992), 205–9; also a sun boat built by Amenhotep III for Amen-Re from the "chiefs of all foreign lands" (*AEL* 2:45).

There are also plenty of records of war spoil being used to build temples for one's god. Examples are especially abundant in the Assyrian annals, which almost always recount spoil taken and end with the construction of a temple or palace.[81] One explicit example is Stela K 3751, which records Tiglath-pileser III's construction of a temple in Kalḫu with war spoil.[82] In Egypt, the "Poetical Stela of Thutmose III" records despoiling and then the construction of a temple, which seems to imply it was built with spoil.[83] This text is important because the second part, the triumphal poem, was later used by Amenhotep III, Seti I, and Ramses III, who adapted it to their use.[84] Amenhotep III built a temple to Amun with war spoil and perhaps also tribute, which the stela emphasizes.[85]

This evidence demonstrates that it was common to build temples with gifts given by a god's devotees, as well as with war spoil. Not all ancient Near Eastern temples were built with gifts given by a god's devotees because not all rulers demanded or requested that they do so. But in the OT accounts, Moses and David placed the demand on the people, who gave freely. So the gifts received by God in Ps 68:19 should be understood in light of these accounts, that he received the gifts from the Israelites. He received these gifts "in order to dwell" (לִשְׁכֹּן). Since receiving gifts does not further God's ability to dwell anywhere, the telic *lamed* must imply that the purpose of the gifts is "[in order to construct God's temple] in order to dwell." The gifts were also given בָּאָדָם. The four possible interpretations here are "among men" (locative, ESV; CJB; NAU; Kraus[86]), "in spite of men" (adversative), "because of men" (causative), or "by/from men" (instrumental, HCSB; NIV; NET; NLT; NRSV). My proposal makes the popular instrumental translation even more likely: it was through the Israelites that gifts were given to God.[87]

But as both ideas of building temples with gifts from devotees and with war spoil are evident in ancient Near Eastern texts, there is no reason both ideas cannot be present in Ps 68. Certainly, the Israelites gained all their construction materials for the tabernacle when they despoiled Egypt (Exod 3:22; 11:2–3; 12:35–36). They gained more materials by despoiling the Canaanites through their various battles on their journey to taking Jerusalem (e.g., Josh 7:21; 8:27; Judg 8:24–25; 1 Sam 14:30; Ps 68:13). Surely the superfluous precious contributions given by the Israelites for the construction of the temple also consisted in large part of these war spoils. So God's reception of gifts in Ps 68:19 may be considered free gifts from his devotees that were acquired as war spoil,

---

[81] These will be examined in detail in Chapter 3.
[82] Tiglath-pileser III 47 rev. 17 in Hayim Tadmor and Shigeo Yamada, eds., *The Royal Inscriptions of Tiglath-pileser III (744-727 BC) and Shalmaneser V (726-722 BC), Kings of Assyria*, RINAP 1 (Winona Lake, IN: Eisenbrauns, 2011), 123.
[83] The translation may be found in *AEL* 2:35–59.
[84] Ibid., 35.
[85] Ibid., 44–46. He also built a gate with war spoil.
[86] Kraus, *Psalms 60–150*, 44.
[87] One might object by suggesting that the mention of rebels (וְאַף סוֹרְרִים) evokes the idea of the defeated enemies bringing tribute and by noting that foreign kings bring tribute in v. 30. But the word for "tribute" in v. 30 (שַׁי) is different than "gifts" (מַתָּנָה) in v. 19, and סוֹרְרִים could just as well refer to the rebellious Israelites, as they are so portrayed throughout the wilderness period (e.g., Ps 95:7–11). As noted earlier, Dahood believes the rebels are the Israelites, although he thinks this section refers to their time at Sinai.

but the emphasis falls on the fact that the gifts are from the Israelites for the purpose of building their glorious God a temple in which he may dwell forever.[88]

The strongest objection to this view is that the word for "gifts" in Ps 68:19 is מַתָּנָה, which is not used in the tabernacle or temple contribution narratives. The word מַתָּנָה refers to the "general idea of 'gift,' with the specific nuance provided by the respective context."[89] It can refer broadly to gifts of an inheritance, something beyond an inheritance, gifts for the poor, a bribe, gifts offered at the sanctuary of Yahweh or an idolatrous sanctuary, or to the Levites as a gift to Israel.[90] The noun used in Exod 25:2–3; 35:5 is תְּרוּמָה, which, in the OT, refers to holy (but not most holy) offerings which are removed from oneself to present to God as a special contribution. It is generally used for contributions for priests (e.g., Lev 7:14; Num 5:9; Ezek 44:30).[91] The narrative in 1 Chr 29 does not use a noun for the contributions, but repeatedly uses the verb נדב ("to give freely").

However, the psalmist need not use the exact word in Exod 25:2–3 (תְּרוּמָה) to refer to the concept that is there expressed. Moreover, the psalmist is not referring to the tabernacle construction but to the temple construction, which is recounted in the later 1 Chr 29 (which uses neither תְּרוּמָה nor מַתָּנָה but only the verb נדב). The noun מַתָּנָה in Ps 68:19 can therefore legitimately refer to the gifts for the construction of the temple which, as 1 Chr 29 records, were "freely given." It also legitimately evokes the similar narrative in Exod 25 and 35, since the tabernacle construction foreshadowed the temple construction and the nouns תְּרוּמָה and מַתָּנָה have similar meanings.

Conclusion

I set out to discuss in turn the six sections of vv. 1–19 in order to argue that each section contributes to a progressive narrative that climaxes at v. 19. This narrative begins with God's rescue of Israel from Egypt, progresses to his leading in the wilderness to Sinai where he manifested his theophanic presence. From there, Israel marched into Canaan and occupied the land, defeated Sisera and Jabin, and eventually made it to Jerusalem, where they took captive their captives and gave gifts to God for him to build his temple. My contention is that this is how Paul read the psalm, or at the very least how he understood v. 19.

Many may not be convinced by all the minutia of the above exegesis. Since Ps 68 has so frequently been taken as incoherent and impossible to interpret, I will now provide corroborative evidence to support this narrative reading. The following chapter

---

[88] I subsequently found that Briggs and Briggs also held that the gifts were given as tributes *and* as "offerings from His people made at the sacred place" (*Psalms*, 2:101). They also take the rebels to refer to the Israelites, although they think it is an editorial addition (ibid., 102). However, they do not explicitly state that the gifts from his people were the materials given to build the temple.

[89] Willem VanGemeren, ed., *New International Dictionary of Old Testament Theology & Exegesis* (Grand Rapids, MI: Zondervan, 1997), 3:207.

[90] Ibid., 3:207. The author also lists "tribute" as one meaning but mentions only Ps 68:19, the occurrence currently in question. This fact should cause one to be suspicious of the gloss "tribute," which connotes a begrudging, subjected giver.

[91] Ibid., 4:355–56.

demonstrates the literary topos of ancient Near Eastern victory songs with divine temple building and argues that Ps 68 shares the features of that topos, particularly the climax of temple building. The fourth chapter examines Ps 68's use of OT traditions in order to support my narrative reading of Ps 68:1–19 and to lay a foundation for understanding the second division of the psalm.

3

The Divine Builder Literary Topos

The previous chapter argued that Ps 68:1–19 is a narrative of God's military victories culminating in the establishment of his temple in Jerusalem. Yahweh saves Israel out of Egypt, provides for them in the wilderness and at Sinai, conquers Canaan, and ascends Mount Zion to receive gifts from his people in order to build his temple and dwell in it forever. This chapter will argue that Ps 68 shares a literary topos that was common in the ancient Near East (ANE), the "divine builder" topos.[1] It will also examine Ps 68 in light of the Ugaritic Baal traditions, since the *Baal Cycle* itself shares the literary topos, and some evidence suggests literary dependence between the two texts.

This chapter will thus serve two purposes. First, it will corroborate my divine builder narratival reading of Ps 68. The pervasive literary topos, by which ANE cultures consistently expressed the pattern of military victories followed by a king or god (or both) building a temple, provides support for accepting my reading of Ps 68, based on the many similarities between Ps 68 and the other divine builder accounts. Their distinctives, on the other hand, point to their underlying theological diversity. Since my main thesis relies on reading Ps 68:19 as portraying Yahweh as a victorious divine warrior building himself a temple with gifts from his people, this chapter plays an important corroborative role. Recall that Ps 68:19 reads, "You ascended to the height; you took captive captives; you received gifts among men, indeed, among those who are stubborn, in order to dwell, O Yah God."

The second purpose of this chapter is to examine the evidence for linking Ps 68 with the Baal traditions. If parts of the psalm are borrowed from these traditions, my distinctively Hebrew reading of the psalm (a sort of "salvation-historical" reading, anachronistically so-called) may be endangered. For a long time I saw echoes and allusions to Baal traditions in Ps 68, and wondered how to interpret such language, but I now think there is good reason to believe there is no literary dependence. There is far greater, and quite explicit, evidence to show that the language that seems reminiscent of Baal traditions comes not from there but from other Israelite traditions. If the psalmist depended on the Baal traditions, my reading is not nullified but would require further

---

[1] By "divine builder," I refer both to the occasion of a god building himself a temple or commissioning the building of his temple and to the occasion of a king building a temple in honor of a god. As we will see, cultures and myths vary in the way they tell the story of celebrating military victories by building temples. But in general, the deity is involved somehow, hence "divine builder."

argumentation that each section of the psalm is indeed part of an Israelite narrative, not a patchwork of borrowed religious language. My argument in the second part of this chapter will suggest that the psalmist is not dependent on Ugaritic traditions, obviating the need for further exploration.

The Divine Builder

The divine builder topos occurs in various ANE cultures, each with its own emphases and characteristics. The pervasiveness of this literary topos provides corroborative evidence for a similar reading of Ps 68, which I have argued to be structured as a divine builder narrative.

Egyptian Texts

At least two Egyptian texts portray a victorious pharaoh building a temple. On the "Poetical Stela of Thutmose III," the god Amen-Re delivers a long speech to the king about his conquests.[2] The narratival prologue recalls how Amen-Re gave the king strength to defeat his enemies, to take a hundred thousand captives, to subdue his enemies under his feet, and to cause his enemies to bear tribute to him on their backs. The second poetic portion is written in quatrains that consist of two distichs introduced by anaphora. The first anaphora is "I came to let you tread on . . ." followed by a region or peoples, while the second is "I let them see your majesty as . . ." followed by a war image, such as "a fearsome lion" or "a crocodile." The second and fourth lines of the quatrains tell further of the king's conquering, which includes smiting Asians' heads, standing on his victim's backs, and binding captives. In the epilogue, the god reiterates his support of the king and notes that the king built his temple "as a work of eternity, [and] made [it] longer and wider than it had been." Amen-Re says he commanded the king to make him monuments, which would surpass those of all former kings. So here the god gives the king victory, who in response builds the god a temple; the god then commands the king to build further monuments. That this triumphal poem was well known and influential in Egyptian culture is evidenced by its later use by Amenhotep III, Seti I, and Ramses III.[3]

A second text celebrates Amenhotep III's temple-building efforts for Amun, but the victory element is implicit.[4] The king was not too hyperbolic to say the temple was one "the likes of which had not existed since the beginning of the Two Lands."[5] Its workhouse was filled with male and female slaves who were despoiled through battles, which justifies our inferring that the other materials were also spoils of war. He states explicitly that he built a great gate for Amun with "the gold [brought] for it from the land of Kry on his first victorious campaign of slaying vile Kush."[6] Likewise, he built

---

[2] *AEL* 2:35–39.
[3] Each later king adapted it for his own use (*AEL* 2:35).
[4] "Stela of Amenhotep III" (*AEL* 2:43–48).
[5] Ibid., 43.
[6] Ibid., 46.

for Amen-Re a bark on the river from timber brought to him from foreign chiefs. The king also built a viewing place for Amun, which included "a place for receiving the produce of all foreign countries, as many gifts are brought before my father [Amun] from the tribute of all lands." At the end of the stela's text, Amun speaks to Amenhotep, saying that he caused various peoples to come to the king, "carrying all their tribute on their backs," including Kush, Asia, Tjehenu, and Punt, which covers all four corners of the earth (south, north, west, and east, respectively). Thus, after building a temple for Amun to celebrate the victory given him by the god, using materials taken as spoil from the defeated enemies, Amun then brings the four corners of the earth to the king with tribute. Since there is not a military record at the front of the inscription, this writing does not fit the exact topos, but the implicit defeat is prerequisite to building Amun's temple since the war spoil constituted the temple's building materials.

Assyrian Texts

Numerous Assyrian texts record military victories followed by temple-building. We get the first detailed narrative of military exploits of an Assyrian king on an inscription from the reign of Adad-narari I (1307–1275 BC). He defeated the king Hanigalbat and his son, both of whom brought him tribute throughout his reign. The inscription closes by recording briefly that he built a palace in the ruined city Taidu.[7] This inscription is the earliest extant example of what became a standard literary form in Assyrian inscriptions with the pattern of military conquest, spoil, tribute, and building activities.

Nearly every Assyrian king recorded annals of this type, showing that the divine builder topos was integral to Assyrian royal records. Shalmaneser I (1274–1245 BC) recorded that he defeated several enemies, despoiled and captured them, and finished by restoring the temple Ehursagkurkurra at Ashur. Shalmaneser's inscription is more pious than the others, which usually mention briefly (if at all) that the temple is for the god.

> I put a great deal of effort into building, for Ashur my lord, the holy temple, the high shrine, . . . When Ashur, the lord, enters that temple and joyfully takes his place on the lofty dais, may he see the brilliant work of that temple and rejoice. May he receive my prayers, may he hear my supplications. For eternity may he greatly decree with his mighty voice a destiny of well-being for my vice-regency and for the vice-regency of my progeny (and) abundance during my reign.[8]

A royal inscription of Tukulti-Ninurta I (1244–1208 BC) describes his military exploits, followed by the tantalizing clause "at that time in [*the area*] of my city Ashur . . . I cleared away . . . ,"[9] but the rest is lost—there is only a lacuna where the building

---

[7] LXXVI, 3 (Albert Kirk Grayson, *From the Beginning to Ashur-resha-ishi I*, ARI 1 [Wiesbaden: Otto Harrassowitz, 1972], 60–61).
[8] LXXVII, 1 §535 (ARI 1:84).
[9] LXXVIII 1 §696 (ARI 1:104).

report probably stood. It concludes with the standard curse formula for those who would remove the stela, so it is likely that this inscription told of the building of a "victory temple." Another, briefer inscription on a stone tablet found at Ashur lists the nations that Tukulti-Ninurta subdued and the palace he built for himself and the gods.[10] Elsewhere he says Ashur asked him to build the cult center.[11] Several other extant texts record this same pattern of victory followed by spoil or tribute followed by temple-building.[12]

Tiglath-pileser I (1114–1076 BC) leaves us the first Assyrian annal, which is the direct literary descendent of this royal inscriptional pattern.[13] It is longer than its predecessors and provides extensive information about the king's victories and enemies. The building section at the end is more extensive and lists the king's epithets and genealogy. The section begins by describing an impressive amount of building, including at least seven temples and reparations to the royal palaces. It concludes with the typical (although expanded) curse formulae for those who would remove the stela.[14]

Without detailing every inscription, I can mention many more that follow the divine builder topos. A stela from Ashur-dan II (934–912 BC), a lengthy annal from Adad-nerari II (911–891 BC), and some shorter inscriptions from Assurnasirpal II (883–859 BC) describe their military exploits followed by their temple-building efforts.[15] A hymn celebrating Assurnasirpal II (883–859 BC) portrays him conquering Carchemish, after which multiple nations bring him war spoils: "ebony and lapis lazuli he constantly received."[16] Although the latter part of the text is fragmented, it is reconstructed as praising Assurnasirpal for taking wood to give to various temples, either to help construct them or (more likely) for expansions or repairs. The Kalḫu Annals of Tiglath-pileser III (744–727 BC) are so fragmented that only about one-third remains of the original text, but the divine builder topos is evident.[17] He conquered several Aramean tribes, rebuilt multiple cities, and set up palaces within them.[18] Stela K 3751 is the only complete building account of Tilath-pileser and follows the standard pattern of military victory, tribute from subdued enemies, and temple building (in Kalḫu). He made plans for the temple "with the keen understanding (and) broad knowledge that the sage of the gods, the prince, the god Nudimmud (Ea), granted to me."[19]

---

[10] LXXVIII 3 (ARI 1:106–7).
[11] LXXVIII 16 §777 (ARI 1:119).
[12] LXXVIII 5, 6, 14, 16, 17 (ARI 1:108–10, 115–22).
[13] LXXXVII 1 (ARI 2:1–20).
[14] Other texts from Tiglath-pileser I with the same literary topos are LXXXVII 2, 4 (ARI 2:20–29). See also Victor Hurowitz and Joan Goodnick Westenholz, "LKA 63: A Heroic Poem in Celebration of Tiglath-Pileser I's Muṣru-Qumanu Campaign," *JCS* 42 (1990): 1–49.
[15] XCVIII 1 (ARI 2:74–78); XCIX 2 (ARI 2:83–92); CI 25, 28, 36 (ARI 2:183–87, 193–94).
[16] "A Hymn Celebrating Assurnasirpal II's Campaigns to the West," trans. V. Hurowitz (*COS*, 1:471).
[17] Hayim Tadmor and Shigeo Yamada, eds., *The Royal Inscriptions of Tiglath-pileser III (744-727 BC) and Shalmaneser V (726-722 BC), Kings of Assyria*, RINAP 1 (Winona Lake, IN: Eisenbrauns, 2011), 19.
[18] Tiglath-pileser III 5, 17 (RINAP 1:26–28, 51–54).
[19] Tiglath-pileser III 47 rev. 17 (RINAP 1:123).

Finally, the detailed "First Campaign Cylinder" (c. 702 BC) of Sennacherib I (704–681 BC) recounts his war against a foreign alliance.[20] Sennacherib "slaughtered" them and captured Babylon, although Merodach-baladan escaped. Sennacherib then raided the temple in Babylon to take all its possessions. The cylinder then lists hundreds of cities and settlements that he conquered and records his building activities. When he returned to Nineveh, he realized through the "will of the gods" that the old divine palace was dilapidated and that he should build a new one.[21] So he built a new palace named Egalzagdunutukua ("The Palace without a Rival") as his royal residence, into which he invited the god Ashur and Assyria's other gods and goddesses after it was finished. He then "made splendid offerings and presented [his] gift(s)" to the deities.[22] This palace is mentioned in nine different royal inscriptions, which shows that it was integral to the presentation of Sennacherib's military victories.[23]

In summary, the divine builder topos is integral to Assyrian royal records and historiography. Its main features include victory over enemies, taking captives, collecting spoil, receiving tribute from foreign leaders, building temples for gods, and sometimes giving gifts to the gods in their new dwelling places. The prominence of Assyria in the ANE and their lengthy hegemony makes it no surprise that this divine builder topos permeated the ancient world.

Ugaritic *Baal Cycle*

The Ugaritic *Baal Cycle* uses the literary topos of divine victory followed by temple-building. This text differs from the Egyptian and Assyrian texts in that it is mythological, dealing only with the gods. Baal's desire to build a temple for himself forms what may be the "central theme . . . of the mythological folklore current among the Semites of Ugarit."[24] His battle with Yam and Mot, as well as his rise to kingship, are also central motifs. This much is clear.

However, there are difficulties in making too specific points about the *Baal Cycle* and its relationship to other documents, such as the similar *Enuma Eliš* and divine warrior texts in the OT. It does not help that only about 50 percent of the original text is extant and legible, while much of what is legible is riddled with lacunas and corruption.[25] An additional problem is our limited knowledge of Ugaritic. As one author put it, "[O]ne reads the authoritative translations . . . with a sense of bewilderment and even disbelief: can all these translations be of the same half-dozen or so texts?"[26] Perhaps the

---

[20] The texts used are from Albert Kirk Grayson and Jamie R. Novotny, eds., *The Royal Inscriptions of Sennacherib, King of Assyria (704-681 BC), Part 1*, RINAP 3/1 (Winona Lake, IN: Eisenbrauns, 2012), 32–40.
[21] Sennacherib I, 70 (RINAP 3/1:37)
[22] Sennacherib I, 92 (RINAP 3/1:40).
[23] The texts are listed in RINAP 3/1:17n39.
[24] Julian Obermann, *Ugaritic Mythology: A Study of Its Leading Motifs* (New Haven, CT: Yale University Press, 1948), 1.
[25] N. Wyatt, *Religious Texts from Ugarit* (New York: Sheffield Academic Press, 2002), 36. All quotations from the Ugaritic texts are from Wyatt's edition, unless otherwise specified. The reconstructions placed in square brackets are therefore Wyatt's.
[26] Baruch Margalit, *A Matter of "Life" and "Death": A Study of the Baal-Mot Epic (CTA 4-5-6)*, AOAT 206 (Kevelaer: Butzon und Bercker, 1980), 1.

greatest problem with the *Baal Cycle* is the ordering of its six tablets (KTU 1.1–1.6). Scholars agree that 1.5 and 1.6 belong together in that order.[27] They likewise agree that 1.3 and 1.4 belong together, but some question that order. KTU 1.1 and one section of 1.2 were found in a different physical location from the rest of the tablets, so some question the connection between 1.1 and the sections of 1.2. The first two tablets concern Baal and Yam; the next two tablets concern Baal's palace; the last two tablets concern Baal and Mot.

The secondary literature is voluminous, and various theories of redactions, recensions, and orders for the tablets have been proposed.[28] There seems to be a slight majority among Ugaritic scholars in favor of viewing narrative continuity across the six tablets and in viewing them in their order inherited from CTA and KTU (tablets 1-2-3-4-5-6).[29] This debate is outside the parameters of this study, and so I rely on that slight majority by reading the *Baal Cycle* as a connected narrative, keeping in mind the need to be cautious about basing too much on the supposed narratival order of events.

The cycle has been interpreted in four different ways.[30] Most early interpreters took the cycle of the death and revivification of Baal and Mot as a myth portraying the annual season and attending rituals.[31] However, while this interpretation enjoyed great popularity, many now recognize its weakness and lack of textual support.[32] A second interpretation is that the cycle is a cosmogony, the primary evidence for which is its similarity to *Enuma Eliš*. However, El—not Baal—is the creator god in the *Baal Cycle*, and Baal's palace does not pertain to the creation of the world. A third interpretation is that Baal's victory over Yam ("Sea") mythologically portrays Ugarit's successful defeat of the Sea Peoples, who invaded Syria in the late Bronze Age.[33] A related interpretation is that the myth portrays the rise of the dynasty of Niqmaddu II, who is mentioned in the colophon of the *Baal Cycle* and also in KTU 1.161.12, 26.[34] There is merit to this third interpretation, but M. Smith has proposed a fourth interpretation that integrates elements of the previous three and pays more attention to the narrative of the myth, whose principle theme is the limited exaltation of Baal. Baal can only beat Yam with the help of his allies and weapon-maker; he cannot beat Mot decisively; and he only gets a temple after extensive negotiations. After defeating Yam and constructing his temple, he is not enthroned as the most high god but remains El's vassal. Smith suggests

---

[27] Margalit, *Matter of Life and Death*, 9; Mark S. Smith, *The Ugaritic Baal Cycle*, SVT 55 (Leiden: E.J. Brill, 1994), 4.

[28] For this summary of the state of affairs, I have drawn from Smith, *The Ugaritic Baal Cycle*, 2–25; Margalit, *Matter of Life and Death*, 9–11; Wyatt, *Religious Texts from Ugarit*, 34–38.

[29] Smith, *The Ugaritic Baal Cycle*, 4n12. Of course, once the tablets were published in that order, it became the de facto standard and more difficult to challenge.

[30] For what follows, I am indebted to Smith's discussion in *The Ugaritic Baal Cycle*, 1:58–114.

[31] E.g., Arvid Schou Kapelrud, *The Ras Shamra Discoveries and the Old Testament* (Norman: University of Oklahoma Press, 1963), 49. Most comprehensively, see Theodor Herzl Gaster, *Thespis: Ritual, Myth, and Drama in the Ancient Near East* (Garden City, NY: Doubleday, 1961).

[32] Wyatt, *Religious Texts from Ugarit*, 35.

[33] E.g., Julian Obermann, "How Baal Destroyed a Rival: A Magical Incantation Scene," *JAOS* 67 (1947): 205–6.

[34] Scholars question whether the Niqmaddu mentioned in the text is Niqmaddu I, II, III, or IV. Most scholars take the one mentioned in the colophon of the *Baal Cycle* and in KTU 1.161 12, 16 to be Niqmaddu II (Wyatt, *Religious Texts from Ugarit*, 146n132).

that this mirrors the situation of Niqmaddu II, who rose to power between the great Near Eastern kingdoms. He gained the throne and built temples, but he never became the most high king.[35] "In sum, it appears that the *Baal Cycle* expresses the political exaltation of the divine king, and by implication that of the human king, as well as the limits of their kingship."[36]

Whatever the meaning of this mythological narrative, it portrays a conflict between gods, the enthronement of the victorious god, and the construction of his temple. Later, Baal's failed attempt to dispense with Mot may suggest that they are equal in power (Baal brings [vegetative] life, Mot embodies death). This may or may not mirror political situations, agricultural seasons and attending rites, or something else. Given the common link between gods and kings in the ANE, it may relate to a specific or general political situation, with Baal representing a king with limited power. If so, then the *Baal Cycle* is more similar to the Egyptian and Assyrian records than it seems, because the cycles reflect a historical king's military victories followed by his construction of a temple. In any case, the following synopsis will demonstrate that the cycles definitely use the divine builder topos.

In the first cycle, Baal struggles with Yam because El had chosen to build a house for Yam with materials supplied "from the hands of Valiant Ba[al]" (KTU 1.1 iv 20–22).[37] Athtar lobbies for El to build Baal a temple but is unsuccessful, so Baal threatens to smite Yam and crush his skull. Yam requests the divine Council to surrender Baal to him, which El does, but Baal refuses to be subdued. The master temple and weapons builder Kothar-wa-hasis sides with Baal and makes him two weapons. The first weapon, "Expeller," is ineffective on Yam, but the second, "All-Driver," strikes Yam on the skull and kills him. Athtar encourages him and proclaims, "[O]ur captive is Prince Yam" (1.2 iv 30). The last extant text of tablet two proclaims Baal's kingship.

The second cycle concerns Baal's victorious temple-building. Baal complains to Anat that he has no house like the gods. Anat requests of El a temple for Baal, for "our king is Valiant, Baal is our ruler" (1.3 v 30–40). Anat fails, but El's wife Athirat persuades him. Baal enlists Kothar to build his palace, after which Baal presents sacrifices and holds a festival for his brothers. He makes the rounds of nearby cities to quell all rebellion and brings peace, afterward settling peacefully into his palace. This aspect of the myth reflects Assyrian records that record the subdual of many cities to bring peace, such as the "First Campaign Cylinder."

In the third cycle, Mot responds to Baal's challenge (which is missing from the end of the second cycle) by claiming he will devour him. Baal actually surrenders to Mot and descends to the grave. Anat mourns for Baal and buries him but later challenges Mot and destroys him in order to save Baal. There are then about thirty-eight missing lines that must have recounted Baal's resuscitation, because when the text returns, Baal seizes and kills the sons of Athirat. After subduing all his enemies, he sits in peace, enthroned as king in his temple. Yet Mot returns to challenge Baal again. The duel

---

[35] Smith, *The Ugaritic Baal Cycle*, 105–6.
[36] Ibid., 110.
[37] The translation used is that of Wyatt, *Religious Texts from Ugarit*, 39–146.

ends in a stalemate and Mot withdraws at the command of Shapsh, the god of the Luminaries. So in the end Baal is king, but only because Mot feared the greater gods.

In summary, the *Baal Cycle* shares the ANE divine builder topos with both Egypt and Assyria. Baal defeats Yam and earns the right to build a temple, which is executed by the master craftsman Kothar-wa-hasis. But his kingship is limited, since El remains in place over him. He also does not receive rest in his temple through absolute sovereignty. Even after losing and regaining his throne from Mot, his kingdom remains limited since he could not defeat Mot by his own power. In the end, Baal is a king, but a limited one; he has peace, but only because others fight for him and decree his kingship.

Babylonian *Enuma Eliš*

Like the *Baal Cycle*, the Babylonian *Enuma Eliš* tells a divine builder narrative in the mythological realm. It differs from the *Baal Cycle* in that the divine builder, Marduk, ascends to the throne as universal king, whereas Baal was still inferior to El. *Enuma Eliš* also differs by including an account of the creation of the world, thereby connecting victorious temple building with creation.

The seven cuneiform tablets of *Enuma Eliš* were excavated between 1848 and 1876 from Assyrian king Ashurbanipal's (c. 668–630 BC) library at Nineveh. Tablets that date from around 1000 BC were also found at Ashur, but the myth can be traced back further. Since the tale centers around Marduk's rise to supremacy and the establishment of Babylon as the world's first city and Marduk's dwelling place, A. Heidel believes the myth probably arose during the First Babylonian Dynasty (1894–1595 BC) when Babylon rose to prominence and when Marduk became a national god.[38] If this is correct, the myth antedates Ps 68 by at least six hundred years. It was also widespread in the ANE and was so significant that Ashurbanipal wanted a copy in his royal library. The tradition also lasted well into the first millennium of the Common Era. Excerpts of *Enuma Eliš* exist in the eighth century (AD) writings of Syncellus (or Synkellos). He copied the fragments from a lost work of Eusebius of Caesarea, who copied them from Polyhistor (first century BC), who copied them from a third-century (BC) Babylonian priest Berossus.[39] The story is also preserved by the Neo-Platonist Damascius (fifth and sixth centuries AD).[40] So even without the benefit of the seven tablets from Ashurbanipal's library, we see that *Enuma Eliš* was widespread in the ancient world, with its traditions lasting into the eighth century (AD).

The focus of the tale is Marduk's rise to the position of supreme god and king, but the divine builder motif is fundamental to the story. There are actually two divine builder stories, a first brief account with Ea and a second more extensive account with Marduk, based on the first building. The first building account occurs after Ea slays Apsu. After the gods are created, they become clamorous and annoy Apsu, who in

---

[38] Alexander Heidel, *The Babylonian Genesis: The Story of the Creation* (Chicago, IL: University of Chicago Press, 1951), 13–14.
[39] Ibid., 77.
[40] Ibid., 75.

turn asks his wife Tiamat to destroy the gods with him. Tiamat is unwilling, so Apsu undertakes his plan alone. Ea, a younger but wise god, enchants Apsu with a spell and slays him instead. He then establishes on Apsu "shrines," his "chamber," which is called "holy," where he and his wife Damkina "dwelt in splendor" (I, 71–78).[41] His story follows the literary topos: Ea slays his enemy and builds himself a holy place in which to dwell in peace.

In this holy place, Ea and Damkina give birth to the second divine builder, Marduk. His power threatens the gods, so they stir up Tiamat to kill him. Ea and Anu step in to fight or appease Tiamat but fail.[42] Anshar finally calls on Marduk, who agrees to fight Tiamat, but only on the condition that they give him supreme authority to determine destinies. The gods fear Tiamat and agree to give Marduk "kingship over the totality of the whole universe" (IV, 14) if he defeats Tiamat. Marduk gathers his weapons and mounts his storm chariot to meet Kingu and Tiamat in battle. He indicts Tiamat for usurping authority and plotting evil, so she becomes enraged and attacks him. Marduk uses the winds to forcefully keep Tiamat's mouth open and shoots an arrow through her innards, piercing her heart and killing her. He splits her head with a club and sends her blood away with the north wind. The gods in response rejoice and send him "dues (and) greeting-gifts" (IV, 134). He splits Tiamat in half and uses half of her to create the heavens and the earth. After creating the heavens and the earth, the Anunnaki—the gods of the underworld—determine to honor Marduk by building him a temple that would be a resting place for the gods. When they finish the temple in Babylon in the second year, Marduk "[sits] down before them in majesty" (VI, 65). The Anunnaki create smaller shrines for themselves and the gods all gather to a banquet, where Marduk is praised as their high priest, shepherd, and supreme king. Man is exhorted to praise Marduk, to establish systems of burnt offerings, to maintain the sanctuaries, and to obey him. The myth concludes by proclaiming Marduk's fifty names and praising him.

In summary, *Enuma Eliš* contains two divine builder narratives. The first is brief and concerns only a victorious god building himself a temple. But this first building narrative foreshadows the second, in which the temple is connected to Marduk's supreme kingship and creative activities. The narrative follows the standard pattern: the warrior defeats his enemies, takes them captive, and commissions a temple or accepts that one be built for him, in which he may rest. He also used standard divine weapons to defeat Tiamat, including wind and rain, and is described as a divine charioteer. In contrast to Ea, who had to build his own temple, Marduk's grateful subordinate deities built the temple for him and proclaimed him king.

Aramean Texts

At least one Aramean text records the divine builder topos. A stela of Zakir, king of Hamath (c. 780–775 BC), tells of his successful war against a coalition of several Syrian

---

[41] The translation used is from Heidel, *Babylonian Genesis*, 18–60.
[42] The text recording Ea's failure is broken (II, 59–70), but it is alluded to later in III, 54.

monarchs, led by the king of Damascus.[43] After telling of the defeat of this coalition, the stela records that he rebuilt Hadrach, adding strongholds and integrating it into his kingdom. It continues, "and I built temples for gods throughout my whole [land]. Then I rebuilt ... [and I rebuilt] Afis; and [I gave a resting-place to the gods] in the temple of [Ilwer in Afis]" (B 9–13). The only subsequent notes are that he set up this stela before his god, along with a curse on whoever might remove the stela. Thus, building the temple stands as the climax of the inscription, which culminates in a place of rest for his gods.

Summarizing the Traditions

Despite the cultural differences exhibited by these texts, they follow a common literary topos: a god or king defeats his enemies and then builds a temple for himself (the god) or for his god (the king). That this literary topos existed in so many ancient Near Eastern cultures, and that the texts were either so many or so influential, shows that it was a common way for cultures to express the divine or royal supremacy that results from victorious warfare.

V. Hurowitz's monograph notes the same literary pattern in the description of temple building in Mesopotamian and northwest Semitic writings. His proposed topos is more detailed,[44] including six elements: (1) circumstances of the project and decision to build; (2) preparations, drafting workmen, gathering materials; (3) description of the building; (4) dedication rites and festivities; (5) blessing and/or prayer of the king; and (6) blessing and/or curses of future generations.[45] Not all records contain all six elements, and the sixth is limited mostly to Assyrian royal inscriptions, but there is a tendency to present building reports using this literary topos. He does not include the element of military victory that so often precedes the dedicatory building, which enables him to include more building inscriptions and records than he could have otherwise. However, he does note that this element is present, especially in the Assyrian inscriptions, as well as in mythological texts such as *Enuma Eliš* and the *Baal Cycle*. Military exploits are linked more closely with the building report in some of the Babylonian inscriptions.[46]

Hurowitz's study included twenty extra-biblical records and five biblical accounts, which includes the Priestly account of the Tabernacle construction (Exod 24:15–31:18; 34:29–40:38), the rebuilding of the Jerusalem temple (Ezra 1–6), the repairing of the Jerusalem walls in Nehemiah, and the building of the first temple in 1 Kings 1–8.[47] Hurowitz's research thus verifies my own conclusion that there is a literary topos in the ANE that portrays a victorious battle followed by temple building, which we find in the

---

[43] John C. L. Gibson, ed., *Aramaic Inscriptions Including Inscriptions in the Dialect of Zenjirli*, TSSI 2 (Oxford: Clarendon Press, 1975), 6–7. The text is cited from this translation.
[44] It is unnecessary to study this further for the purposes of this study.
[45] Victor Hurowitz, *I Have Built You an Exalted House: Temple Building in the Bible in Light of Mesopotamian and Northwest Semitic Writings*, JSOTSS 115 (Sheffield: JSOT Press, 1992), 64.
[46] Ibid., 82–83.
[47] He claims that these twenty represent a far greater number.

biblical accounts.⁴⁸ Although there are variants within the topos, the general pattern is consistent, as if this were the normal way to describe the building of temples. This section therefore corroborates my narrative reading of Ps 68, which is that Yahweh defeated his enemies through Israel, who collected spoils and presented them to their God after he ascended on high to build his temple in which to dwell forever.

Distinctives in the Traditions

When developing a literary topos across cultures, one must necessarily overlook differences and variations. But now that the topos has been established, I should note a few key differences in the accounts, which point to distinctive theologies. First, the nature of the temple varies. In *Enuma Eliš*, the gods wait to build their own houses until they build Marduk's. Although the text is mythological, the temple refers to the historical temple built in Babylonia. In the *Baal Cycle*, many of the gods already have their houses before Baal gets his. While the temple in the text may represent Baal's temple in Ugarit, it may have been a mythological temple, since it is said to be on Mount Saphon in the north. The temple is a heavenly one, from which Baal sends rain and thunder. In the Assyrian, Egyptian, and Aramean inscriptions, the temples are historical, but there is no exclusivity. That is, although credit for victory is usually given to the prominent deity, temples may be built or restored for any number of deities. In the OT accounts, the Israelites build the temple, although Yahweh is also credited with building it (Exod 15:17; Ps 78:69; 121:1). He receives credit for the victory and the temple may only be built unto (or for) him. The Israelite temple was historical, built in Jerusalem, and was to be the only one of its kind (Deut 12).

Second, the nature of the enemy varies. In *Enuma Eliš* and the *Baal Cycle*, the enemy is divine and mythological. But after Baal's temple is built, he does not establish peace but is killed by a second enemy and only later is reinstated with the help of other, more powerful gods. In the Assyrian, Egyptian, and Aramean inscriptions, although the god is given credit for empowering the king, the human king battles human enemies and builds a house for his god. In the OT accounts, Yahweh himself fights against Israel's human enemies. Of course, the enemies are sometimes portrayed mythologically (e.g., Rahab and Leviathan), which creates an affinity with other similar mythological battle accounts.

Third, there is an important difference in the idea of kingship among the various traditions. In Egypt, the king was identified with God; therefore, his victory was the god's victory.⁴⁹ While his reign was supposedly eternal, the king would eventually die and be replaced. His victories in battle did not earn kingship, but confirmed it, yet only temporally. In the *Baal Cycle*, Baal is a lower deity than El and nearly lost the right to build a temple when El favored Yam. Even after he defeats Yam, he does not become the supreme god, even if he is referred to as a king who owns a palace. Also, soon

---

⁴⁸ Hurowitz focuses only on the building reports, but throughout he notes that a victorious battle generally preceded the building report.
⁴⁹ Egypt's kings are "like divinities," and "a king is counted among the gods" ("Dedication Inscriptions of Seti I" [*AEL* 2:55]). The king is made in the image of Aten ("Hymn to the Aten and the King," East Wall cols. 1–5 [*AEL* 2:93]).

after his victory, he acquiesces to Mot with no resistance, displaying his weakness. In Assyria and Aram, the king fought at the command of and on behalf of the god. The gods were subsequently housed in a temple, signifying their kingship, but the deities are downplayed in the inscriptions. The king was considered more worthy of praise than the gods, suggesting their lack of grandeur. In the Aramean text above, the king must give rest to the god, as though the god could not attain it himself.

In the OT, Yahweh is the indisputable king of the universe, signified first by placing Adam in and over his creation as his image. The psalms confirm his universal reign over the universe (Pss 10:16; 24:8–10; 95:3). In this sense, he never becomes king, but is king.[50] Yet he also became king over Israel when he "created" (קנה) them as his covenant people (Deut 32:6, 33:5). In the historical texts (e.g., Exod 1–14), we see Yahweh fighting for his people to deliver them from their duress.[51] Similarly, in the psalms, Yahweh hears his peoples' pleas and rescues them (Ps 44:4; 74:12). His divine warfare is historical, while his divine building is for his glory but also for the great benefit of his people (Exod 29:45–46). He does not need the king to give him rest, but he gives rest to the king through his power (Exod 15:17; 2 Sam 7:1).

Yahweh as Baal?

While various texts share the divine builder topos, scholars have seen a special affinity between Ps 68 and the Ugaritic Baal traditions. Evidence suggests dependence, but there is difficulty in discerning exactly how much evidence is legitimate or forced. This evidence includes (1) the "rider" language (vv. 5, 18, 34–35); (2) words or ideas throughout the psalm that are reminiscent of Ugaritic mythology; and (3) the similarity of the divine building motif. If this language depends on (or polemicizes against) the Baal traditions, my exegetical reading of Ps 68 might require some nuancing or revision. However, I will argue that the language is derived from OT traditions and is not dependent on Ugaritic traditions.[52]

Who Is Riding on What?

The phrase לרכב בערבות ("to the Rider on the Clouds / over the Deserts") in Ps 68:5 resembles Baal's epithet "Rider on the Clouds," *rkb 'rpt* in Ugaritic (e.g., KTU 1.2 iv 8, 29; 1.3 ii 40). (Note that the only orthographical difference is Hebrew *b* for Ugaritic *p*.) This evidence has been interpreted variously.

---

[50] As I mentioned in the last chapter, I find too little evidence for Mowinckel's Enthronement Festival thesis, so I think the best translation of יהוה מלך is "Yahweh is king," not "Yahweh has become king."
[51] On Exod 1–14 as a divine warrior text, see Charlie Trimm, *"YHWH Fights for Them!": The Divine Warrior in the Exodus Narrative*, GBS 58 (Piscataway, NJ: Gorgias Press, 2014).
[52] As I will note later, this does not preclude the psalmist from knowing the Ugaritic traditions. Given the prominence of Baal worship in Israel, he surely did know them. However, even if he is aware of similarity of language between his psalm and the Ugaritic traditions, this does not signify dependence or even necessitate polemic.

B. Arnold and B. Strawn argue the psalm originally read לרכב בערפות, "to the rider on the clouds," borrowing from a Canaanite *Vorlage*. The phrase ביה שמו ("Yahweh is his name"),[53] which directly follows לרכב בערבות in Ps 68:5, was added as a theological gloss to clarify that the psalm refers to Yahweh, not to Baal. The phrase לרכב בערפות ("to the Rider on the Clouds") was later modified to לרכב בערבות ("to the Rider on the Deserts," changing only the *p* to *b*) to conform to the references to the desert (vv. 8–10).[54]

O. Loretz argues, against Arnold and Strawn, that Ps 68:5 is not based on a Canaanite-Ugaritic *Vorlage*.[55] Rather, he believes the Canaanite-Ugaritic character of Baal was appropriated under Israel's monotheism to apply to Yahweh theologically but in the form of the one who "rides through the deserts." He points specifically to vv. 7–8, which speak of Yahweh going before Israel in the wilderness after the Exodus, which shows that the core of the psalm is concerned with Yahweh, not Baal. The Yahwistic bent of the psalm, as well as the Israelite absorption of Baal's characteristics into their conception of Yahweh, means that the two expressions רכב בערפות ("Rider on the Clouds") and רכב בערבות ("the Rider in the Deserts") are equivalent. The textual similarity did not arise from literary dependence; instead, it arose because Yahweh had long ago appropriated Baal's "rider" attribute but with Yahweh's distinctive desert locale rather than the clouds. Loretz holds לרכב בערבות to be original in Ps 68:5. He corroborates this with the belief that vv. 32–35, particularly v. 33 ("to the one who rides in the heavens, the ancient heavens"), are postexilic redactions made to conform to v. 4, although he provides no evidence of such redaction.

Another possibility is that ערבה ("desert") may be a homonym of another Hebrew word ערבה ("cloud").[56] The word ערבה meaning "cloud" would then be a cognate of Ugaritic *'rpt* ("cloud"), with a nonphonemic interchange of the bilabial consonants *b* and *p*. According to Dahood, there are numerous instances of such interchange in northwest Semitic.[57] Whether by emending בערבות to בערפות or by deciding that ערבה is a homonym, several commentators and modern translations render the phrase "Rider on the Clouds."[58] Verses 34–35 may support this view: "to the one who rides in the heavens, the ancient heavens; behold, he sends out his voice, a voice of strength. Give strength to God; his majesty is on Israel and his strength is in the clouds."

Those who see a reference here to Baal interpret the evidence variously. Some see direct absorption of Ugaritic theology into conceptions of Yahweh.[59] Others see the

---

[53] The ב is a *Beth essentiae*, which introduces the predicate in which the subject ("rider") consists (HALOT, s.v. בְּ).

[54] Bill T. Arnold and Brent A. Strawn, "Beyāh šemô in Psalm 68,5: A Hebrew Gloss to an Ugaritic Epithet?," *ZAW* 15, no. 3 (2003): 428–30.

[55] Oswald Loretz, "Der ugaritisch-hebräische Parallelismus rkb rpt // rkb b rbwt in Psalm 68,5," *UF* 34 (2002): 521–26.

[56] This would be the only use of ערבה to mean "cloud" in an extant Hebrew text.

[57] Mitchell J. Dahood, *Psalms*, 3d ed., AB 17 (Garden City, NY: Doubleday, 1966), 2:136.

[58] CJB; HCSB; NAB; NIV; NLT; NRSV; Hans-Joachim Kraus, *Psalms 60–150*, trans. Hilton C. Oswald (Minneapolis, MN: Fortress Press, 1993), 46nf; Tremper Longman III, *Psalms: An Introduction and Commentary*, TOTC (Downers Grove, IL: IVP Academic, 2014), 258.

[59] Kraus, *Psalms 60–150*, 52; Yitshak Avishur, *Studies in Hebrew and Ugaritic Psalms* (Jerusalem: Magnes Press, 1994), 45; Kapelrud, *Ras Shamra Discoveries*, 32–37.

psalmist making a conscious polemic against Baal.[60] There are, however, other ways—more creative or sensitive uses of the comparative method— to explain the evidence. If v. 5 is in fact influenced by Ugaritic traditions, it is unclear how the psalmist is using the traditions, and one's view will likely be determined by one's prior commitments to certain theological traditions or to a larger scheme of Israelite history.

However, while Yahweh's and Baal's epithets are orthographically similar, there are actually several reasons to doubt whether there is any explicit Ugaritic influence here at all. First, Loretz correctly accepts the MT's בערבות as original, meaning "desert," since the psalm in that section speaks of the Exodus and God's guidance and provision through the desert to Sinai and then to Canaan (vv. 7–14). As we have seen, the *Baal Cycle* occurs solely in the mythological realm. His warfare involves the gods, and his temple is built in the heavens. Yahweh's warfare, by contrast, is thoroughly historical. He is the Desert Charioteer. There still may be either implicit or subconscious echoes of Baal here, but the psalm's focus in this section is Israel in the desert, not the heavens and Baal. The word ערבה ("desert") is also used in Jer 2:6 in conjunction with the Exodus: "Where is the LORD who brought us up from the land of Egypt, who led us in the wilderness (מדבר), in a land of deserts (ערבה) and pits." These same two terms are found together also in Isa 40:3, "prepare the way of the LORD in the wilderness (מדבר); make straight a highway for our God in the desert (ערבה)." The redemption prophesied in Isa 40–66 is envisioned as a second Exodus, which strengthens the association of ערבה with the Exodus, as in Ps 68.[61] Such strong associations strengthens Loretz's contention that the original term in Ps 68:5 is the MT's ערבה, meaning "desert."

Second, the term "rider" (רכב) is commonly applied to warriors in the ANE, especially given the superiority of cavalry and chariots over foot soldiers (Exod 15:1; Job 39:18; Ps 76:6; Jer 51:21; etc.). Even Marduk rides a chariot (*Enuma Eliš* IV 50). So it is not unusual to see Yahweh "riding" in battle metaphorically: he rides a cherub (2 Sam 22:11 = Ps 18:11), the heavens (Deut 33:26), a swift cloud (עב קל, Isa 19:1), horses (Hab 3:8), and a chariot of salvation (Hab 3:8). That רכב in Ps 68 is not necessarily tied to the Baal epithet is suggested by v. 18, where God's chariots (רכב) are mentioned, but no Baal language is connected with it. So the term "rider" is applied to warriors in the ANE generally, and to Yahweh throughout the OT poetic texts. Its use in v. 5 therefore need not be influenced by the Baal "rider" epithet.

Nevertheless, even if רכב is a generic term and ערבה means "desert," not "cloud," the conjunction of the two terms and the orthographic similarity between the two epithets of Yahweh and Baal is still striking. So a third reason for considering Ps 68:5 to be independent of Baal's cloud epithet is the weighty evidence that the psalmist drew the "rider" language from Deut 33.[62] Deut 33:26 says Yahweh "rides (רכב) the

---

[60] For a full treatment of Baal polemic in the OT, see Norman C. Habel, *Yahweh Versus Baal: A Conflict of Religious Cultures* (New York: Bookman Associates, 1964). On Ps 68:5 specifically as polemic, see, e.g., Ballard, *The Divine Warrior Motif in the Psalms*, 58.

[61] For the second Exodus in Isa 40–66, see 40:3–11; 41:17–20; 42:14–16; possibly 43:1–3; 43:14–21; 44:24–28; 48:20–21; 49:8–12; 51:1–13; 52:7–12; 55:12–13.

[62] The psalmist could have drawn from Deut 33 if (1) Deuteronomy is pre-Davidic (assuming the psalm is Davidic or later); (2) Deuteronomy is exilic and the psalm is later, either exilic or post-exilic; (3) the tradition recorded in Deut 33 is pre-Davidic. On any account, (3) is likely true, given Deut 33's archaic language, similar to Gen 49, Exod 15, Num 23–24, Judg 5, and perhaps Deut 32,

heavens (שמים) to your help, [he rides] the clouds (שחק) in majesty (גאוה)." These four Hebrew terms all appear in Ps 68:34–35: Yahweh rides (רכב) in the heavens (שמים); his majesty (גאוה) is over Israel; and his strength is in the clouds (שחק). That the terms רכב, שמים, שחק, and גאוה all occur in Deut 33:26 and Ps 68:34–35 suggests strongly that the psalmist borrowed the riding imagery from Deuteronomy, not from Ugaritic texts. If so, Ps 68:5 should also be seen as an allusion to Deut 33:26. While the psalmist retains "heavens" in v. 34, he substitutes "deserts" in v. 5 because the psalm there is concerned with the Exodus-wilderness motif (as Loretz noted). The psalmist in v. 35 retains the term "heavens" (שמים) from Deut 33:26 (rather than changing it to "desert") because the end of the psalm concerns God's universal kingship, not a historical deliverance from Egypt through the desert. Psalm 68:33 commands everyone, "Kingdoms of the earth, sing to God! Praise the Lord."[63]

Further support for seeing Ps 68:5, 34–35 as borrowing from Deut 33:26 is Deut 33's context. Deuteronomy 33:27–29 contains the following elements: (1) Yahweh will defeat their enemies; (2) he will give Israel their land; and (3) Israel is a people "saved" by Yahweh. Psalm 68 contains all these elements. He defeats Egypt (implicit, vv. 6–7), the Canaanites (vv. 12–15), and the Jebusites (vv. 18–19); he gives Israel their land (v. 9); and Yahweh is Israel's "salvation" (v. 20). So there was good reason for the psalmist to draw on Deut 33, especially the last few verses, for his poetic formulation of the psalm.

Finally—and perhaps this may be considered the clinching evidence that the "rider" language comes from Deut 33—Ps 68:18, the third רכב passage in the psalm, borrows directly from Deut 33:2. The psalm says, "[T]he chariots (רכב) of God are ten thousand thousands multiplied; Yahweh is among them, Sinai is in the holy place." This is a clear allusion to Deut 33:2: "Yahweh came from Sinai and shone from Seir upon him; he shone forth from Mount Paran and he came from among tens of thousands of his holy ones [or 'of the sanctuary']."[64] Since Deut 33:2 does not use rider language, he likely had the whole of Deut 33 in mind when he used the rider concept three times in the psalm. The evidence for the psalmist's use of Deut 33 is summarized in Table 3.1.

So while there is a superficial similarity between Baal's epithet "Rider on the Clouds" and Yahweh's epithet "Rider in the Deserts," the evidence from the psalm itself does not necessitate borrowing one way or the other. To the contrary, the psalmist derived his rider language and accompanying militant and royal concepts from Deut 33. Deut 33:26 and Ps 68:35 do name Yahweh as the "cloud rider," but the word for "cloud" in these verses (שחק) is not a cognate of Ugaritic *rpwt*. The use of רכב, we have seen, could be applied to any warrior; it is therefore not surprising that it was applied to both Yahweh and Baal in divine warrior poems.

---

which can all be dated with some confidence to the late second millennium. I will discuss the dates of these passages in the next chapter.

[63] This argument is the opposite of Edmond Jacob, who argued that v. 5 originally read רכב ערפות, borrowing from Baal's epithet, and the psalmist changed ערפות to שמים in v. 34, which he also linked to "Baal Shamayim" (*Ras Shamra-Ugarit et l'Ancien Testament*, Cahiers d'Archéologie Biblique 12 [Neuchâtel, Suisse: Editions Delachaux et Niestlé, 1960], 68–69). By contrast, I am arguing that the psalmist drew שמים from Deut 32:26 and changed שמים to ערבות in v. 5 to fit the wilderness context.

[64] If "of the sanctuary" is the right translation, then my argument that the climax of the psalm is the divine building of the temple is strengthened, since one of the psalmist's sources emphasizes Yahweh's sanctuary.

Table 3.1 "Rider" Passages in Psalm 68 as Allusions to Deuteronomy 33. Similar or synonymous lexemes are underlined.

Ps 68:5	לרכב בערבות	To the one who rides in the deserts
Deut 33:26	רכב שמים	The one who rides the heavens
Ps 68:18	רכב אלהים רבתים אלפי שנאן אדני בם סיני בקדש	The chariots of God are ten thousand thousands multiplied. The Lord is among them, *as at* Sinai, in the sanctuary.
Deut 33:2	יהוה מסיני בא וזרח משעיר למו הופיע מהר פארן ואתה מרבבת קדש	The LORD came from Sinai and shone from Seir upon him; he shone forth from Mount Paran and he came from among tens of thousands of his holy ones.[65]
Ps 68:34–35	לרכב בשמי שמי־קדם הן יתן בקולו קול עז: תנו עז לאלהים על־ישראל גאותו ועזו בשחקים	To the one who rides in the heavens of the ancient heavens; behold, he sends out his voice, a voice of strength. Give strength to God; his majesty is on Israel and his strength is in the clouds.
Deut 33:26–27	אין כאל ישרון רכב שמים בעזרך ובגאותו :שחקים	There is none like God, Jeshurun, who rides the heavens for your help, and in the clouds in his majesty.

That a deity would ride the clouds is also not surprising, since deities resided in the heavens. Moreover, both Baal and Yahweh gave rain, but in different ways. Baal's rain was simply a function of the vegetative cycle, while Yahweh's rain was a covenant blessing (Deut 11:11; Ps 68:10). Given all the evidence, there is no necessary connection between the two "rider" epithets. They were probably developed independently, both gods being warriors and both living in the heavens. The orthographic similarity between Ugaritic *rkb b ʿrpwt* and Hebrew *rkb b ʿrbwt* is simply a coincidence of the similar spelling of Ugaritic "cloud" with Hebrew "desert."[66]

This point needed extensive attention because it is the common starting point for finding parallels to Baal traditions in Ps 68. As we will see, after "finding" an epithet of Baal in Ps 68, scholars have readily found other parallels to Baal traditions in the psalm as well, even if they require emendations or ingenious comparative philology, as I will demonstrate below. If the above argument is correct—that the epithet "Rider in the Deserts" does not depend on Ugaritic tradition—then the plausibility of the next two categories of parallels decreases significantly.

---

[65] Although קדש probably has a different meaning in the two passages, it is probably not coincidental that the same root appears in both since the psalmist drew other language from the Deuteronomy passage. It is possible that קדש in Deut 33:2 does mean "sanctuary" as in Ps 68:18, or that the psalmist read it as "sanctuary." In this case, Yahweh was coming with tens of thousands of his angelic hosts that have access to Yahweh in his heavenly sanctuary ("tens of thousands of the sanctuary").

[66] Since Deut 33:26 speaks of Yahweh riding a שחק ("cloud"), which is not a cognate of Ugaritic *ʿrpwt*, there is also no reason to suspect that the author of Deut 33 borrowed from Baal rider language. Some commentators see a parallel idea or even appropriation (e.g., Duane L. Christensen, *Deuteronomy 21:10–34:12*, WBC 6B [Nashville, TN: Thomas Nelson, 2002], 860; Jeffrey H. Tigay, *Deuteronomy* דברים: *The Traditional Hebrew Text with the New JPS Translation* [Philadelphia, PA: Jewish Publication Society, 1996], 334). But as I have argued, the concept of a deity riding is ubiquitous because of the war imagery conjured by charioteer language.

Words and Ideas Possibly Reminiscent of Baal

Psalm 68:10 refers to "abundant rain," which God poured down. As the storm god, Baal sends rain and dew from heaven (KTU 1.3 ii 39–41) and appoints the season of his rains (1.4 v 6–7).[67] Although there is a superficial similarity between Yahweh's and Baal's control of rain, I noted above the difference in the traditions. Baal's rain was simply a function of the vegetative cycle, while Yahweh's rain was a covenant blessing (Deut 11:11; Psalm 68:10). Moreover, the psalm connects rain with Yahweh's Sinaitic theophany (v. 8) and with the rain that he used as a weapon in the Exodus narrative (Exod 9:33–34). Yahweh controls all factors, including the weather, which meant that any deity that controlled some aspect of the natural world could be compared with Yahweh. That does not mean that the deity's characteristics were absorbed into Yahweh, nor does it seem to be the case here, given the difference in the function of rain in connection with Yahweh and Baal.

Verse 21 says "to Yahweh the Lord belongs escaping from death (תוצאות למות)." The reference to death could be taken as a personified reference, alluding to the god Mot (מות) in the *Baal Cycle*. After Baal built his house, Mot challenged Baal, who acquiesced and descended to the underworld. Later, he ascended from the underworld, thereby escaping death. Psalm 68:21 could be another identification of Yahweh with Baal.[68] However, the verse begins, "God is for us a God of salvation." So it speaks of God delivering Israel from death, paradigmatically from Egypt, not of saving himself from death (nor do the Hebrew Scriptures entertain the possibility of Yahweh's death). Without presupposing Ugaritic influence in the rider language, there is no reason to personify death into a mythological god here.

Many emendations have been proposed for v. 23 (אשיב מבשן, "I will bring back from Bashan"), because of the lack of a direct object for אשיב. Several attempts have been made to emend the text so that God says he will bring back "the Serpent," that is, "the Sea," which reflects Baal mythology.[69] Most suggestions involve unnecessary emendations of MT, which makes sense as it is. The direct object may be omitted to allow for an open class that God can bring back from the heights of Basham, should he so choose. Alternatively, one could consider בשן a case of nonphonemic interchange of *s* for *t*, so that *bšn* would be the Hebrew equivalent to Ugaritic *btn* ("Serpent"). But it would be strange for Bashan to be a mythological god here, yet a historical mountain in v. 15. It is also unlikely the psalmist would use *bāšān* to refer to Ugaritic *btn* when the Hebrew cognate *peten* ("serpent") was available.[70]

The reference in v. 30 to the "beast of the reeds" could possibly be a reference to the chaos myth, since "Behemoth" in the Ugaritic texts was a single, ox-like creature.[71] But, this

---

[67] The point of the window argument between Baal and Kothar-wa-hasis seems to be that Kothar knew Baal would need a place from which to send storms and showers from his heavenly temple (KTU 1.4 v 59–vi 15; vii 14–27).
[68] So Kraus, *Psalms 60–150*, 54.
[69] See proposals summarized and critiqued by John R. Gray, "Cantata of the Autumn Festival: Psalm 68," *JSS* 22 (1977): 10; John Day, *God's Conflict with the Dragon and the Sea: Echoes of a Canaanite Myth in the Old Testament*, UCOP 34 (Cambridge: Cambridge University Press, 1985), 118–19.
[70] Day, *God's Conflict*, 115.
[71] Ibid., 120.

phrase refers to a great national power, probably Egypt, given the association of reeds with Egypt in the OT (2 Kgs 18:21; Isa 19:6; 36:6–7; Ezek 29:6).[72] Targum *Tehillim* 68:15 also interpreted the beast as a national power, but as the nation of Edom. The best argument for seeing a chaos monster here is to note the representation of Egypt as a mythological dragon figure elsewhere in the OT (Isa 30:7; Ps 87:4; Isa 51:9). The psalmist would then have had Egypt in mind as the referent of "beast of the reeds" but would have understood Egypt mythologically, alluding to the chaos monster. But even if this were not too much of a stretch (which I think it is), Yam is not a "chaos monster" in the *Baal Cycle* (El was going to build him a palace and make him a king), and there is no creation theme in the *Baal Cycle* as is usually associated with the *Chaoskampf* motif that appears in *Enuma Eliš*.

Verse 34 says Yahweh יתן בקולו קול עז ("sends forth his voice, a mighty voice"). This phrase is similar to Ugaritic *tn qlh b ʿrpwt* ("the utterance of his voice is in the clouds").[73] In this case, there may be some influence from Canaanite poetic expression, given the linguistic and poetic influence between the two cultures.[74] But there is nothing distinctive about a deity's mighty voice coming from heaven. The psalmist may simply be using a common ANE poetic expression to express Yahweh's heavenly power.

Finally, J. Gray takes references to God's kingship over and subdual of the nations (vv. 25, 30) as obvious parallels to Baal.[75] However, we saw in the first part of this chapter that these two notions are sufficiently common in the ANE that they need not be borrowed from any one tradition. Moreover, as the next chapter will argue, the psalmist drew on Exod 15:1–18 for its narrative structure, and it may have been one of the psalmist's sources for the concepts of God's kingdom and subdual of the nations (see especially Exod 15:14–16, 18). Yahweh will bring Israel in and plant them on his own mountain, "the place, O Yahweh, which you have made for your abode; the sanctuary, O Lord, which your hands have established" (15:17). From there he will "reign forever and ever" (15:18).

In summary, the supposition that Yahweh's epithet "Rider in the Deserts" was borrowed from the Ugaritic Baal traditions has caused scholars to find several other parallels in Ps 68 to the same traditions. None of these, however, are entirely persuasive on their own. They are also severely undercut if the "rider" epithet does not stem from the Baal traditions.

Similarity of the Divine Builder Motif

The last similarity between Ps 68 and the Baal traditions that could suggest that the traditions were borrowed by the psalmist is the similarity of the divine builder motif.

---

[72] Kraus, *Psalms 60–150*, 55; Dahood, *Psalms*, 2:150; Charles A. Briggs and Emilie Grace Briggs, *A Critical and Exegetical Commentary on the Book of Psalms*, ICC (Edinburgh: T&T Clark, 1906–1907) 2:96. Professor Fred Putnam also alerted me to the association of cows with reeds in Egyptian art (cf. Pharaoh's dreams).

[73] Gray, "Cantata of the Autumn Festival," 9.

[74] See, e.g., Oswald Loretz and Ingo Kottsieper, *Colometry in Ugaritic and Biblical Poetry: Introduction, Illustrations, and Topical Bibliography*, UBL 5 (Altenberge: CIS-Verlag, 1987). As with most cultural influences, the influence would likely have gone both ways.

[75] Gray, "Cantata of the Autumn Festival," 8–9.

However, if the arguments above are correct, neither the rider epithet nor any of the possible allusions to Baal traditions are actually borrowed by the psalmist. Also, as we saw above, the divine builder motif is ubiquitous throughout the ANE war traditions, including at least Egyptian, Assyrian, Aramean, Ugaritic, Babylonian, and Israelite traditions. I also noted three categories of differences between all six of these different divine builder traditions. Since the divine builder theme is a literary topos with a set outline for telling the story (albeit with peripheral variations among the traditions), and since all the traditions vary in their theology and emphases, there is no reason to suppose the psalmist borrowed the divine builder motif from the Baal traditions. The divine builder motif was simply a common ANE means of proclaiming that their god was a mighty king with a grand temple.

Conclusion on Psalm 68 and Baal Traditions

While the psalmist may well have been aware of the Baal traditions—his characteristics, accomplishments, and epithets—it does not seem that he borrowed intentionally from those traditions. At the most, he may have been aware of the superficial similarities, but he gives no mind to Baal, for Yahweh is the king of the universe and he will reign forever. While this helps us understand the psalm more precisely, it also means that there is no need to revise my exegetical reading of Ps 68 by accounting for language borrowed from Baal traditions. The psalm is thoroughly Hebrew, with a narrative of salvation that traces Yahweh's favor on Israel from Egypt to Zion.

Psalm 68 would not be the first psalm whose supposed Ugaritic influence was overplayed or misleading. For example, while previous scholars universally accepted Ps 29's reliance on Ugaritic ideas and poetic terms, scholars recently have begun to see Ps 29 as more independent.[76] So in spite of the academic consensus that Ps 68 is dependent on the Ugaritic materials, it is not unprecedented to suggest otherwise.

Conclusion

This chapter has served two purposes. First, I documented the divine builder theme throughout the ANE, spanning cultures and millennia. That this theme was so widespread and existed for so long corroborates my divine builder narratival reading of Ps 68. Second, in order to safeguard my interpretation of the psalm as thoroughly Hebrew, rather than a hodgepodge of Canaanite language and ideas loosely applied to Yahweh, I argued against any influence of the Baal traditions in Ps 68. Although there are unmistakable linguistic affinities between Hebrew and Ugaritic, which may coincidentally lead to similarity of expression, there is no explicit evidence in the psalm of direct borrowing or appropriation of the Baal traditions in Ps 68. This chapter, then, serves to corroborate my reading of the psalm and to guard that reading against potential objections.

---

[76] Peter C. Craigie, *Ugarit and the Old Testament* (Grand Rapids, MI: Eerdmans, 1983), 68–71.

4

Old Testament Scripture in Psalm 68

This chapter has one objective and three purposes. The objective is to explore the psalmist's use of prior OT traditions in Ps 68. The purpose for this objective is threefold. First, I have not yet finished the narrative of the psalm, because I contend that the use of OT traditions in Ps 68 is the main key to correctly interpreting the second half of the psalm. Second, in addition to showing the influence of Deut 33 in the previous chapter, demonstrating Ps 68's use of Judg 5 and Exod 15 will add further corroboration to my narratival argument in the second chapter. Specifically, these three texts are all ANE "victory songs," a genre that existed at the time of the psalmist.[1] The psalmist has appropriated aspects of Judg 5 and Exod 15—albeit in different ways—to compose his own victory song. Third, Ps 68:19, which Paul quotes in Eph 4:8, is itself at least an allusion to Judg 5:12. Indeed, there are many allusions to Judg 5 in the psalm, which we saw in Chapter 2. To understand Paul's use of the psalm properly, we must at least explore the psalm's use of Judg 5:12 to understand how much meaning, if any, has been transferred from Judg 5:12 to Ps 68:19 to Eph 4:8.

It is no secret that the author of Ps 68 has integrated several passages of OT Scripture into its composition. This fact has been used to date the psalm late, used to suggest various redactional phases, or in some cases has been ignored as simple borrowing of language. A more thoughtful investigation of the use of the OT in Ps 68 reveals the author's conscious intention to fall in line with an Israelite and, more broadly, an ANE tradition of composing victory songs after successful military campaigns. Whether Ps 68's *Sitz im Leben* is rooted in a military victory must be considered later. What is more certain is that Judg 5 and Exod 15—the two models for Ps 68—are rooted in such a military experience. I will argue this point in spite of those who have tended to date these two songs late or root them in a cultic or a liturgical setting.

I endeavor to suggest that Moses's Song of the Sea in Exod 15 was the model for Deborah's Song in Judg 5 and that both were models for Ps 68, though in different ways. Psalm 68 draws language more freely from Judg 5, but draws its narrative pattern and ideology more from Exod 15. Both Judg 5 and Ps 68 comprise a prophetic announcement of partial fulfillment of the narratival movement in Exod 15. The psalm also alludes to other passages, particularly Gen 49, Num 24, and, as we have seen, Deut

---

[1] Victory songs need not contain a "divine builder" topos, and divine builder narratives need not be composed as songs, but divine builder narratives do often employ hymnic language as in Ps 68.

33. These songs are not patterns for Ps 68 but rather a source for certain poetic, militant imagery. These three passages hold the key to interpreting the second half of the psalm. I will begin by demonstrating the common "victory song" genre for our three odes, which will assist us in dating the songs and arguing for their dependence.

Three Victory Songs

The proposed "victory song" genre has several distinctive characteristics. Of course, this genre is a modern category, and I am not suggesting that these three authors intentionally molded their song to fit a strict genre. Rather, these three authors lived in a similar cognitive environment that expressed the joy and praise of military successes in ways similar to one another and to their ancient neighbors.

Characteristics of Victory Songs

Several general features may be derived from ancient Egyptian and Assyrian victory songs. To begin with Egyptian accounts, several writings remain from the Asiatic campaigns of Thut-mose III of Egypt (c. 1490–1436 BC).[2] The Armant stela begins with a hymnic introduction including several epithets to Horus and continues with an account of victorious campaigns but not in a strict chronological sequence. A hymn of victory for Thut-mose III praises him as a god, describes his establishment in his temple after his victories, notes the nations' fear of him, depicts the enemy as being taken captive and bringing tribute, records his heroic military victories, and concludes with an affirmation of Thut-mose's eternal kingship. In structure, the song begins with narrative, switches to a lengthy hymnic form, and concludes with narrative. A hymn of victory of Mer-ne-Ptah (the "Israel Stela") from c. 1230 BC also fluidly mixes prose and poetry, as well as a taunt to the enemy whose god deserted them.[3] One hymnic section breaks into exultant praise of Mer-ne-Ptah for his exploits:

> How amiable is he, the victorious ruler!
>   How exalted is the king among the gods!
> How fortunate is he, the lord of command!
>   Ah, how pleasant it is to sit when there is gossip![4]

The song concludes with another hymn, cataloguing the subdued nations and their fear of Pharaoh.

The "Annals in Karnak," which is not strictly a victory song, does describe the military campaigns of Thut-mose III and further enlightens what would be included in the narrative portion of a victory song. The Annals describe Thut-mose's role in leading the forces at the head of the battle. He is often named "king" in connection with his

---

[2] *ANET*, 234–41.
[3] Ibid., 376–78.
[4] Ibid., 378.

battle victories. The enemy is taunted throughout by their depiction as being subjected and by acclamations of Thut-mose's arm (power) being greater than the enemy kings. Pharaoh is "a king, valiant like Montu; a taker, from whom no one can take, who crushes all rebellious countries."[5] When taking Megiddo, Thut-mose's presence caused fear to enter the bodies of his enemies, who became petrified. The enemy's "chariots of gold and silver were captured" easily, and the Egyptians "counted up their possessions," that is, divided the spoil. They praised Pharaoh and his father, Amon, for giving them the victory and then brought the plunder to Thut-mose as gifts. After the Egyptians had the town of Megiddo surrounded, Pharaoh gave a rally cry, "Capture ye [effective, my] victorious [army]! . . . Capture ye firmly, firmly!"[6] After the victories described in the Annals, the author lists the spoil taken from the enemy, including the amount and type of booty. These accounts are similar to divine builder texts, but some lack a building report and are written as least partially in hymnic fashion.

P. Craigie's article comparing Judg 5 to the Tukulti–Ninurta Epic provides several features of ancient Assyrian victory songs, some of which we have already seen in Egyptian odes. These include invoking divine aid in battle based on a previous covenant, the use of war cries, the depiction of a pathetic flight of the enemy, taunt songs, and metaphorical language describing natural phenomena (e.g., wind, water) destroying the enemy.[7] Thus, in addition to these five Assyrian elements, we have the others found in Egyptian literature, including (sometimes) lack of strict chronological sequence, possibly a construction narrative, taking captives and dividing the spoil, subjected enemies bringing tribute, the nations' fear of the victor, and unadulterated praise for the divine warrior god who gave the victory to his people. Not every victory song has all of these elements; we will see that Exod 15, Judg 5, and Ps 68 do not have them all. However, all three songs contain enough of these features to be unmistakably classed as ANE victory songs.

Exodus 15, Judges 5, and Psalm 68 as Songs of Victory

A brief survey of the content of Exod 15, Judg 5, and Ps 68 will demonstrate that they fit nicely into the victory song genre.

In the Song of the Sea, Yahweh is clearly the "divine warrior": "Yahweh is a man of war" (Exod 15:3). Whereas Moses stretched his hand over the sea in 14:21 to send the waves over the Egyptians, Yahweh's nostrils blow the waters into a heap (15:8, 10). Water is the means of destroying the enemy, who is subsequently taunted. The Egyptians thought they would divide the spoil; they thought their hand would destroy Israel (15:9). In fact, this was their last moment of confidence; the song taunts their fragility as v. 10 depicts Yahweh's hand burying them in the sea. After the victory, the nations tremble (15:14–16). Yahweh then leads Israel to his holy mountain sanctuary, where he will reign forever in the temple he will build himself (15:13, 17–18).[8] Hymnic

---

[5] Ibid., 240. Montu is the Egyptian god of war.
[6] Ibid., 237.
[7] Peter C. Craigie, "Song of Deborah and the Epic of Tukulti–Ninurta," *JBL* 88, no. 3 (1969): 256–63.
[8] Thus, Exod 15 is both a song of victory and a divine builder narrative.

praise opens the song (15:1–2) and interjects in the middle as a polemical blast against foreign gods (15:11).

In Deborah's song, Yahweh again plays the divine warrior, though emphasis is also given to human participation by mentioning all the characters from the prose account in Judg 4.[9] God's theophanic phenomena, manifested at Sinai and now in the battle (Judg 5:4–5), foreshadow the natural phenomena later in the poem that defeat the enemy: the stars fight Sisera and the torrent Kishon sweeps away the enemy (5:20–21). Deborah is summoned to bring the war cry and inspire the troops with her prophetic voice (5:12; also possibly 5:21c). Although the song only presupposes it (5:24–25), Judg 4 records Sisera's pathetic flight from Israel's army. The song taunts the enemy kings, who fought but "took no spoils of silver" (5:19). The song makes two more taunts, first against the petrified tribes who failed to join the battle (5:15–17), and second against Sisera's mother with his harem (5:28–30). These women await Sisera's return when he will bring the divided spoil, but it is the Israelite women Deborah and Jael who have won the battle, killed Sisera, and divided the spoil. Deborah's Song also exhibits lack of strict chronological sequence, as when v. 19 suggests Sisera's defeat but vv. 20–27 rewind to describe the battle. Although the final phrase "and the land had rest forty years" probably relates to the same theme in Judges, it is possible that it hints at the peace typically following a god's or a king's victory. Hymnic elements open and close the song (5:2–3, 31)

In Ps 68, we meet again at the outset the divine warrior, whose enemies are scattered and flee before him (68:2–3). Praise is then given in response (68:4–5). Like Exod 15, human participants in this battle are overlooked; Yahweh is the hero. Again we meet water, but this time as a merciful means of sustaining Israel (68:10). As God battles, the enemy kings lead a pathetic retreat (68:13). These kings presumably thought they would divide the spoil (like the Egyptians in Exod 15:9), but instead the psalmist taunts the defeated kings by portraying the tranquil, domestic Israelite women as peacefully dividing the spoil in the safety of their homes (68:13). Yahweh comes from Sinai to defeat the enemy and take captives (68:18–19). He receives gifts from his worshipers in order to build his temple (68:19), where he will reign "forever" (68:17). Praise interrupts the narrative in vv. 20–21 and concludes the song in vv. 33–36. Between this praise, the psalm continues with vague references to God's attributes and power over enemies, as well as a victory processional. Foreign kings will bring tribute to God at his temple in Jerusalem (68:30).

While these three songs do not each contain every feature of early ANE victory songs, they all display enough features to be classed in this genre.[10] Next, since I am going to discuss Judg 5's use of Exod 15, and then Ps 68's use of both songs, I first have

---

[9] James W. Watts, *Psalm and Story: Inset Hymns in Hebrew Narrative*, JSOTSS 139 (Sheffield: JSOT Press, 1992), 84.

[10] Charlie Trimm has recently included all three poems under the rubric of the Divine Warrior and sees them as hymns of victory (*"YHWH Fights for Them!": The Divine Warrior in the Exodus Narrative*, GBS 58 [Piscataway, NJ: Gorgias Press, 2014], 11–28). Craigie also discusses an ANE victory song genre and includes both Exod 15 and Judg 5 in that genre ("Song of Deborah and the Epic of Tukulti-Ninurta," 265).

to argue for a chronology that permits such use. That Ps 68 is an ancient victory song will aid us greatly in determining its date and *Sitz im Leben*.

Dating Ancient Poetry

To date these three ancient songs is no easy task, for they have all been dated variously. We shall see that it was primarily older commentators who dated these songs later, and in light of our recently acquired knowledge of early ANE poetry and detailed linguistic investigation, most scholars have reconsidered these late dates.

Characteristics of Ancient Poetry

F. M. Cross Jr. and D. N. Freedman have discussed the essential features of ancient Israelite poetry, based especially on parallels with Ugaritic poetry near the turn of the first millennium B.C.[11] A common feature is balanced metrical structure, either 3:3 or 2:2, or sometimes 3:3:3 or 2:2:2. Common grammar, vocabulary, and style features include energic *nun*, old case endings, archaic pronominal suffixes, longer and shorter particles appearing in the same poem due to metrical requirements, lack of direct object marker את and relative אשר, occasional use of relative זו or ש, vari-temporal *yqtl* forms (the *waw*-consecutive had not evolved yet), archaic vocabulary, and certain parallel expressions. Cross and Freedman's study examined Exod 15; Gen 49; Num 23–24; Deut 33; Judg 5; 2 Sam 1:19–27; and 2 Sam 22 = Ps 18, which they believed exhibited archaic features. These features were explored at length and corroborated by D. A. Robertson in his *Linguistic Evidence in Dating Early Hebrew Poetry*.[12] Of these features, metrical considerations have now become less important as a standard by which to measure Hebrew poetry, but the other features hold.[13]

Dating Exodus 15

B. Baentsch's dating of the Song of the Sea characterized older critical scholarship: "kann es jedenfalls nicht älter als die salomonische Zeit sein."[14] Critical commentators have assumed 15:1b–18 is an independent tradition woven into its narrative context by the Pentateuchal editor(s). A typical redactional view was that v. 1a is a later narrative introduction, vv. 1b–18 is the song proper, and v. 19 is a gloss coinciding with 14:29.[15]

---

[11] Frank Moore Cross Jr. and David Noel Freedman, *Studies in Ancient Yahwistic Poetry*, BRS (Grand Rapids, MI: Eerdmans, 1997), 1–25.

[12] David A. Robertson, *Linguistic Evidence in Dating Early Hebrew Poetry*, SBLDS 3 (Missoula, MT: Society of Biblical Literature, 1972), 7–28, 57–110, 135–46.

[13] For the failure of metrical analysis, see, e.g., Oswald Loretz and Ingo Kottsieper, *Colometry in Ugaritic and Biblical Poetry: Introduction, Illustrations, and Topical Bibliography*, UBS 5 (Altenberge: CIS-Verlag, 1987), 18.

[14] Bruno Baentsch, *Exodus-Leviticus-Numeri*, HAT 2 (Göttingen: Vandenhoeck und Reprecht, 1903), 128. Similarly, Georg Beer, *Exodus*, HBAT I/3 (Tübingen: J. C. B. Mohr, 1939), 83–84; Marie-Joseph Lagrange, *Le Livre Des Juges*, EB (Paris: Librairie Victor LeCoffre, 1903), 117.

[15] Beer, *Exodus*, 83; George W. Coats, *Exodus 1–18*, FOTL 2A (Grand Rapids, MI: Eerdmans, 1999), 117–18; Bernhard W. Anderson, "The Song of Miriam," in *Directions in Biblical Hebrew Poetry*,

Miriam's song (15:20–21) was considered the older original, on which the Song of the Sea was based. One reason the Song of the Sea was considered later than Miriam's song is that v. 18 culminates in Israel's arrival and enthronement of Yahweh in Jerusalem, which suggests a post-Davidic era.[16] Some scholars supposed v. 17 ("you will bring them in and plant them on the mountain of your inheritance") reflected Israel's return from Babylonian exile and dated the song to the postexilic period.[17] A second reason for dating the Song of the Sea later is that its first line is virtually the same as Miriam's entire song (15:21), and form criticism tends to date the shorter of two similar accounts as earlier.[18] Not all completely denied Mosaic authorship to the Song of the Sea. A. Dillmann supposed that an older, shorter version of Moses's song consisted of vv. 1–3, to which the rest of the song was added in the Davidic or Solomonic times to form a *Festgesang*.[19] Nevertheless, the standard account of the song has been that it is a post-Davidic composition based on Miriam's song.

While many modern scholars still retain the redaction–critical consensus on these poems, they are no longer considered post-Davidic. The Song of the Sea exhibits several archaic poetic features and is now considered by consensus to be among the earliest poems in the OT.[20] For example, the song features the relative זו (Exod 15:13, 16), a consistent use of מו as a verbal suffix (15:5, 9[x2], 10, 12, 15, 17), and a balanced meter.[21] D. Robertson's linguistic study in Hebrew poetry resulted in finding no standard poetic forms (i.e., forms characteristic of the eighth century or later) in Exod 15, and he dates Exod 15 as the oldest Israelite poem to the twelfth century.[22] Miriam's song is too brief to subject to a linguistic analysis, but it is considered early, perhaps even from Miriam herself.[23] Thus, the two songs in Exod 15 are the most ancient *poetic* witnesses to Yahweh's saving power in the OT, dated by linguistic data to the twelfth century (Song

---

ed. Elaine R. Follis, JSOTSS 40 (Sheffield: JSOT Press, 1987), 288; Brevard S. Childs, *The Book of Exodus: A Critical, Theological Commentary*, OTL (Louisville, KY: Westminster, 1974), 248. Werner Fuss assigns the gloss to JE (*Die deuteronomistische Pentateuchredaktion in Exodus 3–17* [Berlin: de Gruyter, 1972], 326).

[16] Baentsch, *Exodus-Leviticus-Numeri*, 128; Beer dates the poem as early as Solomon's reign (c. 970–930 BC); to ascribe the song to Moses is "ein historischer Irrtum" (*Exodus*, 83–84). Many recent commentators have retained this view: Anderson, "The Song of Miriam," 288; John I. Durham, *Exodus*, WBC 3 (Waco, TX: Word Books, 1987), 205, who dates vv. 13–18 to a postconquest time, when it was added to vv. 1–12; Watts, *Psalm and Story*, 49–51; John Day, *God's Conflict with the Dragon and the Sea: Echoes of a Canaanite Myth in the Old Testament*, UCOP 34 (Cambridge: Cambridge University Press, 1985), 100.

[17] Heinrich Holzinger, *Exodus*, KHCAT 2 (Tübingen: J. C. B. Mohr, 1900), 49–50; H. Bender, "Das Lied Exodus 15," *ZAW* 23 (1903): 46–48; P. Haupt, "Moses' Song of Triumph," *AJSLL* 20 (1904): 150–58; Georg Fohrer, *Überlieferung und Geschichte des Exodus: Eine Analyse von Ex 1–15*, BZAW 91 (Berlin: A.Töpelmann, 1964), 115.

[18] E.g., ibid., 111.

[19] August Dillmann and August Knobel, *Die Bücher Exodus und Leviticus für die zweite Auflage*, KEHAT 12 (Leipzig: S. Hirzel, 1880), 154.

[20] Daniel Block notes most scholars agree that Gen 49, Exod 15, Num 23–24, Deut 33, Judg 5, and perhaps Deut 32 are among the oldest in Hebrew literature (*Judges, Ruth*, NAC [Nashville, TN: Broadman & Holman, 1999], 213).

[21] Cross and Freedman, *Studies in Ancient Yahwistic Poetry*, 35–38.

[22] Robertson, *Linguistic Evidence*, 154.

[23] Anderson says Miriam's song was "an immediate poetic response to the event of Yahweh's liberation that it celebrates. In song and dance Miriam and her companions celebrated with the people the wonder of the event at the sea" ("The Song of Miriam," 290–91).

of Moses) and perhaps even the thirteenth or fifteenth century, depending on the date of the Exodus (Song of Miriam).[24]

The final issue is authorship. Scholars now admit the antiquity of both songs, but who authored them? Fohrer and Anderson are surely correct that Miriam's song was authored shortly after the Exodus, probably from Miriam herself. As for the Song of the Sea, the supposition that 15:1b–18 was a later expansion of 15:21 because of the latter's brevity is correctly chided by Anderson as a "weak premise of past form criticism."[25] As for content, the mention of Yahweh's mountain, sanctuary, and kingship in 15:17–18 are no evidence of a post-Mosaic date of composition for several reasons. Israel already had a conception of Yahweh's kingship prior to their monarchy (1 Sam 8:7, 12:12).[26] The lack of any specific details about the Jerusalem temple, the fact that "sanctuary" appears rather than "temple," and the lack of any mention of Zion or Jerusalem tell against a postconquest perspective that older critical scholarship supposed. Moreover, Exod 15 is using the divine builder topos, so the prediction of building a temple is not surprising; it is the expected activity following God's defeat of Egypt.

As for the prophecy that God would lead them to his mountain (Exod 15:17), God told Moses prior to the Exodus that he would lead them back to Sinai: "this will be the sign that I have sent you: when you have brought out the people from Egypt, you will serve God on this mountain (הר)" (3:12). It is therefore not strange that the song mentions God planting them on his mountain.[27] Cross and Freedman also noted Yahweh's close connection with mountains "in the earliest sources (cf. Jud. 5:4–5; Pss. 18:7–15; 68:7–9, 15–17; Hab. 3:3–15; etc.)."[28] There is therefore no content in the song that could not have been composed by Moses just after crossing the Red Sea. In fact, in the period before David, Moses is the most qualified Israelite (and perhaps the only one) who could sing prophetically about Yahweh bringing Israel to his holy mountain-sanctuary. He also would have known that Horeb (i.e., Sinai) would not be a permanent stop for the Israelites, since God's promise to the Patriarchs was to give them Canaan. Thus, the "mountain" in Exod 15:17 has primary reference to Sinai and secondary reference to the final and permanent mountain-sanctuary, Zion.

My final judgment is that the songs are indeed independent and were authored by Moses and Miriam just after the exodus. If Robinson's dating of the song to the twelfth century is correct, then it may be the case that poetic features in Israel were the same

---

[24] Cross and Freedman argued the two songs are actually one. The same phrase appearing in 15:1b, 21 ("I will sing to Yahweh . . . he has thrown into the sea") is the title for the entire song—a typical custom in ANE poetry—preserved in two different traditions. However, it would be strange if the two traditions were brought together with the entire song being preserved from one tradition alongside only the title from the other tradition. It is more likely these are two distinct songs (Anderson, "The Song of Miriam," 290).

[25] Anderson, "The Song of Miriam," 289. Similarly, Childs, *The Book of Exodus*, 247.

[26] Nahum M. Sarna, *Exodus* שמות: *The Traditional Hebrew Text with the New JPS Translation*, JPSTC (Philadelphia, PA: Jewish Publication Society, 1991), 82.

[27] Thus, הר probably does not refer to the mountainous terrain of Canaan, as some commentators believe, e.g., Beer, *Exodus*, 83. I subsequently found that Umberto Cassuto draws the same conclusion that the mountain is Sinai, which Moses deduced from Exod 3:12 (*A Commentary on the Book of Exodus*, trans. Israel Abrahams [Jerusalem: Magnes Press, 1967], 176).

[28] Cross and Freedman, *Studies in Ancient Yahwistic Poetry*, 45n56.

at the time of the exodus as in the twelfth century, or that the language of the song evolved with the Israelite's natural language. Thus, the content of the song could have been sung by Moses and linguistic dating does not preclude Mosaic authorship. Even if this is incorrect, for the purposes of this work, it is enough to show that Exod 15 is earlier than Judg 5 and Ps 68.

Dating Judges 5

Traditionally, Samuel wrote Judges (*b. Bat.* 14b), but critical scholarship (particularly in nineteenth- and twentieth-century commentaries) has found in Judges a fragmented and heavily redacted text.[29] M. Noth's Deuteronomistic History ("DH"), which includes Judges, has helped maintain interest in diachronic studies in Judges. Noth believed the Deuteronomist shaped Judg 4–5 by adding 4:1a, 2, 3a, 17, and 5:31b, and Noth dated the compilation of DH (and thus of the final form of Judges) to the exilic period.[30] A more recent redaction–critical investigation of Judg 3–8 by A. Scherer built on Noth's DH theory. He argues for three redactional phases in Judg 5. The original song was a Yahweh–War–Ballad (vv. 6–30), dated to the last third or quarter of the eleventh century BC. The ballad was then subjected to a hymnic redaction when a hymnic frame was added (vv. 2–5, 31a). Finally, the Deuteronomist added v. 1 to connect the redacted song with chapter 4 and v. 31b to provide the note of "rest" expected after chapter 4.[31] Verses 2–5 are generally considered to be a different battle report than the original ballad.

Although Judges has been atomized for diachronic investigation, critical scholars have been less prone to date Judg 5 late than they have been with Exod 15. E. Bertheau stated flatly in 1883, "Die Dichterin des Liedes ist Debora; so die moisten Ausleger..."[32] In 1903, M.-J. Lagrange argued that the ancient Hebrew style and raw emotion of the poem suggests that its composition is contemporaneous with the events, and that "[c]ette conclusion est toujours celle de la critique moderne dans l'immense majorité."[33] As noted with Scherer, even those who posit redaction layers in Judg 5 still generally see the core ballad as ancient. Robertson's linguistic study of Israelite poetry has confirmed the early date for Judg 5, dating it to the end of the twelfth century BC, just after Exod 15, since it exhibits "numerous early forms, a very few standard ones."[34] D. Block believes both traditions probably descend from Deborah, perhaps through Ephraimites (Deborah dwelt between Bethel and Ramah) or the prophetic

---

[29] Alexander Globe, "Literary Structure and Unity of the Song of Deborah," *JBL* 93, no. 4 (1974): 493. See a history of diachronic interpretation in Barry G. Webb, *The Book of Judges: An Integrated Reading*, JSOTSS 46 (Sheffield: Sheffield Academic Press, 1987), 13–40.

[30] Martin Noth, *The Deuteronomistic History*, JSOTSS 15 (Sheffield: Sheffield Academic Press, 1981), 45, 79.

[31] Andreas Scherer, *Überlieferungen von Religion und Krieg: Exegetische und religionsgeschichtliche Untersuchungen zu Richter 3–8 und verwandten Texten*, WMANT 105 (Neukirchen-Vluyn: Neukirchener, 2005), 161.

[32] Ernst Bertheau, *Das Buch der Richter und Ruth*, KEHAT (Leipzig: S. Hirzel, 1883), 93.

[33] Lagrange, *Le Livre Des Juges*, 105.

[34] Robertson, *Linguistic Evidence*, 154.

guild.³⁵ G. Taylor also argues for a date contemporaneous with Israel's struggle to expel the Canaanites because the song presents Jael akin to a Canaanite goddess, Athtart.³⁶

Those who argue for a later date or for later redactional layers in Judg 5 rely mostly on the mixture of ballad and hymn in the song, suggesting the two would not be mixed in a single composition. H.-P. Mathys has recently perpetuated this argument, noting mixed genres in the song and finding the older report in vv. 2–5, 9–11, 31a, and possibly vv. 13 and 23.³⁷ However, we have seen that ANE victory songs often mix hymn and ballad, and other studies have made the same observation.³⁸ Globe's article is particularly important. He notes, first, that it was customary in Israel from the Exodus to David, and in other ANE cultures, for women to meet their victorious warriors with dancing and songs that they had composed (Exod 15:20–21; Judg 11:34; 1 Sam 18:6–8). He also notes "a dozen, perhaps as many as twenty" archaic forms in the poem (for example, אז, energic *nun*, etc.) as well as repetitive parallelism similar to second millennium Ugaritic poetry.³⁹ Thus, "there is nothing impossible in the traditional view that Deborah composed Judges 5 shortly after the battle it commemorates."⁴⁰ He also argues for distinct literary features in all three parts of the poem (vv. 2–11d, 11e–18, 19–31), which suggests that, even if a later redactor did add a bicola here or there, it would be difficult to add much without disrupting the distinct literary features of each part. Globe concludes, "[T]he stylistic coherence of Judges 5 gives the impression of a single poetic intelligence mustering all the craft at its disposal, always varying the technique, but often returning to devices used earlier."⁴¹ Thus, Judg 5 exhibits features of unity that suggest one author of the entire song.⁴²

The strongest factor in favor of its unity is that the details of all three parts of Judg 5 are incoherent in isolation and presuppose knowledge of the account in Judg 4.⁴³ Moreover, composing a prose and narrative account of the same battle was a common

---

³⁵ Block, *Judges, Ruth*, 184. Block provides six reasons why Deborah's authorship of the song is likely, and suggests that it comprises her prophetic interpretation of the event in chapter 4 (ibid., 214–15).

³⁶ J. Glen Taylor, "The Song of Deborah and Two Canaanite Goddesses," *JSOT* 23 (1982): 99–108.

³⁷ Hans-Peter Mathys, *Dichter und Beter: Theologen aus spätalttestamentlicher Zeit*, OBO 132 (Freiburg: Universitätsverlag, 1994), 174–76.

³⁸ See, e.g., Watts, *Psalm and Story*, 206–20, which describes the phenomenon of inset hymns in literature of various ANE cultures. See also Craigie, "Song of Deborah and the Epic of Tukulti-Ninurta," 253–65.

³⁹ Globe, "Literary Structure and Unity in the Song of Deborah," 509.

⁴⁰ Ibid., 495.

⁴¹ Ibid., 508.

⁴² Recent interest in Judges has also begun shifting away from diachronic to synchronic studies in Judges, likely as a result of the increased influence of literary methods in OT studies. For example, Serge Frolov, in his recent form-critical study of Judges, says, "[T]heoretical advances have massively shifted [form-criticism's] emphasis towards the final form of the [Hebrew Bible]" (*Judges*, FOTL 6B [Grand Rapids, MI: Eerdmans, 2013], 3). In 1987, B. G. Webb authored a monograph on the literary unity of the entire book (*The Book of Judges*). See also Susanne Gillmayr-Bucher, *Erzählte Welten im Richterbuch: Narratologische Aspekte eines polyfonen Diskurses*, BIS 116 (Leiden: Brill, 2013), which uses a sophisticated multi-narratival-world approach but which I was not able to engage in time. In light of these studies and others like them, many factors considered as evidence for redactional layers, such as repetition and literary framing, may be interpreted equally as careful crafting by the author or narrator for rhetorical effect.

⁴³ Webb, *The Book of Judges*, 139; Watts, *Psalm and Story*, 85; Frolov, *Judges*, 137–38, who says "5:2–31a must presuppose Judges 4 (or, rather, an audience familiar with it) unless proven otherwise." See the helpful chart that places Judg 4–5 in parallel in Block, *Judges, Ruth*, 176–84.

practice in the ANE, so Judg 4–5 were likely composed together originally.[44] The song may have been transmitted orally until it was put into writing alongside the prose account in Judg 4.

I conclude that Judg 5 was composed by Deborah just after the victory over Sisera and Jabin, in accord with the Israelite custom for women to compose and sing victory odes after successful campaigns (Exod 15:20–21; Judg 11:34; 1 Sam 18:6–8). Deborah, as a prophetess (Judg 4:4), would have been equipped to compose hymnic oracles, as were Israel's other prophets. Her poem fits linguistically and stylistically in her second-millennium ANE milieu. As with Exod 15, even if the above dating of Judg 5 is incorrect and the song was composed a century or two later, it still holds that Judg 5 was composed later than Exod 15 and earlier than Ps 68.

Dating Psalm 68

Although the title is ascribed to David's handiwork (לְדָוִד), most critics have not accepted his authorship. The language of the psalm is difficult, which led many older commentators to see the psalm as corrupted or even as no psalm at all. T. H. Robinson (in Oesterley's commentary) agreed with H. Schmidt that Ps 68 constituted a "collection of sentences and phrases taken from a number of different poems, and strung together haphazardly."[45] He says, "*[I]t is generally agreed* that the text must have suffered considerably in the course of transmission."[46] The final form of the psalm dates to the latest psalm era possible. Other commentators dated the psalm late based on its contents. D. B. Duhm interpreted vv. 19–36 as a rehearsal of Israel's history from the fall of northern Israel to the time of Alexander Jannaeus: "Es ist demnach einer der jüngsten Psalmen und feiert und unterstützt die Unternehmungen des Alexander Jannäus."[47] Briggs and Briggs believed the psalm was heavily redacted and was not based on any specific historical victory. The sections on what seem to be "thoroughly organised temple worship" suggest a fourth century date, when Persia and Egypt were at war (they saw Egypt as the chief enemy in the psalm).[48] Thus, several older commentators viewed Ps 68 as one of the latest compositions in the Psalter.

Another group of commentators gave a cultic *Sitz im Leben* to the psalm, dating it as preexilic, but were not afraid to suggest later redactions. H. Schmidt saw Ps 68 as a fragmented psalm but one whose parts all shared a similar *Sitz im Leben* in the autumn festival.[49] S. Mowinckel then developed his thesis that the enthronement festival was part of the autumn festival. He thought the "procession" to the temple in Ps 68:25–26 referred to the enthronement procession: Ps 68 is "undoubtedly a procession psalm

---

[44] Block, *Judges, Ruth*, 184; Sarna, *Exodus*, 75.
[45] W. O. E. Oesterley, *The Psalms* (London: Society for Promoting Christian Knowledge, 1939), 2:320.
[46] Ibid., 321, emphasis added.
[47] D. Bernhard Duhm, *Die Psalmen*, KHCAT (Leipzig: J. C. B. Mohr, 1899), 178. Justus Olshausen (*Die Psalmen*, KHCAT [Leipzig: S.Hirzel, 1853], 284–89) also dated the psalm to the Maccabean period, following the work of Eduard Ruess, *Der acht-und-sechzigste Psalm: Ein Denkmal exegetischer Noth und Kunst zu Ehren unsrer ganzen Zunft* (Jena: Friedrich Mauke, 1851).
[48] Charles A. Briggs and Emilie Grace Briggs, *A Critical and Exegetical Commentary on the Book of Psalms*, ICC (Edinburgh: T&T Clark, 1906–1907), 2:95–96.
[49] Hans Schmidt, *Die Psalmen*, HBAT I 15 (Tübingen: Mohr Siebeck, 1934), 127–28.

at Yahweh's triumphal entry as king."[50] Mowinckel, in a small monograph on Ps 68, argued that the psalm was written originally for the cult of the sanctuary at Tabor, when Benjamin held pride of place as the tribe does in the psalm (v. 28).[51] It was later transferred to the Jerusalem cult and was redacted to reflect the prominence of Jerusalem (e.g., v. 30) and Judah (v. 28). Mowinckel was followed, with minor scruples, by J. Gray, H.-J. Kraus, and A. Weiser.[52]

Another set of commentators have fought for the antiquity of the psalm primarily on the basis of Ugaritic linguistic parallels.[53] Albright's oft-cited article took Ps 68's ambiguity to the extreme, arguing that Ps 68 was actually a compilation of thirty incipits.[54] He dated the original poems belonging to these thirty incipits between the thirteenth and tenth century BC, and the final edition of the psalm to the Solomonic period.[55] His early dating depended on the frequent defective spelling in the psalm, which accords with the "fully defective orthography of Phoenecia and early Israel, which was replaced by the standard spelling of the Divided Monarchy in the course of the ninth century B.C.E."[56] He further cited the consistent misunderstanding of the Hebrew by the Septuagint translators, which would be inconceivable if the poem had been postexilic, "even assuming deliberate archaism."[57] M. Dahood built on Albright's work by arguing for the presence of Ugaritic-Phoenician elements in Ps 68, such as "third person singular suffix -*y* (vss. 11, 31, 34, 36), vocative *lamedh* (vss. 5, 33, 36), precative perfect (vs. 10), Phoenician ending of feminine singular nouns (vss. 12, 21, 36), [and] double-duty suffixes (vss. 10, 21, 24)."[58] He believes these Ugaritic-Phoenician parallels clarify much of the psalm's obscurity, resulting in a "greater conceptual unity throughout the composition" than Albright's incipit theory allowed.[59]

Many commentators wrote before psalms studies were transformed by Gunkel and Mowinckel, and therefore sought a *Sitz im Leben* in the life of David, due to the authorial inscription. H. Dimock in 1791 noted, "The best critics and commentators agree that this psalm was composed on David's bringing back the ark to Zion."[60] Hengstenberg and Delitzsch make the most forceful arguments for a Davidic *Sitz im Leben*, based

---

[50] Sigmund Mowinckel, *The Psalms in Israel's Worship* (1962; repr. Grand Rapids, MI: Eerdmans, 2004), 1:170.

[51] Sigmund Mowinckel, *Der achtundsechzigste Psalm* (Oslo: I kommisjon hos J. Dybwad, 1953), 19, 72.

[52] John R. Gray, "Cantata of the Autumn Festival: Psalm 68," *JSS* 22, no. 1 (1977): 2–26; Hans-Joachim Kraus, *Psalms 60-150: A Commentary*, trans. Hilton C. Oswald (Minneapolis, MN: Fortress Press, 1993), 50–51; Artur Weiser, *The Psalms: A Commentary*, OTL (Philadelphia, PA: Westminster Press, 1962), 481–82.

[53] Gray evaluated several of the proposed Ugaritic parallels in his article, accepting many of them as adequate solutions to the interpretive problems of the psalm ("Cantata of the Autumn Festival," 8–20).

[54] An incipit is the first line of a poem used as its title. Incipits were common in Sumerian, Akkadian, and probably Canaanite poetry.

[55] William F. Albright, "A Catalogue of Early Hebrew Lyric Poems (Psalm LXVIII)," *HUCA* 23 (1951): 7–10.

[56] Ibid., 10.

[57] Ibid., 5n7.

[58] Mitchell J. Dahood, *Psalms*, AB 17 (Garden City, NY: Doubleday, 1966), 2:133.

[59] Ibid.

[60] Henry Dimock, *Notes Critical and Explanatory on the Book of Psalms and Proverbs* (Glocester: R. Raikes, 1791), 116.

on internal evidence. Verse 28 shows four tribes together, suggesting a date prior to the split of the kingdom, but not as late as the rise of Assyria, since Egypt represents the current world power ("beast of the reeds," v. 31). Since Solomon did not win a war as celebrated in the psalm, it must have been composed after a Davidic victory when Israel returned the ark to Zion.[61] The sanctuary must already have been on Mount Zion (vv. 17–19, 30, 36), which leaves only the Syrian-Edomite and the Ammonitic-Syrian victories. The ark of the covenant, which is mentioned in the psalm (v. 2), was present in the Ammonitic war (2 Sam 11:11). Hengstenberg concludes that the psalm was written after the capture of Rabbah, when the ark was returned to Jerusalem (2 Sam 12:26–31). The procession mentioned in the psalm refers to an actual procession to celebrate the victory that occasioned the psalm. F. Delitzsch agrees with Hengstenberg that the psalm refers to the Ammonitic-Syrian war, but he differs by suggesting it was written in the middle of the war, and the victory of the psalm is prophesied through the eyes of faith.[62]

Deciding how to date the psalm and uncover its *Sitz im Leben* depends largely on the methodology one applies to the psalms. The group headed by Mowinckel relies largely on the enthronement festival hypothesis, which we have seen is suspect. The major support is the mention of a "procession" in v. 25, but I will argue later that this is not a new year's enthronement procession. Those who favor maximizing Ugaritic parallels in the psalms have given strong evidence supporting an early date, but these linguistic parallels do not help us with the *Sitz im Leben*. Those who had dated the psalm late would surely reverse their conclusions in light of modern linguistic research.

The best approach to the psalm is to derive the date and *Sitz im Leben* from internal evidence. Important is our classification of Ps 68 as an ancient victory song, resembling especially Egyptian and Assyrian victory songs from the late second and early first millennium BC. The linguistic affinities to Ugaritic literature also suggest an early date. Thus, the psalm's most likely occasion for composition was an Israelite military victory around the turn of the millennium, and there is no reason not to look to David's battles for a fitting occasion. It is unnecessary to pinpoint a specific battle, so we could suppose that it was written after any battle subsequent to the taking of Jerusalem from the Jebusites (1 Chr 11:4–9), since Ps 68:18–19 depicts YHWH as the divine warrior ascending Jerusalem and taking captives, presumably the Jebusites. It may in fact have been written to celebrate the victory over the Jebusites once David was established in the city (1 Chr 11:8–9). Although the ark had not yet been brought up, God is depicted as the divine warrior who ascended with David, just as 1 Chr 11:9 says "YHWH of hosts was with him."

If one wanted more specificity, there is one victory that fits well as the possible occasion for Ps 68. Shortly after David took Jerusalem, he defeated a host of Philistines and decided to bring up the ark from Baale-judah (cf. 1 Chr 13:5, "Kiriath-jearim") to Jerusalem (2 Sam 6 // 1 Chr 13). They celebrated "with songs and lyres and harps and tambourines and castanets and cymbals" (2 Sam 6:5) "with all their might" (1 Chr

---

[61] Ernst Wilhelm Hengstenberg, *Commentary on the Psalms* (Cherry Hill, NJ: Mack, 1975), 2:335–36.
[62] Franz Delitzsch, *Biblical Commentary on the Psalms*, trans. Francis Bolton, 2nd rev. ed. (Edinburgh: T&T Clark, 1880), 2:244–47.

13:1, which also adds trumpets). While the episode with Uzzah prevented the ark from getting to Jerusalem immediately, after three months David took up the ark again and brought it to Jerusalem and placed it in the tent he had prepared for it (2 Sam 6:17). There was a grand procession that involved all the tribes (6:1–5). Since Ps 68 begins with an allusion to the taking up of the ark in Num 10:35, it is possible that it was composed in honor of this occasion to move the ark into Jerusalem. This occasion also fits much of the internal data of the psalm.

Whether this move of the ark or some other victory was the psalm's occasion, the psalmist writes in the midst of the fulfillment of Ps 68:19. The apex of the psalm is YHWH's ascent to Mount Zion and his taking captives, which had already occurred when David took Jerusalem. But this apex also includes Israel's generous gifts to build their God a temple in which he would dwell forever. If my general time period for the psalm's composition is correct, the temple had not yet been built. Hence, the psalm begins with a call to move the ark, which was the final step needed to bring Ps 68:19 to completion. This means that everything in the psalm after v. 19 is future from the perspective of the author, an important detail that will cohere with my reading of the second half of the psalm, which I base partly on its use of Pentateuchal passages.

One might object with Hengstenberg and Delitzsch that the temple seems already to be standing when the psalm is written. But we have seen the same issue with Exod 15. The author uses the divine builder topos to describe the near future when he knew they would give their God a permanent and majestic home in Jerusalem. Moreover, as we will see in the rest of this chapter, the psalmist is borrowing the narrative structure of the Song of the Sea, which concludes with a prophecy that God would build a temple. The Jerusalem temple therefore need not be standing at the time of the psalm's composition.

Conclusions to Dating

After first demonstrating that Exod 15, Judg 5, and Ps 68 all share characteristics of ANE victory songs, I have now argued for a chronological order of composition of Exod 15, followed by Judg 5, followed by Ps 68. The Song of the Sea was authored after the crossing of the Red Sea to celebrate the victory over Pharaoh. Deborah's song was probably authored by her shortly after the victory over Sisera. Psalm 68 was most likely written in response to a Davidic military victory after he took Jerusalem, which is depicted in v. 19, but before Solomon had built the temple with gifts from the Israelites, which is also depicted in prophetic fashion in v. 19. We are now poised to explore the possibility that Deborah used Exod 15 as a model to compose her victory song and that Ps 68 used both, albeit in different ways.

Deborah's Use of the Song of the Sea

Exod 15 and Judg 5 display many differences. Some of these were already noted, such as Judg 5's more paratactic chronology and its inclusion of human agents.[63] It also is

---

[63] See especially Alan J. Hauser, "Judges 5: Parataxis in Hebrew Poetry," *JBL* 99, no. 1 (1980): 23–41.

longer, exhibits a different structure, and does not clearly conclude with the temple-rest theme. However, their similarities are so many that it seems undeniable that Deborah developed Exod 15's victory theme. Both songs begin with grounds for praise and a first-person cohortative giving intent to praise. Both songs begin with two parties—Moses and the sons of Israel, Deborah and Barak—singing (שׁיר), although Judg 5 adds "I will make music to Yahweh" (v. 3). If Miriam's song (Exod 15:20–21) is considered also, then both passages have women singing. A. J. Hauser lucidly compared the two songs and demonstrated five common themes, all of which I noted above in the genre discussion.[64] R. O'Connell has compared the common narrative and poetic features of Exod 14–15 and Judg 4–5 in parallel columns spanning a page and a half.[65] Just some of these include: God predicting his victory to his prophet; several mentions of the enemy army, of chariots and horses and officers; the use of mud and water to defeat chariots; and the enemy's fleeing. Similar wording also occurs: aside from Pharaoh and Sisera, "not one was left" (לא נשאר עד־אחד; Exod 14:28; Judg 4:16); the Egyptians and Sisera were found dead (מת; Exod 14:30; Judg 4:23–24); YHWH's and Jael's "right hand" (ימין) defeated the enemy (Exod 15:6, 12; Judg 5:26); and the songs taunt the enemy, who intended to divide the spoil (חלק שלל; Exod 15:9; Judg 5:19b, 30). Many more parallels can be seen in O'Connell's work. Block notes the role of waters in the victory as well as "colorful and mythological imagery."[66] Finally, Exod 14–15 and Judg 4–5 are the only two instances in the OT where a song recapitulates prose.

The common themes, genre, and language between these two songs suggest that Deborah intentionally modeled her song after Moses's Song of the Sea. Indeed, what better song to be the paradigm for later Israelite victory songs than the song celebrating the paradigmatic Israelite deliverance? Deborah as a prophetess has intentionally developed Exod 15 by singing about the fulfillment of God's defeat of the Canaanites, which was prophesied in Exod 15:13–16.

Psalm 68's Use of Judges 5 and Exodus 15

Table 4.1 displays eight possible allusions to Judg 5. If all of these proposed allusions to Judg 5 are correct, there are eight, with one at the climax of the psalm: "You ascended to the height; you took captive captives; you received gifts among men" (Ps 68:19; cf. Judg 5:12). Some of the proposed allusions may not be only to Judg 5 but also to several poetic contexts that share the same idea or language. For example, the division of the spoil in Ps 68:12 may allude to Judg 5:30, to Exod 15:9, or may only reflect a common idea in ancient victory songs and therefore be no allusion at all. Likewise, Yahweh's epiphany from Sinai to the battlefield in Ps 68:7–8 may borrow from Judg 5:4–5, from

---

[64] Alan J. Hauser, "Two Songs of Victory: A Comparison of Exodus 15 and Judges 5," in *Directions in Biblical Hebrew Poetry*, ed. Elaine R. Follis, JSOTSS (Sheffield: JSOT Press, 1987), 266–80. I am indebted greatly to this article for my discussion on the genre of the psalms. See even further comparisons of the two songs in Trimm, *YHWH Fights for Them*, 22–23.

[65] Robert H. O'Connell, *The Rhetoric of the Book of Judges*, SVT (Leiden: Brill, 1996), 134–35.

[66] Block, *Judges, Ruth*, 213n304.

Table 4.1 Allusions to Judges 5 in Psalm 68.

Psalm 68 MT	Judges 5 Source
As smoke is driven away, you will drive away; as wax melts before the fire, the <u>wicked</u> will <u>perish</u> (יֹאבְדוּ רְשָׁעִים) before God (68:3).	So may all your <u>enemies perish</u> (יֹאבְדוּ כָל־אוֹיְבֶיךָ), O Yahweh (5:31).
O <u>God, when you went out</u> (בְּצֵאתְךָ) <u>before your people</u>, when you marched in the desert—Selah!—the <u>earth quaked</u> (אֶרֶץ רָעָשָׁה), indeed, the <u>heavens dripped</u> (שָׁמַיִם נָטָפוּ) before <u>God</u>—<u>this One of Sinai, before God, the God of Israel</u> (זֶה סִינַי מִפְּנֵי אֱלֹהִים אֱלֹהֵי יִשְׂרָאֵל) (68:8–9).	<u>Yahweh, when you went out from Seir</u> (יְהוָה בְּצֵאתְךָ מִשֵּׂעִיר), when you marched from the region of Edom, the earth quaked and the <u>heavens dripped</u> (שָׁמַיִם נָטָפוּ), yes, the clouds <u>dripped</u> water. The mountains quaked before <u>Yahweh, this One of Sinai, before Yahweh, the God of Israel</u> (זֶה סִינַי מִפְּנֵי יְהוָה אֱלֹהֵי יִשְׂרָאֵל) (5:4–5).
Kings of armies flee, they flee! The dweller (fem.) of the house <u>divides the spoil</u> (שָׁלָל תְּחַלֵּק) (68:13).	Have they not found and <u>divided the spoil</u> (יְחַלְּקוּ שָׁלָל)?—A womb or two for every man; <u>spoil</u> (שָׁלָל) of dyed materials for Sisera, <u>spoil</u> (שָׁלָל) of dyed materials embroidered, two pieces of dyed work embroidered for the neck as <u>spoil</u> (שָׁלָל)? (5:30).
Kings of armies flee, they flee! The <u>dweller (fem.) of the house</u> (וּנְוַת בַּיִת) divides the spoil (68:13).	Jael, the wife of Heber the Kenite, is most blessed among <u>tent-dwelling women</u> (מִנָּשִׁים בָּאֹהֶל) (5:24).
when <u>you lie among the sheepfolds</u> (אִם־תִּשְׁכְּבוּן בֵּין שְׁפַתָּיִם)—the wings of a dove covered in silver and its pinions with yellowish green gold (68:14).	Why did <u>you sit among the sheepfolds</u> (לָמָּה יָשַׁבְתָּ בֵּין הַמִּשְׁפְּתַיִם), to hear the bleating of flocks? Among the clans of Reuben there were great searchings of heart (5:16).
You ascended to the height; you <u>took captive captives</u> (שָׁבִיתָ שֶּׁבִי); you received gifts among men, indeed, *among* those who are stubborn, in order to dwell, O Yah God (68:19).	Awake, awake, Deborah! Awake, awake, break out in a song! Arise, Barak, <u>take captive</u> your <u>captives</u> (שֲׁבֵה שֶׁבְיְךָ), O son of Abinoam (5:12).
Surely God will <u>smash</u> the <u>head</u> (יִמְחַץ רֹאשׁ) of his enemies, the hairy <u>skull</u> (קָדְקֹד) walking in his guilt (68:22).	She sent her hand to the tent peg and her right hand to the workmen's mallet; she struck Sisera; she crushed his <u>head</u> (רֹאשׁ); she <u>smashed</u> (מָחֲצָה) and pierced his temple (5:26).
There is insignificant <u>Benjamin</u> ruling (בִּנְיָמִן רֹדֵם), the princes of Judah *in* their throng, the chiefs of <u>Zebulun</u>, the chiefs of <u>Naphtali</u> (68:28).	From Ephraim their root they marched down into the valley, <u>Benjamin following you</u> (אַחֲרֶיךָ בִנְיָמִין), with your kinsmen . . . from <u>Zebulun</u> . . . <u>Zebulun</u> is a people who risked their lives to the death; <u>Naphtali</u>, too, on the heights of the field (5:14, 18).

Note: Corresponding types of underlining signal similar or synonymous lexemes and referents.

Deut 33:2, or from both. In any case, Ps 68 alludes more frequently to Judg 5 than to any other Israelite tradition.

Most important for our project is the psalmist's use of Judg 5:12 in Ps 68:19, quoted by Paul in Eph 4:8. Judges 5 consists of an introductory doxology (vv. 4–5), a poetic account of the campaign against Sisera (vv. 6–30), and a concluding doxology (v. 31a). Judges 5:12 falls within the account of the campaign. After the author describes the prewar conditions in Israel (vv. 6–11), v. 12 summons both Deborah and Barak to action: Deborah to sing with a prophetic rallying cry for the troops and Barak to "arise" and to "take captive (שְׁבָה) your captives (שֶׁבְיְךָ)." The song then continues to describe the battle, including the tribes that took part and God's use of the stars and the river Kishon to defeat the enemy. Of course, Barak does not get the glory of taking captive the enemy, but Jael does, as Deborah had prophesied (Judg 4:9). Psalm 68:19 changes the agent of the verb from Barak to God. The psalm describes an action already accomplished (he had already taken captive the Jebusites), so the imperatival form of Judg 5:12 changes to a 2ms perfect form in Ps 68:19 (שָׁבִיתָ). The 2ms pronominal suffix from Judg 5:12 ("*your* captives") also disappears in Ps 68:19.

This psalmist thus alludes to Judg 5:12 analogically, borrowing language from the record of a previous battle to apply it to God's fulfillment of the prophecy from Exod 15:13–18, which declared that he would defeat the Canaanites and build his temple. The change in agent of the verb "take captive" from Barak to Yahweh is ironic: Barak received no glory in Judg 4–5, but Yahweh receives all the glory in Ps 68. Hence, Yahweh is the victorious divine warrior who triumphs over evil, despite whether his human agents are obedient and follow his will. The rhetorical effect of this allusion is to inspire both confidence and praise in Israel. God was the true warrior among Israel, and they do not accomplish victory by their own might. By drawing language from a previous victory song, the psalmist reminds Israel that God has fought for them all along. By implication, he will also continue to fight for them. The same God who fought for their fathers and who was faithful to his promises will be faithful to the younger generations as well. So Judg 5 is important for Ps 68's militant language and imagery, with probably eight allusions and a significant use of Judg 5:12 at the climax of the psalm.

The psalmist uses Exod 15 in quite a different way, by borrowing its ideological and structural features. The psalmist (in Ps 68:19) does draw at least the name "Yah" from Exod 15:2 and perhaps alludes to the same verse in 68:20, but the structural and conceptual similarities are more important.[67] The structural background is apparent when the structure of both songs is compared. While Exod 15 has been the victim of many structural schemes, G. W. Coats's is most faithful to its hymnic elements.[68] He sees an introduction (v. 1a), the song (1b–18), which includes five parts (vv. 1b, 2–3, 4–10, 11, 12–17), and a concluding narrative gloss (v. 19).[69] Coats's analysis helpfully demonstrates two "epic narrations" whose apexes include a polemic against the gods (vv. 4–10, 12–17), joined together by a "hymnic transition" (v. 11). Psalm 68 similarly exhibits epic narrations with at least implicit polemic at its climax in v. 19, where Yahweh takes captive the enemy (taunt) and establishes his eternal temple to celebrate his sovereignty over all gods (polemic).

Second, and more importantly, the Song of the Sea makes the same narratival movement as Ps 68. Both songs begin with reasons for and commencement of praise,

---

[67] Ps 68:20: "God is for us a God of salvation." Exod 15:2: "YHWH is my strength and my song, and he has become my salvation."

[68] For proposed structures, see Holzinger, *Exodus*, 49; Dillmann and Knobel, *Die Bücher Exodus und Leviticus für die zweite Auflage*, 153; Beer, *Exodus*, 83; Fohrer, *Überlieferung und Geschichte des Exodus*, 113–14. Fohrer lists three other structures from three other scholars on p. 113n7, all differing; Sarna, *Exodus*, 76; Cassuto, *Exodus*, 173.

[69] Coats, *Exodus 1–18*, 117–18.

move to a narration of God's deliverance from Egypt, continue with a narration of the conquest of Canaan, and conclude with Yahweh establishing his eternal kingship over Israel by having his temple built on his holy mountain. The narrative movements of the two songs are almost exactly the same. There are surely differences between the two songs in their diverse poetic expression and their temporal perspectives. The conquest of Jerusalem and construction of the temple are completely future in Exod 15, while partially fulfilled in the psalm. Even so, they are remarkably similar in their structure and ideology. The psalmist looks back on God's nearly complete fulfillment of the prophecy in the Song of the Sea and narrates these feats using the original prophecy as its paradigm.

The use of these two songs also suggests one final point, that Israel based their past memory and future hope on the covenantal loyalty and unchanging goodness of their one God. God's defeat of Pharaoh was surely a prototypical event. It simultaneously displayed his awesome power to defeat his enemies while also impressing itself upon the future, when he must again go out from Seir (Judg 5:4) to conquer the Canaanites (Exod 15:13–17) and then take Mount Zion from the wicked nations (Ps 68:19) in order to establish his eternal reign from his sanctuary (Exod 15:17–18; Ps 68:17). God's consistent nature guaranteed that he would deal with the Canaanites as he did with Pharaoh, which assured Deborah that she could enshrine her victory in a song composed in the style of Exod 15. That same nature assured the psalmist that the pleasure Israel experienced by dwelling in the promised land was only won through the same arousal of God's warrior nature that Israel experienced in Egypt. The defeat of Pharaoh and Israel's liberation was therefore inherently prophetic. It declared that God would fight for Israel while also prophesying about future enemies to be overcome. Judges 5 declares the fulfillment of the prophecy of the land conquest from Exod 15, while Ps 68 declares the nearly complete fulfillment of this same prophecy but with more detail about God's eternal temple-kingship on Mount Zion. Psalm 68 also adds a more detailed vision of its consummation and what would follow.

Psalm 68's Vision of the Latter Days

Finally, we come to the task of interpreting the second half of the psalm. I have argued that even the consummation of Ps 68:19 is future from the poet's perspective, so everything beyond v. 19 must also be a vision of the future after God's eternal kingship is established. This is partially confirmed by the use in the second half of the psalm of the three Pentateuchal passages that describe what will happen "in the latter days": Gen 49, Num 23–24, and Deut 32–33 (for "in the latter days," see Gen 49:1; Num 24:14; Deut 31:29). The psalmist draws the epithet "rider in the heavens" (68:34) from Deut 33:26 and had already possibly drawn language from Deut 33:2 in Ps 68:18. Psalm 68:22 says God will "smash (מחץ) the head of his enemies, the hairy skull (קדקד) walking in his guilt." The verb מחץ appears in Num 24:8 and Deut 32:39 and 33:11 with reference to God smashing his enemies, while קדקד is an ancient poetic word that appears in Gen 49:26; Num 24:17; and Deut 33:16 (developing Gen 49:26) and 33:20.[70] The psalmist therefore draws this significant and violent war imagery from these three eschatological passages.[71] Thus, Ps 68 alludes to Gen 49, Deut 33, and Num 24 in minor fashion.

These passages are not unrelated. J. Sailhamer has demonstrated a general pattern in the Pentateuch of narrative, poetry, and epilogue.[72] This pattern occurs on the microlevel, for example, with Gen 1–2 (prose), Adam's song in 2:23 (poetry), and the epilogue in 2:24. He finds the same micro-pattern in Gen 3 and 4. On the macro-level, he notes the poems at Exod 15, Num 23–24, and Deut 32–33. These all follow narrative sections of the Pentateuch, and each "calls an audience together (imperative: Ge 49:1; Nu 24:14; Dt 31:28) and proclaims (cohortative: Ge 49:1; Nu 24:14; Dt 31:28) what will happen (Ge 49:1; Nu 24:14; Dt 31:29) in "the end of days" (Ge 49:1; Nu 24:14; Dt 31:29)."[73] Hence, the binding element for these three texts is their use of the expression "in the latter days" (באחרית הימים), which on an eschatological interpretation or not refers to an indeterminate time in the future when the prophecy will be fulfilled.

So we can now understand the second half of the psalm. The author is composing a victory song to celebrate God's capture of Jerusalem where his temple will soon be built as an eternal monument to his sovereignty. This vision accords with the typical divine builder topos of the ANE. But not all the land had been conquered, and the promise to Abraham had not yet been completely fulfilled. The rest of the land must be conquered and the rest of the enemies smashed before peace would be established. This futuristic vision is in perfect accord with the standard divine builder topos. The psalmist therefore draws imagery both from prior "latter day" OT prophecies and from typical ANE expectations following the construction of a divine temple to commemorate military victories. The OT traditions provide the war imagery, while typical expectations include the reception of tribute from neighboring kings (Ps 68:30, 32) and universal homage (68:33–36). Such an eschatological tinge, rather than past historical reference, helps clarify the vagueness of the language of the second half of the psalm as well as its confusing interchangeability of *qtl* and *yqtl* verbal forms in these verses.

This reading also provides an alternative explanation to the "procession" that accords with the Targum's ancient interpretation. Mowinckel relied heavily on this processional to classify the psalm as one for the enthronement festival. But one cannot read "the singers went in front; the musicians behind; virgins beating tambourines" (68:26) without thinking of Miriam's classic victory song in Exod 15:20–21, complete with tambourines. The Targum explicitly interprets it in this way: "They rose up early and uttered a song after Moses and Aaron who were playing melodies before them,

---

[70] Cross and Freedman, *Studies in Ancient Yahwistic Poetry*, 1–25; HALOT s.v. קדק. The reference in Num 24:17 depends on an emendation from קרקר to קדקד, which seems correct.

[71] Although v. 14 lies in the first half of the psalm, the word it uses for "sheepfolds" (שְׁפַתָּיִם) occurs elsewhere only in Gen 49:14 and Judg 5:16 (although there it is spelled מִשְׁפְּתָיִם; the psalmist may have used an alternative spelling or the מ may have been lost in transmission; see HALOT s.v. שְׁפַתָּיִם). In any case, Ps 68:14 serves as further evidence that the psalmist alluded to or was cognizant of Gen 49 as he composed the psalm.

[72] John Sailhamer, *The Pentateuch as Narrative: A Biblical-Theological Commentary* (Grand Rapids, MI: Zondervan, 1992), 35–37.

[73] Ibid., 36.

in the midst of the righteous women who were with Miriam playing timbrels." The Targum further elaborates that Benjamin was the first to go into the sea out of Egypt. It therefore understands this processional as a reference to the exodus. Midrash Tehillim 68:12–14 also takes several of these verses to refer to the first Exodus (vv. 22, 23, 25, 26, 28).

I believe vv. 19b–36 comprise the psalmist's religious and prophetic imagination mixed with eschatological hope for the future—a future prophetically stamped by God's paradigmatic victory over Pharaoh at the sea and over the Canaanites through Deborah. Under this reading, Ps 68 concludes like its prototype, by prophesying about God's future victory over the enemy and establishment of his eternal kingship, celebrated poetically in the religious mind with images from Israel's past. As we will see in the next chapter, some Jewish interpreters seem to have read the psalm in just such a manner.

5

Psalm 68 in Early and Late Judaism

Early and late Judaism interpreted Ps 68 in two distinct ways. Modern studies of the psalm and studies of its use in Eph 4 have only noticed the interpretations of Ps 68 in late Judaism, particularly, the Targum and midrashim. This avenue has produced various theories about Paul's reliance on or interaction with these texts, but my thesis in this chapter is that these sources are a false lead. Rather, attention to early Jewish interpretations of Ps 68 demonstrate an understanding of the psalm in line with the eschatological and prophetic orientation of the psalm for which I have argued in the last three chapters. The main evidence for this interpretation of the psalm comes from the Dead Sea Scrolls, but evidence suggests the editor(s) of the Psalter and possibly the Septuagint translator(s) also interpreted the psalm this way. Rather than working through the sources chronologically, I divide this chapter into the two streams of interpretation of Ps 68: Mosaic (late Judaism) and eschatological (early Judaism).

Mosaic Interpretation of Psalm 68

The Mosaic interpretation has attracted the attention of numerous scholars who believe that it may be the key to Paul's use of Ps 68. The tradition of interpreting the mountain in Ps 68:19 as Sinai stretches back perhaps to the third century AD, as we will see. By the time of the compilation of the Targum and the Babylonian Talmud, Moses is interpreted as the one who "went up on high" (in Ps 68:19) in order to receive the law. Later midrashim follow this tradition uniformly, although many embellish the account, and each is selective in its details.[1]

Evidence of the Mosaic Interpretation of Psalm 68

The earliest account of interpreting the mountain in Ps 68:17-19 as Sinai is in the Mekilta de R. Ishmael, whose final literary form solidified probably in the early third

---

[1] For two other detailed surveys of this literature, see Rainer Schwindt, *Das Weltbild des Epheserbriefes: Eine religionsgeschichtlich-exegetische Studie*, WUNT 148 (Tübingen: Mohr Siebeck, 2002), 403–12; W. Hall Harris, *The Descent of Christ: Ephesians 4:7–11 and Traditional Hebrew Imagery*, BSL (Grand Rapids, MI: Baker Books, 1998), 65–95.

century AD after several redactions.² Baḥodesh 4.18 is a midrash on Exod 19, in which God comes down on Mount Sinai. R. Ishmael compares it to Judg 5:5, in which all the mountains, including Sinai, quake at his presence. Ishmael continues, "And it also says: 'Why look ye askance, mountain of peaks'" (Ps 68:16). He compares the Hebrew term גבננים ("many-peaked") in Ps 68:16 with the term "crook-backed" (גבן) in Lev 21:20, which renders one unclean and unqualified for housing the presence of God. Thus, Sinai was the one mountain that was not unclean, so God chose it as his abode, as Ps 68:17 says, "the mountain on which God desired to dwell."

The next relevant text to be composed was probably the Pesikta de R. Kahana, in which Piska 12 is a midrash on Exod 19. This text was probably compiled in Palestine in the fifth century AD, since the most recent rabbi cited lived in the last part of the fourth century AD and because Palestinian rabbis are cited far more than Babylonian.³ In Piska 12.22, the author compiles several interpretations of Ps 68:18, "the chariots of God are twice ten-thousand multiplied." The author assumes that God is coming in his chariots to Mount Sinai to give the law, citing at one point Deut 33:2, to which Ps 68:18 alludes. One teaching says that the angels were intent on destroying Israel, but they did not because Israel accepted Torah. Like Mek. R. Ishmael, this midrash interprets Ps 68:18–19 as God's giving the law at Sinai, but there is still no mention of Moses as the one who ascends on high.

Moses finally enters into the interpretation of Ps 68:19 in the Talmud and Targum. It is difficult to decide which tradition arose first, but since the Talmud compiles tannaitic traditions and the Targum's range for date of completion spans much later than the Talmud's (see below), the tradition in the Talmud is probably earlier. B. Šabb. 88–89a contains the most expansive account of Moses' reception of the law that uses Ps 68 as supporting Scripture. The long account, attributed to R. Joshua b. Levi, begins with Moses ascending (Exod 19:3) and the angels immediately interceding. They challenge Moses as being a mere man, citing Ps 8:5 (MT), who should not be worthy to receive the Torah. Because Moses fears even to speak, the Lord tells him to cling to the Throne of Glory and cites Job 26:9 ("he . . . spreads his cloud over him"), which R. Naḥman interprets as God spreading his presence over Moses to protect him. Moses then replies to the angels with six citations from the Pentateuch to prove that the Law was given for men, not for angels. The angels concede immediately and were "moved to love" Moses. They "transmitted something to him, for it is said, 'You have ascended on high . . . ,'"

---

[2] The Mekilta was not authored by R. Ishmael, who taught in the early second century AD, but is named after him because he is mentioned early in the work. The core of the traditions probably extend back to Ishmael or at least his school, since its *halakhah* often contradict later tannaitic *halakhah*, since it preserves many old legends not preserved elsewhere, and since it uses an unsophisticated interpretation of Scripture that largely agrees with early versions. See H. L. Strack and G. Stemberger, *Introduction to the Talmud and Midrash*, trans. Markus Bockmuehl (Edinburgh: T&T Clark, 1991), 278; Jacob Z. Lauterbach, ed., *Mekilta de-Rabbi Ishmael*, trans. Jacob Z. Lauterbach (Philadelphia, PA: Jewish Publication Society of America, 1976), 1:xviii–xxviii. Lauterbach gives no final date but believes the first redaction was undertaken by R. Joḥanan b. Nappaḥa and subsequent redactions were undertaken by his school. "When and by whom this final redaction was made cannot be ascertained" (ibid., xxvi).

[3] William G. Braude and Israel J. Kapstein, eds., *Pesikta de-Rab Kahana: R. Kahana's Compilation of Discourses for Sabbaths and Festal Days* (Philadelphia, PA: Jewish Publication Society of America, 1975), xlv–xlvi.

citing Ps 68:19. Moses received these gifts from the angels as a recompense for their demeaning him as a man. Moses then descended to give the law to Israel. He says he could not keep such a treasure for himself, implying that he had shared it with Israel. Because of Moses's humility, God declares the law will be called by his name, citing Mal 3:22 ("law of Moses"). Thus, Ps 68:19 is used as a supplemental text to fill out the details of what happened when Moses ascended in Exod 19:3 to receive the law.

The minor tractate 'Abot de R. Nathan 2.3 (18b) contains a similar tradition to b. Šabb. 88–89a but in more concise form. While commenting on how it came about that Moses broke the tablets, the tractate notes (almost as an aside) that the angels arraigned Moses at the time when he received them, citing Ps 8:5–9 (MT). The author clarifies that the angels were citing Ps 8 disparagingly, saying, "What virtue is there in man born of woman that he has ascended on high, as it is stated, *Thou art ascended on high, thou hast led captivity captive, thou has received gifts?*"[4] The tractate then continues to explain how it came about that Moses broke the tablets, saying he took the tablets and descended with them, rejoicing exceedingly, until he saw the golden calf. He had come to give the tablets (Torah) to the people but broke them instead.

The Psalms Targum followed the tradition in the Talmud but is unique in the way it cited Ps 68:19. As mentioned earlier, it is likely later than the tradition in the Talmud. According to D. Stec, the Targum seems unknown to Rashi, Qimhi, Ibn Ezra, and Nahmanides. Considering additional internal evidence, he estimates a date of composition in the fourth to sixth century AD but acknowledges that it is "possible and even likely that it contains material belonging to more than one period."[5] P. Flesher and B. Chilton have dated the Targum even as late as the fourth to the ninth century AD based on its linguistic style and dialect.[6]

The Targum correctly interprets much of the narrative structure in the first half of the psalm from the Exodus to the taking of the land. The author seems to have felt the tension in Ps 68:16 with the phrase הר אלהים הר בשן (likely read as "the mountain of God is Mount Bashan") and interprets the verse as follows: "Mount *Moriah*, the place where the patriarchs worshipped in the presence of the LORD, was chosen for the building of the sanctuary."[7] That is, the interpreter probably read הר אלהים as "mountain of God" and was disturbed to see the following phrase claim Mount Bashan as God's mountain, and thus commented instead on Mount Moriah as God's mountain. But in v. 16, instead of moving forward in Israel's history to Yahweh's ascension to the heights of Zion, the Targum interprets vv. 17–19 as referring to "Mount Sinai for the giving of the Law." God desired Mount Sinai because she is humble (v. 17) and he dwells "on Mount Sinai in the sanctuary" (v. 18). Moses ascended to the firmament, took

---

[4] Translation in A. Cohen, ed., *The Minor Tractates of the Talmud* (London: Soncino Press, 1965), 1:1. Emphasis in original.

[5] David M. Stec, *The Targum of Psalms*, TAB (Collegeville, MN: Liturgical Press, 2004), 2.

[6] Paul V. M. Flesher and Bruce Chilton, *The Targums: A Critical Introduction* (Waco, TX: Baylor University Press, 2011), 230–31. For more on the date of the Targum, all putting it fourth century AD or later, see Roger Le Déaut, "Targum," in *Supplément au Dictionnaire de la Bible: Targum*, ed. Henri Cazelles and Jacques Briend (Paris: Letouzey & Ané, 2002), 308–9; Martin McNamara, *Targum and Testament Revisited: Aramaic Paraphrases of the Hebrew Bible: A Light on the New Testament*, 2nd ed. (Cambridge: Eerdmans, 2010), 235.

[7] Translation in Stec, *The Targum of Psalms*. Emphasis in original.

captives, taught the words of the Law, and *gave* them as gifts to the sons of man (v. 19). The Targum is unique here in being the only source that alters the verb "received" in Ps 68:19 to "gave," which is significant for Paul's similar verbal change in Eph 4:8, which will be explored later. The Targum continues by interpreting the rebellious in v. 19 as the rebellious who are converted and repent, among whom God's presence dwells. It is possible that Moses replaces Yahweh in the psalm (both here and in the Talmud) because the authors found the idea of Yahweh receiving gifts unbecoming of his majesty.[8] Perhaps also the mention of God's myriads in v. 17 evoked Deut 33:1–3, as it did in Mek. R. Kah., which led the authors to interpret Ps 68:17–19 as the giving of the law.

Notably, in the second half of the psalm, the Targum reverts to Exodus imagery, as noted in the previous chapter. When the psalm reads "the singers went in front; the musicians behind; virgins beating tambourines" (68:26), the Targum interprets it as follows: "They rose up early and uttered a song after Moses and Aaron who were playing melodies before them, in the midst of the righteous women who were with Miriam playing timbrels." It could be that the Targum simply evokes the imagery of the Exodus as a sign of God's power, but the chronological narrative of the psalm suggests that the Targum is continuing on into the future, understanding the psalm to be predicting a time when God would defeat all of Israel's enemies and consummate his kingdom. While for the psalmist this future victory would be over the Canaanites and other nations, for the Targum author(s) this victory would truly be another exodus to restore them out of political domination and bring them into their own land and kingdom.

The subsequent midrashim follow the traditions of the Talmud and Targum by interpreting Ps 68:19 as Moses ascending on high, but none of them follow the Targum's eschatological interpretation of the second half of the psalm. Pesikta Rabbati is a Palestinian set of homilies compiled somewhere between the fourth and ninth centuries AD.[9] In 20.4, the story of Moses's bout with the angels from b. Šabb. 88–89a is greatly elaborated. When Moses was to go up, a cloud descended to him and he entered it. The cloud took him to the firmament where he was challenged by several angels, from whom God protected Moses. He spread his splendor over him (citing Job 26:9, as in b. Šabb. 88–89a). The angels around God's throne sought to burn Moses with the breath of their mouths, but God told Moses to answer them. So, as in b. Šabb. 88–89a, Moses cited six passages from the Pentateuch to show that the Law was for men, not for angels. They have no reply, and the angel of death even gives to Moses the gift of the secret of preserving life. At this point, it quotes Ps 68:19 with an interpretive alteration of wording: "You ascended on high, you took *the Torah* into captivity, you received gifts *as a mere man*" (emphasis added). The word "captives" is exchanged for its interpretation, Torah. The "gifts" are the secret of life from the angel of death (cf. Num 17:11–13). When the Lord then thundered "I am the Lord your God" to

---

[8] Similarly, Schwindt, *Das Weltbild des Epheserbriefes*, 403.
[9] See the discussions in William G. Braude, ed., *Pesikta Rabbati: Discourses for Feasts, Fasts, and Special Sabbaths* (New Haven, CT: Yale University Press, 1968), 1:20–26; Strack and Stemberger, *Introduction to the Talmud and Midrash*, 325–29. A date in the ninth century was formerly more popular, but a sixth or seventh century dating is now gaining ground.

Israel (Exod 20:2), they fainted, but God revived them as Ps 68:10 says, "You, O God, sent bounteous rain, whereby you restored your inheritance when it fainted away." The midrash cites Ps 68:19 again later when interpreting the word "this" in Lev 16:3 ("with this shall Aaron come into the holy place"). The word "this" implies the merit of Israel, to whom it was said "This thy stature is like to a palm tree" (Song 7:8). R. Phinehas said that, indeed, Moses who ascended on high and took the Torah captive and brought it down was able to do so not by virtue of his own strength but by virtue of Israel's merit, citing Ps 68:19, with באדם interpreted as "by virtue of men." Israel can be said to be the אדם of Ps 68:19 because they are called men in Ezek 34:31.

Shir ha-Shirim Rabbah was likely written in Palestine and was late enough to draw from Seder Olam, Sifre, Mekilta, the Palestinian Talmud, and Leviticus Rabbah among other sources.[10] Strack and Stemberger date its original composition to around AD 650.[11] When commenting on the identification of Solomon's vineyard (Song 8:11) as the Sanhedrin (because it is arranged in rows like a vineyard), the midrash says that swarms of kings longed for the Torah, citing Ps 68:13 as proof. R. Judan took "kings of armies" to refer to kings of angels, that is, Gabriel and Michael. The midrash then comments on the second clause of Ps 68:13, "the fair one in the house divides the spoil," as it cites the verse. The "fair one of the house" is interpreted as the Torah, in one tradition, and Moses, according to another, in which he takes the Torah and divides it as spoil among the dwellers of the earth. It cites Ps 8:2, "you have set your majesty above the heavens," with "majesty" interpreted as Torah. Despite God's pleasure to keep Torah there, he sought against the will of the angels to give it to Israel, so the angels thrust themselves before the Lord to beg that he leave the Law in heaven with them. God cites Lev 15:25 (about unclean women) and Num 19:14 (about men dying) to demonstrate that the Law does not apply to them. The midrash concludes that this is why Scripture praises Moses with the words of Ps 68:19, "You ascended on high . . .," which R. Aḥa interprets as the giving of the law.

Pirqe de R. Eliezer is the next midrash to interpret Ps 68:19. It mentions the date AD 776 at one point and its final redaction probably occurred in the first half of the ninth century AD.[12] Section 19 discusses the Sabbath and, in connection with it, creation. God created seven firmaments, the seventh and highest being ʿAraboth, as Ps 68:5 says that God rides on the ʿAraboth. God also created seven lands, and of them all he chose the desert of Sinai, where he gave the Torah, just as Ps 68:17 says "the mountain on which God desired to dwell [is Sinai]." In Pirqe R. El. 46, a *haggadah* on Moses's reception of the law details his spat with the angels. They claimed that the Law was written for them, but Moses rebutted their claim by citing two passages from the Pentateuch that cannot apply to them. "The sages" say Moses went up to the heavenly regions with his wisdom and brought down the might of the trust of the angels, citing

---

[10] H. Freedman and Maurice Simon, eds., *Song of Songs*, trans. Maurice Simon, Midrash Rabbah 9 (London: Soncino Press, 1983), vii; Strack and Stemberger, *Introduction to the Talmud and Midrash*, 342.

[11] Strack and Stemberger, *Introduction to the Talmud and Midrash*, 342.

[12] Gerald Friedlander, ed., *Pirḳê De Rabbi Eliezer: (The Chapters of Rabbi Eliezer the Great) According to the Text of the Manuscript Belonging to Abraham Epstein of Vienna* (New York: Hermon Press, 1970), xx, liv.

in this connection Prov 21:22 ("a wise man goes up to the city of the mighty, and brings down the strength in which it trusts"). When the angels gave the Torah to Moses, they also gave him "presents and letters and tablets for healing the sons of man, as it is said, 'Thou hast ascended on high . . .,'" citing Ps 68:19.[13]

Midrash Tehillim was compiled probably in Italy as late as the ninth century AD. Evidence includes a possible allusion to the Muslim caliphate (6:2), a possible reference to Apulia and Sicily (9:8), and some "local and temporary coloring."[14] It is a running commentary on verses and phrases throughout the Psalter. Its commentary on Ps 68 insightfully notes many sources used by Ps 68, such as Judg 5, Num 10:35, and others. When commenting on v. 16, the author imagines a dialogue between Mount Carmel and Mount Tabor, fighting for God's presence. Their haughtiness rules them out, and Sinai wins God's favor because it is the lowliest of all, as Isa 57:15 says that the Lord will dwell with the contrite and lowly. Yet the author sees the problem with v. 17, which says he has chosen the mountain on which he will dwell forever, so he translates it as "But the Lord will dwell in eternity," meaning God's presence soon left Sinai and returned to heaven. Sinai itself came out of Mount Moriah, plucked out of it as a priest's portion is plucked out of bread. For the author, Isa 2:2 proved that Moriah was the true mountain of God. Since the author interprets God's mountain in the psalm as Sinai, not Moriah, this allows him to continue to see Sinai as the focus in vv. 18–19. God came to Sinai with myriads of angels. By mutually interpreting Ps 68:19 with Prov 21:22 (as in Pirqe R. El. 46) and Exod 19:3 ("and Moses went up to God"), he takes "you ascended on high" in Ps 68:19 to refer to Moses's ascension to receive Torah, which was bestowed on Israel as a gift, at no cost.

Midrash Tehillim cites Ps 68:19 once elsewhere in 22.19. R. Joshua b. Levi says he never looked into a book of 'Aggadah, except once, which said the 175 sections of the Pentetuech in which the words "speech," "saying," and "command" occur correspond in number to the 175 years of Abraham. As proof, it cites Ps 68:19 as what God said to Moses. The law was given as a gift because of Abraham, who is described as "the greatest man among the Anakim" in Josh 14:15.[15] B. Sof. 16.10 (41b) includes this same tradition from R. Joshua and adds that it was "on this account the Rabbis instituted one hundred and seventy-five orders in the Torah [to be read in public worship] every Sabbath [as regularly as the] continual burnt-offering."[16]

The latest rabbinic source to interpret Ps 68:19 is Exodus Rabbah, a compilation of Haggadic material from the eleventh to the twelfth centuries.[17] Exodus Rab. 28.1 interprets Exod 19:3 ("Moses ascended") through the lens of Ps 68:19. Moses's ascension is metaphorical: he is exalted because he wrestled with the angels and won the right to deliver the law to Israel. Because Moses labored for forty days and forty nights, fasting and suffering, he won Torah as a gift for this price of his hardship. He

---

[13] Translation from ibid., 362.
[14] Leon Nemoy, ed., *The Midrash on Psalms*, trans. William G. Braude (New Haven, CT: Yale University Press, 1959), 1:xi.
[15] It may be that the author, intentionally or not, misread Arba (ארבע) as Abram (אברם) in order to make this connection.
[16] Translation from Cohen, *The Minor Tractates of the Talmud*, 1:292.
[17] S. M. Lehrman, ed., *Midrash Rabbah: Exodus*, 3rd ed. (New York: Soncino Press, 1983), vii.

took it captive in order to deliver it to Israel. The angels then tried to attack Moses, but God caused him to resemble Abraham and rebuked the angels, telling them they should not seek to attack one in whose home they ate (cf. Gen 18). Thus, the midrash interprets באדם as "for the sake of Abraham." The author here follows Midr. Teh. 22.19 by interpreting the "man" (אדם) Arba as Abraham.

The evidence from these late Jewish sources demonstrates that the mountain in vv. 17–19 was consistently interpreted not as Zion but as Sinai. The first such extant interpretation was produced in literary form by the early third century AD (Mek. R. Ishmael) but may have existed in oral or traditional form for some time prior, perhaps as early as Ishmael's school in the late second century. Yet Moses did not become the agent of the verbs in Ps 68:19 until the Babylonian Talmud, which used the psalm as a supplemental text to elaborate details of Moses's ascension to receive the law in Exod 19. After the Talmud and the Targum, all midrashim interpreted Ps 68:19 as Moses receiving the law. The Targum is unique in altering the verb "you received" to "you gave." The most important point to make about this evidence, though, is that it is all significantly later than the NT period. Even if the tradition in the Talmud does stem from R. Joshua b. Levi, the Mosaic interpretation of Ps 68:19 could only be traced back to around the turn of the third century.

Pushing the Mosaic Tradition Back

Yet, H. Harris has made one of the most influential arguments regarding the dating of this Mosaic tradition, namely, that the tradition enshrined in the Targum was available and widespread at least in oral form during the NT period. His argument proceeds in three steps, the evidence for which I will examine closely. First, legends of Moses's ascent to heaven to receive the law were widespread in the NT period and before. Second, Ps 68 became associated with Pentecost before the NT period. Third, in this same period, Pentecost became associated with the giving of the law. Given these three arguments, it would follow that Ps 68 naturally became associated with the giving of the law prior to the NT period and the tradition was later solidified in the Targum.

Harris's evidence for a heavenly Mosaic ascent to receive the law includes the *Exagoge* of Ezekiel the Tragedian, Philo (*Somn.* 1.36; *Mut.* 7; *Mos.* 1.158; *QE.* 2.27–52; *QG.* 4.29), Pseudo-Philo (*Bib. Ant.* 11:15), and 2 Bar. 4:2–7; 59:3–11.[18] The ascent in the *Exagoge* is to the top of Mount Sinai, where Moses is seated on a throne and given a crown and scepter. Yet this ascent occurred in a dream, which Moses's father-in-law interpreted as his accession to be ruler. Although the ascent occurred in a dream, we may charitably take this text from around the second century BC as one instance of Moses ascending into heaven to sit on the divine throne.

Philo's texts, though, are more ambiguous. Moses on Mount Sinai was "incorporeal" as he heard the heavenly music (*Somn.* 1.36), which relates more to Philo's Platonism than to Moses being in heaven. *Mut.* 7 refers to Moses peering "into the darkness"

---

[18] Harris, *The Descent of Christ*, 123–42. Harris mentions many other passages that he admits do not speak of Moses visiting heaven, so there is no need to discuss them here (e.g., Josephus, *Ant.* 3.5.3, 8; 4.8.48; *Test. Mos.* 1:15; 11:8; 2 Bar. 4:2–7; Clement, *Strom.* 6.15).

and searching for the incorporeal God not in heaven but at the base of Mount Sinai (Exod 20:21) and in the camp (Exod 33:13). *Mos.* 1.158 also refers to Moses peering "into the darkness where God was," but this again alludes to Exod 20:21, and the point of the passage is that Moses through his divine communion with God transformed his mind into one of perfect virtue to be imitated (*Mos.* 1.159). QG. 4.29 places in parallel the descent and ascent of angels on Jacob's ladder and Moses's descent and ascent, presumably at Sinai. But the point is that the pure mind should be mixed with the moral for "necessary uses," of which Jacob's ladder provides allegorical grounds. Moses's ascent and descent then demonstrates that he has both a pure mind and a moral element; no ascent to heaven is evident or necessarily inferable. The evidence from Philo is therefore ambiguous. Charitably, perhaps one or two references might suggest a heavenly ascent at Sinai, but no references are clear.

The reference in Pseudo-Philo probably uses temple imagery atop Sinai rather than describing a heavenly ascent. In *Bib. Ant.* 11:15, Moses sees the tree of life on Sinai, which Harris takes to signal heavenly paradise. But the tree of life evokes the Garden of Eden, which itself is described as a temple in Genesis.[19] The temple imagery here is made clear when immediately afterward God commands Moses about the tabernacle and the ark (11:15). Harris takes 12:1—"he went down to the place where the light of the sun and the moon are"—to mean Moses was above the sun and the moon in heaven. But the phrase could equally mean that he descended to the earth where the light of the sun and moon shines. The following phrase suggests as much: "and the light of his face surpassed the splendor of the sun and the moon." The author's point is not that Moses was in heaven but that he descended to the earth where the light shines, where the Israelites were when they saw his face.

The two passages in 2 Baruch are also ambiguous. In 2 Bar. 4:2–7, God showed the heavenly Jerusalem to Moses when he was on Mount Sinai, but Moses did not enter heaven, as Harris also admits. In 2 Bar. 59:3–11, the author describes the things Moses saw on Mount Sinai, such as the depths of the abyss, the number of the raindrops, the truth of judgment, and the worlds not yet come. As Harris admits, these may only

---

[19] Much evidence exists for seeing Eden as the first temple. If Gen 1 portrays God's victory over chaos, Eden would be his temple of victory in which he would "rest" (recall the divine builder topos in Chapter 3). Eden is entered from the east and is guarded by cherubim, as were later sanctuaries (Gen 3:24; Exod 25:18–22; 26:31–36:35; 1 Kgs 6:23–29; 2 Chr 3:14). The tabernacle menorah or lampstand may symbolize the tree of life (Gen 2:9; 3:22; cf. Exod 25:31–35). The Hebrew verbs in 2:15 (שׁמר; אבד) are used later in the Pentateuch to describe priestly activities of keeping and guarding the temple (e.g., Num 3:7–8; 8:25–26; 18:5–6; 1 Chr 23:32; Ezek 44:14). Gold and onyx are used to describe the garden (Gen 2:11–12) and to decorate priestly garments and the sanctuary of the tabernacle and temple (e.g., Exod 25:7, 11, 17, 31). Moreover, there is an abundance of arboreal imagery in the temple, connecting it to the garden. God walks in Eden as he does later in the tabernacle (Gen 3:8; Lev 26:12; Deut 23:15; 2 Sam 7:6–7). The future temple in Ezek 47:1–2 has a river flowing from it, which alludes to the river flowing from Eden in Gen 2:10. Ezekiel 28:13–16 refers to Eden as the "holy mountain of God," which phrase elsewhere describes the temple or Jerusalem (e.g., Ps 3:5; 15:1; 24:1; 43:3; Isa 27:13; etc.). More explicitly, 28:18 refers to Eden as "your sanctuaries," which may refer to Adam. The same person referred to here is also pictured as dressed like a priest in 28:13. The evidence is taken from T. Desmond Alexander, *From Eden to the New Jerusalem* (Grand Rapids, MI: Kregel, 2008), 21–31; G. K. Beale, *The Temple and the Church's Mission: A Biblical Theology of the Dwelling Place of God*, NSBT 17 (Downers Grove, IL: InterVarsity Press, 2004), 66–80.

be visions and not a physical entrance into heaven. His argument that Moses was in heaven because the powers of heaven were shaken is unconvincing.

A few passages also speak of Moses ascending into heaven at his death (Josephus, *Ant.* 4.8.48; *Strom.* 6.15; Ps.-Philo, *Bib. Ant.* 19:10–12), which Harris takes to suggest a parallel to an ascent to heaven at Sinai, but there is no reason to believe any author, besides perhaps Philo, connected the two events.[20] Harris tries to bolster this suggestion by arguing that texts that record Moses's death and burial may have been polemics against a tradition that Moses did not die but rather ascended into heaven at his death. This claim is the most problematic of all, since it uses silence about a tradition as positive evidence for a tradition. In sum, prior to the second century there is only one clear reference to a heavenly ascent by Moses, and even that ascent in the *Exagoge* occurs only in a dream.

Harris's evidence for connecting Ps 68 with Pentecost and the giving of the law prior to the second century is just as problematic as his evidence for a Mosaic ascent to heaven in the same period.[21] In the Pentateuch, Pentecost was a festival to commemorate the harvest seven weeks after harvest began (Num 28:26–31; Deut 16:9–12). The earliest extant source associating Pentecost and the giving of the law is the Babylonian Talmud (b. Meg. 31a; b. Pesaḥ 68b). In b. Meg. 31a, Exod 19 is included as one of the alternative Pentecostal readings from the Pentateuch, the other being Deut 16:9. In b. Pesaḥ 68b, the statement that Pentecost is the day on which the law was given is attributed to R. Eliezer, whom H. Strack places in the third Tannaitic generation (c. AD 130–160).[22] One might then consider the association of Pentecost with the giving of the law to be as early as the mid-second century. But the authorial attribution of teachings in the Talmud is notoriously difficult to verify, and the fact that Pentecost is not associated with the giving of the law in the Mishnah suggests the tradition may not extend back to R. Eliezer. Indeed, in m. Meg. 3:5, only Deut 16:9–12 (referred to as "Seven Weeks") is listed as the reading for Pentecost. However, to be as charitable as possible, we might concede that, at best, the association is as old as the mid-second century AD, even though it was not recorded in the Mishnah.

Harris reviewed attempts to push back this connection between Pentecost and the giving of the law to the first century or earlier. The arguments, however, are either inaccurate, speculative, or inconclusive. G. B. Caird claimed that Exod 19 would have been part of the reading for Pentecost in the triennial lectionary system but offered no evidence or sources for his claim and, as Harris notes, the nature and date of the triennial cycle is disputed and probably not as early as the first century.[23]

---

[20] *Test. Mos.* 1:15; Josephus, *Ant.* 4.8.48. Philo, *Mos.* 1.158; 2.288; *QG* 1.86; *Sacr.* 8. In Philo's texts, Harris claims the language used for Moses's ascent to heaven at his death is similar to the language used for Moses ascending Sinai and that this similarity suggests that "Philo was aware of traditions which associated Moses with a heavenly ascent" (*The Descent of Christ*, 130). However, he does not demonstrate the similarity of terminology. Even if he is correct, there is no evidence that Philo was evoking a tradition rather than simply interpreting the OT himself by connecting, perhaps only subliminally, the two ascents of Moses via similar language.

[21] Harris, *The Descent of Christ*, 143–70.

[22] Hermann Leberecht Strack, *Introduction to the Talmud and Midrash* (New York: Atheneum, 1969), 115.

[23] G. B. Caird, "The Descent of Christ in Ephesians 4, 7–11," in *Studia Evangelica*, ed. F. L. Cross (Berlin: Akademie, 1964), 2:540n1; Harris, *The Descent of Christ*, 145–46.

H. St. J. Thackeray argued that, since b. Meg. 31a claimed the festival lasted two days but Jubilees emphasized that Pentecost lasted only one day in the year (Jub. 6.17–22): the author was polemicizing against the two-day tradition that was solidified in the Talmud.[24] Such a conclusion is not impossible but also not warranted or likely. Thackeray also incorrectly claimed Ps 68 was read on Pentecost (this is nowhere stated in the Mishnah, the Talmud, or the rabbis). He tried to support his claim by arguing that the *Sitz im Leben* of Ps 68 was the Maccabean victory in Gilead (1 Macc 5:45–54; 2 Macc 12:27–32), after which they ascended Jerusalem as it was almost time to celebrate Pentecost. However, we saw in Chapter 4 that a date for Ps 68 in the Maccabean period is untenable. Caird also suggested that the tradition from b. Pesaḥ 68b, which claimed the law was given on Pentecost, could be seen behind the connection between Pentecost and Acts 2. His claim relies on similar language between the giving of the law in Philo (*Dec.* 9, 11) and Luke's account of the giving of the Spirit in Acts 2, but to assume that Luke alluded to Philo's writings *and* that this reflected an early oral version of the latter Talmudic tradition puts too much strain on the evidence.[25]

Harris then turns to Jubilees, which places Moses's ascent of Sinai (1:1) on the same day as Abraham's celebration of Pentecost (15:1). Harris concludes, "[I]t is clear that the author of Jubilees believed (or wanted those for whom he was writing to believe) that the giving of the Torah to Moses and the celebration of the feast of Pentecost coincided."[26] If Harris were correct, then a Pentecost–Torah tradition could be found in the second century BC and in the Talmud, which might suggest that it existed all along, at least orally. But the intentions of the author of Jubilees are not as clear as Harris makes it. The two verses stand far apart, and 1:1 places Moses's ascent on the sixteenth day of the third month while 15:1 places Abraham's celebration of Pentecost "in the third month, in the middle of the month." If the author wanted to stress the connection between Pentecost and the giving of the law, he could have been clearer by stating exactly the sixteenth day in 15:1 rather than a vague "middle of the month." He also could have made an explicit connection in 15:1 with Moses's ascent in 1:1 if he desired his audience to make the connection, which would have been difficult to discern when the references were placed so far apart. Moreover, Moses did not receive the law on the sixteenth day when he ascended. He waited on the mountain for seven days to hear from God and then received the law some time during the next forty days and forty nights on the mountain (1:2–4). If, as it seems, Moses received the law at the

---

[24] H. St. J. Thackeray, *The Septuagint and Jewish Worship: A Study in Origins* (London: Oxford University Press, 1921), 47–54.

[25] In fact, the similarity in language between Acts 2 and some Jewish sources more likely stems from Luke's attempt to portray the church as being formed into God's temple. E.g., the phrase "tongues of fire" is used in second temple documents in temple contexts (1 En. 14:15; 71:5; 108:4–5; 1Q29). For much more evidence, see Gregory K. Beale, "The Descent of the Eschatological Temple in the Form of the Spirit at Pentecost. Part 1, The Clearest Evidence," *TynBul* 56, no. 1 (2005): 73–102; Gregory K. Beale, "The Descent of the Eschatological Temple in the Form of the Spirit at Pentecost. Part 2: Corroborating Evidence," *TynBul* 56, no. 2 (2005): 63–90. Philo and Luke are likely drawing from such traditional imagery for their own distinct purposes.

[26] Harris, *The Descent of Christ*, 153.

end of the forty days, the covenant at Sinai was actually established forty-seven days after the day on which Jubilees places Pentecost (1:5). According to Jubilees, then, the law was not given on Pentecost.

Harris is correct that Pentecost has a significant role in Jubilees as the celebration of God's covenant with Israel, a covenant inaugurated with Noah and renewed with all the Patriarchs (Jub. 6:1–16; 14:10–20; 15:1–16; 16:13; 22:1–2). He errs, though, when he sees the celebration of the covenant as synonymous with the celebration of the giving of the law. The celebration of Pentecost in Jubilees is not as straightforward as Harris makes it. Jubilees opens with the ratification of the Mosaic covenant and the giving of the law, but as we just noted, the ratification probably occurred on the forty-seventh day after Pentecost. Noah's covenant was ratified on the first day of the third month, fifteen days before Pentecost (6:1). Isaac was born on the day of Pentecost (16:13), perhaps signaling God's fulfillment of his covenantal promises. Strangely, 22:1–2 places Pentecost in the "first week of this forty-fourth jubilee in the second year," "when Isaac and Ishmael came from the Well of the Oath of Abraham, their father, to observe the feast of Shebuot." Thus, there is no consistent scheme for Pentecost in Jubilees. Abraham's covenant is ratified on Pentecost (14:10–20; 15:1–16) but not the others. As noted above, Isaac is born on Pentecost, and at one point Pentecost is given a different date. The claim that the author of Jubilees associates Pentecost with the giving of the law is therefore suspect. Even for the Qumran community, who possessed several copies of Jubilees, Pentecost was likely the occasion of annual covenant renewal and was not associated with the giving of the law.[27]

We may now summarize Harris's case. The only clear evidence he marshals for an ascent by Moses into heaven prior to the second century is the *Exagoge*, which presents the ascent as a dream. The earliest extant source associating Pentecost and the giving of the law is the Babylonian Talmud (b. Meg. 31a; b. Pesaḥ 68b). B. Pesaḥ 68b refers to Eliezer as the one who taught that the law was given on Pentecost, so we might charitably date the tradition to his time period, the mid-second century. But there is no convincing argument from the available evidence that Pentecost was associated with the giving of the law prior to the second century or as early as the NT period. There is also, then, no convincing case for associating Ps 68 with Pentecost or with the giving of the law by the NT period.

The earliest date at which we may say confidently that Ps 68 became associated with the giving of the law to Moses is, as we concluded above, the Babylonian Talmud and Targum Psalms. If this tradition really did stem from R. Joshua b. Levi, then it would have existed around the turn of the third century, but we can say nothing more definite than that. There is, though, another stream of Jewish interpretation of Ps 68 that definitely predates the authorship of Ephesians. To these earlier interpretations of Ps 68 we now turn.

---

[27] 1QS I, 8–17; 4Q275; 4Q320 frg. 4 III, 1–5; 321 2 II, 4–5. See James C. VanderKam, "Sinai Revisited," in *Biblical Interpretation at Qumran*, ed. Matthias Henze, SDSSRL (Grand Rapids, MI: Eerdmans, 2005), 48–51.

Eschatological Interpretation of Psalm 68

The earliest evidence of an eschatological interpretation of the psalm comes from the canonical order of the Psalter. I also will discuss some tentative evidence in the Septuagint translation of Ps 68, but this is followed by important evidence in the Dead Sea Scrolls.

The Editors of the Hebrew Psalter

As I described in Chapter 2, G. Wilson's 1985 monograph launched a new phase of psalms studies that sought to identify a new level of meaning that is derived from the intentions of the editors of the Psalter. I chose not to interpret Ps 68 with this hermeneutical approach because I believe it only gives us veiled and somewhat speculative insight into the theology or beliefs of the Psalter editors. But the canonical approach is useful here, since it provides us a window into the earliest interpretation of the psalm.[28]

Psalms 65–68 sit oddly in their canonical context.[29] This becomes evident when one considers the Psalter as a whole and the major theme of Books I–II. Scholars studying the shape and shaping of the Psalter are in broad agreement that Pss 1–2 should be read in tandem and that they introduce the Psalter as a whole. The major idea becomes that the Davidic king in Ps 2 is one who meditates on the law day and night (cf. Deut 17) and is therefore righteous. He will trample his enemies (Ps 2), who are the wicked that will be blown away like the chaff (Ps 1).[30] The rest of the Psalter is the historical dialectic between failure to reach this ideal and the attempt to revive the ideal.

Books I (Pss 1–41) and II (Pss 42–72) relate David's struggle to fulfill the ideal of Pss 1–2. Each psalm in Book I either overtly mentions the wicked or mentions David's suffering from his implied enemies.[31] Psalms 42–43, which open Book II, are probably

---

[28] It is almost certain that the placement of Ps 68 in its current context occurred before the translation of Ps 68 into the Septuagint. As G. Wilson showed, Books I–III were virtually fixed by the second century BC, while Books IV–V may or may not have still been in flux (*The Editing of the Hebrew Paslter*, SBLDS [Chico, CA: Scholars Press, 1985], 120–21). See also his article "The Qumran Psalms Manuscripts and the Consecutive Arrangement of Psalms in the Hebrew Psalter," *CBQ* 45, no. 3 (1983): 377–88.

[29] Recall that in this study I use MT versification unless otherwise noted.

[30] See, e.g., Gianni Barbiero, *Das erste Psalmenbuch als Einheit: Eine synchrone Analyse von Psalm 1–41*, ÖBSB 16 (Frankfurt am Main: Peter Lang, 1999), 725; Patrick D. Miller, "The Beginning of the Psalter," in *The Shape and Shaping of the Psalter*, ed. J. Clinton McCann, JSOTSS 159 (Sheffield: JSOT Press, 1993), 83–92; John H. Walton, "Psalms: A Cantata about the Davidic Covenant," *JETS* 34, no. 1 (1991): 23; Nancy L. DeClaisse-Walford, Rolf A. Jacobson and Beth LaNeel Tanner, *The Book of Psalms*, NICOT (Grand Rapids, MI: Eerdmans, 2014), 56; Gerald T. Sheppard, *Wisdom as a Hermeneutical Construct: A Study in the Sapientializing of the Old Testament*, BZAW 151 (New York: Walter de Gruyter, 1980), 140–41; Robert Cole, *Psalms 1–2: Gateway to the Psalter* (Sheffield: Sheffield Phoenix Press, 2013).

[31] The following verses are according to English versification: Pss 3:3, 8; 4:2; 5:5–7; 6:9, 11; 7:6; 8:3; 9:4, 7; 10:2–18; 11:2; 12:2–3, 9; 13:3, 5; 14:1–4; 15:4; 16:4; 17:9; 18 *passim*; 19:13–14; 20:7–9; 21:9; 22:8, 16–22; 23:5; 24:5; 25:2, 19; 26:1–5, 9–10; 27:2, 6; 28:3–5; 29:10 (the enemy is chaos); 30:2; 31:9, 16; 32:7, 10; 33:16–19; 34:4, 16–22; 35 *passim*; 36:1–4, 11–12; 37 *passim*; 38:13, 17, 20–23; 39:2, 9; 40:2–3, 5, 10–11, 13–18; 41:2–3, 6–12.

meant to be read in tandem in the same way Pss 1–2 are.³² The same refrain occurs in 42:6, 12; 43:5: "Why are you cast down, O my soul, and why are you in turmoil within me? Hope in God; for I shall again praise him, my salvation and my God." Both psalms express a longing to be with God in his temple again (42:5; 43:3) and feature ungodly adversaries who threaten the psalmist (42:10; 43:1). Thus, Book II opens with the message that, despite the idealized kingship pictured in Pss 1–2, the wicked are flourishing against the righteous (42:10–11; 43:2). "Hope in God" is the threefold refrain (42:6, 12; 43:5).

The rest of Book II can be coherently read through this lens of lament and hope. As with Book I, nearly every psalm of Book II features fools or enemies and adversaries of David.³³ But with every troubling situation, David applies the perspective of Pss 42–43: "hope in God" for salvation and deliverance.³⁴ Many of the psalms elicit praise of Yahweh for his salvation from these enemies. Often, this praise is enacted through cultic sacrifice in the temple.³⁵ Book II concludes with royal Ps 72, titled לשלמה ("by/to/for/concerning Solomon"). Interestingly, Ps 71 presents the prayer of an old man who does not wish to be cast off and forsaken by Yahweh in his old age. Since Ps 71 directly precedes Ps 72 with its reference to Solomon, it may be that the editors read Ps 71 as David's plea in his old age for God to uphold his covenant promises to his descendants.³⁶ This supposition is supported by the LXX, which labels Ps 71 as a psalm of David, whereas the MT does not. By this reading, לשלמה in Ps 72 would mean "for Solomon" or "concerning Solomon" rather than "by Solomon." Taken this way, Ps 72 stands as a prayer of David, at the end of his reign, pleading that Solomon would rule faithfully and righteously.³⁷ David petitions for his son that he would rule justly, have dominion, be blessed, and thus secure for himself the blessing of the covenant.³⁸ Psalm 72:8 ("may he have dominion from sea to sea, and from the River to the ends of the earth") alludes to Ps 2:8 ("I will make the nations your heritage, and the ends of the earth your possession"). David therefore transfers the royal covenant promise of universal dominion to his son, with the hope that Solomon will succeed where his father has failed.

---

[32] Ps 43 lacks a superscription, suggesting that it should be linked to the previous psalm (on the lack of a superscription suggesting psalms should be read as a group, see Wilson, *Editing of the Hebrew Psalter*, 173–81; Miller, "The Beginning of the Psalter," 84–85). In fact, these two psalms were copied as one psalm in several late Hebrew manuscripts (Codices 36; 82; 89; 156; 178; 210; 216; 245; 260; 326; 356; 409; 499; 590; Wilson, *Editing of the Hebrew Psalter*, 134–35).

[33] The following verses are according to English versification: Pss 44:5, 16; 45:7; 46:6; 47:3; 49:13–14; 50:16–22; 52:7; 53:1; 54:3; 55:3, 12–15, 22–23; 56:1–2, 5–9; 57:3–7; 58:3–5; 59 *passim*; 60:11; 61:3; 63:9–10; 64:1–6; 66:3; 68:1–3; 69 *passim*; 70 *passim*; 71 *passim*.

[34] The following verses are according to English versification: Pss 44 *passim*; 46:1; 47:3; 49:15; 53:6; 54:1, 7; 55:16–18; 56:4, 10–11; 57:3; 58:6–11; 59:2, 9–10, 16–17; 60:5, 12; 62:1–2, 5–8; 63:7; 64:7–10; 66:14–20; 67:2; 68:20; 69 *passim*; 70 *passim*; 71 *passim*.

[35] The following verses are according to English versification: sacrifices: Pss 50:8–9, 23; 51:16–17, 19; 54:6; 56:12; 61:8; 65:1; 66:13–15; temple: Pss 46:4–5; 48 *passim*; 50:2; 51:18; 52:8; 63:2; 65:4; 66:13; 68:17–18, 29, 35; 69:9.

[36] DeClaissé-Walford, Jacobson, and Tanner, *The Book of Psalms*, 30.

[37] Brevard S. Childs, *Introduction to the Old Testament as Scripture* (Philadelphia, PA: Fortress Press, 1979), 516–17.

[38] Wilson, *The Editing of the Hebrew Psalter*, 210–11.

Interrupting this neat picture of Books I–II is the strange grouping of Pss 65–68. These psalms provide a strange break from themes of lament and hope by turning toward an idyllic picture of universal praise and worship of God. Wilson suggested that the four psalms alternate between "praise" (Pss 65:2; 67:4, 6) and "blessing" (Pss 66:8, 20; 68:27, 36), but elements of both praise and blessing can be seen in all four psalms.[39] Psalm 65 begins with "all praise is due to you, O God, in Zion" (65:2). "All flesh" shall come to God (65:2), and the one whom God chooses to dwell in his courts is blessed (65:5). God is the "hope of all the ends of the earth and of the farthest seas" (65:6). Those who dwell at the ends of the earth are in awe of his signs (65:9). The psalm concludes with a lengthy description of God's blessing upon the land and its resultant fertility (65:10–14).

Psalm 66 opens with a call to "all the earth" to shout for joy to God and sing the glory of his name, give him glorious praise (66:1–2). All of God's enemies will come cringing to him (66:3). "All the earth worships [God] and sings praises to [him]" (66:4). After rehearsing God's deeds in the exodus, the psalmist again calls the nations to bless God (66:8). Because of God's provision for his people, the psalmist will come into his temple with burnt offerings (66:13–15). The psalm concludes with a blessing for God because of his covenantal loyalty (66:20).

Psalm 67 continues the universal perspective by praying that God's saving power would be known among "all nations" (67:3). The psalmist admonishes all the peoples to praise God (67:4, 6) and to sing for joy because of his righteous judgment and sovereign guidance of the nations (67:5). The Lord has blessed the earth with fruitful increase (67:6) and will continue to bless his people (67:8). The psalm concludes with a universal call to the nations to fear God (67:8).

Psalm 68 shares many of these same themes. The psalm begins and ends by praising God (68:4–5). The psalmist then rehearses God's past victories over Israel's enemies (68:6–15), as in Ps 66:5–7. The first half of Ps 68 culminates with the construction of his holy temple (68:19), where the kings of the nations would later bring their tribute (68:30). God is blessed (68:20) and all the kingdoms of the earth should sing to him (68:33) and ascribe power to him (68:35). The psalm concludes with a blessing (68:36).

Psalms 65–68 contrast starkly with their canonical context. While surrounded by psalms of Davidic lament and hope, Pss 65–68 give a glimpse of what the world might look like if the ideal of Pss 1–2 were realized. All the nations would praise God and ascribe power to him, and they would bring tribute to him in his holy temple. These images evoke the similar prophecies in Isa 2:1–4 and Mic 4:1–4, which might properly be called eschatological. Hence, Pss 65–68 envision, at least in their calls to universal homage to God, an eschatological age at the end of history. The fact that Ps 68 was placed in this grouping suggests that the editor(s) of the Psalter read it in an eschatological manner and intended to highlight these themes by juxtaposing it to Pss 65–67.

Psalm 68 in the Septuagint

An eschatological interpretation may also be present in the Septuagint, as Joachim Schaper attempted to demonstrate in his *Eschatology in the Greek Psalter*.[40] Psalm 68:7

---

[39] Ibid., 191n50.
[40] Joachim Schaper, *Eschatology in the Greek Psalter*, WUNT II/76 (Tübingen: Mohr Siebeck, 1995), 85–93.

refers to the Exodus: "God causes the lonely to dwell in a home; he brings out the prisoners with prosperity; surely those who are stubborn dwell in scorched land." The Septuagint translates this phrase as "God places the lonely in a house; he liberates the prisoners in manliness, likewise the rebellious ones who live in tombs." Thus, the LXX translates the MT's "stubborn" (סוררים) as "rebellious" (παραπικραίνοντας) and also adds "in tombs" (ἐν τάφοις). Whereas the MT says the "stubborn dwell in scorched land," the LXX has God placing in a house both the lonely and the rebellious ones who live in tombs. Thus, the Septuagint translators may have given this Exodus imagery an eschatological interpretation by applying God's saving power of the Israelites to the dead; God will save them from the bondage of death. Such an eschatological application of the Exodus imagery would cohere with the psalm's own eschatological use of the Exodus imagery in vv. 25–28.

Again, when Ps 68:13 MT reads "Kings of armies flee, they flee!" the LXX renders it strangely as "the king of the forces of the loved one" (ὁ βασιλεὺς τῶν δυνάμεων τοῦ ἀγαπητοῦ). The translation of "kings" (מלכי) as singular βασιλεὺς may have been an attempt to harmonize the noun with the surrounding divine epithets ("God," vv. 10–11; "Lord," v. 12; "Almighty," v. 15). According to Schaper, the translators then read some form of יְדִיְ ("loved one," from ידד) for the MT's יִדּדוּן ("they flee," from נדד). They chose Greek ἀγαπητός, which in that period approached the meaning of μονογενής and is used messianically (purportedly) in Ps 28:6 (LXX) and (definitely) in T. Benj. 11.2 and T. Jud. 24:1, both modeled on Num 24:7, 17. Thus, the Septuagint translators render Ps 68:13 MT to say that the king of the Messiah's forces will let them divide the spoil. Schaper's arguments are unique and he argues for many instances of such eschatological interpretations of the psalms in the Greek Psalter. Nevertheless, reception of his methodology is divided: some highly critical and some praising it.[41] Most problematic is that Schaper circularly assumes the Septuagint translators engaged in intentionally interpretive translation and then proves his assumption by finding rabbinic-style interpretation throughout the psalms. Thus, while his arguments are suggestive of an eschatological interpretation of Ps 68 by the Septuagint translators, we must hold such a possibility tentatively.

The Dead Sea Scrolls

The canonical placement of Ps 68 and its Septuagintal translation are possible evidence for an early eschatological interpretation, but the evidence in the Dead Sea Scrolls is perhaps more important.

1. Qumran's Pesher on Psalm 68. The first and most immediately telling use of Ps 68 at Qumran is found in 1Q16 (1QpPs), which provides a fragmented record of a pesher on Ps 68. The parts that remain include quotations of Ps 68:13, 26–27, 30, 31. Unfortunately, the majority of these are too fragmented to compare to the psalm, but the word "pesher" does occur twice clearly and perhaps once more in reconstruction. Fragment 9 quotes Ps 68:31 and seems to read that the *pesher* of the "beast of the reed"

---

[41] Critical: reviews by Albert Pietersma, *BO* 54 (1997): 185–90; Melvin K. H. Peters, *JBL* 116 (1997): 350–53; Eberhard Bons, *RevScRel* 71 (1997): 257–58; John W. Wright, *CBQ* 59, no. 2 (1997): 357–59. Praising: reviews by Alison Salvesen, *JTS* 47, no. 2 (1996): 580–83; P. W. van der Horst, *JSJPHRP* 28, no. 1 (1997): 123–24; Folker Siegert, *TLZ* 122 (1997): 39–41.

is the Kittim (the words "pesher," "beast," and "Kittim" are all preserved). It is therefore possible that 1Q16 applied Ps 68:31 to the Kittim, whom they believed God would destroy in the latter days. However, it is not certain that the word "Kittim" belongs to the same sentence as the one with "pesher" and "beast," so we cannot be certain. Since the pesher cites lines from Ps 68 and then inserts פשרו ("its interpretation [is]") at two or three locations that are extant, it seems this was a line-by-line pesher rather than a topical pesher. If so, then the Qumran community took special interest in all of Ps 68 and sought for the fulfillment of all or many of its verses in their contemporary community, just as they did with prophets such as Habakkuk (1QpHab).

That a pesher was written on Ps 68 shows that the covenanters considered it prophetic. The term פשר used at Qumran is a Hebraization of the Aramaic cognate used in Daniel and thus has its semantic basis in the "loosening" of a dream's interpretation.[42] It is therefore connected with the interpretation of cryptic revelation. Moreover, all pesher texts at Qumran were written on prophetic books, with the exception of three psalms peshers (1Q16; 4Q171; 4Q173). All three psalms are ascribed to David, who was considered a prophet in some early and late Jewish sources and explicitly in 11QPsa XXVII, 2-11 [11Q5], which says that his psalms were composed through prophecy (11QPsa).[43] Thus, while 1Q16 is unfortunately fragmented, it demonstrates that the covenanters read Ps 68 as prophetically as they read the biblical prophets.[44]

2. *The Influence of Psalm 68 on 1QM XII, 7-16.* While it is unfortunate that the pesher was not preserved so that we could see clearly how the Qumran community interpreted Ps 68, it is plausible that the psalm was a major influence in the production of an important prayer for war in the War Scroll (1QM). There is possibly one direct allusion to Ps 68 in 1QM, and there is a clear allusion to Judg 5:12 in the prayer in 1QM XII, 7-16, which is repeated in XIX 1-8 with little variation. 4Q492 contains a text parallel to 1QM XIX, also with little variation. The variations between these three versions of the prayer are slight enough that they do not affect my argument, so I will focus only on the prayer as it appears in 1QM XII, 7-16. Given its repetition in col. XIX of 1QM and its existence in 4Q492, it is indeed an important prayer for the Qumran community.

---

[42] Shani Berrin, "Qumran Pesharim," in *Biblical Interpretation at Qumran*, ed. Matthias Henze, SDSSRL (Grand Rapids, MI: Eerdmans, 2005), 124.

[43] For David as a prophet, see Josephus, *Ant.* 6.166; Tg. Ps. 14:1; 18:1; 45:3; 49:16, 17; 51:13, 14; 103:1; Acts 2:30; *b. Sot.* 48b.

[44] There are a couple of other texts in which Ps 68 might possibly have been in mind. An allusion to Judg 5:12 (cf. Ps 68:19) may occur in 11Q14 fr. 2, 2, although it is too damaged to make out the context: "[Arise, war]rior, take captive the Phili[stines] . . ." ([· · ·]פל שבה ור[· · ·]). 11 Q14 is part of the War Texts and is associated with 4Q285 and the War Scroll (1QM). The allusion to Judg 5:12 occurs in a separate fragment and the text cited here is all that remains. However, given the similar use of Judg 5:12 in 1QM XII, 10 and its parallels (as we will see later), it is likely that either "take captive your captives," "collect your spoil," or both occurred after "take captive the Philistines." Since the community studied Ps 68 closely (as is evident from the existence of 1Q16), any allusion to Judg 5:12 may have also been a combined allusion with Ps 68:19. The cognate accusative phrase "when you take captive your captives" (ושביתה את שביו) occurs in 11Q19 LXIII, 10, which the author likely drew from Judg 5:12 or Ps 68:19. 4Q365 6c line 6 is an expanded version of the Song of Miriam. It says that, because of God's deliverance from Egypt, his people will exalt him to the heights (למרומם), the same expression used in Ps 68:19 "you ascended to the height" (למרום). Since Exod 15 was a prototype for Ps 68, it is not implausible that the author here has read the two passages in concert.

While this prayer alludes directly to Judg 5:12, we will have reason to suspect that Ps 68 might have been in mind secondarily, or that it might have influenced the author in some way. Our suspicion is first aroused when we remember that Ps 68:19 also directly alludes to Judg 5:12 by adapting its language, just as we will see 1QM XII, 10 does. Our suspicion is heightened when we notice the OT passages on which 1QM draws to compose this prayer: many of the contexts are exactly the same, and in a couple of cases the verses are exactly the same, as those used by the author of Ps 68. When we keep in mind that the covenanters had executed what was probably a line-by-line pesher, and thus developed a keen awareness of Ps 68's language, we have even greater reason to suspect that Ps 68 loomed large as an influence for the author of this prayer in 1QM.

First, I will discuss the role of XII, 7–16 within 1QM. The document's literary unity is disputed, so I must first explain its broad structure and how the prayers in cols. X–XIV function in the document as a whole. I will then examine closely the prayer that contains the combined allusion to Judg 5:12 and Ps 68:19. I will demonstrate a slew of allusions to the five passages on which Ps 68 mainly relies for its language and ideas: Exod 15, Judg 5, and the three Pentateuchal "latter days" passages (Gen 49, Num 23–24, Deut 32–33). When this fact is combined with a couple of potential allusions to Ps 68, it is plausible that the author of 1QM used Ps 68 as one of his major sources of inspiration in this prayer. His use of it is also clearly eschatological and in line with the original meaning of the psalm as I have laid it out in the previous three chapters.

1QM presents an eschatological war of the sons of light against the sons of darkness, the nations, and Belial. It divides generally into four sections. Columns I–II provide an overview of the war and its chronology; III–IX present military tactics and army descriptions; X–XIV present hymns and prayers; and XV–XIX describe the final war, but in slightly different terms than col. I. Literary unity has been disputed for reasons such as a seemingly contradictory timeline and different enemies in cols. I–II, difficulty understanding how cols. III–IX relate to the war(s) in cols. I–II, the lack of explanation regarding the function of the prayers in the document or in the actual war, and the differences between the war in col. I and cols. XV–XIX.[45]

However, as I have argued elsewhere, the document can be read as a unity, depicting a three-stage war.[46] Column I envisions a defensive battle against the king of the Kittim and his allies, which lasts a "day." Since col. II opens with renewed temple service, the missing end of col. I either explicitly or implicitly tells of the sons of light retaking Israel completely, including Jerusalem, and reestablishing temple worship. There are then six years of preparation for the War of the Divisions followed by a Sabbath year. The War of the Divisions is an offensive war against the nations that lasts forty years and is the subject of cols. III–IX. Columns XV–XIX then depict a third stage of

---

[45] See, e.g., J. van der Ploeg, *Le Rouleau de la Guerre*, STDJ 2 (Leiden: Brill, 1959), 12–22; Philip R. Davies, *1QM, the War Scroll from Qumran: Its Structure and History*, BibOr 32 (Rome: Biblical Institute Press, 1977); Brian Schultz, *Conquering the World: The War Scroll (1QM) Reconsidered*, STDJ 76 (Leiden: Brill, 2009), 86–239; Jürgen Becker, *Das Heil Gottes: Heils- und Sündenbegriffe in den Qumrantexten und im Neuen Testament*, SUNT 3 (Göttingen: Vandenhoeck & Ruprecht, 1964), 43–50.

[46] Todd A. Scacewater, "The Literary Unity of 1QM and its Three Stage War," *RevQ* 27, no. 2 (2015): 225–48.

the war that includes a final eschatological battle against the nations and Belial, who empowers the nations. This defeat will be final, "removing forever the enemy do[mi]nion" (XVIII, 11).

The prayers found in cols. X–XIV contain lexemes and themes that share affinities with all three stages of the war. They are best understood to have been composed for the priest to recite before any battle during the War of the Divisions (cols. III–IX) and during the final battle against the Kittim and Belial (cols. XV–XIX). Deuteronomy 20:2–5 stipulates that the priest is to stand and speak a prayer whenever Israel is approaching the battle against their enemies. 1QM X, 2–5 records this brief prayer from Deut 20:2–5, and it seems that the prayers in the rest of cols. X–XIV are an expansion of the prayer from Deuteronomy. The sect believed in a strict adherence to the law and would therefore not fail to have the priest recite a hortatory prayer before any battle. The prayers are omitted in col. I because the sons of light are at that point exiled from Jerusalem, with no organized priestly service.

Since 1QM XII, 7–16 is part of the set of prayers in cols. X–XIV, it would be recited as part of that set before each battle. This prayer, repeated in col. XIX, is therefore a key part of exhorting Israel as they defeat each wicked nation and, eventually, the Kittim and Belial. But the repetition of the prayer demonstrates its importance for the eschatological war. It is in fact the only prayer repeated fully in 1QM. The prayer in col. XIX comes after the sons of light defeat the Kittim and must pursue them for final destruction (XVIII, 12). It is therefore the last prayer to be recited in the war and functions to exhort God to arise and destroy evil once and for all. There is no more important prayer in the eschatological war than this repeated prayer. Now we may evaluate the prayer closely to illuminate the allusion to Judg 5:12 and also to argue for Ps 68's broader influence on the author's production of the prayer.

The repeated prayer divides into three parts. The first part (XII, 7–10a) establishes assurance of victory and is inspired by several OT allusions describing God as a feared warrior who will give them success over the enemy:

> [7] Now you, O God, are f[eared] in the glory of your kingdom, and the congregation of your holy ones is in our midst for everlastin[g] help. [Therefore] we will [gi]ve contempt to the kings, mocking [8] and deriding to the warriors. For holy is our Lord and the King of Glory is with us, a holy people. Warr[iors and] a host of angels are among our numbered men. [9] And a warrior of wa[r] is in our congregation, and an army of his spirits is with our foot-soldiers and o[ur] cavalry, [like] clouds and fogs of dew covering the earth, [10] and like a storm of spring showers to water justice for all its produce.

The most prominent statement in this first section is the confident expectation of victory: "we will give contempt to the kings, mocking and deriding to the warriors." This assertion is surrounded on both sides by four reasons for such confidence.[47]

---

[47] I have translated "[Therefore]" in line 7 because it seems most likely a *waw* was written where the text is now worn away, and I have taken the *waw* as resultant since what comes before and after the clause functions logically as reasons or grounds.

First, God is feared (ירא), or terrifying in the glory of his kingdom (cf. Ps 145:11; Ps 89:9), and his angels are among Israel's army to help them.[48] Second, God is holy and he is with them (cf. Ps 99:9).[49] Third, warriors (גבור, here probably the four angels Michael, Gabriel, Sariel, and Raphael) are among the angels with God. Fourth, the prayer reiterates the presence of God and his angels among them but expands it greatly with a host of metaphors drawn from Ezek 38:9, 15–16; Isa 18:4; Mic 5:7 [5:6 MT]. So this first part of the prayer expresses confident expectation of victory because God is with them as a divine warrior, a theme that resonates with Israel's divine warrior texts, which includes Exod 15, Judg 5, and Ps 68.

The second part of this prayer (XII, 10b–13a) calls God to action. There is no linguistic indication of how the author intended these first two sections to be connected, but it seems that the first part functions as the grounds for the exhortations in the second part:

Arise, O Warrior, take captive your captives, O Man of Glory, and plunder [11] your plunder, O Performer of Valiance. Place your hand on the neck of your enemies and [place] your foot on the back of the slain. Smash the nations of your adversaries, and let your sword [12] devour guilty flesh. Fill your land with glory and [fill] your inheritance with blessing, a multitude of cattle in your fields, silver, gold, and pleasurable stones [13] in your palaces.

The first six imperatives are requests for the Warrior to act in war, and they do not follow a sequential pattern but are instead drawn together from various OT passages. The final imperative seems to be the logical result of the Warrior's actions in war: "Fill your land with glory . . ." This part of the prayer therefore contains six imperatives to move the Warrior to action, resulting in his filling the earth with his glory.[50]

Commentators question the identity of the Warrior. According to Y. Yadin, there is no Messiah in this section, as there is in 4Q285 (a related "War Text"); here, God is the hero.[51] Similarly, P. Davies denies any agency (angelic or Messianic) in this section and believes the imperatives must only be applied to God in order to fit the context

---

[48] The verb is reconstructed and has been conjectured as either נורא or נערץ. Bastiaan Jongeling opts for נורא, with the majority of commentators, since it appeared already in 10:1 (*Le Rouleau de la Guerre des Manuscrits de Qumrân*, SSN 4 [Assen, Netherlands: Van Gorcum, 1962], 281).

[49] The phrase "King of Glory is with us" involves the word עם, which has been vocalized as "with" or "people." Daniel 7:27 and 8:24 refer to Israel as a "people of holy ones," and on this likely allusion עם should be vocalized "people" rather than "with" (Jean Carmignac, *La Règle de la Guerre des Fils de Lumière contre les Fils de Ténèbres* [Paris: Letouzey et Ané, 1958], 179). Jongeling is not certain it is an allusion to Daniel and believes קדושים relates to the angels here rather than the community. He reads "with the saints *as* our heroes," reconstructing the lacuna as גבורינו (*Rouleau de la Guerre*, 283–84). However, the allusion to Daniel is likely, given the author's reliance on Dan 11–12, especially in col. I, and I have therefore translated עם as "people."

[50] The final word translated "palaces" could also be "temples," which could possibly evoke the divine builder topos of the psalm. However, since the word is plural (היכל[ו]תיכה), it probably does not refer to the Jerusalem temple.

[51] So also, Yigael Yadin, *The Scroll of the War of the Sons of Light against the Sons of Darkness* (London: Oxford University Press, 1962), 215n3.

of the entire hymn.[52] A. Dupont-Sommer notes that calling God "man (איש) of glory" should not be strange, since this may allude to "man (איש) of war" in Exod 15:3.[53] J. Carmignac believes it could refer both to God and Israel as his agent.[54] B. Jongeling similarly holds that God and Israel are so closely related that "ce qui concerne Dieu concerne également son peuple."[55] Alternatively, it could be the prince of the whole congregation from V, 1–2, who is possibly a messianic figure. This prince appears in CD VII, 18–21 as the scepter of the prophecy in Num 24:17 and is implied in 1QM XI, 6–7, which explicitly quotes the scepter prophecy in Num 24:17. However, on balance the Warrior is likely God because of the preceding appellations "King of glory" and "Hero of War" in XII, 8–9, which refer to God. Moreover, no studies have uncovered a significant strand of messianic thought in 1QM, so it is unlikely a messianic figure would figure here in so prominent a role.[56] The hero here is therefore God.

The most important phrase for our purposes appears in 1QM XII, 10: "arise, O Warrior, take captive your captives" (קומה גבור שבה שביכה). The cognate accusative שבי שבה occurs in the OT seven times (Num 21:1; Deut 21:10; Judg 5:12; Ps 68:19; 2 Chr 6:37, 38; 28:17). The only context that includes "arise" in conjunction with the command to take captives is Judg 5:12, and a comparison of Judg 5:12 with 1QM XII, 10 makes it evident that the author adapted Judg 5:12: "Arise, Barak, and take captive your captives, O son of Abinoam (קום ברק ושבה שביך בן־אבינעם)." If the author does allude to Judg 5:12 here, he adds a paragogic ה to קום and adds a ה to שביך for full spelling, in accord with 1QM's style. He also changes the appellation "Barak" to "Warrior," a frequent word in 1QM, and changes "Son of Abinoam" to איש כבוד. This title "man of glory" may be an adaptation of "man of war" (איש מלחמה) in Exod 15:3, since it is otherwise odd to call God a man.[57]

That 1QM XII, 10 alludes to Judg 5:12 and not Ps 68:19 is evident for multiple reasons. First, the 2ms pronominal suffix on שבי is present in 1QM XII, 10 and Judg 5:12, but absent in Ps 68:19 (שבית שבי). Second, Ps 68:19 does not use an epithet for God, while Judg 5:12 and 1QM do. A third possible reason could be that the phrase "plunder your plunder" (שללכה ושול) is inspired by Judg 5:30, which uses שלל ("plunder") four times. However, שלל also appears in Ps 68:13 ("the women at home divide the spoil"), which itself probably alludes to Judg 5:30. So the clause "plunder your plunder" in 1QM XII, 10–11 may have borrowed from the wider context of Judg 5, or it may be evidence that Ps 68 was also in mind.[58] Similarly, while "arise, O Warrior" (1QM XII, 10) is part of the allusion to Judg 5:12's "arise, Barak," it may also have evoked in the author's mind the beginning of Ps 68:1, "let God arise" (יקום אלהים). Additionally, in

---

[52] Davies, IQM, 97.
[53] André Dupont-Sommer, The Essene Writings from Qumran, trans. G. Vermes (Cleveland, OH: World Publishing, 1962), 187n2.
[54] Carmignac, Règle de la Guerre, 181.
[55] Jongeling, Rouleau de la Guerre, 287.
[56] 1QM deserves a thorough examination for any messianic ideas.
[57] Similarly, Dupont-Sommer, The Essene Writings from Qumran, 187n2.
[58] Alternatively, the primary source of this phrase could be Ezek 38:12, 13; 39:10, since Ezek 38–39 is a consistent influence throughout 1QM (on which, see Scacewater, "The Literary Unity of 1QM," 239–42). However, since the allusion is directly to Judg 5:12 with Ps 68:19 secondarily in mind, and since both songs use the plundering imagery, they are the more likely source of the phrase.

Judg 5:12, Barak takes captives, while in Ps 68:19 and 1QM XII, 10, God takes captives. While it is uncertain that Ps 68:19 was the linguistic source for 1QM XII, 10, I find it at least plausible, since the community had studied Ps 68 carefully enough to compose a pesher on it. At this point, we have seen some glimpses of Ps 68's possible influence on this prayer, including this significant adaptation of Judg 5:12, which Ps 68:19 also adapts in a similar fashion. These observations provide a hint that perhaps Ps 68 influenced the author, but more convincing evidence is forthcoming. We will now complete our literary analysis of the prayer and then turn to the author's use of OT texts to demonstrate further evidence of Ps 68's influence.

The third part of the prayer (XII, 13b–16) continues with commands for the sons of light to rejoice and reign forever. There are seven imperatives. The first and last three are brief phrases, while the fourth imperative is followed by a purpose clause with three intended results. The result is a well-balanced paragraph.

> O Zion, rejoice exceedingly!
> And shine in jubilance, O Jerusalem!
> And rejoice, all cities of Judah!
> Open ¹⁴ your gates continually in order to bring in the wealth of the nations,
>   so that their kings shall serve you,
>   and all your oppressors shall bow down before you,
>   and the dust ¹⁵ [of your feet they shall lick.]
> [O daught]ers of my people, shout with a jubilant voice,
> adorn yourselves with glorious jewelry,
> and rule over the king[dom of] ... ¹⁶ [... *to your camps, in order for*] Israel to reign forever.

The imperatives seem to move progressively—if not chronologically, then at least logically. They begin with rejoicing over Israel's victory, move toward opening Jerusalem's gates for the nations to flow in and bow down to God, move again to rejoicing, then call for Israel to adorn themselves with jewelry and reign forever. This progression therefore climaxes at the end of the prayer, where Israel is said to reign forever. While again it is unclear how this part of the prayer relates to the second part, it seems that the second part is the grounds for this third part of the prayer. The flow of the entire prayer therefore moves toward a climax in this third part, where Israel rejoices over the enemy's defeat and enjoys their everlasting reign. As with the rest of the prayer, the majority of the language comes from the OT.[59] Thus the fragmented final imperative exhorts Israel to rule over the kingdom of someone (perhaps "the nations"), then do something (perhaps "return") to their camps, so that the reconstituted Israel will reign forever, probably from Jerusalem. Here then is the climax of the entire prayer, that Israel would rule over the nations and reign forever from Jerusalem.

The strongest evidence that Ps 68 influenced the author's composition of this prayer is his similar use of the five major passages used by the psalmist. We saw already that

---

[59] Primarily Ps 97:8; Zech 9:9; Isa 60:11, 14; 61:10; Isa 49:23.

"Man of Glory" probably alludes to Exod 15:3 and that XII, 10 adapts Judg 5:12 in a similar manner to Ps 68:19. We also saw that "plunder your plunder" *could* allude to Ps 68:13, and that "arise, O Warrior" might have some connection with Ps 68:1. But now we will see that this prayer also draws language from the same three Pentateuchal "latter days" passages (Gen 49; Num 23–24; Deut 32–33) that help form the eschatological, militant vision of the future in the second half of Ps 68.

The appellation "Performer of Valiance" (XII, 11) could come from either Ps 118:15–16 or Num 24:18.[60] The phrase occurs twice in the psalm to say that the right hand of Yahweh does valiantly (עשה חיל). Since it is a victory song, it would fit 1QM's purpose well and is a good candidate as the language's source. However, 1QM XI, 6–7 quotes Num 24:17–19 directly, showing the author's interest in the prophecy in Num 24. Numbers 24:18 says Israel does valiantly, which the author may have adapted and applied to the Warrior. This transference of description from Israel to God is not problematic, just as the end of the prayer says not that God will reign forever (as we might expect) but that Israel will reign forever. One further consideration is a clear allusion in the prayer to Num 24:8, which we will examine below. The decision is difficult, but 1QM's prior interest in Num 24 and the following clear allusion to Num 24:8 gives the edge slightly to Num 24:18 as the source of "Performer of Valiance."

The next imperative in 1QM XII, 11 is drawn directly from Gen 49:8 (the underlining in each of these parallel citations indicate corresponding lexemes and concepts):

1QM XII, 11:	Place <u>your hand</u> on the <u>neck of your enemies</u>
	תן ידכה בעורף אויביכה
Gen 49:8:	<u>Your hand</u> shall be <u>on the neck of your enemies</u>
	ידך בערף איביך

The nouns "neck" and "enemy" are collocated only seven times in the OT (Gen 49:8; Exod 23:27; Jos 7:8, 12; 2 Sam 22:41; Ps 18:41; Jer 18:17). Every instance except Gen 49:8 refers to someone turning their back to their enemies to retreat or flee. Genesis 49:8 is the only context in which the words are collocated to refer to militant violence toward one's enemy and is therefore the source for this command in 1QM.

The next command is drawn from Deut 33:29:

1QM XII, 11:	[place] your <u>foot</u> on the <u>back</u> of the slain
	תן . . . ורגלכה על במותי חלל
Deut 33:29:	and you shall <u>tread</u> on their <u>backs</u>
	ואתה על־במותימו תדרך

The noun בָּמָה occurs 105 times in the OT. Of these, only one instance refers to a literal back: Deut 33:29. And in that context, the back of the enemy is being trampled on. It seems clear then that this command in 1QM XII, 11 alludes to Deut 33:29.

---

[60] The participle "performers" (עושי) is oddly in the plural, which can be explained in several ways. See Carmignac, *Règle de la Guerre*, 181.

The following command is clearly drawn from Num 24:8:

1QM XII, 11–12: Smash (מחץ) the nations (גוים) of your adversaries (צר)
Num 24:8: He shall consume the nations (גוים), his adversaries (צר), and shall break their bones in pieces and pierce (מחץ) them through with his arrows.

The verb מחץ occurs only fifteen times in the OT.[61] Interestingly, two of these uses are in Num 24 and Ps 68. But Num 24:8 is the only passage that collocates מחץ ("smash"), צר ("enemy"), and גוים ("nations"), which makes it clear that 1QM is alluding to it. But since מחץ is a rare word, other passages may have been in mind secondarily. Psalm 68:22 is the strongest candidate, since it collocates מחץ with a synonym of צר, namely, איב ("enemy"). It seems for this reason that Ps 68:22 alludes directly to Num 24:8, so again we may have an instance of the author of 1QM choosing to allude to a specific verse to which Ps 68 also alludes. Numbers 24:17 may also be in mind, since it is quoted in 1QM XI, 6–7. It says the star and scepter from Jacob will smash (מחץ) the forehead of Moab. Deuteronomy 32:39 says that God alone smashes (מחץ) and heals, while Deut 33:11 says God will smash (מחץ) the loins of those who rise against him (קמיו), perhaps another development of Num 24:8 with קמיו substituting as a synonym of צר. Although there is probably no connection besides the militant use of the word, it is worth noting that Judg 5:26 says Jael smashed (מחץ) Sisera's head. Thus, 1QM's "smash the nations of your adversaries" alludes directly to Num 24:8 with its collocation of מחץ, צר, and גוים but may have had in mind secondarily any of Ps 68:22; Num 24:17; Deut 32:39; 33:11; or Judg 5:26.

The next command likely pulls language from Deut 32:42 and Ps 68:22:

1QM XII, 11–12: and let your sword consume guilty flesh
(תואכל בשר אשמה וחרבכה)
Deut 32:42: I will make my arrows drunk with blood, and my sword shall devour flesh (וחרבי תאכל בשר)
Ps 68:22: But God will smash the heads of his adversaries, the hairy skull of him who walks in his guilty (אשם) ways.

The allusion to Deut 32:42 is clear; it is the only place in the OT that the terms "sword," "consume," and "flesh" are collocated in same clause.[62] The previous allusion to Deut 33:29, which is part of this long "latter days" prophecy (Deut 32–33), also demonstrates the author's attention to this context. The likelihood that "guilty" is drawn from Ps 68:22 stems from two considerations. First, we have seen possible glimpses of Ps 68 already, including 1QM's allusion to Num 24:8, to which Ps 68:22 also likely alludes with its collocation of מחץ and אָיָב. Thus, the author may have already had Ps 68:22 in mind. Second, the word אשם refers to "guilt" only four times in the OT (Gen

---

[61] Num 24:8, 17; Deut 32:39; 33:11; Judg 5:26; 2 Sam 22:39; Job 5:18; 26:12; Pss 18:39; 68:22, 24; 110:5–6; Isa 30:26; Hab 3:13.
[62] All three terms occur also in Jer 12:12, but "flesh" is part of a separate clause from "the sword of Yahweh consumes."

26:10; Jer 51:5; Ps 68:22; Prov 14:9). Only in Ps 68:22 does "guilt" relate to enemies who will be destroyed, as it does in 1QM XII, 11–12. We have here, therefore, an echo or possible allusion to Ps 68:22, along with a clear allusion to Deut 32:42.

The final OT allusion that draws from similar contexts as Ps 68 is in the third part of the prayer:

1QM XII, 14:   all your oppressors <u>shall bow down before you</u> (לך והשתחוו)
Gen 49:8:   the sons of your father <u>will bow down before you</u> (לך ישתחוו)

The phrase "all your oppressors shall bow down to you" comes primarily from Isa 60:14, "The sons of those who afflicted you shall come bowing low [lit. "bowing on hands"] to you." That Isa 60:14 is 1QM's source here is evident because all of 1QM XII, 14–15a is inspired by Isa 60:11–14.[63] However, after the verb "shall bow down," 1QM curiously exchanges Isa 60:14's "on hands" (על־כפות) for the prepositional phrase לך. This exchange suggests the author may again have been pulling language from multiple contexts with similar phraseology. The phrase "bow down to you" (חוה + לך) occurs in the OT only in Gen 27:29; 37:10; 49:8; and Ps 66:4. In Gen 27:29, Isaac prays that all nations would bow down to Jacob. In Gen 37:10, Jacob's parents ask if they will indeed bow down to Joseph, in accord with his dream. In Ps 66:4, the psalmist states or requests that all the earth worship God. Genesis 49:8 is Jacob's blessing of Judah, that all his brothers would bow down to him. If 1QM's "all your oppressors shall bow down to you" draws the prepositional phrase לך from any of these passages, it is most likely Gen 49:8, since the same verse has already been alluded to in 1QM XII with the phrase "place your hand on the neck of your enemies." As with the transference of valiant action from Israel (Num 24:18) to God (1QM XII, 11), so here also the reception of bowing can be transferred from Judah (Gen 49:8) to God (1QM XII, 14). Thus, while the phrase "all your oppressors shall bow down to you" comes primarily from Isa 60:14, the author may have had the prophecy about Judah secondarily in mind.

One last reason to suspect that the author may have had Ps 68 in mind is the emphasis on the temple in and around this prayer. 1QM XII, 1 says a host of angels is in God's sanctuary (קודש). This verse resembles Ps 68:18, "The chariots of God are ten thousand thousands multiplied, the Lord is among them, Sinai is in the sanctuary." 1QM's language could also, though, be drawn from Deut 33:2, from which Ps 68:18

---

[63] Isa 60:11–14:

> <u>Your gates shall be open continually;</u> day and night they shall not be shut, <u>that people may bring to you the wealth of the nations, with their kings led in procession</u>. For the nation and kingdom that will not serve you shall perish; those nations shall be utterly laid waste. The glory of Lebanon shall come to you, the cypress, the plane, and the pine, to beautify the place of my sanctuary, and I will make the place of my feet glorious. The sons of those who afflicted you shall come bending low to you, and <u>all who despised you shall bow down at your feet</u>; they shall call you the City of the LORD, the Zion of the Holy One of Israel.

> 1QM XII, 14–15a: "<u>Open your gates continually in order to bring in the wealth of the nations, so that their kings shall serve you</u>, and <u>all your oppressors shall bow down before you</u>, and the dust [of your feet they shall lick.]" The final line is restored on the basis of 4QM2 frg. 1 line 7.

draws its language. 1QM XII, 2 says the names of these great angels are with him in his holy sanctuary. Lines 12–13 of col. XII exhort God to fill his palaces (היכל) with silver, gold, and precious stones. We have seen a similar idea in Chapter 3 with war spoil being used to build temples or palaces for gods after war victories. The next phrase in line 14 is "Rejoice, Zion," which is where the temple is envisioned in Ps 68:17–19. This emphasis on God's temple does not necessarily point to Ps 68, but when read in the light of all the other evidence pointing to the author's inspiration from Ps 68, the temple language is provocative.

To summarize, we have analyzed the use of OT traditions in 1QM XII, 7–16 that relate to the traditions used in Ps 68. I contend that the following evidence is sufficient to establish the probability that the author of 1QM was inspired by Ps 68 as he composed this prayer for his community's future eschatological battles. God is throughout this prayer the divine warrior, as in Ps 68 and its two prominent sources, Exod 15 and Judg 5. 1QM adapts the language of Judg 5:12 ("take captive your captives") and applies it to God, just as Ps 68:19 has done. The phrase "plunder your plunder" may also allude to Ps 68:13, or might allude to Judg 5:30, to which Ps 68:13 probably alludes. We saw that "Performer of Valiance" likely comes from Num 24:18, a chapter to which the author was attuned in his composition of the War Scroll. The following imperatives allude to Gen 49:8; Deut 33:29; Num 24:8 (perhaps secondarily Ps 68:22; Num 24:17; Deut 32:39; 33:11); Deut 32:42; Ps 68:22; and again probably Gen 49:8. Thus, the author of 1QM has alluded to or adapted language from the exact same OT contexts—and in two cases, the exact same verses (Judg 5:12; Num 24:8)—that the author of Ps 68 used and adapted. There is also the plausibility that the adjective "guilty" was borrowed from or inspired by Ps 68:22. Finally, the use of temple language in and around this part of the prayer evokes similar imagery of the temple in Ps 68.

I contend that this evidence is weighty enough to conclude that the author of 1QM was inspired by Ps 68 and its use of OT sources. The Qumran community had written a pesher on Ps 68, perhaps a verse-by-verse commentary on how the psalm was being fulfilled in the community, so the author likely had an intimate knowledge of Ps 68. Hence, when we see the evidence for Ps 68's influence above, I judge it probable that the author was inspired by Ps 68 when composing this prayer for the eschatological battle against the Kittim and Belial. This use or interpretation of Ps 68 is therefore quite distinct from the Mosaic tradition. Rather, if I am correct, the author has read Ps 68 in accord with its ancient victory song tradition and has appropriated its imagery and traditions to portray God as the divine warrior who will smash his adversaries and bring about the final submission of all nations to his people Israel. Tables 5.1 and 5.2 illustrate the use of OT traditions in both Ps 68 and 1QM XII, 7–16 to demonstrate their similarity.

Summary of the Eschatological Interpretation

The earliest possible eschatological interpretation is evident in the canonical arrangement of the Psalter, which suggests the possibility that the editor(s) of the Psalter read Ps 68 eschatologically and grouped it with three other eschatological psalms. The evidence of an eschatological interpretation in the Septuagint translation

Table 5.1 1QM XII, 7–16's Use of OT Traditions Used by Psalm 68.

OT			1QM XII	
Judg 5:12	Arise, Barak, take captive your captives (קום ברק ושבה שביך)	10	Arise, O Warrior, take captive your captives (קומה גבור שבה שביכה)	
Exod 15:3	Yahweh is a <u>man of war</u> (יהוה איש מלחמה)	10	Arise . . . <u>man of glory</u> (איש כבוד)	
Num 24:18	Israel <u>does valiantly</u> (חיל עשה)	11	<u>Performer of Valiance</u> (חיל עושי)	
Ps 118:15–16	The right hand of Yahweh <u>does valiantly</u> (עשה חיל) (x2)			
Gen 49:8	<u>your hand</u> shall be <u>on the neck of</u> your <u>enemies</u> (ידך בערף איביך)	11	Place <u>your hand on the neck of</u> your <u>enemies</u> (תן ידכה בעורף אויביכה)	
Deut 33:29	and <u>you shall tread on</u> their <u>backs</u> (תדרך ואתה על־במותימו)	11	place . . . <u>your foot on</u> the <u>back</u> of the slain (תן . . . ורגלכה על במותי חלל)	
Num 24:8	he shall eat up the nations, his <u>adversaries</u> (צר), and shall break their bones in pieces and <u>pierce</u> (מחץ) them through with his arrows	11–12	<u>Smash</u> (מחץ) the nations of your <u>adversaries</u> (צר), and let your sword devour guilty flesh	
Ps 68:22	But God will <u>smash</u> (מחץ) the heads of his <u>enemies</u> (איב)			
Deut 32:42	I will make my arrows drunk with blood, and my <u>sword shall devour flesh</u> (בשר תאכל וחרבי)	11–12	and let your <u>sword consume guilty flesh</u> (רשב וחרבכה תואכל המשא)	
Ps 68:22	But God will smash the heads of his adversaries, the hairy skull of him who walks in his <u>guilty</u> (אשם) ways			
Gen 49:8	the sons of your father will <u>bow down before you</u> (ישתחוו לך)	14	all your oppressors <u>shall bow down before you</u> (והשתחוו לך)	

Note: The different types of underlining signal corresponding lexemes and concepts.

is tantalizing, but not certain enough to make any definitive claims. The evidence in the Dead Sea Scrolls, however, is determinative. The Qumran covenanters interpreted Ps 68 prophetically and eschatologically. The ascription to David automatically elevated the psalm to prophetic status, which is confirmed by the pesher on Ps 68 (1Q16). I have argued that the War Scroll uses Ps 68 as one of its main inspirations for crafting the most important prayer in the document, which the High Priest would pray before every battle, including the final destruction of the enemy that would usher in Israel's eschatological kingdom. This use of the psalm would cohere with the existence of the pesher, especially if the pesher did interpret the enemy in v. 31 of the psalm, the "beast of the reeds," as the Kittim. They would have then easily taken the language of Ps 68 and the OT traditions it utilized to develop the prayer for the final destruction of the Kittim, just as the psalm prophesies.

Table 5.2 Psalm 68's Use of Genesis 49, Numbers 23–24, and Deuteronomy 32–33.

OT		Ps 68	
Exod 15:2	Yah is my strength and my song, and he has become my salvation (ישועה)	v. 19	In order that Yah, God, might dwell there
		v. 20	God is for us a God of salvation (ישועה)
Gen 49:14	Issachar is a strong donkey, lying among the sheepfolds	v. 14	when you lie among the sheepfolds
Num 24:8	He shall eat up the nations, his adversaries (צר), and shall break their bones in pieces and pierce (מחץ) them through with his arrows	v. 22	But God will smash (מחץ) the heads of his adversaries (איב), the hairy skull (קדקד) of him who walks in his guilty ways
Num 24:17	it shall smash (מחץ) the forehead of Moab and the hairy skull (קדקד) of all the sons of Seth		
Deut 32:39	I smash (מחץ) and I heal		
Deut 33:11	Smash (מחץ) the loins of those who rise against him		
Gen 49:26	May they be on the head of Joseph, and on the hairy skull (קדקד) of him who was set apart from his brothers	v. 22	the hairy skull (קדקד)
Num 24:17	it shall smash the forehead of Moab and the hairy skull (קדקד) of all the sons of Seth		
Deut 33:16	May these come on the head of Joseph, on the hairy skull (קדקד) of the prince among his brothers		
Deut 33:20	Gad lies like a lion and tears arm and skull (קדקד)		
Deut 33:26	There is none like God, O Jeshurun, who rides in the heavens to your help, through the clouds (שחק) in his majesty	v. 34	rider in the heavens
		v. 36	his power is in the clouds (שחק)
Deut 33:2	The LORD came from Sinai (מסיני בא) and rose from Seir . . . he came from the ten thousands (רבבה) of holy ones	v. 18	The chariots of God are ten thousand thousands (רבתים אלפי) of myriads; the Lord is among them; Sinai is in the holy place (אדני בם סיני בקדש)

Note: The different types of underlining signal corresponding lexemes and concepts.

Conclusion

Two divergent streams of interpretation of Ps 68 emerged in Judaism. Early Jews at Qumran read the psalm in line with its original meaning, that of an ancient war song celebrating God's victory over the enemy sources and his subsequent eternal dwelling in his temple. The author of 1QM appropriated this imagery and Ps 68's other sources to compose a prayer for God to do to the sons of darkness and Belial as he had done to the Canaanites in the past. Evidence suggestive of an eschatological interpretation of Ps 68 is found even earlier among both the canonical arrangement of the Psalter and the Septuagint translation. On the other hand, later Jewish sources beginning with the Targum interpreted the climax of the psalm as referring to Moses ascending Mount Zion to receive the law. While the Mosaic interpretation lived on among the rabbis, the eschatological interpretation died out with the Qumran covenanters. That is, until a Jew named Paul interpreted the psalm eschatologically through the lens of what Jesus Christ had accomplished on a cross. To Paul's use of the psalm we now turn.

6

Psalm 68 in Ephesians 4:8–10

The preceding five chapters have set us up to complete our full analysis of Ps 68's meaning in its ANE context, its interpretation in early and late Judaism, and (now in this chapter) its interpretation and application in Ephesians. We have seen that Ps 68 is an ANE victory song that presents the narrative of God's defeat of Israel's enemies, culminating in his ascending Zion and receiving gifts from the Israelites to build his temple. The second half of the psalm reuses Exodus imagery and eschatological passages from the Pentateuch to shape a vision for God's final defeat of Israel's enemies in the future. Early Judaism latched onto this future vision of the psalm, and the War Scroll in particular used Ps 68 and language from its major sources to present the fulfillment of the psalm's eschatological vision. Late Judaism, centered as it became on the law, reinterpreted the climax of the psalm (and of Israelite history as told in the psalm) as Moses' ascending Sinai to receive the law.

This chapter will focus on Paul's use of Ps 68:19 in Eph 4:8 and his interpretation or application of the psalm in Eph 4:9–10. I will first survey previous understandings of Paul's use of Ps 68:19. After suggesting deficiencies in each of these views, I will express my own view, evaluating the amount of thematic coherence between Eph 4:8 and Ps 68:19, the transformation of the "gifts" and their purpose, and the reason for the verbal change from "you received" to "he gave." This analysis will allow us to see how Paul compares to his fellow Jewish interpreters before him and after him. I will discuss the various views of Eph 4:9–10 and explore how Paul could have derived the idea of Christ's descent and ascent from the psalm. Finally, I will suggest some ways that Paul's use of the psalm contributes to Pauline theology and to his address of the socio-religious situation in Asia Minor.

Previous Views of the Use of Psalm 68:19 in Ephesians 4:8

Interpreters through the ages have handled Eph 4:8 and Paul's use of Ps 68 diversely. The earliest interpretation comes in Justin's *Dialogue with Trypho*. While in the last few decades a flurry of articles has appeared, there still is no consensus on how Paul used the psalm and why he changed the verb from "you received" (Ps 68:19) to "he gave"

(Eph 4:8). There is a definite recent trend, as we will see, toward exploring the OT context for a rationale for the verb change, but not all agree with this approach.

Psalm 68:19 as Directly Prophetic of Christ

Writers in the early church unanimously understood Ps 68:19 to be a prophecy about Christ. In Justin's *Dialogue with Trypho*, he uses Eph 4:8 as a proof text to prove that believers would receive gifts after Christ's ascent into heaven (*Dial*. 39). Twice he labels this passage "prophecy," by which he certainly means *logoi*, verbal prophecies of Christ, rather than *typoi*, persons or actions that foreshadow Christ.[1] Later in *Dial*. 87, he connects the psalm's prophecy with Joel 2:28–29, which is cited at the distribution of gifts at Pentecost, but he does not explain how he understands the connection between Ps 68:19 and Joel 2:28–29.

Origen interpreted Ps 68:19 as predicting Christ's resurrection and his rescue of those in captivity. He cites in this connection Matt 27:52–53, where the saints are resurrected with Christ. These saints were held in bondage in the underworld, where Christ descended and freed them from captivity.[2] Origen gives different accounts of when and where Christ gave gifts. In his homilies on Luke, he says that the gifts mentioned in Eph 4:8 were given by Christ in the form of the Spirit at his resurrection (citing John 20:22, where Jesus breathes on his disciples to give them the Spirit).[3] But in his commentary on John, he says that after Christ ascended to the height when he led captivity captive, he then descended bearing various gifts, including the gift of tongues at Pentecost.[4] Perhaps this contradiction may be resolved by supposing that he understood the distribution of gifts not to be a one-time event.

Irenaeus interprets Ps 68:18–19 in his *Demonstration of the Apostolic Preaching* and gives more exegetical attention to the psalm than his predecessors.[5] He had already mentioned Christ's descent to hell earlier in the document (*Dem*. 78) and here presupposes it, as he does elsewhere.[6] He claims "captivity" refers to the "destruction of the rule of the apostate angels" and the ascension is Christ's ascent from Mount Zion to heaven. He then relates Christ's ascension to his gathering of the disciples on Mount Olives after his resurrection, from where he ascended into heaven. Thus, his interpretation of the psalm is unique in its treatment of the ascension clause, but he still interprets it as Christ's ascent to heaven and understands the "captivity" as the rule of demons. While his interpretation is more elaborate and unique, he still understands

---

[1] Justin distinguishes between *logoi* and *typoi* in *Dial*. 114. The Holy Spirit sometimes brought about things that were types of what would come in the future and sometimes speaks words about what would happen. "For the Holy Spirit sometimes brought about that something, which was the type of the future, should be done clearly; sometimes He uttered words about what was to take place, as if it was then taking place, or had taken place." For further discussion *logoi* and *typoi* in Justin's writings, see Joseph Trigg, "The Apostolic Fathers and Apologists," in *The Ancient Period*, ed. Alan J. Hauser and Duane Frederick Watson, HBI (Grand Rapids, MI: Eerdmans, 2003), 320–21.

[2] Origen, *Comm. Rom*. 5.1.37.

[3] Origen, *Hom. Luke* 27.5.

[4] Origen, *Comm. John* 6.292.

[5] Irenaeus, *Dem*. 83.

[6] *Adv. Haer*. 3.20; 4.22. He also cites Eph 4:8 in *Adv. Haer*. 2.20 but simply uses the language to refer to the ascension.

the psalm to prophesy directly of Christ's ascent to the heavens and defeat of the devil's rule over men.

Tertullian used Eph 4:8 as a proof text that Christ gave spiritual gifts. After returning to heaven, Christ would send these gifts, which are the *charismata*, the gifts of the Spirit. The "captivity" refers to "death or slavery of man."[7] In this same passage, like Justin, he cites Joel 2:28–29 as another proof text that Christ gave spiritual gifts, which he says was fulfilled when Christ dispensed gifts. It is unclear whether he understands Christ to have dispensed these gifts at Pentecost (Acts 2) or more generally. But in favor of the latter is his interpretation of the phrase "to the sons of men" (which he takes from Ps 68:19) as the converts of the apostles, who were begotten through their preaching of the gospel. So Ps 68:19 prophesies directly that Christ would dispense gifts to the converts of the apostles, perhaps initially at Pentecost.

One last early text, the Apocalypse of Elijah, which dates between the first and fourth centuries AD, interprets Eph 4:8 as Christ delivering us from "the captivity of this age" (Apoc. El. 1:4). Because of the devil's work and because he desires to "consume men like a fire which rages in stubble, and he desires to swallow them like water," God has "sent his son to the world so that he might save us from the captivity" (1:5).[8]

Summarizing the early Fathers, they see in the ascent language of the psalm a direct verbal prophecy of Christ's ascension and his later distribution of spiritual gifts. Moreover, early interpreters did not only see Christ as the agent in vv. 18–19 of the psalm but also understood the entire psalm to speak of Christ. Methodius applies the "cloud rider" epithet (Ps 68:34) to Christ.[9] Cyprian interpreted the theophanic language of Ps 68:2–8 as a prophecy of Christ's second coming as judge.[10] Augustine applied Ps 68:20 ("our God is the God of salvation, and to the Lord belongs the escape of death") to Christ, "whose name means 'savior' or 'saving'" (*Civ.* 17.18). So the psalm throughout spoke of Christ. Yet, despite all this early attention to Eph 4:8 and its quotation of Ps 68:19, these earliest interpreters made no attempt to resolve the problem of Paul's verbal change in Eph 4:8.

Later Patristics still interpreted Ps 68:19 as a direct prophecy of Christ but began wrestling with the verbal change. For Augustine, both the prophetic psalmist and the apostolic writer possess the authority of divine utterance and, when their statements are taken together, we may gather the full sense. The "gift" is the Holy Spirit, whom Christ distributed to his church after his ascension. "Captivity" refers to the captivity of Christ's people, whom he freed from the devil.[11] John Chrysostom resolved the issue of the verbal change by claiming that "the one is the same as the other."[12] His rationale was that "the whole is of God," so anything given must have been previously received from God. The captivity again refers to the devil's hold on humanity. Theodoret of Cyrus

---

[7] *Adv. Marc.* 5.8. Translation from ANF 3:446.
[8] Translation from O. S. Wintermute, "Apocalypse of Elijah: A New Translation and Introduction," in *The Old Testament Pseudepigrapha*, ed. James H. Charlesworth (Peabody, MA: Hendrickson, 1983), 1:736. This section is probably a Christian interpolation in an originally Jewish text.
[9] *Oration on the Psalms* 2 (*ANF* 6:395).
[10] *The Treatises of Cyprian*, Treatise 12, Second Book, Testimony 28 (*ANF* 5:526).
[11] *Ex. Ps.* 68.22–23; *De Trin.* 15.19.33.
[12] Chrysostom, *Hom. Eph.* 11. Translation from *NPNF* 13:103.

gave a similar rationale. He says both the receiving and the giving happened: "accepting faith from those who made their approach, he accords them grace."[13] He did not say explicitly who is receiving and who is giving, but commenting on Ps 68:19, he said that he who appeared to our ancestors will "in his own person guide the latter as well; they are not different beings: 'The same Lord is Lord of all,' remember, 'generous to all who call upon him.'"[14] Thus, he draws no distinction between Christ and Yahweh in the psalm, which allows him to see Christ receiving faith in the psalm and later giving grace to the church.

Some modern scholars, represented by John Eadie, have advanced this prophetic reading and its solution to the verbal change by arguing that לקח ("to receive") in Ps 68:19 is proleptic, meaning the "receiving" anticipates the "giving," and should be translated "to fetch."[15] The translation ἔδωκεν in Eph 4:8 would then legitimately carry over the meaning of לקח from Ps 68's context. A few of Eadie's examples of a proleptic לקח include Gen 15:9, 18:5, and 27:13. Several modern authors have held this view, including John Owen, Hugo Grotius, and Paul Baynes.[16]

Based on the background work of the previous five chapters, I see several fatal problems for the directly prophetic view. First, the psalm refers to Yahweh as the divine warrior who ascends Mount Zion to build a temple for himself. It is not prophesying directly about Christ's resurrection or ascension.[17] Second, the gifts received in the psalm are not faith or the Holy Spirit but gifts from the Israelites (perhaps including war spoil) for Yahweh to build his temple. Third, the claim fails that, if לקח in the psalm is proleptic and means "to fetch," then Paul can use δίδωμι legitimately in Eph 4:8. In none of the adduced cases of proleptic לקח does the LXX translate with δίδωμι but rather with verbs such as λαμβάνω (Gen 15:9) or φέρω (Gen 27:13). Also, wherever לקח does have the meaning "to fetch," there is almost always a prepositional phrase using ל plus a pronominal suffix to indicate for whose benefit the fetching occurs, which is missing in Ps 68:19.[18] The preposition ב does modify לקח, but this construction does not mean "to fetch," and the preposition likely is instrumental (Yahweh received gifts *through* men). The LXX's ἔλαβες ἐν ἀνθρώπῳ suggests the translator also understood the ב as instrumental or locative, not as part of a proleptic לקח formula. Thus, the

---

[13] *Comm. Ps.* 68. Translation from FC 101:387.

[14] Ibid.

[15] John Eadie, *Commentary on the Epistle to the Ephesians* (1883; repr. Minneapolis, MN: James & Klock, 1977), 282.

[16] Paul Baynes, *An Commentary upon the Whole Epistle of St. Paul to the Ephesians* (Edinburgh: James Nichol, 1866), 250; Hugo Grotius, *Annotationes in Vetus Testamentum* (Groningen: Zuidema, 1875), 1:395; William H. Goold, ed., *The Works of John Owen* (London: Banner of Trust, 1967), 4:422. These sources were found in Martin Foord, "Taking with One Hand, and Giving with the Other? The Use of Psalm 68:18 in Ephesians 4:8," in *All That the Prophets Have Declared*, ed. Matthew R. Malcolm (Croydon: Paternoster, 2015), 129, and were subsequently consulted. Charles Hodge also follows the proleptic interpretation of לקח but does not interpret the psalm as directly prophetic of Christ (*A Commentary on the Epistle to the Ephesians* [1856; repr. Grand Rapids, MI: Baker, 1980], 212–16).

[17] By the term "directly prophetic," I refer to Justin's *logoi*, which are verbal predictions of exactly what will happen in the future.

[18] Both of these criticisms are taken from Richard A. Taylor, "The Use of Psalm 68:18 in Ephesians 4:8 in Light of the Ancient Versions," *BS* 148, no. 591 (1991): 327. The first is noted also by Foord, "Taking with One Hand," 129, following Taylor.

directly prophetic view fails as an adequate explanation. This view does correctly discern a prophetic element to the psalm. Unfortunately, the Fathers do not pick up on (or do not feel the need to explicitly mention) the hermeneutical axiom that Paul uses to apply the psalm prophetically to Christ.

Borrowing from an Alternative Text Form

One of the most popular solutions to the problem of the verbal change in modern scholarship has been to suppose that Paul borrowed the wording from the Targum, which reads, "You ascended to the firmament, O prophet Moses; you captured captives, you taught the words of Torah, you gave gifts to the sons of men."[19] J. Gnilka could say emphatically, "Es besteht kein Zweifel, daß der Verf. in dieser Auslegungstradition des Psalms steht."[20] Similarly, L. Jacquet says there is no doubt that this Mosaic tradition is the source of Paul's use of the psalm.[21] Many proponents of this view believe the Targum interpreters saw it too unfit for God to receive gifts, so they transposed (intentionally or not) the letters from לקח ("to take") to חלק ("to distribute").[22]

Yet, not all who claim Targumic influence agree on Paul's hermeneutical point. Some argue that Paul uses the verse polemically against contemporary Mosaic interpretations of Ps 68:19 enshrined in the Targum.[23] Others believe Paul was using "midrash pesher," borrowing the verb from the Targum.[24] Midrash pesher is a Jewish exegetical technique that allows the theological conclusions seen in the OT text to determine the wording of the citation. Often the interpreter speaks from an inspired revelatory stance and the wording of the citation is drawn from whichever contemporary text-form makes the theological point the author desires.[25] In this case, Paul wanted to make the theological

---

[19] Although many of the authors referenced in this chapter do not hold to Paul's authorship of Ephesians, for the sake of convenience I will continue to refer to the author as Paul without intending to attribute the same view to these authors.

[20] Joachim Gnilka, *Der Epheserbrief*, 2nd ed., HTKNT 10 (Freiburg im Breisgau: Herder, 1977), 207.

[21] Louis Jacquet, *Les Psaumes et le Cœur de l'Homme: Étude Textuelle, Littéraire et Doctrinale* (Gembloux: Duculot, 1977), 354.

[22] For a further explanation and proponents of this view, beginning with H. St. J. Thackeray, see Ryszard Rubinkiewicz, "Ps 68:19 (Eph 4:8) Another Textual Tradition or Targum?," *NovT* 17, no. 3 (1975): 221; Taylor, "The Use of Psalm 68:18 in Ephesians 4:8 in Light of the Ancient Versions," 333. M. Silva says Eph 4:8 is the "most convincing example of targumic influence" among Paul's uses of the OT ("Old Testament in Paul," in *DPL*, §3). H. Hübner is less certain that Eph 4:8 is influenced by the Targum, concluding "werden wir die Frage unbeantwortet sein lassen müssen" (*An Philemon, an die Kolosser, an die Epheser*, HNT 12 [Tübingen: Mohr Siebeck, 1997], 205). The latest advocate of the use of the Targum's language in Eph 4:8 (of which I am aware) is Hanna Stettler, *Heiligung bei Paulus: Ein Beitrag aus biblisch-theologischer Sicht*, WUNT II/368 (Tübingen: Mohr Siebeck, 2014), 598n119.

[23] Markus Barth, *Ephesians: Introduction, Translation, and Commentary*, AB (Garden City, NY: Doubleday, 1974), 2:476; Craig S. Keener, *The IVP Bible Background Commentary: New Testament* (Downers Grove, IL: InterVarsity Press, 1993), 93; John C. Kirby, *Ephesians, Baptism and Pentecost: An Inquiry into the Structure and Purpose of the Epistle to the Ephesians* (London: SPCK, 1968), 146.

[24] Andrew T. Lincoln, *Ephesians*, WBC 42 (Dallas, TX: Word Books, 1990), 243; E. Earle Ellis, *Paul's Use of the Old Testament* (Eugene, OR: Wipf & Stock, 1957), 144; Jean-Noël Aletti, *Saint Paul, Épître aux Éphésiens: Introduction, Traduction et Commentaire*, EB 42 (Paris: J. Gabalda, 2001), 215–16.

[25] Scholars define midrash pesher differently, but see especially Richard Longenecker, *Biblical Exegesis in the Apostolic Period* (Grand Rapids, MI: Eerdmans, 1975), 38–45.

point that Christ did not receive gifts, but gave them, so he borrowed the verb "gave" from the Targum. Whether Paul used the Targum polemically or as an instance of midrash pesher, some see Paul using Moses typology: Moses and Torah in the Targum are replaced with Christ and grace in Ephesians, making Christ a "greater than Moses" (cf. John 1:17).[26]

One last group of commentators who believe Paul is building on the Mosaic tradition of a heavenly ascent holds that Ephesians utilizes the Gnostic redeemer myth. The author is so concerned to find a "descent" for Christ because he needs it to match the myth. For Gnilka, the author found support for the descent in v. 24 (MT) of the psalm, "The Lord said, 'I will bring back from Bashan, I will bring back from the depths of the sea.'" In Gnilka's view, the author saw God rising to the highest point, Mount Bashan, and descending to the lowest point in the depths of the sea.[27] This reading could not apply to God in the MT, which uses the hiphil form of שׁוּב, "bring back." Although there is no direct object, the hiphil form suggests that one is implied. However, the Septuagint translates the verb with ἐπιστρέφω and no direct object, which could then be understood as God himself returning from the top of Bashan and the depths of the sea. H. Schlier argued that the author of Ephesians could not have anything but the ascent-descent pattern from John in mind, which R. Bultmann convinced many of his era to believe reflected the Gnostic-redeemer myth. So for Schlier, "καταβαίνειν und ἀναβαίνειν sind hier termini technici für die Herabkunft des Erlösers auf die Erde und seinen Aufstieg von der Erde zum Himmel."[28]

The problems with these various views, all relating to supposed Targumic influence, are formidable. As we saw in the last chapter, the final form of the Psalms Targum dates between the fourth and ninth centuries AD, and there is no convincing evidence that the Mosaic interpretation of Ps 68 existed in Paul's day.[29] In fact, what we have seen is that Judaism prior to and contemporaneous with Paul interpreted the psalm eschatologically, in line with the psalm's original meaning. If Paul were using a Moses typology, it is unclear how this fits into the immediate context (Eph 4:7–16) or into Ephesians as a whole.[30] Moreover, it is unlikely Paul would expect his predominantly Gentile audience to know an interpretive tradition preserved only in an Aramaic paraphrase of the psalms.[31] Targumic influence on Eph 4:8 therefore remains unlikely, unconvincing, and fails to cohere with the context of Ephesians.

---

[26] E.g., Lincoln, *Ephesians*, 243; Aletti, *Éphésiens*, 215–16; W. Hall Harris, *The Descent of Christ: Ephesians 4:7-11 and Traditional Hebrew Imagery* (Grand Rapids, MI: Baker, 1996), 171; W. Hall Harris, "The Ascent and Descent of Christ in Ephesians 4:9–10," *BS* 151, no. 2 (1994): 208–12; Martin Pickup, "New Testament Interpretation of the Old Testament: The Theological Rationale of Midrashic Exegesis," *JETS* 51, no. 2 (2008): 370–71.

[27] Gnilka, *Epheserbrief*, 207–9.

[28] Heinrich Schlier, *Christus und die Kirche im Epheserbrief*, BHT 6 (Tübingen: Mohr Siebeck, 1930), 3. See also Petr Pokorný, *Der Epheserbrief und die Gnosis: Die Bedeutung des Haupt-Glieder-Gedankens in der entstehenden Kirche* (Berlin: Evangelische Verlagsanstalt, 1965), 77.

[29] Similarly, Frank Thielman, "Ephesians," in *Commentary on the New Testament Use of the Old Testament*, ed. G. K. Beale and D. A. Carson (Grand Rapids, MI: Baker Academic, 2007), 823.

[30] Similarly, Timothy G. Gombis, "Cosmic Lordship and Divine Gift-Giving: Psalm 68 in Ephesians 4:8," *NovT* 47, no. 4 (2005): 370; Jonathan M. Lunde and John Anthony Dunne, "Paul's Creative and Contextual Use of Psalm 68 in Ephesians 4:8," *WTJ* 74 (2012): 105.

[31] Thielman, "Ephesians," 823.

Another group of authors has recognized the weaknesses of positing Targumic influence, so they supposed instead that the author had access to other textual traditions of Ps 68:19, from which he borrowed the verb "gave." B. Lindars argued that he borrowed the verb from an earlier Christian tradition, but his theory involves speculative and dubious redactions of hypothetical early Christian traditions and has not won much favor with subsequent interpreters.[32] R. Taylor argued that Paul borrowed the verb from an earlier (hypothetical) textual tradition of Psalm 68:19 that was later enshrined in the original reading of the Peshitta.[33] But Taylor's argument that the original reading of the Peshitta was "gave" is not absolutely convincing, and to suppose that Paul drew from a hypothetical text tradition is so non-verifiable that other solutions should be sought. R. Rubinkiewicz argued that Paul borrowed from an earlier Targum manuscript that lacked any mention of Moses and Torah.[34] Supposedly, this earlier Targum saw a problem with God receiving gifts, so it changed the verb to "gave." Later tradition then added Moses and Torah into the Targum. Here again the realm of speculation and non-verifiability looms large, and his supposition that Paul borrowed ἐδωκεν from T. Dan 5:2 has no evidence to commend it.[35]

Apart from internal problems with these theories, looming large over all of them is the fact that these scholars give almost no consideration to the context of the psalm whatsoever. The change of the verb from "received" to "gave" provides such an opposite meaning that the possibility that Paul was using the psalm contextually was ruled out a priori.[36] But these scholars focused too narrowly on v. 19 of the psalm, without considering whether much thematic coherence existed between the entire psalm and Eph 4:7–16. In fact, W. Hall Harris's oft-cited dissertation *The Descent of Christ*, published in 1996, contains no sustained exegesis of the psalm at all.[37] It may be that Eph 4:8 distorts the context of the psalm or that the psalm's context matters little, but that no one would make the effort to engage the entire contextual meaning of the psalm is troubling. Indeed, in 1952 C. H. Dodd published his *According to the Scriptures*, whose lasting contribution (although it was not the main argument) was to

---

[32] Barnabas Lindars, *New Testament Apologetic: The Doctrinal Significance of the Old Testament Quotations* (London: SCM Press, 1961), 52–54. See criticisms in, e.g., Gary V. Smith, "Paul's Use of Psalm 68:18 in Ephesians 4:8," *JETS* 18, no. 3 (1975): 188–89. For a position similar to Lindars, see also Rudolf Schnackenburg, *Der Brief an die Epheser*, EKKNT (Zürich: Benziger, 1982), 179–80.

[33] The date of the translation of the Old Testament into Syriac, which is known as the Old Testament Peshitta, is uncertain. It probably goes back to the second century AD (Sebastian P. Brock, "The Earliest Syriac Literature," in *The Cambridge History of Early Christian Literature*, ed. Frances Young, Lewis Aryes, and Andrew Louth [Cambridge: Cambridge University Press, 2004], 163). H. J. Holtzmann had earlier noted the possible connection between the Targum and the Peshitta (*Kritik der Epheser- und Kolosserbriefe: Auf Grund einer Analyse ihres Verwandtschaftsverhältnisses* [Leipzig: Wilhelm Engelmann, 1872], 244).

[34] Rubinkiewicz, "Ps 68:19 (Eph 4:8) Another Textual Tradition or Targum?," 219–24.

[35] Lincoln also finds Rubinkiewicz's argument from T. Dan. 5:10–11 unconvincing, saying it "will not bear the weight he places on it" (*Ephesians*, 243). Taylor calls Rubinkiewicz's line of argumentation "faulty" ("The Use of Psalm 68:18 in Ephesians 4:8 in Light of the Ancient Versions," 335n45). See further criticism in Lunde and Dunne, "Paul's Creative and Contextual Use of Psalm 68 in Ephesians 4:8," 104n24.

[36] E.g., Holtzmann says flatly that Paul used the psalm arbitrarily (*Kritik der Epheser- und Kolosserbriefe*, 6).

[37] Harris, *The Descent of Christ*.

demonstrate the plausibility that when the NT authors cite from the OT, they usually have the wider context in mind.[38] Reception of Dodd's conclusions have been mixed,[39] but in my opinion the enduring lesson from Dodd is that one must *at least consider* whether the NT author has cited an OT passage with the context in mind. And indeed, a more recent group of scholars studying Paul's use of Ps 68:19 has heeded Dodd's call to investigate the OT context and determine to what extent, if any, Paul is quoting with regard for the meaning of the psalm. To these commentators we now turn.

Contextual Solutions to Paul's Use of Psalm 68:19

Gary Smith in 1975 argued that Psalm 68:19 refers to God "taking captive" the Levites; he took them to serve him (Num 8:6–11) and then "gave" them as "gifts" to Aaron and his sons for service (Num 8:19, 18:6).[40] Paul thus uses the passage analogically: just as God "took captive" men, gifted them with the ability to serve the people of God, and gave them as a gift to the people, so he has done with the church. Smith was commendably one of the first to explore the psalm's context seriously and suggest a contextually based solution. However, Smith's solution suffers from a couple of problems. First, Num 18:6 says God "took" the Levites and "gave" them as a "gift" to Israel. But the psalm says God *received* gifts, not that he *took and then gave* gifts. This proposal is too similar to the "proleptic לקח" solution. Second, he interprets "he took captive captives" as God taking captive the Levites. But "take captive" is militant language of defeating enemies and does not fittingly describe God's setting apart of the Levites for service. Moreover, Ps 68:19 is an allusion to Judg 5:12, which does not refer to the Levites but rather to Barak taking captive the enemy in war.

Rainer Schwindt in 2002 paid even more attention to the psalm's context than did Smith. He sees the narrative movement in the psalm from the Exodus, through the wilderness, to the taking of the land, and to the battle against Sisera in vv. 12–15.[41] The psalm borrowed from Ugaritic mythology in order to characterize Yahweh as a new Baal figure, who descends to the realm of the dead but then ascends to defeat Mot. Schwindt then delineates three strands of interpretation in Judaism: a Yahwistic interpretation similar to the original meaning of the psalm, a Mosaic-law interpretation, and a Mosaic-mystic interpretation. Ephesians' use of the psalm appears to follow the OT meaning insofar as the ascent of Christ manifests his victory over the powers in the entire cosmos, but there appears to be more of an echo with the "Mose-Tora-Soteriologie" tradition since "Christus fungiert wie Mose als Heilsmittler der Menschen."[42] But the tradition is altered: Christ's gift is not the Torah but himself in

---

[38] C. H. Dodd, *According to the Scriptures: The Sub-Structure of New Testament Theology* (London: Nisbet, 1952), esp. 47–59, 72–73, 102–3, 109, 128–33.
[39] For one of the earliest and harshest criticisms of Dodd's conclusions, see Albert C. Sundberg Jr., "Response Against C. H. Dodd's View: On Testimonies," in *The Right Doctrine from the Wrong Texts: Essays on the Old Testament in the New*, ed. G. K. Beale (Grand Rapids, MI: Baker Books, 1994), 182–94.
[40] Gary V. Smith, "Paul's Use of Psalm 68:18 in Ephesians 4:8," *JETS* 18, no. 3 (1975): 181–89.
[41] Rainer Schwindt, *Das Weltbild des Epheserbriefes: Eine religionsgeschichtlich-exegetische Studie*, WUNT 148 (Tübingen: Mohr Siebeck, 2002), 400.
[42] Ibid., 430.

his pneumatical existence acquired through his death and resurrection. In this sense, Ephesians sets itself apart from the Moses–Torah tradition, which bloomed fully in the rabbinic period. Schwindt uses a strong methodology with careful attention to ancient Near Eastern and Jewish sources. But he misses much in his analysis, including the centrality of the gifts for the temple in both Ps 68 and Eph 4:7–16, the eschatological sections of the psalm, and the eschatological interpretations in Judaism. Also, his reliance on Baal traditions is misguided, as I have argued in Chapter 3.

In 2005, Timothy Gombis engaged the psalm's context by first noting the ancient Near Eastern divine warfare topos that is present in Ps 68. He claims that the topos concludes with the deity blessing his people with gifts.[43] Gombis proposes that Paul employed this myth in Eph 4, as well as in Eph 2, and views Christ as the highest deity who has triumphed over the cosmic powers (Eph 1:20–23) and who subsequently gives gifts to his people.[44] Paul changed the verb "received" to "gave" because at the end of the psalm Yahweh gives gifts to his people (68:36), namely, "strength" and "power." Paul was thus not only quoting from Psalm 68:19 but also "appropriating the narrative movement of the entire psalm."[45] Gombis's proposal is much stronger than Smith's and correctly identifies the divine builder topos in the psalm, although he misses the temple connotations in Eph 4:11–16. Also, it is questionable whether the "strength" and "power" in Ps 68:36 should be considered "gifts" to the people. Giving strength and power to the people refers not to literal gifts but metaphorically to God's exercise of his power on behalf of Israel as depicted throughout the psalm. The gifts in Ps 68:19 are not strength and power but rather materials for building God's temple. Gombis advanced our understanding of this quotation, but more work was to be done.[46]

Jonathan Lunde and John Dunne have recently argued that Paul's use is typological and his change of verb a form of midrash pesher. Paul sees Yahweh's ascent to the temple, his subjugation of enemies, and subsequent blessing of his people from his temple (Ps 68:30, 36) as a type of Christ's ascent to the heavenly temple at the right hand of God, subjugation of spiritual powers, and subsequent blessing of his people with the Spirit from the heavenlies.[47] Paul reflected on the entirety of the psalm and interpreted it in light of Christ's fulfillment, hence the change of agent from Yahweh to Christ and of verb from "received" to "gave." Lunde and Dunn correctly bring out much of the thematic coherence between the two passages, but they rely on Ps 68:30, 36, which express God's giving nature, as the rationale for Paul's verbal change. As I noted regarding Gombis's use of these verses, they simply cannot bear the weight of Paul's intentional change of "received" to its complete opposite "gave." Even if the typological pattern that Lunde and Dunn discern exists in the psalm, there must be a more persuasive reason for Paul to have changed the verb.

---

[43] Gombis, "Cosmic Lordship and Divine Gift-Giving," 374.
[44] Ibid., 373. On this theme in Ephesians 2, see Gombis's article "Ephesians 2 as a Narrative of Divine Warfare," *JSNT* 26 (2004): 403–18.
[45] Ibid., 375.
[46] William N. Wilder followed Gombis's proposal that the "strength" and "power" in Ps 68:36 are the key to Paul's verbal change, but his article focuses on tenuous links between Ephesians and Isaiah and gives no sustained exegesis of the psalm ("The Use (or Abuse) of Power in High Places: Gifts Given and Received in Isaiah, Psalm 68, and Ephesians 4:8," *BBR* 20, no. 2 [2010]: 185–99).
[47] Lunde and Dunne, "Paul's Creative and Contextual Use of Psalm 68 in Ephesians 4:8," 99–117.

The most recent study of Ps 68:19 in Eph 4:8 comes from Martin Foord, who most fruitfully explores the context of the psalm.[48] He argues for a narrative reading of the psalm culminating in the reception of gifts from the Israelites to build God's temple. He connects these temple-gifts with the church as a temple in Eph 2:19–22. Foord therefore corroborates my reading of the psalm, but he fails to see the same temple concept in Eph 4:11–16, which is essential to understanding how Paul is using the psalm. He helpfully points to several instances of God "giving" throughout the psalms and the typological connection between Yahweh's ascent to Zion and Jesus's ascent to the heavenlies. He also correctly interprets the "gifts" in Ephesians as the ministers of the church and suggests that the reason for the change to "gave" is to emphasize "*the difference and superiority of Christ's ascension* compared to the ark's ascension to Zion. Christ's ascension is superior because he as ruler not only receives tribute gifts but also shares them with his people."[49] Foord, then, like Dunne and Lunde, believes the rationale for the verb change is that Paul is quoting the psalm in the language with which, retrospectively, Paul understands it to be fulfilled. Rather than slavishly quoting the psalm, Paul cites it using language to express the way it was actually fulfilled. Foord's analysis is similar in many ways to my own and I commend his article as a fruitful investigation of the psalm's context for insights on why Paul chose to cite Ps 68:19.[50] Nevertheless, his paper would have improved had he discussed the divine builder motif in the psalm and observed that the church is described as a temple in Eph 4:11–16. Furthermore, (1) his analysis of Ps 68's use of the OT is relegated to a couple of sentences on its use of Judg 5:12; (2) he is missing a thorough examination of Judaism's use of the psalm (especially the eschatological tradition); and (3) he does not provide adequate prophetic basis in the psalm for Paul's eschatological application of it. Thus, Foord's article is in my view the best essay written to date on this issue and is correct as far it goes, but many key pieces of the puzzle are still missing.

One could draw several implications from this history of research section, but I propose one that I find particularly important and foundational for my own thesis. As one follows the discussion of Ps 68:19 in Eph 4:8, one sees that as scholars began spending more effort exploring the context of the psalm, more light has been shed on the thematic coherence between the two passages and on Paul's rationale for citing Ps 68:19. Proposals to explain Paul's change of the verb have also become more insightful and plausible. Thus, those who have followed in Dodd's footsteps by at least considering the possibility that the NT authors cite the OT contextually (to more or less degrees) have greatly enhanced our understanding not only of Paul's use of the psalm but of the psalm itself. Notably, several NT scholars examining Eph 4:8 have correctly discerned the Exodus to Zion narrative in the psalm, while such a reading continues to elude OT

---

[48] Foord, "Taking with One Hand," 127–38.
[49] Ibid., 137, emphasis original.
[50] I have been shaping my view of Eph 4:8 since 2012 and had never encountered any of Foord's ideas until his essay was published in 2015. His brief argumentation provides some corroboration for my views, even though the brevity of his essay lacks the rigor required to defend his views of Ps 68 against the majority of critical commentators who would disagree with his interpretation of the psalm.

scholars. If the narratival reading is correct, as I have argued, then we see here support for the idea that the two testaments are mutually enlightening. While one does not want to read the NT completely into the OT, one should take seriously how the NT authors understand the OT, since it may lead to new vistas in our own quest for the meaning of OT passages.

In this next section, I build on this tradition of exploring the psalm's context for thematic coherence with Eph 4:7–16 and for a rationale for Paul's use of Ps 68:19 and his verbal change. The previous five chapters have laid the groundwork for comprehending the major themes of the psalm and its reception among Jewish interpreters. I will now demonstrate that the major themes of the psalm are similarly found in Eph 4:7–16 and that the main point of Ps 68:19 is also the same main point of Paul's citation in Eph 4:8, although eschatologically reconfigured. My interpretation of Paul's use of the psalm must also make sense of the descent in Eph 4:9–10, which will constitute the next section. Finally, I will conclude by discussing how Paul's use of the psalm contributes to his overall theology and how Eph 4:7–16 speaks powerfully to the socioreligious situation of Christians in Asia Minor.

Paul's Use of Psalm 68:19 in Ephesians 4:8

Paul's citation of the psalm largely follows the Greek versions, but he makes several changes (more or less depending on which Greek version he was reading or had memorized). The following Greek text of Ps 67:19 (Rahlfs) is used as a hypothetical base text, but variants are also mentioned below:

Ps 67:19:   ἀνέβης εἰς ὕψος ᾐχμαλώτευσας αἰχμαλωσίαν ἔλαβες δόματα ἐν ἀνθρώπῳ.[51]

Eph 4:8:   ἀναβὰς εἰς ὕψος ᾐχμαλώτευσεν αἰχμαλωσίαν, ἔδωκεν δόματα τοῖς ἀνθρώποις.

The first change he makes is from the indicative ἀνέβης to the participial form ἀναβὰς, which subordinates the ascension clause to ᾐχμαλώτευσεν so that "he took captive captives" receives more emphasis. The participial change also more closely correlates the ascension with the taking of captives, so that Christ took captives while or by means of ascending.[52] This change is pragmatic, not semantic, and is therefore not problematic in any sense. The second change that Paul makes is to alter the second-person verbs to third-person verbs, thereby shifting agents from Yahweh to Christ.[53]

---

[51] This Greek text is found in Alfred Rahlfs, *Septuaginta: id est Vetus Testamentum graece iuxta LXX interpretes* (Stuttgart, Deutsche Bibelgesellschaft, 1935).

[52] The aorist ἀναβὰς could express an event antecedent to the aorist ᾐχμαλώτευσεν, but more likely it expresses contemporary time, as often in Paul's letters (Daniel B. Wallace, *Greek Grammar beyond the Basics: An Exegetical Syntax of the New Testament* [Grand Rapids, MI: Zondervan, 1996], 624–25).

[53] The assumption that Yahweh was the agent of the assent in the Hebrew version of the psalm depends on my earlier exegesis of the psalm in Chapter 2.

Again, this is not a problematic alteration since Paul sees the verse somehow fulfilled in Christ, and thus he alters the grammar accordingly.

A third alteration depends on the Greek version Paul was reading or had memorized, since Sinaiticus has ἀνθρώποις and Vaticanus has ἀνθρώπῳ. Both manuscripts have ἐν for the Hebrew ב. Sinaiticus's plural ἀνθρώποις captures the collective sense of אדם better than Vaticanus's ἀνθρώπῳ, but it is difficult to know which rendering Paul had before him or had memorized. If Paul did alter ἀνθρώπῳ to ἀνθρώποις, it is insignificant since it was grammatically required for the noun to function as an indirect object of ἔδωκεν. Ephesians 4:8 has a minor variant ἐν ἀνθρώποις (as opposed to τοῖς ἀνθρώποις in all other manuscripts), but only in some citations from Jerome (d. AD 420) and late manuscripts such as F, G, 614, 630, 2464, which are likely conforming Paul's τοῖς to the ἐν of the Greek psalm manuscripts. So whether Paul altered ἀνθρώπῳ to ἀνθρώποις, he definitely changed ἐν to τοῖς.[54] Yet this change is also insignificant, since it is virtually dictated by ἔδωκεν. In other words, one can *receive* "among," "through," or "because of" men (בָּאָדָם), but *giving* requires an indirect object (either implicitly or explicitly), lest we be left wondering *to whom* Christ gave these gifts. Any issue with alterations from ἐν ἀνθρώπῳ to τοῖς ἀνθρώποις is therefore pushed back to the issue of Paul's use of ἔδωκεν instead of ἔλαβες.

This change from ἔλαβες to ἔδωκεν is the final alteration, and the one that has caused most of the theological and academic discussion on this quotation. As noted earlier, ἔλαβες in Ps 68:19 cannot be interpreted proleptically to mean "to fetch" so that ἔδωκεν is virtually equivalent. In fact, ἔδωκεν signifies the exact opposite meaning of ἔλαβες. In what follows, I will summarize the major themes excavated throughout this study in order to explain and provide sufficient warrant for Paul's verbal change.

We saw in Chapter 1 that Eph 4:7–16 speaks of the gifts that Christ has given the church in order that it might grow up into Christ in every way as the eschatological temple. These gifts are technically the *charismata*, the gifts of the Holy Spirit. Among these gifts are the gifts related to teaching and leading—the gifts of apostleship, prophecy, evangelism, shepherding, and teaching—which are given to a specific set of believers to equip the saints so that they might achieve their goal of becoming a mature temple and body of Christ. Paul, via metonymy, refers to the individuals who have received these teaching-specific gifts as the gifts themselves. Likewise all Christians, because they have received *charismata*, can be referred to as gifts via metonymy. Thus, Christ gives gifts in order to build up his church as the eschatological temple of God, or as 2:21–22 refers to the church, a "holy temple" and "dwelling place" for God.

While Eph 4:8 speaks of giving gifts for building up the temple, so also Ps 68:19 speaks of the reception of gifts for building up the temple. Those who have focused on the verbal change have often seen little thematic coherence between these two verses in

---

[54] A choice of ἀνθρώποις over ἀνθρώπῳ makes little semantic difference, except to pluralize the recipients of Christ's gifts. In fact, the Vaticanus's ἀνθρώπῳ may simply be an attempt to render literally the singular word אדם, despite its collective nature. This alteration (if indeed Paul's Greek text read ἀνθρώπῳ) is therefore not problematic. Nevertheless, it may provide a hint to the solution to Paul's major change of ἔλαβες to ἔδωκεν. I discuss this in full below, but the nature of Christ's fulfillment of the psalm (that he gave gives to *men*, not to *a man*, as ἀνθρώπῳ could be understood) necessitated the way in which Paul had to cite the verse.

their respective contexts. But apart from the difference between "received" and "gave," the idea of each verse is exactly the same. In fact, in both verses, *someone* is giving gifts: in the psalm, the Israelites give the gifts, while in Ephesians, Christ gives the gifts. Thus, the idea of gifts being given to constitute the building blocks of the temple is the point of both Ps 68:19 and Eph 4:8. This conclusion is important for understanding why Paul chose to cite Ps 68:19 and why he chose to change the verb.

Another point of thematic coherence between the two passages is the divine builder topos. Chapter 3 documented this topos thoroughly in five different ANE cultures and in the OT itself. The topos is clear in the psalm also: Yahweh defeats his enemies in Egypt, the wilderness, Canaan, and Jerusalem; he then receives gifts from his devotees (at least partially consisting of war spoil) in order to build himself an eternal temple in which he will receive tribute from foreign kings who submit to him.

Writing in the first century, Paul does not use a strict divine warrior topos, but he definitely presents Christ as the divine warrior extraordinaire. Christ's resurrection and ascension has placed him "far above all rule and authority and power and ruling power" (Eph 1:21). Through his resurrection and ascension, he took these spiritual powers captive (4:8) by defeating them on the cross (cf. Col 2:15). By being united to their master warrior (i.e., being "in Christ"), the church is empowered to "be strong" (Eph 6:10) and to "stand against the schemes of the devil" (6:11). Although Christ has won the decisive victory over the evil powers, the church still struggles against them until the consummation (6:12). The major source for the "armor of God" language in 6:11–18 is Isa 59:17 ("righteousness as a breastplate . . . helmet of salvation"), and the armor is God's as he fights for Israel: "his own arm brought him salvation, and his righteousness upheld him" (59:16). Ephesians 5:14 also likely taps into this section of Isaiah to construct an interpretive and conflated citation of Isa 26:19 and 60:1–2, drawing on themes such as the believers' resurrection and calling to light on the basis of God's redemption through war against his peoples' enemies.[55] Christ's depiction as the divine warrior is therefore rooted in God's warfare on behalf of Israel, and the church is to be empowered by its head, who supplies them with the power they need to wage the remaining warfare until the consummation.

A third point of thematic coherence is the ascension. In the psalm, Yahweh's ascent to Mount Zion is the capstone of the narratival movement. Both before and after Yahweh's ascension in the psalm is a record of God's faithful protection of Israel in the past and future, and bookending the entire psalm are calls to praise. Likewise in Paul's depiction of Christ in Ephesians, the ascension stands at the center of much of his theological discourse. As Yahweh's ascent in the psalm leads to his taking captives, so also in Ephesians Christ's resurrection and ascension are tied directly to his defeat of the spiritual powers (Eph 1:20–22; 4:8–10).

The thematic continuities might lead one to believe that Paul is simply drawing an analogy: Christ's ascension and taking captive of the spiritual powers is analogically comparable to what Yahweh did in the psalm. But for several reasons, I believe Paul correctly read the psalm as more than a historical analogy to his knowledge and

---

[55] See especially Jonathan Lunde and John Anthony Dunne, "Paul's Creative and Contextual Use of Isaiah in Ephesians 5:14," *JETS* 55, no. 1 (2012): 87–110.

experience of Christ's work. First, Ps 68:17 says that Yahweh will reign on Mount Zion in his temple "forever." This claim is perhaps a reinforcement of Exod 15:17–18, which prophesies that God will build his temple and rule "forever and ever."[56] But following the destruction of the first temple, God no longer dwelt on Mount Zion. The temple was rebuilt, but the result was clearly anticlimactic and lacked the fulfillment of previous promises regarding the temple for which the Israelites longed (Hag 2:9; Ezra 3:12). There is also a question of whether God's glory had ever returned to the second temple, since such an event is not recorded as it was with the first temple (Exod 40:34–35; 1 Kgs 8:11). The political subjugation of Israel in Paul's day would lead him to disappointment in the psalm's claims about God's eternal dominion and reign from Mount Zion (vv. 30, 33, 36). This unfulfilled claim would lead Paul to reflect on God's faithfulness to fulfill these promises made by the psalmist. Paul therefore infers that this promise has been fulfilled through Christ by his building up an indestructible and eternal temple and dwelling place for God. No longer does God physically defeat Israel's foes and subsequently establish a physical temple to declare his majesty and dominion over nations. Now God, in Jesus, has defeated the principalities and powers, and Christ has ascended to the heavenlies and reigns over the nations with an eternal dominion. Jesus has constituted a new temple in himself, and all who are united with him through faith are part of that temple. Jesus's inaugurated reign will be consummated when all the nations worship him, just as the psalm declares: "Kingdoms of the earth, sing to God! Praise the Lord!" (v. 33; cf. Phil 2:11).

A second reason for seeing more than just an analogy between Ps 68:19 and Eph 4:8 is that, as I argued in Chapter 4, the second half of the psalm prophesies about God's provision for his people in the future. Part of that provision involves his eternal dwelling among them, and part of it includes his continued warfare on their behalf. The eschatological interpretation of the psalm in the Qumran community and the possible eschatological interpretation by the editors of the psalter and the Septuagint translator(s) provides a precedent for Paul to understand the psalm similarly. That is, it is not unreasonable to believe Paul read it prophetically in the same manner as some of his predecessors.

Perhaps the strongest reason to support the idea that Paul read the psalm prophetically is his use of διό before his introductory formula λέγει in Eph 4:8.[57] Most translations render διό as "therefore," but many commentators find this odd: Christ gave gifts, *and this is why Scripture says* that Yahweh ascended on high and received

---

[56] Exod 15:18 uses לְעֹלָם וָעֶד, "forever and ever," while Ps 68:16 uses לָנֶצַח, "forever." The word עוֹלָם can refer to (1) a long duration of the past; (2) a long duration of the future, either as long as one's lifetime or for eternity; (3) an age; (4) the world or created order; (5) the underworld; or (6) to the Lord as the Eternal or Ancient One (David J. A. Clines, ed., *The Dictionary of Classical Hebrew* [Sheffield: Sheffield Phoenix Press, 2007], 6:300–307). Its use in Exod 15:18, coupled with עֶד, suggests "unto everlastingness" or "forever and ever" (ibid., 305). It is therefore equivalent to לָנֶצַח in Ps 68:16, which elsewhere is used to express "in perpetuity" or "everlastingness" (e.g., Isa 13:20, 25:8; Ps 9:7; Job 4:20; Amos 8:7).

[57] Recall that while most consider διό λέγει the introductory formula in Eph 4:8 and 5:14, Paul often uses only λέγει as an introductory formula (e.g., 2 Cor 6:2; Gal 3:16; Rom 15:10), so διό is best understood as a discourse marker expressing the relationship between v. 7 and the quotation of Ps 68:19 in Eph 4:8.

gifts. How could a future event be the reason a Scripture was written a thousand years before? Many commentators try to work around the oddity by interpreting διό as signaling grounds or proof to support v. 7, making διό into a γάρ.[58] But διό cannot signal grounds or proof; it is a strong inferential particle.[59] Rather than attempting to interpret the particle contrary to its meaning, we should understand it to function as strong evidence that Paul read Ps 68 prophetically. Just as the Qumran community felt that Ps 68 was written to predict what would be fulfilled in their day (hence the pesher on Ps 68), and just as Paul says elsewhere that Israel's wilderness episodes were recorded for "our instruction" (1 Cor 10:11), so also he believed that the psalm was written for the sake of its future fulfillment. The reason Ps 68 was recorded was to establish a historical type that would later elucidate the significance of the death and resurrection of Christ and his distribution of gifts to build up the eschatological temple. Paul's odd use of διό therefore enlightens us to his understanding of God's providence over the minute details of history, including even the selection of the very words preserved in our Scriptures.

In sum, the combination of thematic continuity, the inherently prophetic element of the psalm (v. 19 and especially vv. 20–36), and the διό in Eph 4:8 leads to the conclusion that Paul interpreted the psalm typologically. Paul understood many OT events, persons, or institutions to be impresses on history that created a pattern that must necessarily be fulfilled in God's divine plan (οἰκονομία, Eph 1:10; 3:2; 3:9). The word τύπος in classical Greek could mean "blow," "the effect of a blow," "cast (replica made in a mold)," "carved figure," "form, style (grammatical)," "archetype," "outline, sketch," or "prescribed ethical model."[60] In the NT, τύπος could mean "mark" (John 20:25), "moral example" (1 Pet 5:3; Phil 3:17; 1 Thess 1:7; 2 Thess 3:9; Titus 2:7), "norm" (Rom 6:17) and "type."[61] The last definition of "type" is the technical theological term that Paul uses in Rom 5:14 and 1 Cor 10:6 (cf. τυπικῶς in 10:11) to refer to persons or events in the past that became a historical pattern to be fulfilled by Christ or the church. This technical meaning is related closely to the classical meaning "mold" in that the event, person, or institution creates a mold in history that must be fulfilled later.[62] Paul therefore read the psalm such that Yahweh impressed a mold on history through his actions. Promises were made in the psalm that were not fulfilled, but

---

[58] E.g., William J. Larkin, *Ephesians: A Handbook on the Greek Text*, BHGNT (Waco, TX: Baylor University Press, 2009), 74; Horacio E. Lona, *Die Eschatologie im Kolosser- und Epheserbrief*, FB 48 (Würzburg: Echter Verlag, 1984), 323; Hübner, *Epheser*, 204; Andreas Lindemann, *Die Aufhebung der Zeit: Geschichtsverständnis und Eschatologie im Epheserbrief*, SNT 12 (Gütersloh: Gütersloher Verlagshaus, 1975), 84. The CSB translates it as "for."

[59] All the standard lexicons list it as inferential or resultant: BDAG, s.v. διό; Joseph Henry Thayer, *A Greek-English Lexicon of the New Testament*, electronic edition (International Bible Translators, 1998–2000), s.v. διό; Henry George Liddell, Robert Scott, Henry Stuart Jones, and Roderick McKenzie, eds., *A Greek-English Lexicon* (Oxford: Clarendon Press, 1996), s.v. διό; J. P. Louw and Eugene Albert Nida, *Greek-English Lexicon of the New Testament: Based on Semantic Domains* (Swindon: United Bible Societies, 1999), 89.47 διό.

[60] Richard M. Davidson, *Typology in Scripture: A Study of Hermeneutical τύπος Structures*, AUSDDS (Berrien Springs, MI: Andrews University Press, 1981), 115–90.

[61] Leonhard Goppelt, "τύπος," *TDNT* 8:246–52.

[62] I say "must" because types are prophetic, since they are intended by God to foreshadow his future intended acts in history. See further in Todd A. Scacewater, "The Predictive Nature of Typology in John 12:37–43," *WTJ* 75, no. 1 (2013): 129–43.

because God's nature is consistent and his covenantal loyalty does not fail, his people can know that he will act similarly in the future as he has in the past. The ascension to Mount Zion to build his temple was a pattern firmly fulfilled by Christ when he rose to the heavenlies after his resurrection and gave gifts to build up the eschatological temple of God. One can also see the essential typological feature of escalation since Christ's ascension and temple-building were not temporary as in the OT but were irreversible, eschatological acts in the beginning stages of "the latter days" alluded to throughout the latter half of Ps 68.[63]

Paul's Change from "Received" to "Gave"

Before providing my rationale for Paul's verbal change, I suggest first that if the bulk of my work thus far is on the right track, the verbal change is far less important than it has been made out to be. I have argued for more thematic coherence between Ps 68:19 and Eph 4:8 than any previous study and have argued that the main point of both verses is the same. Moreover, as I noted earlier, while "received" and "gave" are opposite in meaning, in both verses someone is still giving: the Israelites in the psalm and Christ in Ephesians. The respective verbs used by the psalmist and Paul allow the focus of the verse to remain on Yahweh and Christ, the divine builders. Thus, Paul has by no means distorted the meaning of Ps 68:19, nor has he violated its context. Like the author of 1QM, he has read Ps 68 contextually and used it responsibly, yet creatively.

Ultimately, though, a convincing reason for Paul's verbal change must be proposed. I propose that Paul had no other way he could have quoted the psalm because his intention in citing it was to declare the fulfillment of the typological pattern, and that fulfillment had occurred in exactly the way he recorded it. The first temple was physical, made with hands. But when Christ ascended and fulfilled the divine builder pattern set in Ps 68:19, he fulfilled it not by receiving physical gifts with which to build a temple but by giving his own eschatological gifts to believers so that he could build his own temple. He built this temple through the Spirit (Eph 2:22), and it is therefore imperishable, making it greater than the first and second temples, which were destroyed by the hands of men. Paul changed the verb because it was the only way he could cite it in light of the way Christ fulfilled the psalm. God's people did not need to give Christ anything for him to build his temple. He built it by his resurrection from the dead and subsequent gifting of believers with the Spirit. Also, there is no problem

---

[63] Many believe escalation is necessary for typology, for without it the two events would simply be analogous. See Leonhard Goppelt, *Typos: The Typological Interpretation of the Old Testament in the New*, trans. Donald Madvig (1939; repr. Grand Rapids, MI: Eerdmans, 1982), 199; E. Earle Ellis, *Prophecy and Hermeneutic in Early Christianity: New Testament Essays* (Eugene, OR: Wipf and Stock, 2003), 169; R. T. France, *Jesus and the Old Testament: His Application of Old Testament Passages to Himself and His Mission* (Vancouver, B.C.: Regent College, 1998), 38–43; G. K. Beale, *Handbook on the New Testament Use of the Old Testament: Exegesis and Interpretation* (Grand Rapids, MI: Baker Academic, 2012), 13–25. For an extended treatment of typology from an analogical perspective that requires no escalation, see Gerhard von Rad, *Old Testament Theology: The Theology of Israel's Prophetic Traditions*, trans. D. M. G. Stalker, OTL (Louisville, KY: Westminster John Knox Press, 1965), 2:319–87.

with the discontinuity between the typological event and its fulfillment because Ps 68:19 is not a direct prophecy of what will happen specifically but rather an event whose principles and messages about God carry forward to its fulfillment. Typological events never correspond exactly with their antitypes, especially because they are analogically foreshadowing them and because the escalated element in the antitype makes it necessarily unlike its OT corresponding reality to some degree.

Recently, L. Hurtado has noticed a similar phenomenon when Ps 110:1 is quoted or alluded to in various NT texts. When NT authors quote Ps 110:1, they use the Septuagint's ἐκ δεξιῶν, but when they allude to the verse, they use ἐν δεξιᾷ. He suggests that, just as in the only two times the LXX describes someone ἐν δεξιᾷ to another (1 Esd 4:29; 1 Chr 6:24), the preposition ἐν connotes a more intimate relationship than does ἐκ.[64] So early Christian formulas to express Christ's rule at the right hand were formulated with phraseology (ἐν δεξιᾷ) that cohered more exactly with their convictions arising from their religious experience, rather than using the exact wording of the Scriptures. Early Christians recognized the intimate relationship between the Son and the Father, so when alluding to Ps 110:1 they used language that matched their communal experience, rather than slavishly citing the LXX's ἐκ δεξιῶν, which lacks the intimate connotation they desired to communicate. "They knew very well that their experiences reflected new divine acts, giving a new standpoint from which to approach their Scriptures in the hope of perceiving things anew."[65]

While this phenomena is not an exact parallel because Paul alters the wording of a quotation, the premise is the same. Paul is approaching the quotation from the retrospective view of Jesus's death and resurrection, which resulted in the building of his victorious temple and thus also in the typological fulfillment of Ps 68:19. He is confronted with the reality that Ps 68:19 indirectly prophesied Jesus's ascent to the heavenlies and with the reality that Jesus did not need to receive gifts to build his temple because of the mysterious nature of the fulfillment (cf. μυστήριον in Eph 1:9; 3:3, 4, 9; 5:32; 6:19). There is always some discontinuity with a typological fulfillment because the historical situation is necessarily different (no historical moment is exactly the same), so Paul had no issue with altering the wording of Ps 68:19 to express the same truth according to the reality of the historical fulfillment.

Christ's Descent in Ephesians 4:9–10

Any view of how Paul uses Ps 68:19 in Eph 4:8 must deal adequately with Christ's descent in Eph 4:9–10. One must answer what the descent is, how Paul derived it from the psalm (if he did at all), and whether that derivation is legitimate. Ephesians 4:9 follows v. 8 with τὸ δὲ ἀνέβη τί ἐστιν. This phrase can be translated literally as, "Now, this, 'he ascended,' what is it?" However, almost all translations recognize this phrase

---

[64] Larry Hurtado, "Two Case Studies in Earliest Christological Readings," in *All that the Prophets Have Declared*, ed. Malcolm, 12–13.
[65] Ibid., 22.

as signaling Paul's quest for meaning and translate τί ἐστιν as "what does it mean?"[66] It seems he is inquiring only into the phrase "he ascended,"[67] but more likely this is an idiomatic use of the neuter article that asks not for the meaning of "he ascended" but for the meaning of the entire quotation.[68] Similarly, P. T. O'Brien says that Paul now "expounds its meaning," that is, the meaning of the quotation of Ps 68:19.[69] Thus, Eph 4:9–10 expounds the meaning of the quotation of Ps 68:19 in Eph 4:8.

There are some text-critical issues in Eph 4:9 that bear on its interpretation. NA[28] reads κατέβη εἰς τὰ κατώτερα [μέρη] τῆς γῆς. The word μέρη ("parts") is found in ℵ, A, B, C, D², and others, while it is missing in 𝔓[46] and in the first corrector of D and others. External evidence favors the inclusion of μέρη, although one could argue that 𝔓[46] is significant enough to make the decision too difficult to decide. In any case, whether it is original or not, it simply makes explicit the substantival function of the article τά. The phrase τὰ κατώτερα on its own is translated "the lower parts," so whether μέρη is included is not significant for any of the views.

Another important text-critical issue is that πρῶτον is found in the second corrector of ℵ, B, the third corrector of C, the second corrector of D, and almost all Byzantine miniscules. It is also found in early versions such as the Vulgate, some of the Itala (Old Latin) manuscripts, the Peshitta, most of the old Sahidic Coptic manuscripts, and the Gothic and Aramean versions.[70] Yet πρῶτον is lacking in 𝔓[46], ℵ and its first corrector, A, the first corrector of C, D, and other later manuscripts. With Vaticanus being its only solid early support, πρῶτον is surely a scribal gloss to make explicit the logical and temporal relationship between the ascent and descent.[71] It is easier to see how a scribe would add the word to clarify the verse than to see how it came to be omitted. Also, this addition was perhaps facilitated further by the order of descent followed by ascent in the Apostles' Creed.

Ephesians 4:9–10 as a Descent to Hades

There are three interpretations of the descent. Throughout the early Fathers and up until the Reformation, the descent in Eph 4:9 was unanimously understood as Christ's descent to Hades.[72] In this view, τῆς γῆς in Eph 4:9 is interpreted as a partitive genitive ("the lower parts of the earth itself").[73] In Irenaeus's *Demonstration of the Apostolic*

---

[66] This translation is given with slightly different wording and word order by CJB, CSB, ESV, NAB, NASB, NET, NIV, NJB, NLT, and NRSV.
[67] As argued by Schnackenburg, *Epheser*, 174.
[68] Cf. Mark 9:23; Luke 9:46; Rom 13:9. Wallace, *Greek Grammar beyond the Basics*, 238; Thomas Kingsmill Abbott, *A Critical and Exegetical Commentary on the Epistles to the Ephesians and to the Colossians*, ICC 34 (New York: C. Scribner's Sons, 1909), 114.
[69] Peter Thomas O'Brien, *The Letter to the Ephesians*, PNTC (Grand Rapids, MI: Eerdmans, 1999), 293.
[70] Harris, "The Ascent and Descent of Christ in Ephesians 4:9–10," 201.
[71] Similarly, Hübner, *Epheser*, 205; Harris, "The Ascent and Descent of Christ in Ephesians 4:9–10," 201–2.
[72] In what follows, I discuss early sources that explicitly or implicitly interpret Eph 4:9 as Christ's descent to Hades, but there are more sources before Irenaeus that refer to the descent to Hades without connecting them to Eph 4:9. See Jared Wicks, "Christ's Saving Descent to the Dead: Early Witnesses from Ignatius of Antioch to Origen," *ProEccl* 17, no. 3 (2008): 281–309.
[73] The true superlative was fading in the Koine period, by which time the comparative could function as a superlative (Wallace, *Greek Grammar beyond the Basics*, 298–302; F. Büchsel, "κάτω," in *TDNT*

Preaching, he cites a text supposedly from Jeremiah: "And the Lord the Holy One of Israel, remembered his dead, which aforetime fell asleep in the dust of the earth; and he went down unto them, to bring the tidings of his salvation, to deliver them" (*Dem.* 78). Irenaeus interprets the clause "he went down," which is unknown to us yet attributed to Jeremiah, as Jesus's descent into hell. He considers Christ's descent to be "the salvation of them that had passed away" (*Dem.* 78).[74] This same "Jeremiah" text was cited earlier by Justin (*Dial.* 72), but not in connection with the descent to hell. It is also cited by Irenaeus in *Adv. Haer.* 4.22 as from Jeremiah, but in 3.20 as from Isaiah. This popular passage is an enigma, but importantly, in *Adv. Haer.* 4.22 Irenaeus connects this enigmatic quotation to Eph 4:9 and says the descent was "to behold with His eyes the state of those who were resting from their labours."[75] Thus, the "Lord and Holy One of Israel" from the "Jeremiah" passage is equated with Christ in Eph 4:9. In *Adv. Haer.* 5.31, he again quotes Eph 4:9, saying he descended to the place "where the dead were," comparing the descent with Jonah's three days in the fish. In none of these passages does Irenaeus argue that the descent of Eph 4:9 is Christ's descent to Hades; he simply assumes it is true, which suggests it was already part of traditional teaching, at least for his community.

Origen explicitly interprets the "lowest parts of the earth" in Eph 4:9 as Hades.[76] To counter any objections to this interpretation, he cites Phil 2:10 to say that not only knees in heaven and on earth would bow to him in the future but also those under the earth during his descent to the underworld; "some will fall down to him earlier and others later."[77] He reinforces both of these interpretations (of Eph 4:9 and Phil 2:10) in his sixth homily on Luke.[78] Prior to Christ's death and resurrection, all who died were held in Hades.[79] He took his people with him to prepare a place for them in the kingdom of the heavens, but those who do not belong to him bowed the knee to him in Hades.

Augustine used Ps 16:10 as a prophetic proof text that Christ would not be left in hell (which implies he would descend there).[80] Shortly after this reference, in commenting on the Lord's ascension into the heavens and subsequent judgment of the earth in 1 Sam 2:10, he says this order of ascension followed by judgment follows the creed and then quotes Eph 4:9–10.[81] Jonah's three days in the belly of the sea monster also signified that Christ would return from the depths of hell on the third day.[82] Christ delivered the OT saints from hell, although their holding place was not torturous, as was the place of the damned.[83]

3:640). Thus, τὰ κατώτερα τῆς γῆς could be "the lower parts of the earth" or "the lowest parts of the earth." Either meaning works for this ancient view that Christ descended to Hades.

[74] Translation from Irenaeus, *The Demonstration of the Apostolic Preaching*, ed. Armitage Robinson (New York: Macmillan Co., 1920).
[75] Translation from Irenaeus, *Against Heresies*, in *ANF* 1.
[76] *Comm. John* 19.140. *Gen. Hom.* 15.5; *Hom. Lev.* 9:5.
[77] *Comm. John* 19.141. Translation in FC 89:200.
[78] FC 94:27.
[79] *Hom. Exod.* 6.6.
[80] *Civ.* 17.4.
[81] Ibid.
[82] *Civ.* 18.30
[83] *Civ.* 20.15.

Acts of Thomas seems to allude to Eph 4:9–10 when it says, "And Thou didst descend to Sheol, and go to its uttermost end; and didst open its gates, and bring out its prisoners, and didst tread for them the path (leading) above by the nature of Thy Godhead."[84] Later, the author more explicitly speaks of Christ descending to the dead and making them alive through his ascension, rescuing them from the underworld:

> Thou didst descend to Sheol with mighty power, and the dead saw Thee and became alive, and the lord of death was not able to bear (it); and Thou didst ascend with great glory, and didst take up with Thee all who sought refuge with Thee, and didst tread the path for them (leading) up on high, and in Thy footsteps all Thy redeemed followed; and Thou didst bring them into Thy fold, and mingle them with Thy sheep.[85]

Maximus the Confessor (d. AD 662) alluded to Eph 4:9 in *Ad Thal.* 22, saying that Christ "even descended into the lower regions of the earth where the tyranny of sin compelled humanity."[86] Since in this context he is speaking of Christ's incarnation and because these lower regions are where sin tyrannizes humanity, he may understand the descent to be to earth. However, in another passage, Maximus interprets Eph 4:9 as Christ's descent to Hades: "He even descended willingly into the heart of the earth, where the Evil One had swallowed us through death, and drew us up by his resurrection, leading our whole captive nature up to heaven."[87] The reference to our "captive" nature alludes to Eph 4:8, "he took captive captives."

In sum, the early Fathers unanimously believed that Christ descended into Hades (or hell) during the three days between his crucifixion and resurrection.[88] They connected Eph 4:9 with this descent, although it is unknowable whether they derived the descent directly from 4:9 as a proof text or whether they were taught about the descent and read it into Eph 4:9. Since so many other texts are cited to support the descent to Hades, Eph 4:9 is probably only one supporting text among many. The belief that Christ brought captive believers out of Hades when he was resurrected found support in Eph 4:8, "he took captive captives," and this became the standard interpretation of the captivity clause in the ancient church.

Ephesians 4:9–10 as the Incarnation

In the Reformation period and beyond, it became common to interpret τῆς γῆς as a genitive of apposition, "he descended into the lower [parts], that is, the earth." This

---

[84] Translation from W. Wright, *Apocryphal Acts of the Apostles* (Edinburgh: Williams and Norgate, 1871), 2:155. Wright dates this Syriac manuscript to no later than the fourth century AD (ibid., xiv).
[85] Ibid., 288.
[86] *Ad Thal.* 22. Translation from John Behr, ed., *On the Cosmic Mystery of Jesus Christ: Selected Writings from St. Maximus the Confessor*, trans. Paul M. Blowers and Robert Louis Wilken, PPS 25 (Crestwood, NY: St. Vladimir's Seminary Press, 2003).
[87] *Ad Thal.* 64.
[88] Even outside the Fathers, the interpretation is evident, e.g., in *Mart. Isa.* 4:20–21.

interpretation holds that the descent refers to Christ's incarnation, when he descended to the earth. Calvin argued for the incarnation view in his commentary on Eph 4:9:

> These words mean nothing more than the condition of the present life. To torture them so as to make them mean purgatory or hell, is exceedingly foolish. The argument taken from the comparative degree, "the *lower* parts," is quite untenable. A comparison is drawn, not between one part of the earth and another, but between the whole earth and heaven; as if he had said, that from that lofty habitation Christ descended into our deep gulf.[89]

An incarnational descent in Eph 4:9–10 would fit well the pattern of Ps 68 if it can be shown that Yahweh first descended to a lower part of the earth's land to defeat an earthly enemy and to deliver his people before ascending to Mount Zion.[90] Theodoret of Cyrus actually made a similar observation.[91] This view would also explain the purpose of vv. 9–10 in the discourse: to bring attention to the descent in order to imply that this psalm could only be fulfilled in Christ, who is the only one who has descended and ascended like Yahweh. Additionally, one might interpret τὰ κατώτερα as a comparative and argue that a two-tiered cosmology coheres with the same two-tiered cosmology in the rest of Ephesians, which speaks only of the heavens and the earth (e.g., Eph 2:2; 3:10).[92]

For some commentators, the ascent and descent parallel the same movements in John and Phil 2:6–11. Schnackenburg relates the "lowest parts of the earth" (Eph 4:9) with the deep humiliation in Phil 2:6–11, while "filling all things" (Eph 4:10) corresponds to the "exaltation" in Phil 2:9.[93] J. Becker and U. Luz also see the similarity to Phil 2:6–11 and John's Gospel, and believe that the author drew the "ascent and descent" framework from those traditions. For these main reasons, and because of arguments against the traditional descent to Hades view, probably the majority of modern commentators espouse the incarnation view.[94]

---

[89] Translation from John Calvin, *Commentaries on the Epistle of Paul to the Galatians and Ephesians*, trans. William Pringle (Grand Rapids, MI: Christian Classics Ethereal Library, 1948), online at http://www.ccel.org/ccel/calvin/calcom41.iv.v.ii.html.
[90] O'Brien, *Ephesians*, 295.
[91] Theodoret of Cyrus, *Comm. Ps. 68*, 14.
[92] O'Brien, *Ephesians*, 294.
[93] Schnackenburg, *Epheser*, 181.
[94] See Schnackenburg, *Epheser*, 181; Heinrich Schlier, *Der Brief an die Epheser: Ein Kommentar* (Düsseldorf: Patmos, 1957), 192; Harold W. Hoehner, *Ephesians: An Exegetical Commentary* (Grand Rapids, MI: Baker, 2002), 533–36; C. Leslie Mitton, *Ephesians* (London: Oliphants, 1976), 144–49; Andreas Lindemann, *Der Epheserbrief*, ZBK 8 (Zurich: Theologischer Verlag, 1985), 77; Max Zerwick, *The Epistle to the Ephesians*, trans. Kevin Smyth (New York: Herder & Herder, 1969), 106–8; Ernest Best, *A Critical and Exegetical Commentary on Ephesians*, ICC (Edinburgh: Clark, 1998), 383–88; John Paul Heil, *Ephesians: Empowerment to Walk in Love for the Unity of All in Christ* (Atlanta, GA: Society of Biblical Literature, 2007), 173–74; F. F. Bruce, *The Epistles to the Colossians, to Philemon, and to the Ephesians*, NICNT (Grand Rapids, MI: Eerdmans, 1984), 343–45; Barth, *Ephesians*, 432–34; Pheme Perkins, *Ephesians* (Nashville, TN: Abingdon, 1997), 97–99; Richard N. Longenecker, *The Christology of Early Jewish Christianity*, SBT 2/17 (London: SCM, 1970), 60. I owe some of these references to William Bales, "The Descent of Christ in Ephesians 4:9," *CBQ* 72, no. 1 (2010): 85.

Ephesians 4:9–10 as the Descent of the Spirit at Pentecost

A third view has gained some support in the last century, that the descent refers to Christ's descent in the form of the Spirit at Pentecost. This view had a few early advocates, including G. B. Caird, but was developed fully by H. Hall Harris in an article and subsequently in his monograph, *The Descent of Christ*.[95] This view first relies on the exclusion of πρῶτον from Eph 4:9, because the view holds that the descent and distribution of gifts occurred *after* the ascent. If Eph 4:9 says Christ "first descended," this view would not be possible, but we have seen good reason for believing πρῶτον is not original.

Harris's thesis is that Paul borrowed the verb "gave" from the Targum (in oral-traditional form) and replaced Moses with Christ so that, as Moses ascended the mountain and then descended to give the gift of the law, now Christ has ascended to the heavenlies and subsequently descended *in the form of the Spirit* to give spiritual gifts at Pentecost (Acts 2:1–12, 33).[96] I suggested in the last chapter that Harris's attempt to find Pentecost associated with Ps 68 and the giving of the law by the NT period is problematic and uncertain. There is also no guarantee how widespread these traditions would have been, so it is an unsafe assumption to believe that Paul would have been familiar with these traditions. However, the interpretation of the descent as occurring at Pentecost does not rely on Paul borrowing from the Targum. So even if Harris is incorrect about the Targum, his treatment of Eph 4:9–10 deserves close attention.

He argues correctly that the order of the ascent and descent cannot be inferred by the wording of Eph 4:9–10.[97] This matter must be decided by the meaning of the passage and the relationship of vv. 9–10 to the quotation in v. 8. He also argues correctly that Eph 4:9–10 should not be considered parenthetical, since it would add nothing to the discourse to introduce a descent if it had nothing to do with the point being made in the quotation.[98] He suggests that the only reason it is introduced is because the distribution of gifts that is referred to in the citation of Ps 68:19, and also recalled in Eph 4:11, occurred at Christ's descent. The distribution of gifts seems to be connected with the ascent in the psalm, but Paul had to quote it that way. His midrash (as Harris classifies it) in vv. 9–10 clarifies that the one who descended (and gave gifts) is also the one who ascended in v. 8.

This identification of the ascender with the descender is important because the readers would have had problems realizing that the ascending Christ was the same as the descending Spirit. But they could indeed be identified. As G. B. Caird writes,

---

[95] Early advocates include H. von Soden, ed., *Hand-Kommentar zum Neuen Testament*, vol. 3: *Die Briefe an die Kolosser, Epheser, Philemon; die Pastoralbriefe* (Freiburg: Mohr, 1893), 135–36; George B. Caird, "The Descent of Christ in Ephesians 4,7-11," in *Studia Evangelica*, ed. F. L. Cross (Berlin: Akademie, 1964), 2:535–45. Abbott was similar in that he saw the descent and distribution of gifts after the ascent, but he argued that the descent referred to the incarnation with the gifts being Christ's preaching to those who are far and those who are near (Eph 2:17) (*Ephesians and to the Colossians*, 115–16). Harris's work appeared first as his article "The Ascent and Descent of Christ in Ephesians 4:9–10," 198–214, and was followed by his published dissertation, *The Descent of Christ*.

[96] Harris, *The Descent of Christ*, 46–197.

[97] Harris, "The Ascent and Descent of Christ in Ephesians 4:9–10," 206.

[98] Harris, *The Descent of Christ*, 173–75.

let us recall that the first speech of Peter in Acts asserts that it is the exalted Christ who has poured out the Pentecostal gift (Acts 2, 33), that the Fourth Gospel takes the coming of the Paraclete to be at least a partial fulfillment of Christ's promise to come again (Jn. 14, 15-18), that Paul, who regularly fails to draw any distinction between the Spirit and the indwelling Christ (Rom. 8, 9-10; 2 Cor 3, 17), in one passage actually declares that "the last Adam has become a life-giving spirit" (1 Cor 15, 45), and that a coming of Christ which has taken place since the crucifixion is mentioned in an earlier chapter of Ephesians (2, 17).[99]

Evaluating the Three Views of Ephesians 4:9-10

Each view has its problems. The descent to Hades view has against it that it is difficult to see how Paul deduced it from the citation of Ps 68:19.[100] As Harris noted, any advocate of this view would need to explain why Paul even felt the need to mention the descent. H. Hübner claims that this view makes no sense of the context of Eph 4:9 and of the argument of Chapter 4 as a whole, although he does not elaborate to support that claim.[101] Some rejections of this view rise to the level of emotional resistance, as in Calvin's statement, "To torture them so as to make them mean purgatory or hell, is exceedingly foolish."[102] But such a reaction is valid only against the ever-expanding ancient traditions about what Christ did during his three days in Hades. There is nothing foolish about believing that Eph 4:9 relates Christ's descent to Hades, especially if we say nothing more about the descent than what Eph 4:9-10 says. Yet the former problems still remain as obstacles to overcome for advocates of the descent to Hades view.

The biggest problem for the incarnation view is τὰ κατώτερα. This view only works if one assumes a two-tiered cosmology for Ephesians. With a two-tiered cosmology, either the comparative meaning ("the lower parts") or the superlative meaning ("the lowest parts") would refer to the earth. But one can only limit Ephesians' cosmology by assuming non-Pauline authorship, an assumption I have argued has little merit.[103] We should, with Origen, read τὰ κατώτερα in concert with Phil 2:10 and assume that the author of Ephesians held a three-tiered cosmology.[104] With three tiers, a comparative κατώτερα would be ambiguous—would it refer to the second tier (the earth) or

---

[99] Caird, "The Descent of Christ in Ephesians 4, 7-11," 537.
[100] Ibid., 536; Hodge, *Ephesians*, 220.
[101] Hübner, *Epheser*, 205.
[102] As cited above, Calvin, *Galatians and Ephesians*.
[103] Even in Rom 10:6-7, the Pauline passage most parallel to Eph 4:9-10, he refers to an ascent to heaven and a descent into the Abyss, the realm of the dead. The Abyss would constitute τὰ κατώτερα τῆς γῆς, while the earth itself would simply be referred to as ἡ γῆ, had he wanted to refer to a descent to the earth.
[104] *Comm. John* 19.141. To believe Paul wrote Ephesians and had in mind a two-tiered cosmology because of the way he portrays the cosmos in Ephesians would be to overemphasize the literary dimension of interpretation to the exclusion of the historical and theological. Paul, as an avid reader of the OT, believed in Sheol beneath the earth, as is evident from passages in two of his uncontested epistles (Rom 10:6-7; Phil 2:6-11). Thus, despite some statements throughout Ephesians that might suggest a two-tiered cosmology, if Paul wrote Ephesians, we cannot limit his view of the cosmos solely to the literary dimension of Ephesians.

the third tier (the underworld)? Given a three-tiered cosmology, τὰ κατώτερα only unambiguously makes sense as a superlative, referring to the lowest of the three tiers of the cosmos (equivalent to καταχθόνιος, "under the earth," Phil 2:10).[105] The use of τὰ κατώτερα therefore signifies the lowest of three cosmic tiers, namely, the realm of the dead. So the incarnation view is limited in that one must assume a two-tiered cosmology to make good sense of τὰ κατώτερα τῆς γῆς.[106]

Positively, the incarnation view fits well with the typological pattern in the psalm, assuming Paul inferred God's descent from Sinai and his subsequent ascent of Zion. It does fit the pattern of ascending and descending in John's Gospel, although there is no need to fit the context of Eph 4:7–11 into the Johannine motif of Christ's incarnation and ascension. On balance, this view has merit. But its need for a two-tiered cosmology in Ephesians, coupled with its nonexistence until the Reformation period, leaves room for a less problematic view.[107]

The major problem with the Pentecost view is that Paul could in no way infer from Ps 68 a subsequent descent of Christ, even in a typological manner, since Yahweh never descends from Mount Zion. Indeed, according to the psalmist's perspective, he will remain there "forever" and from on high (Ps 68:34) he will bless his people (Ps 68:36). Harris attempted to make the case that Ps 68 became associated with Pentecost as early as the writing of Ephesians and that the author was aware of that association. But we have seen that Harris's case lacks sufficient evidence. Regarding the placement of the ascent first, Harris is correct that the order is not obvious, but it is telling that not until the turn of the twentieth century did anyone think to invert the order. Also, while Caird is correct that Paul can refer to the Holy Spirit as the "Spirit of Christ" (Rom 8:9; cf. 1 Pet 1:11), Paul makes a clear distinction between the Spirit and Christ as different persons throughout his letters.[108] Thus, in no way can Christ really be said to have descended at Pentecost. Caird assumes Christ must descend to give his gifts, but this is a faulty assumption. Christ gives his gifts from his place of enthronement "in the heavenlies," where the spiritual blessings are found (Eph 1:3). A final issue that C. Arnold says is the "chief difficulty of this particular view" is that if the "earth" is what is meant in Eph 4:9, why is the comparative κατώτερα included?[109] To simply

---

[105] A. T. Robertson also interprets it as a superlative (*A Grammar of the Greek New Testament in the Light of Historical Research*, 3rd ed. [London: Hodder & Stoughton, 1919], 668).

[106] One other possibility is to take τῆς γῆς as a partitive genitive so that Eph 4:9 refers to the grave as the lower or lowest parts of the earth. This option again seems limited to the two-tiered cosmology since the grave would not be the lowest part of the earth because Hades is conceived as being below the earth and lower than a shallow grave. The comparative could not unambiguously refer to the grave in a three-tiered cosmology, either. This view was proposed by Chrysostom (*NPNF* 13:103–4).

[107] If there are early interpreters who take this view, I am unaware of them.

[108] E.g., Rom 1:4; 8:2; 15:6; 1 Cor 6:11; 2 Cor 3:3; 13:14; Gal 3:14. Even in Eph 4:7–16, Christ gives the gifts of the *charismata* by sealing believers with the Spirit (Eph 1:13–14). It is difficult for me to see how it is not modalism to collapse Paul's consistent distinction between the Spirit and Christ by saying that Christ descended at Pentecost "as the Spirit."

[109] Clinton E. Arnold, *Ephesians, Power and Magic: The Concept of Power in Ephesians in Light of Its Historical Setting*, SNTSMS (Cambridge: Cambridge University Press, 1989), 57. This critique holds for the incarnation view as well. Büchsel also points out that the opposite of "above the heavens" would not be "the earth" but would be "below the earth," which would require a partitive genitive for τῆς γῆς ("κάτω," *TDNT* 3:641).

say "he descended to the earth" would have been sufficient and less ambiguous. These problems, combined with the novelty of this view, make it more problematic than the incarnation view.

Although the descent to Hades view (i.e., *descensus ad inferos* as it is traditionally called) has fallen out of favor with modern interpreters, for several reasons it is still the best interpretation of Eph 4:9–10. The strongest evidence for the *descensus* interpretation is the use of the κατώτερος word group in the Hellenistic world of Paul's day and in the Septuagint. In the magical papyri, *PGM* LXX combines the term "descend" (καταβαίνω) with "down below" (κάτω), the same combination of roots used by Paul in Eph 4:9.[110] The text is a charm to protect against the fear of Hekate, a god associated with the crossroads to the underworld. The charm includes an initiation rite that would occur in an underground chamber. "I have been initiated, and I went down (καταβαίνω) into the [underground] chamber of the Dactyls, and I saw the other things down below (κάτω) . . . Say it at the crossroad, and turn around and flee, because it is at those places that she appears." H. Betz dates the text to the late third or early fourth century, so it is much later than Ephesians, but there is no indication that the magical papyri was influenced by Ephesians, so the completely independent use of the similar phrase does provide evidence of how it would be understood in ancient Asia Minor and Egypt.[111]

L. Kreitzer has recently demonstrated numismatic evidence for the presence in Hierapolis of the myth of the abduction of Persephone by Hades.[112] Her "descent" into the underworld would last for four months, leaving the land barren, until her "ascent" in the spring, bringing agricultural fruitfulness with her. Since Ephesians was intended for churches generally in Asia Minor, including the church at Hierapolis, the presence of such a myth could suggest that Eph 4:9–10 should be understood likewise as a descent into the underworld.[113] Stories about descents into the underworld in Greco-Roman religions of the first century were also prevalent and widespread. In some of these, the hero figure would also make the return trip out of the underworld. "So prevalent was the idea of an 'underworld' in the Greco-Roman culture of the day that it can be reasonably assumed that the average person would have understood the phrase 'he descended to the lower regions of the earth' as indicating, first and foremost, a descent (of some sort) to the underworld, the realm of the dead."[114]

This usage of the κατώτερος word group in Hellenistic culture is similar to its usage in the Septuagint. W. Bales provides three classes of texts parallel to the phrase "he

---

[110] Ibid. A translation of the text may be found in Hans Dieter Betz, ed., *The Greek Magical Papyri in Translation Including the Demotic Spells*, 2nd ed. (Chicago, IL: University of Chicago Press, 1992), 297–98.

[111] On the dating, see Hans Dieter Betz, "Fragments from a Catabasis Ritual in a Greek Magical Papyrus," *HR* 19 (1980): 287.

[112] Larry J. Kreitzer, *Hierapolis in the Heavens: Studies in the Letter to the Ephesians*, LNTS (London: T&T Clark, 2007), 54–67.

[113] That is, Paul would most likely not use language that so clearly expressed one idea (descent to the underworld) when he meant something completely different (incarnation or descent of the Spirit) without clarifying this difference for his audience. Otherwise, we would have to judge Paul's communication a failure. It is important to note that the phrase τὰ κατώτερα τῆς γῆς is not taken from the psalm but is Paul's own phrase used to describe Christ's descent.

[114] Bales, "The Descent of Christ in Ephesians 4:9," 90.

descended to the lower regions of the earth" in Eph 4:9: (1) texts almost equivalent, lexically and semantically (Ps 62:10 LXX; 138:15; Prayer of Manasseh 13); (2) texts that use τῆς γῆς similarly (Isa 14:15; Ps 70:20 LXX; Ezek 26:20; 32:18); (3) texts referring to a descent to the grave or underworld using the formula καταβαίνω + εἰς + a word or phrase denoting the grave or underworld.[115]

The most instructive of these examples is Ps 62:10 LXX: εἰσελεύσονται εἰς τὰ κατώτατα τῆς γῆς ("they will enter the lowest regions of the earth"). By Paul's time, with the superlative (κατώτατα) being mostly replaced by the comparative (κατώτερος), the words overlapped greatly. Also, when used with the article, a comparative adjective as in Eph 4:9 would generally be taken in the superlative sense.[116] Thus, the two phrases in Eph 4:9 and Ps 62:10 LXX are virtually identical, with εἰσέρχομαι being similar to καταβαίνω (one must "go down" in order to "enter" the underworld). Paul probably is not alluding to Ps 62:10 contextually, since there is no real thematic coherence between the two passages, but it may be the source of his phraseology as a way to refer to the underworld. If so, then the descent cannot refer to the incarnation or to the descent of the Spirit at Pentecost.[117] Following Ps 62:10 in importance is Prayer of Manasseh 13: ἐν τοῖς κατωτάτοις τῆς γῆς. After lamenting his own multitude of sins, for which he has been taken into Babylonian captivity, Manasseh prays that God would forgive him and not condemn him ἐν τοῖς κατωτάτοις τῆς γῆς. Hence, this phrase is a clear reference to the underworld, a locale to which sinners plead not to be condemned. While Paul was surely not alluding to Prayer of Manasseh, the writing serves as evidence of how the phrase would be understood in his day.[118]

Further important support for the *descensus* interpretation is the ἵνα clause in Eph 4:10, "in order that he might fill all things." This clause is generally syntactically subordinated to "the one who ascended above all the heavens," but the phrase is better understood as the purpose of both the ascent and descent: "the one who descended is himself the one who ascended far above all the heavens, [and he did both] in order that he might fill all things." The term "fill" (πληρόω) can be taken as spatial or as a reference to sovereignty, and both meanings seem to apply here. In order to "fill all things," Christ had to actually enter and conquer all locales, both the underworld and the heavenlies. He demonstrated his sovereignty over the underworld through his resurrection, and he demonstrates his sovereignty over the heavenlies by sitting at the

---

[115] Ibid., 91–97. Examples of the third category are Gen 37:35; Num 16:30, 33; Job 17:16; Pss 27:1 LXX; 29:4, 10; 54:16; 62:10; 70:20; 87:5; 113:25; 138:8, 15; 142:7; Isa 14:15, 19; Ezek 26:20; 31:14–18; 32:18, 24, 27, 29, 30; Tob 13:2 (א); Jonah 2:7; Bar. 3:19; Pr. Man. 13.

[116] Robertson, *Grammar of the Greek New Testament*, 668.

[117] Unfortunately, there is too little evidence to make a solid case for Paul borrowing the language from Ps 62:10 LXX; otherwise this would be a nearly insurmountable problem for the other two views.

[118] Dating Prayer of Manasseh is difficult. It is included in some versions of the Septuagint, such as Alexandrinus, but was not *clearly* written before Paul's day. There are no discernible Christian elements, so it was likely written by a Greek-speaking Jew anywhere from the turn of the millennium to the third century AD. Although, the majority of scholars (according to J. Charlesworth) date it prior to the destruction of Jerusalem. He says confidently, "[T]here can be no doubt that the Prayer of Manasseh predates the destruction of Jerusalem" ("Prayer of Manasseh," in *Old Testament Pseudepigrapha*, ed. James H. Charlesworth [Peabody, MA: Hendrickson, 1983], 2:627).

right hand of God.[119] The thought is quite similar to Ps 139:8: "If I ascend to heaven, you are there! If I make my bed in Sheol, you are there!"

Earlier in Ephesians, Paul makes a similar statement about the spatial consequences of the ascension. God raised him from the dead and "seated him at his right hand in the heavenly places, far above all rule and authority and power and dominion . . . and [i.e., "with the result that"] he put all things under his feet and gave him as head over all things to the church" (Eph 1:20–22).[120] Christ had to be raised above all things in order that they could be put "under his feet," which in itself was a typological fulfillment of Ps 8:6. Thus, the ascension in 1:20–22 has significance with regard to space and sovereignty while simultaneously fulfilling Scripture. I suggest that the same three elements are present in the ἵνα clause in Eph 4:10 that refers to Christ's ascension. He ascended and descended spatially to the highest and lowest regions of the earth, thereby filling them with his presence and expressing his sovereignty over them, while simultaneously filling the imprint of history that was created by the mold of his type. This filling of the historical type was part of the divine plan (οἰκονομία) of God (Eph 1:10; 3:2, 9), which included the fulfillment of the divine warrior theme from Ps 68:19. The use of πληρόω in Eph 4:10 probably does not denote all three of these ideas simultaneously. Rather, the word signifies spatial filling, which connotes the idea of sovereignty, and the idea in context also expresses the fulfillment of OT (indirect) prophecy. Eph 4:9–10 thus furthers elaborates on the quotation of Ps 68:19 by expressing the fullness of what Christ has done in history to antitypically fulfill the pattern created by Yahweh's victorious warfare in Ps 68.

That Eph 4:9–10 is elaborating on Christ as the divine warrior is even more evident if O'Brien and Harris are correct that "over the heavens" is a metaphor for "over the spiritual powers," which they claim because the spiritual powers in Ephesians are said to be in the heavenlies (3:10). They could be correct that this is a metaphor, or it could simply be that to be "over the heavens" is to be over the region of the spiritual powers' activity and therefore to be sovereign over them. In either case, the ascension is clearly a spatial movement that expresses sovereignty and fulfills Scripture, the most explicit Scriptures being Ps 8:6 and Ps 68:19. When one reads ἵνα πληρώσῃ τὰ πάντα as subordinated to *both* the ascent and descent as one holistic movement, one sees how the descent is also a spatial movement that expresses sovereignty and fulfills Scripture. The descent fulfills Ps 68 not because Yahweh in the psalm descends to the underworld (he does not) but because the principle in Ps 68 is that Yahweh through his spatial movement conquers his enemies and builds his temple. Christ's historical fulfillment of the psalm has exceeded even Yahweh's great victories over the Egyptians and Canaanites, because Christ traveled to the depths of creation and back and tamed every evil power in his wake, subsequently building an indestructible temple from his heavenly throne at the right hand of God.

---

[119] Similarly, Gnilka, *Epheserbrief*, 208; Büchsel, "κάτω," in *TDNT* 3:641.

[120] H. Lona (*Eschatologie*, 324) observes four similarities between 1:20–23 and 4:9–10. The object of πληρόω in both passages is τὰ πάντα; there is a connection between the fulfilling-function of Christ and the church; the fulfilling-function of Christ is grounded by his ascension; both are connected to OT passages by keywords: Ps 8:7 in Eph 1:23 and Ps 68:19 in Eph 4:10.

Above, I mentioned objections to the *descensus* view and noted that any proponent must answer them satisfactorily. One must explain how Paul deduced the *descensus* from the citation of Ps 68:19, why Paul brings up the descent at all, and how a descent to the underworld makes sense in the context of Eph 4:7–16. I have just answered the last two objections: Paul brings up the descent to emphasize the escalated fulfillment of the psalm, and from this understanding we see how the *descensus* makes sense in its context. But whether Paul deduced the descent from the psalm is a question that requires a clear answer.

It is possible that Paul derived the descent from the psalm, albeit only partially. He may have been considering Yahweh's descent from Mount Sinai and subsequent ascent of Mount Zion as part of the typological pattern established by Yahweh's warfare. Such a descent is not a mere literary feature of the psalm but a significant theological point: God is immanent and will condescend to his creation to fight for his people and to express his sovereignty over all his enemies to magnify his glory. This idea is the point expressed in Phil 2:6–11 regarding Christ's crucifixion: that though he existed in the form of God, he did not consider his equality with God something to be exploited but emptied himself, taking the form of a servant, and humbled himself to the point of death on a cross.[121] Christ condescends for his people, as Yahweh does in the psalm, but Christ reserved his ultimate display of sovereignty and warfare until he conquered the grave through his resurrection and dominated the spiritual powers through his ascension above them, so that they were placed under his feet (Eph 1:22). It is therefore possible that Paul read a descent into the psalm as part of the typological pattern fulfilled in an escalated manner by Christ.

However, since the psalm does not explicitly mention a descent, it is likely the manner of Christ's historical fulfillment of the psalm, by which he descended to Hades, that Paul came to infer such a descent in the psalm. Although the descent is not an explicit point of the psalm, it becomes a significant point of the psalm's fulfillment. Christ did not only descend to the earth but went even further to conquer the very corners of the cosmos. Thus, Paul elaborated on the meaning of the psalm by expressing the fullness of its typological fulfillment. No one could have predicted that Christ would have fulfilled the psalm in precisely *this* way, but that is the teaching that Paul received. It is therefore ultimately not the psalm that necessitates Paul's discussion of the descent, but his retrospective viewpoint of Christ's historical fulfillment of the psalm. This explanation coheres with the verbal change Paul made to the quotation, which stemmed also from his understanding of the historical fulfillment of the psalm.

This interpretation of Eph 4:9–10 also carries power to explain the early generation of the *descensus ad inferos* teaching. It seems unlikely that the earliest Fathers invented the *descensus* apart from apostolic teaching. If my view of Eph 4:9–10 is correct, then Paul believed and taught the *descensus* and assumed that the teaching was common enough that he did not need to elaborate it in Eph 4. Perhaps Paul assumed that they were taught the *descensus* because he taught it to many of them himself. He spent two years and three months teaching in Ephesus (Acts 19:8–10), and being as fervent

---

[121] Taking ἁρπαγμὸν ἡγήσατο τὸ εἶναι ἴσα θεῷ (Phil 2:6) as "he did not consider this equality with God something to be exploited," although there is no need to defend that translation here.

about preaching as he was, it is hard to imagine that during these two years he did not wander around to the other cities in Asia Minor to which he intended Ephesians to be circulated.[122] Assuming the Asian believers had been taught about the *descensus*, the function of the emphatic αὐτός in 4:10 ("the one who descended, *he* is the one who also ascended") is to strengthen the identification of Jesus as the antitypical fulfillment of the psalm. Christ, whom they had been taught had descended to the underworld and conquered it through his resurrection, is himself the one who has ascended far above the heavens and fulfilled the pattern of Ps 68:19. Verse 9 functions similarly, suggesting the logical necessity of a descent before an ascent. How could Christ ever have ascended to fulfill Ps 68:19 if he had not first descended? If a descent is thus required to fulfill the psalm, and they know from apostolic witness that Christ is the one who descended into the underworld, then they can know that the same Christ about whom they have been taught is certainly the same person who has fulfilled this psalm.

Conclusions on Ephesians 4:9–10

The typical meaning of a phrase such as κατέβη εἰς τὰ κατώτερα τῆς γῆς in first-century Hellenistic and Jewish culture would be a descent to the underworld. This interpretation is less problematic than the other two views, it has the support of the entire ancient church, and it fits well in its context. The descent may have been inferred from the psalm, although the typological pattern was fulfilled in an escalated manner through a descent to the very depths of creation rather than simply to the battlefield of the wilderness. The descent clause also identified the ascender who fulfilled the psalm as the same one who, according to apostolic witness, had descended to Hades. The *descensus* interpretation also makes better sense of the ἵνα clause in 4:10. Although many church fathers elaborated on the doctrine of the *descensus ad inferos* by including details such as his preaching to the dead and release of the OT saints, this idea is not expressed by Eph 4:9–10 and may not be part of what Paul meant to communicate.

While the descent in Eph 4:9–10 is not that of the Spirit at Pentecost, we have seen that some early Fathers connected Eph 4:8–10 with Acts 2. The question arises, when did Christ give the gifts mentioned in Eph 4:8? Verses 9–10 do not answer this question, but our knowledge of early Christian history as portrayed in Acts can answer the question. Pentecost was in fact the initial event in which Christ sent the Spirit to his disciples, which empowered them through the *charismata* to carry out their gospel commission. And just as Eph 4:7–16 is about the use of gifts for building up the temple, so also there is good reason to view the church's reception of the Spirit at Pentecost as the formation of the ecclesiological temple.[123] So when Justin, Origen, and Tertullian

---

[122] The passages in Ephesians that suggest he does not know his audience personally does not preclude him from knowing anyone in the cities of Asia Minor, and enough time had elapsed by the time he wrote Ephesians that he could write about "hearing" of their faith (Eph 1:15) since the time he left.

[123] Evidence was cited in the last chapter, but see especially the works cited there, Gregory K. Beale, "The Descent of the Eschatological Temple in the Form of the Spirit at Pentecost. Part 1, The Clearest Evidence," *TynBul* 56, no. 1 (2005): 73–102; Gregory K. Beale, "The Descent of the Eschatological Temple in the Form of the Spirit at Pentecost. Part 2: Corroborating Evidence," *TynBul* 56, no. 2 (2005): 63–90.

cite Acts 2 in connection with Eph 4:8-10, they have good reason, since both passages focus on the gifts of the *charismata*.[124] But Christ's gifts were not only given at that one Pentecost. Even now, he gifts individual believers whenever they hear the gospel and believe (Eph 1:13-14), thus incorporating them into the ecclesiological temple. There is therefore some truth to the descent at Pentecost view, which sees Pentecost as the fulfillment of Eph 4:8, even though advocates of this view are incorrect about vv. 9-10. The partial truth of the view may explain its popularity among modern commentators.

Paul's Theological Use of Psalm 68:19

Paul read Ps 68:19 typologically and applied it eschatologically to Christ's victory over the spiritual powers through his resurrection and ascent. His use is therefore in line with the eschatological stream of early Jewish interpretation of the psalm, which serves as a precedent for Paul. This typological interpretation of Ps 68 contributes to aspects of his theology. The most immediately obvious theological move in this citation is his change of agent from Yahweh to Christ. Paul has no issue with describing Christ's actions with words used to describe Yahweh's actions. Paul does this frequently in his letters, but it remains striking in each instance.[125] This observation leads to the deeper question of how Jesus came to be exalted to an equal status with Yahweh. Various answers are possible. L. Hurtado has emphasized the increasing devotion to intermediary figures in early Judaism so that devotion to Jesus was the final step in raising an intermediary figure to full divine status.[126] N. T. Wright suggests that early Christians recognized Jesus's coming as the promised coming of Yahweh to save his people from exile, and they therefore considered Jesus to be the embodiment of Yahweh.[127] One might also consider the fact that Jesus's appearance after his resurrection was enough to convince early believers that he is God. In whatever way Christ came to be worshiped as God (which is beyond the scope of this work), we see from citations such as Ps 68:19 in Eph 4:8 that Paul was perfectly comfortable treating Jesus with the same worshipful

---

[124] Justin, *Dial.* 87; Origen, *Comm. John* 6.292; Tertullian, *Adv. Marc.* 5.8.

[125] E.g., in Phil 2:10-11, Paul says all knees will bow before Christ, using language from Isa 45:23, which says all knees will bow before Yahweh. In Eph 2:17, Christ came and preached peace to the near and the far, alluding to Isa 57:19, where God speaks peace to the near and the far. In 2 Thess 1:7-8, Paul speaks about Christ's judgment at his parousia using language from Isa 66:4, 15, which speaks of the same judgment at Yahweh's coming. In Rom 10:13, Paul says that everyone who calls on the name of the Lord (Jesus) will be saved, quoting Joel 2:32, which says the same of Yahweh. Examples could be multiplied. R. Hays has also recently argued that the Gospels present Jesus as functionally equivalent to Yahweh through application to Christ of OT passages that speak of Yahweh. "[E]ach of the four Evangelists, in their diverse portrayals, identifies Jesus as the embodiment of the God of Israel" (Richard B. Hays, *Reading Backwards: Figural Christology and the Fourfold Gospel Witness* [Waco, TX: Baylor University Press, 2014], 107).

[126] Larry W. Hurtado. *One God, One Lord: Early Christian Devotion and Ancient Jewish Monotheism* (Philadelphia, PA: Fortress, 1988).

[127] N. T. Wright, *Jesus and the Victory of God*, COQG 2 (Philadelphia, PA: Fortress, 1996), 612-53. See Hurtado's reply in "YHWH's Return to Zion: A New Catalyst for Earliest High Christology?," in *God and the Faithfulness of Paul: A Critical Examination of the Pauline Theology of N.T. Wright*, ed. Christoph J. Heilig, Thomas Hewitt, and Michael F. Bird, WUNT II/413 (Tübingen: Mohr Siebeck, 2016), 417-38.

posture as Yahweh. In fact, we may safely assume that Paul would ascribe the same praise to Christ for his victory over the enemy as the psalmist ascribes to Yahweh at the beginning and end of the psalm (Ps 68:2–4, 33–36).

Not all agree, though, that Paul and the earliest Christians worshiped Jesus as God. J. Dunn, for example, has advanced the entrenched "low early Christology" of critical scholarship. Although he agrees that "Paul seems to have had no qualms about transferring God's role in eschatological salvation to the risen Jesus," he still argues that for early Christians and Paul, Jesus simply shared in God's authority but was not venerated as God.[128] Yet it is difficult to read all the passages in which Paul attributes to Christ what formerly was attributed to Yahweh without concluding that Paul worshiped Christ as God. First Corinthians 8:6 is the most striking passage in this regard, in which Paul modifies the Shema to include Christ while still maintaining there is only one God. Dunn concludes that Christ is simply Lord alongside God, but the NT passages that name Christ "God" suggest that Paul is doing the same in 1 Cor 8:6.[129] Further evidence that Paul viewed Christ as God is that, as C. Tilling has recently argued, the "relational data concerning Christ in Paul's letters corresponds, as a pattern, only to the language concerning YHWH in second Temple Judaism."[130] Additionally, R. Bauckham has argued that the NT authors include Jesus in the "unique, defining characteristics by which Jewish monotheism identified God as unique."[131] Paul's citation of Ps 68:19 is a clear instance of Paul attributing to Jesus functional equality with Yahweh.

Yet, the manner in which Christ fulfilled the psalm is escalated and eschatological. Yahweh defeated his enemies physically and then established his glorious, yet destructible temple. Jesus's victory over the spiritual powers and his subsequent construction of the latter-day temple was part of the broader feat of inaugurating on earth the Kingdom of God, an inauguration that was sealed by his resurrection (2 Cor 5:15–21; 1 Cor 15:20). Christ's resurrection was the firstfruits of the universal resurrection, functioning as the first stage of the restoration of heaven and earth. Paul's use of Ps 68:19 reminds us that part of ushering in the Kingdom of God and bringing about the New Creation is the subdual and eradication of all evil. The construction of the indestructible latter-day temple is essential to the Kingdom in the New Creation, for history concludes with our eternal dwelling with God in the New Jerusalem, which is itself a Holy of Holies.[132] Ephesians 4:7–16 reminds us, then, that Christians are not yet the consummated form of the temple of God. Rather, just as Jesus was God's temple

---

[128] James D. G. Dunn, *The Theology of Paul the Apostle* (Grand Rapids, MI: Eerdmans, 1998), 254–60, quote on 250.

[129] Ibid., 253. Passages in which Jesus is called θεός include Titus 2:13; John 1:1, 18; 20:28; Heb 1:8–9; 2 Pet 1:1; Rom 9:5, which is more likely than not an affirmation that the Messiah is God over all, but the grammatical alternatives must be seriously considered. For alternative views on Rom 9:5, see, e.g., Murray J. Harris, *Jesus as God: The New Testament Use of Theos in Reference to Jesus* (Grand Rapids, MI: Baker, 1992), 143–72; Gordon D. Fee, *Pauline Christology: An Exegetical-Theological Study* (Peabody, MA: Hendrickson, 2007), 272–78, and further studies cited therein.

[130] Chris Tilling, *Paul's Divine Christology*, WUNT II/323 (Tübingen: Mohr Siebeck, 2012), 3.

[131] Richard Bauckham, *Jesus and the God of Israel: God Crucified and Other Studies on the New Testament's Christology of Divine Identity* (Grand Rapids, MI: Eerdmans, 2008), 1–59, quote on ix.

[132] In Rev 21:16, the New Jerusalem is measured at 12,000 stadia cubed. The only other structure in the Bible to have the same length, width, and height is the holy of the holies in Israel's temple. Revelation therefore presents the New Jerusalem as the final temple.

on earth (Col 1:19; 2:9) until God later dwelt in his church, so now the church is God's dwelling on earth until he remakes all of creation into his holy temple.

Ephesians 4:7–16 also reminds us what Paul says explicitly elsewhere, that the church is the temple of God (1 Cor 3:16; 6:19; 2 Cor 6:16; Eph 2:21–22). The temple is only one corporate figure that Paul uses to describe the church. Although the body imagery is evident in Eph 4:11–16, and although Paul's use of body imagery throughout his corpus has received much attention, rarely does anyone see the body and temple imagery intertwined. But Paul's mixture of body and temple imagery grants us a better understanding of what it means for the church to be God's temple. Believers are not a static building that is complete and fully mature. Rather, as a body that is knit together by sinews and joints, and that grows into maturity if nourished and exercised properly, so also the temple of God in this age of the church is an organic structure that shifts and grows with every new member added to it. The work of the teaching ministers equips each member of the temple so they will all attain unity and maturity in Christ (4:11–13). Yet, ultimately, it is the proper functioning of each member of this temple that causes the growth of the body (4:16). In this sense, sanctification is not only individual but also corporate; the growth of individuals depends on the proper functioning of other individuals. Thus, the temple of God is no longer a static building to which the nations must flow to bring their praises, but now the temple is an organically maturing body that takes itself to the ends of the earth as a light to the nations. Jesus said, "[T]he hour is coming when neither on this mountain nor in Jerusalem will you worship the Father" (John 4:21), and indeed that hour has now come.

Another theological contribution this quotation makes is to the *Christus Victor* aspect of the atonement. Whereas Paul has stated factually elsewhere that Christ has defeated the evil powers, disarming them and putting them to open shame (Col 2:15; Eph 1:21–22; etc.), here Paul shows that this victory was prophesied in the OT.[133] Yahweh's deliverances of Israel, combined with the eschatological promises of the psalm, called for a future fulfillment of these promises. Yahweh would once again—this time through Christ—triumph over his foes, deliver his people, establish his temple, declare his eternal reign, and all the nations would praise him. The imagery of Ps 68 also allows one to express the theme of *Christus Victor* in terms of God's past deliverances, specifically, those narrated so poetically throughout the psalm.

Finally, Paul's use of Ps 68:19 demonstrates what D. Moo has called "hermeneutical axioms," which are "statements that express the beliefs about Scripture and about how the Scripture relates to a particular community."[134] Paul obviously believed the OT Scriptures were relevant for him in his day (he says so explicitly in 1 Cor 10:11), although in a more indirect manner than the Qumran interpreters, who seem to have interpreted OT prophecies as relating directly to their community (e.g., in the peshers). Paul also believed that God was sovereignly guiding history according to his divine plan (οἰκονομία, Eph 1:10; 3:2, 9). But, although fulfillment had come in part, it had not yet been consummated, since history still awaits the final destruction of the

---

[133] Technically, the subject in Col 2:15 is probably God, and Jesus is the intermediary agent.
[134] Douglas J. Moo, *The Old Testament in the Gospel Passion Narratives* (Sheffield: Almond Press, 1983), 8.

spiritual powers and of the spirit at work among mankind (Eph 2:2). Paul recognized that there is a new heavens and a new earth in our future (2 Cor 5:17; Gal 6:15), when Christ will fully express his sovereignty and reconcile all things to himself (Col 1:20).

Paul's Rhetorical Use of Psalm 68:19

Assuming that Ephesians was a circular letter to the churches of Asia Minor, this citation would have resonated in many ways with the readers. The Temple of Artemis was one of the seven wonders of the ancient world and loomed large in the religious life of those in Asia Minor. The record in Acts 19:27 says "all Asia and the world" worshipped Artemis and that the Ephesian citizens were disturbed by the first Christian missionary activity in the city because it might strip the temple of honor. Its physical size was so impressive that Antipater of Sidon described it as rising into the clouds:

> I have set eyes on the wall of lofty Babylon on which is a road for chariots, and the statue of Zeus by the Alpheus, and the hanging gardens, and the colossus of the Sun, and the huge labour of the high pyramids, and the vast tomb of Mausolus; but when I saw the house of Artemis that mounted to the clouds, those other marvels lost their brilliancy, and I said, "Lo, apart from Olympus, the Sun never looked on aught so grand."[135]

Perhaps Antipater embellishes here, but obviously the impressive structure struck awe in those who saw it. Paul, either purposefully or subconsciously, confronts those who are tempted to marvel at a physical pagan temple, which was still as frail as Israel's first temple that was destroyed. In fact, the Temple of Artemis had already been destroyed and rebuilt twice by Paul's day. Thus, by presenting the eschatological temple as indestructible because it is composed of Christ's own gifts, he demonstrates that God's temple is more magnificent and eternal than even the greatest physical temple they could possibly lay eyes on.

Another important rhetorical effect of Paul's citation and interpretation of Ps 68 is that it would serve to admonish those in Asia Minor who fear spiritual powers and who participate (or might be tempted to participate in) any magical rites to ward off such spirits. The prevalence of magic in Ephesus is recorded in Acts 19, in which Paul first confronts an evil spirit. Believers in Acts 19:11–19 also confess to their use of magic and burn their magical books, the value of which came to fifty thousand pieces of silver. The Greek magical papyri give us a sense for the extent of the peoples' fear of evil spirits and the measures they took to protect themselves, through initiating rites into mystery religions and through charms that would ward off spirits. Throughout Ephesians, and in 4:8–10, Paul emphasizes Christ's victory over all spiritual powers and over all regions of the universe. Those who belong to Christ are part of his body and part of God's holy temple. The spiritual powers lie underneath Christ's feet, and death could not hold him. While those in Asia Minor resorted to charms and rites to

---

[135] Antipater, *Greek Anthology* IX.58. Translation in *LCL* 84:31.

protect themselves from death, Christians have no need to fear death. Surely, death is the last enemy to be destroyed (1 Cor 15:26), but it has already experienced its death blow through the resurrection. Because Christ is the firstfruits, Christians know that they too will defeat death through their own resurrection.

> When the perishable puts on the imperishable, and the mortal puts on immortality, then shall come to pass the saying that is written: "Death is swallowed up in victory." "O death, where is your victory? O death, where is your sting?" The sting of death is sin, and the power of sin is the law. But thanks be to God, who gives us the victory through our Lord Jesus Christ (1 Cor 15:54–57).

Those in Asia Minor who would have read Eph 4:8–10 therefore would have been admonished to abandon adoration for the Temple of Artemis, to seek the protection of Christ rather than that of charms and rites, and to shake the fear of death. Christ's sovereignty over all powers and every inch of creation provides all the safety, assurance, and empowerment believers need to live a fruitful and flourishing life in their pagan environment.

Conclusion

Although various elements of my proposal for how Paul used Ps 68 may be gleaned from or anticipated by the various explanations from Justin Martyr to the present, no one view has incorporated all the elements pulled together here. The early church understood that Paul read Ps 68 prophetically, but they incorrectly saw it as direct prophecy and also struggled to grasp the rationale for the verbal change. Many scholars wrote on the problem in the twentieth century, with the Targum approach being the most popular until recently. The most recent batch of articles have turned to the context of Ps 68 for clues about why Paul changed the verb as he did, and about how he was interpreting and using the psalm.

Ultimately, Paul read the psalm prophetically, reading the first half of the psalm (especially v. 19) as a type that impressed itself on history and demanded a future fulfillment and the second half of the psalm as a prophecy of God's complete eschatological deliverance of his people. He cited Ps 68:19 in a way that captured the historical fulfillment of the psalm, seen retrospectively. Christ became the divine builder by giving his own gifts to build up his church as a holy temple. And just as Yahweh descended in the psalm before ascending to the height of Mount Zion, so Christ in an escalated manner descended even lower to Hades, where he rose to defeat death and ascended to the highest region of the universe, where all his enemies were put under his feet. The Christological implications are consistent with other similar passages in which Christ is equated functionally with Yahweh. Other theological implications, such as corporate sanctification in Eph 4:11–16 and the *Christus Victor* aspect of the atonement, may be gleaned from this passage. Ephesians 4:8–10 would have had a profound rhetorical effect on its Asian readers, who would have been inundated with the grandeur of the Temple of Artemis and tempted consistently to protect themselves from evil spirits through magic and pagan cultic rites. Paul's use of Ps 68:19 demonstrates to them the irony that they would submit themselves to the same evil spirits who had been taken captive and placed under Christ's feet, as he sits in the heavenlies blessing his people.

Conclusion

Therefore it says, "ascending on high, he took captive captives, he gave gifts to men."
—Paul the Apostle, Eph 4:8

We have come a long way from H. J. Holtzmann's claim that Paul used Ps 68:19 "arbitrarily."[1] We have seen major elements of thematic coherence between the two passages that suggest Paul read the verse in its wider context of the entire narratival sweep of the psalm. That the point of Eph 4:8 and Ps 68:19 is that the divine builder would supply the materials for his temple to honor his victory over his enemies is no coincidence. Moreover, Paul had precedent for applying the psalm to Christ's eschatological victory. The authors of the Qumran pesher on Ps 68 and of the War Scroll applied the psalm in a similar manner. The Mosaic interpretation of the psalm in Jewish writings is therefore a red herring. Many have believed that this tradition held the key to understanding Paul's use of Ps 68:19, but in fact his interpretation agreed with that of the eschatological tradition, which seems to date back as early as the arrangement of the Psalter by its editors. The key is therefore not in some rabbinic hermeneutical principle, in a Jewish interpretive tradition, or in Paul's mishandling of Scripture. The key to understanding Paul's use of Ps 68:19 is the psalm itself.

The conclusions of this study contribute to two of the major issues involved in studying the NT's use of the OT, which I discussed in the introduction. First, do NT authors cite passages contextually? In this one test case, I have argued that Paul did cite Ps 68:19 with great respect for its context. Moreover, the two contexts are mutually illuminating. For example, when I initially began studying Ps 68, I thought vv. 16-19 might be a reprise of the Sinai theme from earlier in the psalm, as some scholars argue. But when I discovered that Paul was portraying the church as the temple in Eph 4:11-16, I then saw that Ps 68:16-19 was also about the (Jerusalem) temple. The nature of the "gifts" in Eph 4:8 as building blocks of the temple led me to reexamine the "gifts" in Ps 68:19, which have always been understood simply as war spoil unrelated to the temple. It was only through a dialectical process involving both contexts that I was able to come to a fuller understanding of the psalm and of Eph 4:7-16. So while there is an apologetic element to understanding citations as contextual, there is also a

---

[1] Heinrich Julius Holtzmann, *Kritik der Epheser- und Kolosserbriefe: Auf Grund einer Analyse ihres Verwandtschaftsverhältnisses* (Leipzig: Wilhelm Engelmann, 1872), 6.

pragmatic reason for giving NT authors the benefit of the doubt. By first looking at the OT context for reasons why an NT author may have cited from there, we are allowing the two contexts to illuminate one another, thereby enriching our understanding of Scripture.

Aside from judging Paul's level of contextuality, we have also seen how the meaning of Ps 68:19 has been transformed by its placement into its new context in Eph 4:8. Much of its meaning has transferred, the majority of it seemingly consciously through Paul, if indeed he read the psalm in a similar narratival way as I have. Indeed, Paul's own use of the psalm led me to my own views of the psalm, so I think it is likely he read it similar to the way I have expounded it. However, it is doubtful that Paul recognized the ancient Near Eastern divine builder topos that has been so important to my own interpretation of the psalm. Paul may have picked up on elements of the topos without consciously recognizing the topos itself, which may be why Ephesians is so filled with ideas of divine warfare, ascension, and the church as a temple.[2] Thus, some meaning possibly transfers from the psalm into Ephesians subconsciously. Finally, while we have seen much continuity between the original and the new meaning of the cited text, there is also the discontinuity, which I discussed above in the last chapter. As the typological pattern was fulfilled, a new agent (Christ, not the Israelites) gave a different kind of gifts (*charismata*, not stones) for a different kind of temple (the church, not the Jerusalem complex). The meaning has indeed been transformed, but the two meanings are connected by the strings of history, as it were. The *oikonomia* of God, his plan for history and the fullness of time, connects the two meanings, even as the text is transformed by its use.

The second issue to which this study contributes is the manner in which Christ is found in the OT. Typology is an historically attested method of interpretation, grounded in the apostle's hermeneutic.[3] Nevertheless, critical scholarship has called into question the legitimacy of using typology to understand how OT events, persons, or institutions might foreshadow Christ.[4] The problem for many scholars lies in accepting God's supernatural governing of history. The project to rid the Bible of the supernatural lends itself to ridding the Bible of any divinely intended glimpses of his future work in Christ. But typology is not so easily set aside. The NT authors employ the τύπος word group and other word groups that fit within a typological framework.[5] Those who invest any normative authority in the apostles' hermeneutic will therefore retain

---

[2] E.g., Eph 1:20–23; 2:6, 16, 19–22; 3:10; 4:7–16; 5:14; 6:10–20. See further, Timothy G. Gombis, *The Drama of Ephesians: Participating in the Triumph of God* (Downers Grove, IL: IVP Academic, 2010).

[3] See especially Richard M. Davidson, *Typology in Scripture: A Study of Hermeneutical Τύπος Structures*, AUSDDS (Berrien Springs, MI: Andrews University Press, 1981); Leonhard Goppelt, *Typos: The Typological Interpretation of the Old Testament in the New*, trans. Donald Madvig (1939; repr., Grand Rapids, MI: Eerdmans, 1982).

[4] E.g., R. E. Clements asserts that, given the advances of critical OT scholarship, "the vagaries of the older patterns of allegorical and typological interpretation which are to be found in abundance in patristic and mediaeval Christian exegesis can now command no confidence" (*One Hundred Years of Old Testament Interpretation* [Philadelphia, PA: Westminster, 1976], 148). Even N. T. Wright, who reads the NT with the OT narrative in its background, is shy of using traditional typology (*The Climax of the Covenant: Christ and the Law in Pauline Theology* [Minneapolis, MN: Fortress Press, 1993], 264).

[5] Σκιά ("shadow," Col 2:17; Heb 8:5); παραβολή ("type, figure," Heb 9:9; 11:19); ἀλληγορούμενα ("spoken allegorically," Gal 4:24); ἀντίτυπος ("antitype," 1 Pet 3:21).

typology within their hermeneutical arsenal. Those who do not take their hermeneutic as normative must still reckon with the fact that the apostles certainly viewed parts of the OT typologically and applied them as such in many of their quotations and allusions. And there is at least one linguistic indicator of typological thinking in Eph 4:8. The "therefore" (διό) of Eph 4:8 connects 4:7 ("grace was given to each of us") with the citation of Ps 68:19. The fact that Christ would—in the future—give gifts to his church to build up his latter-day temple was the reason that the psalmist recorded God's ascension of Zion in the way he did. The inferential διό therefore suggests that Paul is thinking typologically when he cites the psalm. My interpretation of Paul's quotation as applying typologically to Christ's victory and subsequent divine temple-building demonstrates—if it is correct—that typological interpretation is still viable, useful, and necessary for understanding how the NT authors use the OT.

A significant implication of this study is that this understanding of the citation of Ps 68:19 renders more plausible the *descensus* interpretation of Eph 4:9–10. The belief that Christ descended into the underworld after his death is found throughout the early Fathers, and many of the Fathers interpreted Eph 4:9–10 as referring to the *descensus*. The history of the clause in the Apostles' Creed is murkier, but it is found as early as AD 404 in Rufinus's exposition of his local Aquileian creed, written in Latin.[6] The earliest Greek witness to the creed comes from Marcellus of Ancyra (c. AD 340), who does not discuss the *descensus* clause.[7] But as it was later incorporated more widely in both Latin and Greek versions, and eventually became enshrined in the *Textus Receptus* around AD 700, the Greek form of the creed rendered the *descensus* clause as κατελθόντα εἰς τὰ κατώτατα, which is a clear allusion to Eph 4:9. The implication is that, at least according to this Greek tradition, whatever the creed means by the *descensus* clause is whatever Eph 4:9 means.

I hope that my interpretation of Eph 4:8–10 has demonstrated the plausibility of reading the descent in v. 9 as a descent into the underworld, based on the grammatical and lexical evidence, as well as the coherence of such a view with my understanding of how Paul was applying the psalm.[8] While the mythological details about what Christ did in the underworld evolved over the centuries, the passage itself says only that he descended and then ascended for the purpose of expressing his sovereignty over every inch of creation. We can therefore unashamedly recite the Apostles' Creed, descent and all, since its language simply echoes Scripture. I believe many churches today feel uncomfortable with this line of the creed because it is translated into English as "he descended into hell." But the problem has more to do with the English word "hell," which denotes a place of punishment and torment. I suggest that the line be translated

---

[6] Rufinus testified that the *descensus* phrase is not found in the Roman creed or in the creeds of the Eastern churches, but that it is included in his local Aquileian version (*Symb.* 18). Rufinus claimed that the descent was "unmistakably prophesied in the Psalms," citing LXX Pss 21:16, 29:10, 68:3; 15:10; 29:4 (*Symb.* 28). He also cites 1 Pet 3:18–20 as evidence of the *descensus*. For further discussion, see J. N. D. Kelly, "Introduction," in *Rufinus: A Commentary on the Apostles' Creed*, Ancient Christian Writers 20 (New York: Newman Press, 1954), 12–18.

[7] See Tarmo Toom, "Marcellus of Ancyra and Priscillian of Avila: Their Theologies and Creeds," *Vigiliae Christianae* 68 (2014): 60–81.

[8] One might also point to 1 Pet 3:18–19 to support the *descensus*, but its interpretive ambiguities are well known.

and recited as "he descended to the dead," which is a fair translation of Eph 4:9's "lowest parts of the earth." The phrase "to the dead" allows enough ambiguity that those who theologically object to the *descensus* can alternatively understand it to mean "to the grave." Thus, all can recite this ancient creed in unity while allowing for multiple understandings of this phrase from Eph 4:9.

Finally, I hope this study can serve as a model for exploring NT citations and allusions. The OT context should not be ignored but should be explored thoroughly. A purely literary approach is insufficient since it ignores historical aspects of the text, especially its social milieu. Thus, even NT scholars should acquaint themselves with the general worldview of the ancient Israelites and the primary sources of their ancient neighbors, so many of which were only discovered in the nineteenth century or later.[9] The recent trend to explore Jewish interpretive traditions should also be continued, but we must be wary of giving those traditions preference over exploration of the OT context, at least in the beginning of the investigation. This precedence for Jewish traditions to the exclusion of exploring the OT context led H. Harris to include virtually no exegesis of Ps 68 in his entire monograph and to base his entire thesis on the speculative argument that certain Jewish traditions were available in Paul's day.[10] As we have seen, it is highly unlikely those traditions were available in Paul's day. Harris's study deserves careful consideration, but the conclusions of his project would have been more fruitful had he first exegeted Ps 68 and considered whether any thematic coherence existed between the two contexts.

As it turned out, the OT context does hold the keys to understanding Paul's citation, but the complexities of translating and interpreting Ps 68 have masked those keys from commentators. Ancient Near Eastern texts illuminated and corroborated my narrative reading of Ps 68 with its divine builder topos. Jewish traditions previously unnoticed by interpreters of Eph 4:8 supported my eschatological reading of the latter half of the psalm and also provided precedence for Paul's similarly eschatological (yet also Christological) application. Thus, fruitful studies of the NT's use of the OT will respect and explore both contexts while illuminating them with evidence from the social and historical contexts of the OT and NT authors.

---

[9] The exciting tales of the early discoveries have been related in numerous sources. See a very short summary in Alan Lenzi, "Assyriology and Biblical Interpretation," in *The Oxford Encyclopedia of Biblical Interpretation*, ed. Steven L. McKenzie (New York. Oxford University Press, 2013), 42–45.

[10] W. Hall Harris, *The Descent of Christ: Ephesians 4:7–11 and Traditional Hebrew Imagery*, BSL (Grand Rapids, MI: Baker Books, 1998).

Bibliography

Abbott, Thomas Kingsmill. *A Critical and Exegetical Commentary on the Epistles to the Ephesians and to the Colossians*. ICC 34. New York: C. Scribner's Sons, 1909.
Adolfus Busse, ed. *Olympiodori prolegomena et in categorias commentarium*. CAG 12/1. Berlin: Reimer, 1902.
Albright, William F. "A Catalogue of Early Hebrew Lyric Poems (Psalm LXVIII)." *HUCA* 23 (1951): 1–39.
Aletti, Jean-Noël. *Saint Paul, Épître aux Éphésiens: Introduction, Traduction et Commentaire*. EB 42. Paris: J. Gabalda, 2001.
Alexander, T. Desmond. *From Eden to the New Jerusalem*. Grand Rapids, MI: Kregel 2008.
Anderson, Bernhard W. "The Song of Miriam." Pages 285–96 in *Directions in Biblical Hebrew Poetry*. Edited by Elaine R. Follis. JSOTSS 40. Sheffield: JSOT Press, 1987.
Archer, G. L. *Jerome's Commentary on Daniel*. Grand Rapids, MI: Baker, 1977.
Arnold, Bill T., and Bryan Beyer. *Readings from the Ancient Near East: Primary Sources for Old Testament Study*. EBS. Grand Rapids, MI: Baker Academic, 2002.
Arnold, Bill T., and Brent A. Strawn. "Beyāh šemô in Psalm 68,5: A Hebrew Gloss to an Ugaritic Epithet?" *ZAW* 115, no. 3 (2003): 428–32.
Arnold, Clinton E. *The Colossian Syncretism: The Interface between Christianity and Folk Belief at Colossae*. WUNT II/77. Tübingen: Mohr Siebeck, 1995.
Arnold, Clinton E. *Ephesians, Power and Magic: The Concept of Power in Ephesians in Light of Its Historical Setting*. SNTSMS. Cambridge: Cambridge University Press, 1989.
Auffret, Pierre. "Le Dieu d'Israël, c'est lui: Étude structurelle du Psaume 68." Pages 1–30 in *Merveilles a Nos Yuex: Etude Structurelle de Vingt Psaumes Don't Celui de 1Ch 16,8–36*. BZAW 235. New York: Walter de Gruyter, 1995.
Avishur, Yitshak. *Studies in Hebrew and Ugaritic Psalms*. Jerusalem: Magnes Press, 1994.
Baentsch, Bruno. *Exodus-Leviticus-Numeri*. HAT 2. Göttingen: Vandenhoeck und Reprecht, 1903.
Bales, William. "The Descent of Christ in Ephesians 4:9." *CBQ* 72, no. 1 (2010): 84–100.
Ballard, Harold Wayne. *The Divine Warrior Motif in the Psalms*. BIBALDS 6. North Richland Hills, TX: BIBAL Press, 1999.
Barbiero, Gianni. *Das erste Psalmenbuch als Einheit: Eine synchrone Analyse von Psalm 1–41*. ÖBSB 16. Frankfurt am Main: Peter Lang, 1999.
Barth, Markus. *Ephesians: Introduction, Translation, and Commentary*. 2 vols. AB. Garden City, NY: Doubleday, 1974.
Batey, Richard. "Destination of Ephesians." *JBL* 82, no. 1 (1963): 101.
Bauckham, Richard. *Jesus and the God of Israel: God Crucified and Other Studies on the New Testament's Christology of Divine Identity*. Grand Rapids, MI: Eerdmans, 2008.
Baum, Armin D. "Authorship and Pseudepigraphy in Early Christian Literature: A Translation of the Most Important Source Texts and an Annotated Bibliography." Pages 11–63 in *Paul and Pseudepigraphy*. Edited by Stanley E. Porter and Gregory P. Fewster. PAST 8. Leiden: Brill, 2013.

Baum, Armin D. *Pseudepigraphie und literarische Fälschung im frühen Christentum: Mit ausgewählten Quellentexten samt deutscher Übersetzung*. WUNT II/138. Tübingen: Mohr Siebeck, 2001.
Baynes, Paul. *An Commentary upon the Whole Epistle of St. Paul to the Ephesians*. Edinburgh: James Nichol, 1866.
Beale, Gregory K. *Colossians and Philemon*. BECNT. Grand Rapids, MI: Baker Academic, 2019.
Beale, Gregory K. "The Descent of the Eschatological Temple in the Form of the Spirit at Pentecost. Part 1, The Clearest Evidence." *TynBul* 56, no. 1 (2005): 73–102.
Beale, Gregory K. "The Descent of the Eschatological Temple in the Form of the Spirit at Pentecost. Part 2: Corroborating Evidence." *TynBul* 56, no. 2 (2005): 63–90.
Beale, Gregory K. *Handbook on the New Testament Use of the Old Testament: Exegesis and Interpretation*. Grand Rapids, MI: Baker Academic, 2012.
Beale, Gregory K. *The Temple and the Church's Mission: A Biblical Theology of the Dwelling Place of God*. NSBT 17. Downers Grove, IL: InterVarsity Press, 2004.
Beale, G. K., and D. A. Carson, eds. *Commentary on the New Testament Use of the Old Testament*. Grand Rapids, MI: Baker Academic, 2007.
Becker, Jürgen. *Das Heil Gottes: Heils- und Sündenbegriffe in den Qumrantexten und im Neuen Testament*. SUNT 3. Göttingen: Vandenhoeck & Ruprecht, 1964.
Becker, Jürgen, and Ulrich Luz. *Die Briefe an die Galater, Epheser, und Kolosser*. NTD 8. Güttingen: Vandenhoeck & Ruprecht, 1998.
Beekman, John, John Callow, and Michael Kopesec. *The Semantic Structure of Written Communication*. 5th rev. ed. Dallas, TX: Summer Institute of Linguistics, 1981.
Beer, Georg. *Exodus*. HAT I/3. Tübingen: J. C. B. Mohr, 1939.
Beetham, Christopher A. *Echoes of Scripture in the Letter of Paul to the Colossians*. BIS 96. Leiden: Brill, 2008.
Behr, John, ed. *On the Cosmic Mystery of Jesus Christ: Selected Writings from St. Maximus the Confessor*. Edited by John Behr. Translated by Paul M. Blowers and Robert Louis Wilken. PPS 25. Crestwood, NY: St. Vladimir's Seminary Press, 2003.
Bender, H. "Das Lied Exodus 15." *ZAW* 23 (1903): 1–48.
Berner, Christoph. *Die Exoduserzählung: Das literarische Werden einer Ursprungslegende Israels*. FAT 73. Tübingen: Mohr Siebeck, 2010.
Berrin, Shani. "Qumran Pesharim." Pages 110–33 in *Biblical Interpretation at Qumran*. Edited by Matthias Henze. SDSSRL. Grand Rapids, MI: Eerdmans, 2005.
Bertheau, Ernst. *Das Buch der Richter und Ruth*. 2nd ed. KEHAT. Leipzig: S. Hirzel, 1883.
Best, Ernest. *A Critical and Exegetical Commentary on Ephesians*. ICC. Edinburgh: Clark, 1998.
Best, Ernest. *Essays on Ephesians*. Edinburgh: T&T Clark, 1997.
Best, Ernest. "Who Used Whom? The Relationship of Ephesians and Colossians." *NTS* 43 (1997): 72–96.
Betz, Hans Dieter. *Fragments from a Catabasis Ritual in a Greek Magical Papyrus*." *HR* 19 (1980): 287–95.
Betz, Hans Dieter, ed. *The Greek Magical Papyri in Translation Including the Demotic Spells*. 2nd ed. Chicago, IL: University of Chicago Press, 1992.
Biber, Douglas. *Variation across Speech and Writing*. Cambridge: Cambridge University Press, 1988.
Biber, Douglas. "Register and Discourse Analysis." Pages 191–208 in *The Routledge Handbook of Discourse Analysis*. Edited by James Paul Gee and Michael Handford. New York: Routledge, 2012.

Biber, Douglas, and Susan Conrad. *Register, Genre, and Style*. CTL. Cambridge: Cambridge University Press, 2009.

Block, Daniel I. *Judges, Ruth*. NAC. Nashville, TN: Broadman & Holman, 1999.

Block, Daniel I. "Recovering the Voice of Moses: The Genesis of Deuteronomy." *JETS* 44, no. 3 (2001): 385–408.

Bons, Eberhard. "Review of Eschatology in the Greek Psalter, by Joachim Schaper." *RevScRel* 71 (1997): 257–58.

Braude, William G., ed. *Pesikta Rabbati: Discourses for Feasts, Fasts, and Special Sabbaths*. New Haven, CT: Yale University Press, 1968.

Braude, William G., and Israel J. Kapstein, eds. *Pesikta de-Rab Kahana: R. Kahana's Compilation of Discourses for Sabbaths and Festal Days*. Philadelphia, PA: Jewish Publication Society of America, 1975.

Briggs, Charles A., and Emilie Grace Briggs. *A Critical and Exegetical Commentary on the Book of Psalms*. 2 vols. ICC. Edinburgh: T&T Clark, 1906–1907.

Brock, Sebastian P. "The Earliest Syriac Literature." Pages 161–71 in *The Cambridge History of Early Christian Literature*. Edited by Frances Young, Lewis Aryes, and Andrew Louth. Cambridge: Cambridge University Press, 2004.

Brown, Gillian, and George Yule. *Discourse Analysis*. CTL. New York: Cambridge University Press, 1983.

Brown, Raymond E. *An Introduction to the New Testament*. New York: Doubleday, 1997.

Bruce, F. F. *The Epistles to the Colossians, to Philemon, and to the Ephesians*. NICNT. Grand Rapids, MI: Eerdmans, 1984.

Buch, Kai Rander. "A Note on Sentence-Length as Random Variable." Pages 76–79 in *Statistics and Style*. Edited by Lubomír Doležel and Richard W. Bailey. MLALP 6. New York: American Elsevier, 1969.

Caird, George B. "The Descent of Christ in Ephesians 4,7–11." Pages 535–45 in *Studia Evangelica*. Vol. 2. Edited by F. L. Cross. Berlin: Akademie, 1964.

Calvin, John. *Commentaries on the Epistle of Paul to the Galatians and Ephesians*. Translated by William Pringle. Grand Rapids, MI: Christian Classics Ethereal Library, 1948. Online at http://www.ccel.org/ccel/calvin/calcom41.iv.v.ii.html.

Carmignac, Jean. *La Règle de la Guerre des Fils de Lumière contre les Fils de Ténèbres*. Paris: Letouzey et Ané, 1958.

Carr, Wesley. "Two Notes on Colossians." *JTS* 23 (1973): 492–500.

Cassuto, Umberto. *A Commentary on the Book of Exodus*. Translated by Israel Abrahams. Jerusalem: Magnes Press, 1967.

Chen, Kevin. *Eschatological Sanctuary in Exodus 15:17 and Related Texts*. SBL 154. New York: Peter Lang, 2013.

Charlesworth, James H., ed. *The Old Testament Pseudepigrapha*. 2 vols. Peabody, MA: Hendrickson, 1983–2011.

Charlesworth, James H. "Prayer of Manasseh." Pages 625–37 in *Old Testament Pseudepigrapha*. Vol. 1. Edited by James H. Charlesworth. Peabody, MA: Hendrickson, 1983.

Childs, Brevard S. *The Book of Exodus: A Critical, Theological Commentary*. OTL. Louisville, KY: Westminster, 1974.

Childs, Brevard S. *Introduction to the Old Testament as Scripture*. Philadelphia, PA: Fortress Press, 1979.

Christensen, Duane L. *Deuteronomy 21:10–34:12*. WBC 6B. Nashville, TN: Thomas Nelson, 2002.

Clements, R. E. *One Hundred Years of Old Testament Interpretation*. Philadelphia, PA: Westminster, 1976.
Clines, David J. A., ed. *The Dictionary of Classical Hebrew*. 8 vols. Sheffield: Sheffield Phoenix Press, 2007.
Coats, George W. *Exodus 1–18*. FOTL 2A. Grand Rapids, MI: Eerdmans, 1999.
Cohen, A., ed. *The Minor Tractates of the Talmud*. 2 vols. London: Soncino Press, 1965.
Cole, Robert. *Psalms 1–2: Gateway to the Psalter*. Sheffield: Sheffield Phoenix Press, 2013.
Cole, Robert Luther. *The Shape and Message of Book III: Psalms 73–89*. JSOTSS 307. Sheffield: Sheffield Academic Press, 2000.
Craigie, Peter C. "Song of Deborah and the Epic of Tukulti-Ninurta." *JBL* 88, no. 3 (1969): 253–65.
Craigie, Peter C. *Ugarit and the Old Testament*. Grand Rapids, MI: Eerdmans, 1983.
Cross, Frank Moore, Jr., and David Noel Freedman. *Studies in Ancient Yahwistic Poetry*. 2nd ed. BRS. Grand Rapids, MI: Eerdmans, 1997.
Dahood, Mitchell J. *Psalms*. 3 vols. AB 17. Garden City, NY: Doubleday, 1966.
Dahl, Nils Alstrup. "Einleitungsfragen zum Epheserbrief." Pages 3–105 in *Studies in Ephesians: Introductory Questions, Text- & Edition-Critical Issues, Interpretation of Texts and Themes*. Edited by David Hellholm, Vemund Blomkvist, and Tord Fornberg. Tübingen: Mohr Siebeck, 2000.
Dahl, Nils Alstrup. "The Letter to the Ephesians: Its Fictional and Real Setting." Pages 451–59 in *Studies in Ephesians: Introductory Questions, Text- & Edition-Critical Issues, Interpretation of Texts and Themes*. Edited by David Hellholm, Vemund Blomkvist, and Tord Fornberg. Tübingen: Mohr Siebeck, 2000.
Dalton, W. J. "Pseudepigraphy in the New Testament." *CTR* 5 (1983): 29–35.
Davidson, Richard M. *Typology in Scripture: A Study of Hermeneutical Τύπος Structures*. AUSDDS. Berrien Springs, MI: Andrews University Press, 1981.
Davies, Philip R. *IQM, the War Scroll from Qumran: Its Structure and History*. BibOr 32. Rome: Biblical Institute Press, 1977.
Day, John. *God's Conflict with the Dragon and the Sea: Echoes of a Canaanite Myth in the Old Testament*. UCOP 34. Cambridge: Cambridge University Press, 1985.
De Wette, Wilhelm Martin Leberecht. *Kurze Erklärung der Briefe an die Colosser, an Philemon, an die Ephesier und Philipper*. Leipzig: Weidmann'sche Buchhandlung, 1847.
DeClaissé-Walford, Nancy L., ed. *The Shape and Shaping of the Book of Psalms: The Current State of Scholarship*. AIL 20. Atlanta, GA: Society of Biblical Literature, 2014.
DeClaissé-Walford, Nancy L., Rolf A. Jacobson, and Beth LaNeel Tanner. *The Book of Psalms*. NICOT. Grand Rapids, MI: Eerdmans, 2014.
Delitzsch, Franz. *Biblical Commentary on The Psalms*. Translated by Rev. Francis Bolton. 2nd rev. ed. 3 vols. Edinburgh: T&T Clark, 1880–81.
DeMaris, Richard E. *The Colossian Controversy: Wisdom in Dispute at Colossae*. JSNTSS 96. Sheffield: JSOT Press, 1994.
le Déaut, Roger. "Targum." Pages 1–344 in *Supplément au Dictionnaire de la Bible: Targum*. Edited by Henri Cazelles and Jacques Briend. Paris: Letouzey & Ané, 2002.
Dibelius, Martin. *Die Isisweihe bei Apuleius und verwandte Initiations-Riten*. Heidelberg: Carl Winters, 1917.
Dillmann, August, and August Knobel. *Die Bücher Exodus und Leviticus für die zweite Auflage*. 2nd ed. KEHAT 12. Leipzig: S. Hirzel, 1880.
Dillon, John M., and Jackson P. Hershbell. *Iamblichus, On the Pythagorean Way of Life: Text, Translation, and Notes*. TT 29. Atlanta, GA: Scholars Press, 1991.

Dimock, Henry. *Notes Critical and Explanatory on the Book of Psalms and Proverbs*. Glocester: R. Raikes, 1791.
Dodd, Charles H. *According to the Scriptures: The Sub-Structure of New Testament Theology*. London: Nisbet, 1952.
Dodd, Charles H. "The Old Testament in the New." Pages 171–72 in *The Right Doctrine from the Wrong Texts: Essays on the Old Testament in the New*. Edited by G. K. Beale. Grand Rapids, MI: Baker Books, 1994.
Dooley, Robert A., and Stephen H. Levinsohn. *Analyzing Discourse: A Manual of Basic Concepts*. Dallas, TX: SIL International, 2001.
Donelson, Lewis R. *Pseudepigraphy and Ethical Argument in the Pastoral Epistles*. HUT 22. Tübingen: J.C.B. Mohr, 1986.
Duff, Jeremy. "A Reconsideration of Pseudepigraphy in Early Christianity." DPhil thesis, University of Oxford, 1998.
Duff, Jeremy. "A Reconsideration of Pseudepigraphy in Early Christianity." *TynBul* 50, no. 2 (1999): 306–9.
Duhm, D. Bernhard. *Die Psalmen*. KHCAT. Leipzig: J. C. B. Mohr, 1899.
Dunn, James D. G. *The Theology of Paul the Apostle*. Grand Rapids, MI: Eerdmans, 1998.
Dupont-Sommer, André. *The Essene Writings from Qumran*. Translated by G. Vermes. Cleveland, OH: World Publishing, 1962.
David, Durell. *Critical Remarks on the Books of Job, Proverbs, Psalms, Ecclesiastes, and Canticles*. Oxford: Clarendon, 1772.
Durham, John I. *Exodus*. WBC 3. Waco, TX: Word Books, 1987.
Eadie, John. *Commentary on the Epistle to the Ephesians*. 1883. Reprint, Minneapolis, MN: James & Klock, 1977.
Ehorn, Seth. "The Use of Psalm 68(67).19 in Ephesians 4.8: A History of Research." *CBR* 12, no. 1 (2013): 96–120.
Ehrman, Bart D. *Forgery and Counterforgery: The Use of Literary Deceit in Early Christian Polemics*. Oxford: Oxford University Press, 2014.
Ellegård, Alvar. *A Statistical Method for Determining Authorship: The Junius Letters, 1769–1772*. AUGGSE 13. Göteborg, 1962.
Ellis, E. Earle. *History and Interpretation in New Testament Perspective*. BIS 54. Atlanta, GA: Society of Biblical Literature, 2001.
Ellis, E. Earle. *The Making of the New Testament Documents*. BIS 39. Leiden: Brill, 1999.
Ellis, E. Earle. *Paul's Use of the Old Testament*. Eugene, OR: Wipf & Stock, 1957.
Ellis, E. Earle. *Prophecy and Hermeneutic in Early Christianity: New Testament Essays*. Eugene, OR: Wipf and Stock, 2003.
Emerton, John Adney. "The 'Mountain of God' in Psalm 68:16." Pages 24–37 in *History and Traditions of Early Israel: Studies Presented to Eduard Nielsen*. Edited by André Lemaire and Benedikt Otzen. SVT 50. Leiden: Brill, 1993.
Evanson, Edward. *The Dissonance of the Four Generally Received Evangelists and the Evidence of their Respective Authenticity, Examined; With That of Some Other Scriptures Deemed Canonical*. 2nd ed. Gloucester: D. Walker, 1805.
Fee, Gordon D. *God's Empowering Presence: The Holy Spirit in the Letters of Paul*. Peabody, MA: Hendrickson, 1994.
Fee, Gordon D. *Pauline Christology: An Exegetical-Theological Study*. Peabody, MA: Hendrickson, 2007.
Fischer, Karl. "Anmerkungen zur Pseudepigraphie im Neuen Testament." *NTS* 23 (1977): 76–81.

Fischer, Karl Martin. *Tendenz und Absicht des Epheserbriefes*. FRLANT 111. Göttingen: Vandenhoeck und Ruprecht, 1973.

Flesher, Paul V. M., and Bruce Chilton. *The Targums: A Critical Introduction*. Waco, TX: Baylor University Press, 2011.

Flint, Peter W., and Patrick D. Miller, eds. *The Book of Psalms: Composition and Reception*. SVT 99. Boston, MA: Brill, 2005.

Fohrer, Georg. *Überlieferung und Geschichte des Exodus: Eine Analyse von Ex 1–15*. BZAW 91. Berlin: A.Töpelmann, 1964.

Fokkelman, J. P. "The Structure of Psalm lxvii." Pages 123–40 in *In Quest of the Past: Studies on Israelite Religion, Literature, and Prophetism: Papers Read at the Joint British-Dutch Old Testament Conference, Held at Elspeet, 1988*. Edited by A. S. van der Woude. OS 26. Leiden: E.J. Brill, 1990.

Foord, Martin. "Taking with One Hand, and Giving with the Other? The Use of Psalm 68:18 in Ephesians 4:8." Pages 127–38 in *All That the Prophets Have Declared*. Edited by Matthew R. Malcolm. Croydon: Paternoster, 2015.

France, R. T. *Jesus and the Old Testament: His Application of Old Testament Passages to Himself and His Mission*. Vancouver, BC: Regent College, 1998.

Freedman, H. and Maurice Simon, eds. *Song of Songs*. Translated by Maurice Simon. Midrash Rabbah 9. London: Soncino Press, 1983.

Friedlander, Gerald, ed. *Pirḳê De Rabbi Eliezer: (The Chapters of Rabbi Eliezer the Great) According to the Text of the Manuscript Belonging to Abraham Epstein of Vienna*. New York: Hermon Press, 1970.

Frolov, Serge. *Judges*. FOTL 6B. Grand Rapids, MI: Eerdmans, 2013.

Fuss, Werner. *Die deuteronomistische Pentateuchredaktion in Exodus 3–17*. Berlin: de Gruyter, 1972.

García Martínez, Florentino, and Eibert J. C. Tigchelaar, eds. *The Dead Sea Scrolls Study Edition*. 2 vols. Leiden: Brill, 2000.

Gaster, Theodor Herzl. *Thespis: Ritual, Myth, and Drama in the Ancient Near East*. Rev. ed. Garden City, N.Y.: Doubleday, 1961.

Gehring, Roger W. *House Church and Mission: The Importance of Household Structures in Early Christianity*. Peabody, MA: Hendrickson, 2004.

Gesenius, Wilhelm, E. Kautzsch, and A. E. Cowley. *Gesenius' Hebrew Grammar*. 2nd English ed. Oxford: Clarendon Press, 1909.

Gibson, John C. L., ed. *Aramaic Inscriptions Including Inscriptions in the Dialect of Zenjirli*. TSSI 2. Oxford: Clarendon Press, 1975.

Gillmayr-Bucher, Susanne. *Erzählte Welten im Richterbuch: Narratologische Aspekte eines polyfonen Diskurses*. BIS 116. Leiden: Brill, 2013.

Globe, Alexander. "Literary Structure and Unity of the Song of Deborah." *JBL* 93, no. 4 (1974): 493–512.

Gnilka, Joachim. *Der Epheserbrief*. 2nd ed. HTKNT 10. Freiburg im Breisgau: Herder, 1977.

Goldingay, John. *Psalms*. 3 vols. Grand Rapids, MI: Baker Academic, 2006.

Goodspeed, Edgar J. *The Key to Ephesians*. Chicago: University of Chicago Press, 1956.

Goold, William H., ed. *The Works of John Owen*. 16 vols. London: Banner of Trust, 1967.

Gombis, Timothy G. "Cosmic Lordship and Divine Gift-Giving: Psalm 68 in Ephesians 4:8." *NovT* 47, no. 4 (2005): 367–80.

Gombis, Timothy G. *The Drama of Ephesians: Participating in the Triumph of God*. Downers Grove, IL: IVP Academic, 2010.

Gombis, Timothy G. "Ephesians 2 as a Narrative of Divine Warfare." *JSNT* 26 (2004): 403–18.
Goppelt, Leonhard. *Typos: The Typological Interpretation of the Old Testament in the New.* Translated by Donald Madvig. 1939. Reprint, Grand Rapids, MI: Eerdmans, 1982.
Gray, John. "Israel in the Song of Deborah." Pages 421–55 in *Ascribe to the Lord: Biblical & Other Essays in Memory of Peter C. Craigie.* Edited by Lyle M. Eslinger and Glen Taylor. JSOTSS 67. Sheffield: JSOT Press, 1988.
Gray, John R. "Cantata of the Autumn Festival: Psalm 68." *JSS* 22, no. 1 (1977): 2–26.
Grayson, Albert Kirk. *From the Beginning to Ashur-resha-ishi I.* ARI 1. Wiesbaden: Otto Harrassowitz, 1972.
Grayson, Albert Kirk. *From Tiglath-pileser I to Ashur-nasir-apli II.* ARI 2. Wiesbaden: Otto Harrassowitz, 1976.
Grayson, Albert Kirk, and Jamie R. Novotny, eds. *The Royal Inscriptions of Sennacherib, King of Assyria (704-681 BC), Part 1.* RINAP 3/1. Winona Lake, IN: Eisenbrauns, 2012.
Gregg, J. A. F. "The Commentary of Origen upon the Epistle to the Ephesians." *JTS* (1902): 233–44, 398–420, 554–76.
Grindheim, Sigurd. "A Deutero-Pauline Mystery? Ecclesiology in Colossians and Ephesians." Pages 173–95 in *Paul and Pseudepigraphy.* Edited by Stanley E. Porter and Gregory P. Fewster. PAST 8. Leiden: Brill, 2013.
Grotius, Hugo. *Annotationes in Vetus Testamentum.* 3 vols. Groningen: Zuidema, 1875.
Gunkel, Hermann. *The Psalms: A Form-Critical Introduction.* Translated by Thomas M. Horner. Philadelphia, PA: Fortress Press, 1967.
Gunkel, Hermann, and Joachim Begrich. *Introduction to Psalms: The Genres of the Religious Lyric of Israel.* Translated by James D. Nogalski. MLBS. Macon, GA: Mercer University Press, 1998.
Habel, Norman C. *Yahweh Versus Baal: A Conflict of Religious Cultures.* New York: Bookman Associates, 1964.
Haefner, A. E. "A Unique Source for the Study of Ancient Pseudonymity." *ATR* 16 (1934): 11–15.
Hallo, William W. "Compare and Contrast: The Contextual Approach to Biblical Literature." Pages 1–30 in *The Bible in the Light of Cuneiform Literature.* Edited by William W. Hallo, B. W. Janes, and G. L. Mattingly. SC 3. Lampeter: Edwin Mellen, 1990.
Harris, Murray J. *Jesus as God: The New Testament Use of Theos in Reference to Jesus.* Grand Rapids, MI: Baker, 1992.
Harris, R. J. *Testimonies.* 2 vols. Cambridge: Cambridge University Press, 1916–1920.
Harris, W. Hall. "The Ascent and Descent of Christ in Ephesians 4:9–10." *BS* 151, no. 2 (1994): 198–214.
Harris, W. Hall. *The Descent of Christ: Ephesians 4:7–11 and Traditional Hebrew Imagery.* BSL. Grand Rapids, MI: Baker Books, 1998.
Hasel, Gerhard F. *New Testament Theology: Basic Issues in the Current Debate.* Grand Rapids, MI: Eerdmans, 1978.
Haupt, P. "Moses' Song of Triumph." *AJSLL* 20 (1904): 49–72.
Hauser, Alan J. "Judges 5: Parataxis in Hebrew Poetry." *JBL* 99, no. 1 (1980): 23–41.
Hauser, Alan J. "Two Songs of Victory: A Comparison of Exodus 15 and Judges 5." Pages 265–84 in *Directions in Biblical Hebrew Poetry.* Edited by Elaine R. Follis. JSOTSS. Sheffield: JSOT Press, 1987.
Hay, David M. *Glory at the Right Hand: Psalm 110 in Early Christianity.* SBLMS 18. Nashville, TN: Abingdon Press, 1973.

Hays, Richard B. *Reading Backwards: Figural Christology and the Fourfold Gospel Witness.* Waco, TX: Baylor University Press, 2014.
Heidel, Alexander. *The Babylonian Genesis: The Story of the Creation.* 2nd ed. Chicago, IL: University of Chicago Press, 1951.
Heil, John Paul. *Ephesians: Empowerment to Walk in Love for the Unity of All in Christ.* Atlanta, GA: Society of Biblical Literature, 2007.
Heilig, Christoph, J. Thomas Hewitt, and Michael F. Bird, eds. *God and the Faithfulness of Paul: A Critical Examination of the Pauline Theology of N.T. Wright.* WUNT II/413. Tübingen: Mohr Siebeck, 2016.
Hengstenberg, Ernst Wilhelm. *Commentary on the Psalms.* 4th rev. ed. 3 vols. Cherry Hill, NJ: Mack, 1975.
Hengstenberg, Ernst Wilhelm. *Christology of the Old Testament and a Commentary on the Messianic Predictions.* Translated by Theodore Meyer and James Martin. 4 vols. 1872–1878. Reprint, Grand Rapids, MI: Kregel, 1956.
Hentschel, Anni. *Gemeinde, Ämter, Dienste: Perspektiven zur neutestamentlichen Ekklesiologie.* BTS 136. Neukirchen-Vluyn: Neukirchener Verlag, 2013.
Hodge, Charles. *A Commentary on the Epistle to the Ephesians.* 1856. Reprint, Grand Rapids, MI: Baker, 1980.
Hoehner, Harold W. *Ephesians: An Exegetical Commentary.* Grand Rapids, MI: Baker Academic, 2002.
Holmstedt, Robert D. "Analyzing זֶה Grammar and Reading זֶה Texts of Ps 68:9 and Judg 5:5." *JHS* 14 (2014): 1–26.
Holtzmann, Heinrich Julius. *Kritik Der Epheser- Und Kolosserbriefe: Auf Grund Einer Analyse Ihres Verwandtschaftsverhältnisses.* Leipzig: Wilhelm Engelmann, 1872.
Holzinger, Heinrich. *Exodus.* KHCAT 2. Tübingen: J. C. B. Mohr, 1900.
Horsley, Samuel. *The Book of Psalms: Translated from the Hebrew with Notes, Explanatory and Critical.* 2nd ed. Edinburgh: C. Stewart, 1815.
Howard, David M. Jr. "Editorial Activity in the Psalter: A State-of-the-Field Survey." Pages 52–70 in *The Shape and Shaping of the Psalter.* Edited by J. Clinton McCann. JSOTSS 159. Sheffield: JSOT Press, 1993.
Howard, David M. Jr. "Recent Trends in Psalms Studies." Pages 329–68 in *The Face of Old Testament Studies.* Edited by David W. Baker and Bill T. Arnold. Grand Rapids, MI: Baker, 1999.
Howard, David M. Jr. *The Structure of Psalms 93–100.* Biblical and Judaic Studies from the University of California, San Diego 5. Winona Lake, IN: Eisenbrauns, 1997.
Hübner, Hans. *An Philemon, an die Kolosser, an die Epheser.* HNT 12. Tübingen: Mohr Siebeck, 1997.
Hurowitz, Victor. *I Have Built You an Exalted House: Temple Building in the Bible in Light of Mesopotamian and Northwest Semitic Writings.* JSOTSS 115. Sheffield: JSOT Press, 1992.
Hurowitz, Victor, and Joan Goodnick Westenholz. "LKA 63: A Heroic Poem in Celebration of Tiglath-Pileser I's Muṣru-Qumanu Campaign." *JCS* 42 (1990): 1–49.
Hurtado, Larry W. *One God, One Lord: Early Christian Devotion and Ancient Jewish Monotheism.* Philadelphia, PA: Fortress, 1988.
Hurtado, Larry W. "Two Case Studies in Earliest Christological Readings." Pages 3–23 in *All that the Prophets Have Declared: The Appropriation of Scripture in the Emergence of Christianity.* Edited by Matthew R. Malcolm. Bletchley, England: Paternoster, 2015.
Hurtado, Larry W. "YHWH's Return to Zion: A New Catalyst for Earliest High Christology?" Pages 417–38 in *God and the Faithfulness of Paul: A Critical Examination*

of the Pauline Theology of N.T. Wright. Edited by Christoph J. Heilig, Thomas Hewitt, and Michael F. Bird. WUNT II/413. Tübingen: Mohr Siebeck, 2016.

Irenaeus. *The Demonstration of the Apostolic Preaching*. Edited by Armitage Robinson. New York: Macmillan, 1920.

Jacob, Edmond. *Ras Shamra-Ugarit et l'Ancien Testament*. Cahiers d'Archéologie Biblique 12. Neuchâtel, Suisse: Éditions Delachaux et Niestlé, 1960.

Jacquet, Louis. *Les Psaumes et le Cœur de l'Homme: Étude Textuelle, Littéraire et Doctrinale*. Gembloux: Duculot, 1977.

Jirku, Anton. "Zu Psalm 68:3a," *VT* 5, no. 2 (1955): 203–4.

Jongeling, Bastiaan. *Le Rouleau de la Guerre des Manuscrits de Qumrân*. SSN 4. Assen, Netherlands: Van Gorcum, 1962.

Joüon, Paul, and T. Muraoka. *A Grammar of Biblical Hebrew*. SB. Roma: Pontificio intituto biblico, 2006.

Kapelrud, Arvid Schou. *The Ras Shamra Discoveries and the Old Testament*. Norman: University of Oklahoma Press, 1963.

Keener, Craig S. *The IVP Bible Background Commentary: New Testament*. Downers Grove, IL: InterVarsity Press, 1993.

Kenny, Anthony. *A Stylometric Study of the New Testament*. Oxford: Oxford University Press, 1986.

Kirby, John C. *Ephesians, Baptism and Pentecost: An Inquiry into the Structure and Purpose of the Epistle to the Ephesians*. London: SPCK, 1968.

Knohl, Israel. "Psalm 68: Structure, Composition and Geography." *JHS* 12 (2012): 1–21.

Köstenberger, Andreas, and Richard Patterson. *Invitation to Biblical Interpretation: Exploring the Hermeneutical Triad of History, Literature, and Theology*. Grand Rapids, MI: Kregel Academic, 2011.

Kraus, Hans-Joachim. *Psalms 60–150: A Commentary*. Translated by Hilton C. Oswald. Minneapolis, MN: Fortress Press, 1993.

Kreitzer, Joseph L. *Hierapolis in the Heavens: Studies in the Letter to the Ephesians*. LNTS. London: T&T Clark, 2007.

Kümmel, Werner G., and Paul Feine. *Introduction to the New Testament*. 17th rev. ed. Translated by Howard C. Fee. Nashville, TN: Abingdon Press, 1975.

Lagrange, Marie-Joseph. *Le Livre Des Juges*. EB. Paris: Librairie Victor LeCoffre, 1903.

Larkin, William J. *Ephesians: A Handbook on the Greek Text*. BHGNT. Waco, TX: Baylor University Press, 2009.

Lauterbach, Jacob Z., ed. *Mekilta de-Rabbi Ishmael*. Translated by Jacob Z. Lauterbach. Philadelphia, PA: Jewish Publication Society, 1976.

Lehrman, S. M., ed. *Exodus*. 3rd ed. Midrash Rabbah 2. New York: Soncino Press, 1983.

Lenzi, Alan. "Assyriology and Biblical Interpretation." Pages 42–52 in *The Oxford Encyclopedia of Biblical Interpretation*. Edited by Steven L. McKenzie. New York. Oxford University Press, 2013.

LePeau, J. P. "Psalm 68: An Exegetical and Theological Study." PhD diss., University of Iowa, 1981.

Levenson, Jon Douglas. *Sinai and Zion: An Entry into the Jewish Bible*. NVBS. Minneapolis, MN: Winston Press, 1985.

Lichtheim, Miriam. *Ancient Egyptian Literature: A Book of Readings*. 3 vols. Berkeley, CA: University of California, 2006.

Liddell, Henry George, Robert Scott, Henry Stuart Jones, and Roderick McKenzie, eds. *A Greek-English Lexicon*. Oxford: Clarendon Press, 1996.

Lincicum, David. "Paul and the Testimonia: Quo Vademus?" *JETS* 51, no. 2 (2008): 297–308.
Lincoln, Andrew T. *Ephesians*. WBC 42. Dallas, TX: Word Books, 1990.
Lindemann, Andreas. *Die Aufhebung der Zeit: Geschichtsverständnis und Eschatologie im Epheserbrief*. SNT 12. Gütersloh: Gütersloher Verlagshaus, 1975.
Lindemann, Andreas. *Der Epheserbrief*. ZBK 8. Zürich: Theologischer Verlag, 1985.
Lindars, Barnabas. *New Testament Apologetic: The Doctrinal Significance of the Old Testament Quotations*. London: SCM Press, 1961.
Lona, Horacio E. *Die Eschatologie im Kolosser- und Epheserbrief*. FB 48. Würzburg: Echter Verlag, 1984.
Longenecker, Richard N. *Biblical Exegesis in the Apostolic Period*. Grand Rapids, MI: Eerdmans, 1974.
Longenecker, Richard N. *The Christology of Early Jewish Christianity*. SBT II/17. London: SCM, 1970.
Longman, Tremper, III. *Psalms: An Introduction and Commentary*. TOTC. Downers Grove, IL: IVP Academic, 2014.
Loretz, Oswald. "Der ugaritisch-hebräische Parallelismus rkb rpt // rkb b rbwt in Psalm 68,5." *Ugarit-Forschungen* 34 (2002): 521–26.
Loretz, Oswald, and Ingo Kottsieper. *Colometry in Ugaritic and Biblical Poetry: Introduction, Illustrations, and Topical Bibliography*. UBL 5. Altenberge: CIS-Verlag, 1987.
Louw, J. P., and Eugene Albert Nida. *Greek-English Lexicon of the New Testament: Based on Semantic Domains*. Swindon: United Bible Societies, 1999.
Lunde, Jonathan M., and John Anthony Dunne. "Paul's Creative and Contextual Use of Psalm 68 in Ephesians 4:8." *WTJ* 74 (2012): 99–117.
Lunde, Jonathan M., and John Anthony Dunne. "Paul's Creative and Contextual Use of Isaiah in Ephesians 5:14." *JETS* 55, no. 1 (2012): 87–110.
Macaskill, Grant. *Union with Christ in the New Testament*. Oxford: Oxford University Press, 2013.
MaGee, Gregory S. *Portrait of an Apostle: A Case for Paul's Authorship of Colossians and Ephesians*. Eugene, OR: Wipf & Stock, 2013.
Margalit, Baruch. *A Matter of "Life" and "Death": A Study of the Baal-Mot Epic (CTA 4-5-6)*. AOAT 206. Kevelaer: Butzon und Bercker, 1980.
Mathys, Hans-Peter. *Dichter und Beter: Theologen aus spätalttestamentlicher Zeit*. OBO 132. Freiburg, Schweiz: Universitätsverlag, 1994.
McNamara, Martin. *Targum and Testament Revisited: Aramaic Paraphrases of the Hebrew Bible: A Light on the New Testament*. 2nd ed. Cambridge: Eerdmans, 2010.
Meade, David G. *Pseudonymity and Canon: An Investigation into the Relationship of Authorship and Authority in Jewish and Early Christian Tradition*. WUNT 39. Tübingen: J.C.B. Mohr, 1986.
McCann, J. Clinton, ed. *The Shape and Shaping of the Psalter*. JSOTSS 159. Sheffield: JSOT Press, 1993.
McKelvey, Michael G. *Moses, David, and the High Kingship of Yahweh: A Canonical Study of Book IV of the Psalter*. GDBS 55. Piscataway, NJ: Gorgias Press, 2010.
Miller, Patrick D. "The Beginning of the Psalter." Pages 83–92 in *The Shape and Shaping of the Psalter*. Edited by J. Clinton McCann. JSOTSS 159. Sheffield: JSOT Press, 1993.
Mitchell, David C. *The Message of the Psalter: An Eschatological Programme in the Books of Psalms*. JSOTSS 252. Sheffield: Sheffield Academic Press, 1997.
Mitton, C. Leslie. *Ephesians*. London: Oliphants, 1976.

Mitton, C. Leslie. *The Epistle to the Ephesians: Its Authorship, Origin, and Purpose.* Oxford: Clarendon Press, 1951.
Moo, Douglas J. *The Old Testament in the Gospel Passion Narratives.* Sheffield: Almond Press, 1983.
Mowinckel, Sigmund. *Der achtundsechzigste Psalm.* Oslo: I kommisjon hos J. Dybwad, 1953.
Mowinckel, Sigmund. *The Psalms in Israel's Worship.* 2 vols. 1962. Reprint, Grand Rapids, MI: Eerdmans 2004.
Mowinckel, Sigmund. *Psalm Studies.* Translated by Mark E. Biddle. 2 vols. SBLHBS. Atlanta, GA: SBL Press, 2014.
Müller, Hans-Peter. "Zur Grammatik und zum religionsgeschichtlichen Hintergrund von Ps 68,5." *ZAW* 117, no. 2 (2005): 206–16.
Murphy-O'Connor, Jerome. *Paul the Letter-Writer: His World, His Options, His Skills.* Collegeville, MN: Liturgical Press, 1995.
Nemoy, Leon, ed. *The Midrash on Psalms.* Translated by William G. Braude. New Haven, CT: Yale University Press, 1959.
Nes, Jermo van. "The Problem of the Pastoral Epistles: An Important Hypothesis Reconsidered." Pages 153–69 in *Paul and Pseudepigraphy.* Edited by Stanley E. Porter and Gregory S Fewster. Leiden: Brill, 2013.
Niditch, Susan. *Judges: A Commentary.* OTL. Louisville: Westminster John Knox, 2008.
Niehaus, Jeffrey Jay. *God at Sinai: Covenant and Theophany in the Bible and Ancient Near East.* SOTBT. Grand Rapids, MI: Zondervan, 1995.
Nineham, D. E. "The Case against the Pauline Authorship." Pages 21–35 in *Studies in Ephesians.* Edited by F. L. Cross. London: A. R. Mowbray, 1956.
Noth, Martin. *The Deuteronomistic History.* JSOTSS 15. Sheffield: Sheffield Academic Press, 1981.
O'Brien, Peter T. *Colossians, Philemon.* WBC 44. Dallas, TX: Word, 1991.
O'Brien, Peter T. *The Letter to the Ephesians.* PNTC. Grand Rapids, MI: Eerdmans, 1999.
O'Connell, Robert H. *The Rhetoric of the Book of Judges.* SVT. Leiden: E. J. Brill, 1996.
O'Donnell, Matthew Brook. "Linguistic Fingerprints or Style by Numbers? The Use of Statistics in the Discussion of Authorship of New Testament Documents." Pages 206–62 in *Linguistics and the New Testament: Critical Junctures.* Edited by Stanley Porter and D. A. Carson. JSNTSS. Sheffield: Sheffield Academic Press, 1999.
Obermann, Julian. "How Baal Destroyed a Rival: A Magical Incantation Scene." *JAOS* 67 (1947): 195–208.
Obermann, Julian. *Ugaritic Mythology: A Study of its Leading Motifs.* New Haven, CT: Yale University Press, 1948.
Oesterley, W. O. E. *The Psalms.* 2 vols. London: Society for Promoting Christian Knowledge, 1939.
Olshausen, Justus. *Die Psalmen.* KEHAT. Leipzig: S. Hirzel, 1853.
Ouro, Roberto. "Similarities and Differences between the Old Testament and the Ancient Near Eastern Texts." *Andrews University Seminary Studies* 49, no. 1 (2011): 5–32.
Parker, Simon B., ed. *Ugaritic Narrative Poetry.* WAW 9. Atlanta, GA: Scholars Press, 1997.
Percy, Ernst. *Die Probleme der Kolosser- und Epheserbriefe.* Lund: C. W. K. Gleerup, 1946.
Perkins, Pheme. *Ephesians.* Nashville, TN: Abingdon, 1997.
Peters, John P. "Notes on Some Difficult Passages in the Old Testament." *JBL* 11, no. 1 (1892): 38–52.
Peters, Melvin K. H. "Review of Eschatology in the Greek Psalter, by Joachim Schaper." *JBL* 116 (1997): 350–53.

Pfeiffer, Henrik. *Jahwes Kommen von Süden: Jdc 5, Hab 3, Dtn 33, und Ps 68 in ihrem literatur- und theologiegeschichtlichen Umfeld*. FRLANT 211. Göttingen: Vandenhoeck & Ruprecht, 2005.

Pietersma, Albert. "Review of Eschatology in the Greek Psalter, by Joachim Schaper." *BO* 54 (1997): 185–90.

Pickup, Martin. "New Testament Interpretation of the Old Testament: The Theological Rationale of Midrashic Exegesis." *JETS* 51, no. 2 (2008): 353–81.

Pitts, Andrew W. "Style and Pseudonymity in Pauline Authorship: A Register Based Confirguration." Pages 113–52 in *Paul and Pseudepigraphy*. Edited by Stanley E. Porter and Gregory P. Fewster. PAST 8. Leiden: Brill, 2013.

van der Ploeg, J. *Le Rouleau de la Guerre*. STDJ 2. Leiden: Brill, 1959.

Pokorný, Petr. *Der Brief des Paulus an die Epheser*. THNT. Leipzig: Evangelische Verlagsanstalt, 1992.

Pokorný, Petr. *Der Epheserbrief und die Gnosis: Die Bedeutung des Haupt-Glieder-Gedankens in der entstehenden Kirche*. Berlin: Evangelische Verlagsanstalt, 1965.

von Rad, Gerhard. *Old Testament Theology*. Translated by D. M. G. Stalker. 2 vols. OTL. Louisville, KY: Westminster John Knox Press, 1965.

Rahlfs, Alfred. *Septuaginta: id est Vetus Testamentum graece iuxta LXX interpretes*. Stuttgart, Deutsche Bibelgesellschaft, 1935.

Reed, Jeffrey T. *A Discourse Analysis of Philippians: Method and Rhetoric in the Debate over Literary Integrity*. JSNTSS 136. Sheffield: Sheffield Academic Press, 1997.

Reicke, Bo. *Re-examining Paul's Letters: The History of the Pauline Correspondence*. Edited by David P. Moessner and Ingalisa Reicke. Harrisburg, PA: Trinity Press International, 2001.

Reuss, Eduard. *Der acht-und-sechzigste Psalm: Ein Denkmal exegetischer Noth und Kunst zu Ehren unsrer ganzen Zunft*. Jena: Friedrich Mauke, 1851.

Richards, E. Randolph. *Paul and First-Century Letter Writing: Secretaries, Composition, and Collection*. Downers Grove, IL: InterVarsity Press, 2004.

Roberts, J. J. M. "Mowinckel's Enthronement Festival: A Review." Pages 97–115 in *The Book of Psalms: Composition and Reception*. Edited by Peter W. Flint and Patrick Miller Jr. Boston, MA: Brill, 2005.

Robertson, A. T. *A Grammar of the Greek New Testament in the Light of Historical Research*, 3rd ed. London: Hodder & Stoughton, 1919.

Robertson, David A. *Linguistic Evidence in Dating Early Hebrew Poetry*. SBLDS 3. Missoula, MT: Society of Biblical Literature, 1972.

Roller, Otto. *Das Formular der Paulinischen Briefe: Ein Beitrag zur Lehre vom antike Briefe*. BWANT. Stuttgart: W. Kohlhammer, 1933.

Rubinkiewicz, Ryszard. "Ps 68:19 (Eph 4:8) Another Textual Tradition or Targum?" *NovT* 17, no. 3 (1975): 219–24.

Ruess, Eduard. *Der acht-und-sechzigste Psalm: Ein Denkmal exegetischer Noth und Kunst zu Ehren unsrer ganzen Zunft*. Jena: Friedrich Mauke, 1851.

Rufinus, and J. N. D. Kelly. *Rufinus: A Commentary on the Apostles' Creed*. Ancient Christian Writers 20. New York: Newman Press, 1955.

Sailhamer, John. *The Pentateuch as Narrative: A Biblical-Theological Commentary*. Grand Rapids, MI: Zondervan, 1992.

Salvesen, Alison. "Review of Eschatology in the Greek Psalter, by Joachim Schaper." *JTS* 47, no. 2 (1996): 580–83.

Sarna, Nahum M. *Exodus* שמות: *The Traditional Hebrew Text with the New JPS Translation*. JPSTC. Philadelphia, PA: Jewish Publication Society, 1991.

Scacewater, Todd A., ed. *Discourse Analysis of the New Testament Writings.* Dallas, TX: Fontes Press, forthcoming.

Scacewater, Todd A. "The Literary Unity of 1QM and Its Three Stage War." *RevQ* 27, no. 2 (2015): 225–48.

Scacewater, Todd A. "The Predictive Nature of Typology in John 12:37–43." *WTJ* 75, no. 1 (2013): 129–43.

Schaper, Joachim. *Eschatology in the Greek Psalter.* WUNT II/76. Tübingen: Mohr Siebeck, 1995.

Scherer, Andreas. *Überlieferungen von Religion und Krieg: Exegetische und religionsgeschichtliche Untersuchungen zu Richter 3–8 und verwandten Texten.* WMANT 105. Neukirchen-Vluyn: Neukirchener, 2005.

Schlier, Heinrich. *Der Brief an die Epheser: Ein Kommentar.* Düsseldorf: Patmos, 1957.

Schlier, Heinrich. *Christus und die Kirche im Epheserbrief.* BHT 6. Tübingen: Mohr Siebeck, 1930.

Schmidt, Hans. *Die Psalmen.* HBAT I 15. Tübingen: Mohr Siebeck, 1934.

Schnackenburg, Rudolf. *Der Brief an die Epheser.* EKKNT. Zürich: Benziger, 1982.

Schultz, Brian. *Conquering the World: The War Scroll (1QM) Reconsidered.* STDJ 76. Leiden: Brill, 2009.

Schweizer, Eduard. *Der Brief an die Kolosser.* EKKNT. Zürich: Benziger, 1994.

Schwindt, Rainer. *Das Weltbild des Epheserbriefes: Eine religionsgeschichtlich-exegetische Studie.* WUNT 148. Tübingen: Mohr Siebeck, 2002.

Sheppard, Gerald T. *Wisdom as a Hermeneutical Construct: A Study in the Sapientializing of the Old Testament.* BZAW 151. New York, NY: Walter de Gruyter, 1980.

Siegert, Folker. "Review of Eschatology in the Greek Psalter, by Joachim Schaper." *TLZ* 122 (1997): 39–41.

Simpson, E. K., and F. F. Bruce. *Commentary on the Epistles to the Ephesians and the Colossians.* NICNT. Grand Rapids, MI: Eerdmans, 1957.

Singer, P. N., ed. *Galen: Selected Works.* Oxford: Oxford University Press, 1997.

Smith, Gary V. "Paul's Use of Psalm 68:18 in Ephesians 4:8." *JETS* 18, no. 3 (1975): 181–89.

Smith, Mark S. *The Ugaritic Baal Cycle.* SVT 55. Leiden: E.J. Brill, 1994.

von Soden, H., ed. *Hand-Kommentar zum Neuen Testament, Vol. 3: Die Briefe an die Kolosser, Epheser, Philemon; die Pastoralbriefe.* Freiburg: Mohr, 1893.

Stanley, Christopher D. *Arguing with Scripture: The Rhetoric of Quotations in the Letters of Paul.* New York: T&T Clark International, 2004.

Staples, Shelley, Jesse Egbert, Douglas Biber, and Susan Conrad. "Register Variation: A Corpus Approach." Pages 505–25 in *The Handbook of Discourse Anlaysis.* 2nd ed. Edited by Deborah Tannen, Heidi E. Hamilton, and Deborah Schiffrin. Malden, MA: Blackwell, 2015.

Stec, David M. *The Targum of Psalms: Translated, with a Critical Introduction, Apparatus, and Notes.* ArBib 16. Collegeville, MN: Liturgical Press, 2004.

Stettler, Hanna. *Heiligung bei Paulus: Ein Beitrag aus biblisch-theologischer Sicht.* WUNT II/368. Tübingen: Mohr Siebeck, 2014.

Strack, Hermann Leberecht. *Introduction to the Talmud and Midrash.* New York: Atheneum, 1969.

Strack, Hermann, and Paul Billerbeck. *Kommentar Zum Neuen Testament aus Talmud und Midrasch.* 4 vols. München: C. H. Beck, 1922–1928.

Strack, H. L., and G. Stemberger, *Introduction to the Talmud and Midrash.* Translated by Markus Bockmuehl. Edinburgh: T&T Clark, 1991.

Strawn, Brent A. "Comparative Approaches: History, Theory and the Image of God." Pages 129–35 in *Method Matters: Essays on the Interpretation of the Hebrew Bible in Honor of David L. Petersen*. Edited by Joel M. LeMon and Kent H. Richards. SBLRBS 56. Atlanta, GA: Society of Biblical Literature, 2009.

Sundberg, Albert C. Jr. "On Testimonies." *NovT* 3 (1959): 268–81.

Sundberg, Albert C. Jr., "Response against C. H. Dodd's View: On Testimonies." Pages 182–94 in *The Right Doctrine from the Wrong Texts: Essays on the Old Testament in the New*. Edited by G. K. Beale. Grand Rapids, MI: Baker Books, 1994.

Tadmor, Hayim, and Shigeo Yamada, eds. *The Royal Inscriptions of Tiglath-pileser III (744-727 BC) and Shalmaneser V (726-722 BC), Kings of Assyria*. RINAP 1. Winona Lake, IN: Eisenbrauns, 2011.

Tate, Marvin E. *Psalms 51–100*. WBC 20. Dallas, TX: Word Books, 1990.

Taylor, J. Glen. "The Song of Deborah and Two Canaanite Goddesses." *JSOT* 23 (1982): 99–108.

Taylor, Richard A. "The Use of Psalm 68:18 in Ephesians 4:8 in Light of the Ancient Versions." *BS* 148, no. 591 (1991): 319–36.

Thackeray, H. St J. *The Septuagint and Jewish Worship: A Study in Origins*. London: Oxford University Press, 1921.

Thayer, Joseph Henry. *A Greek-English Lexicon of the New Testament*. Electronic edition. International Bible Translators, 1998–2000.

Tigay, Jeffrey H. *Deuteronomy* דברים: *The Traditional Hebrew Text with the New JPS Translation*. Philadelphia, PA: Jewish Publication Society, 1996.

Tilling, Chris. *Paul's Divine Christology*. WUNT II/323. Tübingen: Mohr Siebeck, 2012.

Terrien, Samuel L. *The Psalms: Strophic Structure and Theological Commentary*. ECC. Grand Rapids, MI: Eerdmans, 2003.

Thielman, Frank "Ephesians." Pages 813–34 in *Commentary on the New Testament Use of the Old Testament*. Edited by G. K. Beale and D. A. Carson. Grand Rapids, MI: Baker Academic, 2007.

Toom, Tarmo. "Marcellus of Ancyra and Priscillian of Avila: Their Theologies and Creeds." *Vigiliae Christianae* 68 (2014): 60–81.

Trigg, Joseph. "The Apostolic Fathers and Apologists." Pages 304–33 in *The Ancient Period*. Edited by Alan J. Hauser and Duane Frederick Watson. HBI. Grand Rapids, MI: Eerdmans, 2003.

Trimm, Charlie. *"YHWH Fights for Them!": The Divine Warrior in the Exodus Narrative*. GBS 58. Piscataway, NJ: Gorgias Press, 2014.

Usteri, Leonhard. *Entwickelung des paulinischen Lehrbegriffes mit Hinsicht auf die übrigen Schriften des Neuen Testamentes: Ein exegetisch-dogmatischer Versuch*. Zürich: Orell, Füssli, und Compagnie, 1824.

van der Horst, P. W. "Review of Eschatology in the Greek Psalter, by Joachim Schaper." *JSJPHRP* 28, no. 1 (1997): 123–24.

VanderKam, James C. "Sinai Revisited." Pages 44–60 in *Biblical Interpretation at Qumran*. Edited by Matthias Henze. SDSSRL. Grand Rapids, MI: Eerdmans, 2005.

VanGemeren, Willem, ed. *New International Dictionary of Old Testament Theology & Exegesis*. 5 vols. Grand Rapids, MI: Zondervan, 1997.

van Roon, A. *The Authenticity of Ephesians*. SNT 39. Leiden: Brill, 1975.

Wallace, Daniel B. *Greek Grammar beyond the Basics: An Exegetical Syntax of the New Testament*. Grand Rapids, MI: Zondervan, 1996.

Waltke, Bruce K., and Michael Patrick O'Connor. *An Introduction to Biblical Hebrew Syntax*. Winona Lake, IN: Eisenbrauns, 1990.

Walton, John H. "Psalms: A Cantata about the Davidic Covenant." *JETS* 34, no. 1 (1991): 21-31.
Watts, James W. *Psalm and Story: Inset Hymns in Hebrew Narrative*. JSOTSS 139. Sheffield: JSOT Press, 1992.
Webb, Barry G. *The Book of Judges: An Integrated Reading*. JSOTSS 46. Sheffield: Sheffield Academic Press, 1987.
Weiser, Artur. *The Psalms: A Commentary*. OTL. Philadelphia, PA: Westminster Press, 1962.
Werner, John R. "Discourse Analysis of the Greek New Testament." Pages 213-33 in *The New Testament Student and His Field*. Edited by John H. Skilton. Phillipsburg, NJ: Presbyterian and Reformed, 1982.
Wicks, Jared. "Christ's Saving Descent to the Dead: Early Witnesses from Ignatius of Antioch to Origen." *ProEccl* 17, no. 3 (2008): 281-309.
Wilder, William N. "The Use (or Abuse) of Power in High Places: Gifts Given and Received in Isaiah, Psalm 68, and Ephesians 4:8." *BBR* 20, no. 2 (2010): 185-99.
Wilson, Gerald Henry. *The Editing of the Hebrew Paslter*. SBLDS. Chico, CA: Scholars Press, 1985.
Wilson, Gerald Henry. "King, Messiah, and the Reign of God." Pages 396-405 in *The Book of Psalms: Composition and Reception*. Edited by Peter W. Flint and Patrick D. Miller Jr. SVT 99. Boston, MA: Brill, 2005.
Wilson, Gerald Henry. "The Qumran Psalms Manuscripts and the Consecutive Arrangement of Psalms in the Hebrew Psalter." *CBQ* 45, no. 3 (1983): 377-88.
Wintermute, O. S. "Apocalypse of Elijah: A New Translation and Introduction." Pages 721-53 in *The Old Testament Pseudepigrapha*. Vol. 1. Edited by James H. Charlesworth. Peabody, MA: Hendrickson, 1983.
Wright, John W. "Review of Eschatology in the Greek Psalter, by Joachim Schaper." *CBQ* 59, no. 2 (1997): 357-59.
Wright, N. T. *The Climax of the Covenant: Christ and the Law in Pauline Theology*. Minneapolis, MN: Fortress Press, 1992.
Wright, N. T. *Jesus and the Victory of God*. COQG 2. Philadelphia, PA: Fortress, 1996.
Wright, N. T. *The New Testament and the People of God*. Minneapolis, MN: Fortress Press, 1992.
Wright, W. *Apocryphal Acts of the Apostles*. 8 vols. Edinburgh: Williams and Norgate, 1871.
Wyatt, N. *Religious Texts from Ugarit*. 2nd ed. New York: Sheffield Academic Press, 2002.
Yadin, Yigael. *The Scroll of the War of the Sons of Light against the Sons of Darkness*. London: Oxford University Press, 1962.
Younger, K. Lawson. "The Figurative Aspect and the Contextual Method in the Evaluation of the Solomonic Empire (1 Kings 1-11)." Pages 157-75 in *The Bible in Three Dimensions: Essays in Celebration of Forty Years of Biblical Studies in the University of Sheffield*. Edited by David J. A. Clines, Stephen E. Fowl, and Stanley E. Porter. JSOTSS 87. Sheffield: Sheffield University Press, 1990.
Zahn, Theodor. *Introduction to the New Testament*. 3 vols. Translated by Melancthon Williams Jacobus, John Moore Trout, Charles Snow Thayer, William Arnot Mather, Lewis Hodous, Edward Strong Worcester, William H. Worrell, and Rowland Backus Dodge. Edinburgh: T&T Clark, 1909.
Zenger, Erich. "The Composition and Theology of the Fifth Book of Psalms, Psalms 107-145." *JSOT* 80 (1998): 77-102.

Zerwick, Max. *The Epistle to the Ephesians.* Translated by Kevin Smyth. New York: Herder & Herder, 1969.

Zhmud, Leonid. *Wissenschaft, Philosophie und Religion im frühen Pythagoreismus.* Berlin: Akademie Verlag, 1997.

Scripture Index

Genesis		15:2	38
1–2	88	15:2–3	86
1–3	3	15:3	73, 110, 112
2:23	88	15:4–10	86
2:24	88	15:5	76
3	88	15:6	84
4	88	15:8	73
12–22	3	15:9	73, 76, 84
15:9	122	15:10	73, 76
18	97	15:11	74, 86
18:5	122	15:12	76, 84
23:6	44	15:12–17	86
26:10	114	15:13	73, 76
27:13	122	15:13–16	84
27:29	114	15:13–17	87
30:8	44	15:13–18	86
37:10	114	15:14–16	68, 73
49	71, 75, 87–8, 107, 112	15:15	76
49:1	87–8	15:16	76
49:8	112, 114–15	15:17	61–2, 68, 76–7
49:26	87	15:17–18	39, 44, 73, 76, 87, 132
		15:18	68, 76
Exodus		15:19	75
1–14	62	15:20–21	41, 76, 79–80, 84, 88
3:12	77	15:21	76–7
3:14	16	19	92, 97, 99
3:22	48	19:3	92–3, 96
9:33–34	67	19:16	39
11:2–3	48	20:2	95
12:35–36	48	20:21	98
14:21	73	23:27	112
14:28	84	24:15–31:18	60
14:29	75	25	49
14:30	84	25:1–2	47
14–15	84	25:2–3	49
15	33, 71, 73–8, 80, 83–4, 86–8, 107, 109, 115	29:45–46	62
		31:3	28
15:1	64, 86	33:13	98
15:1–2	74	33:16	87
15:1–3	76	34:29–40:38	60
15:1–18	68, 75, 77, 86	35	49

35:5	49	32:6	62
35:21–29	47	32:29	112
36:1	28	32:39	87, 113, 115
36:6	47	32:42	113–15
40:34–35	132	32–33	87–8, 107, 112–13
		33	64–5, 71–2, 75
Leviticus		33:1–3	94
7:14	49	33:2	40, 65–6, 85, 87, 92, 114
15:25	95		
16:3	95	33:5	62
19:14	95	33:11	87, 113, 115
21:20	92	33:20	88
		33:26	38, 64–6, 87
Numbers		33:26–27	66
5:9	49	33:27–29	65
8:6–11	126	33:29	115
8:19	126		
10:33	37	Joshua	
10:35	37, 83, 95	7:8	112
17:11–13	94	7:12	112
18:6	126	7:21	48
21:1	110	8:27	48
23–24	75, 87–8, 107, 112	12:4–5	43
24	71, 88, 112–13	13:18	40
24:7	105	14:15	96
24:8	87, 112–13, 115		
24:14	87–8	Judges	
24:17	87, 105, 110, 113, 115	3–8	78
24:17–19	112	4	74, 78–9
24:18	112, 114–15	4:1–3	78
28:26–31	99	4:9	86
		4:16	84
Deuteronomy		4:17	78
3:1–10	43	4:23–24	84
4:4	80	4–5	41, 78, 80, 84, 86
4:20	40	5	41, 71, 73–5, 78–80, 83, 84–7, 96, 107, 110, 115
4:21	40		
4:38	40		
4:47–48	43	5:2–3	74
11:11	66–7	5:2–5	78–9
12	61	5:2–11	79
16:9	99	5:3	84
16:9–12	99	5:4	87
17	102	5:4–5	40, 74, 77, 84
20:2–5	108	5:5	39, 92
21:10	110	5:6–11	85
28–32	3	5:6–30	78, 85
31:28	88	5:9–11	79
31:29	87–8	5:11–18	79

5:12	74, 85–6, 106–12, 115, 126, 128	1 Chronicles	
		6:24	135
5:13	79	11:4–9	82
5:15–17	74	11:8–9	82
5:16	41	11:9	82
5:19	41, 74, 84	13	82
5:19–31	79	13:1	83
5:20–21	74	13:5	82
5:20–27	74	26:27	25, 47
5:21	74	29	49
5:23	79	29:2–5	47
5:24	41	29:5–17	47
5:24–25	74	29:6–9	47
5:26	84, 113	29:9	47
5:28–30	74	29:14	47
5:30	41, 84, 110, 115	29:16	47
5:31	74, 78–9, 85		
8:24–25	48	2 Chronicles	
11:34	41, 79–80	6:37–38	110
		28:17	110
1 Samuel			
2:10	137	Ezra	
8:7	77	1–6	60
12:12	77	3:12	132
14:15	44	7:15–16	47
14:30	48		
18:6–8	41, 79–80	Job	
		26:9	92, 94
2 Samuel		39:18	64
1:19–27	75		
6	82	Psalms	
6:1–5	83	1	102
6:5	82	1–2	102–4
6:17	83	1–41	102
7:1	62	2	34, 102
11:11	82	2:8	103
12:26–31	82	8	93
22	75	8:2	95
22:11	64	8:5 MT	92
22:41	112	8:5–9 MT	93
		8:6	145
1 Kings		10:16	62
1–8	60	16:10	137
8:11	132	18	75
		18:7	39
2 Kings		18:7–15	77
18:21	68	18:8–12	39
		18:11	64
		18:41	112

20	33	67:5	104
22	3	67:6	104
24	33	67:8	104
24:8–10	62	67:17 LXX	27, 30
28:6 LXX	105	67:19 LXX	129
28:9	40	68	1, 2, 5–9, 27–8, 30,
29	33, 69		35–6, 40–1, 43, 46,
33	33		48–52, 58, 61–2,
33:12	40		64–6, 68–9, 71–5, 78,
36:7	44		80–2, 85–7, 89, 91,
42:5	103		96–7, 99–102, 104–9,
42:6	103		111, 113–17, 119,
42:10	103		124, 127–8, 133–4,
42:10–11	103		139–40, 145, 148, 152,
42:12	103		155, 158
42–43	102–3	68:1	37, 110, 112
42–72	102	68:1–19	36, 49–51
43:1	103	68:2	37–8
43:2	103	68:2–3	74
43:3	103	68:2–4	149
43:5	103	68:2–8	121
44:4	62	68:3	37
46	33	63:4	37, 63
47	33	68:4–5	74, 104
47:3	46	68:4–19	37
47:6	46	68:5	38, 62–6, 81, 95
47:8	46	68:5–7	38–9, 104
48	33	68:6	38
49:9	46	68:6–7	65
62:10 LXX	144	68:6–15	104
65	104	68:7	38, 104
65:2	104	68:7–8	63, 84
65:5	104	68:7–9	77
65:6	104	68:7–14	64
65:9	104	68:8	39, 67
65:10–14	104	68:8–9	39
65–67	104	68:8–10	63
65–68	102, 104	68:8–11	39
66	104	68:9	39, 45, 65
66:1–2	104	68:10	40, 66–7, 74, 81, 95
66:3	104	68:10–11	39–40, 105
66:4	104, 114	68:11	40–1, 81
66:8	104	68:12	41, 81, 84, 105
66:13–15	104	68:12–14	89
66:20	104	68:12–15	40–1, 44, 65, 126
67	104	68:13	41, 48, 74, 95, 105,
67:3	104		110, 112, 115
67:4	104	68:13–15	41
67:6	104	68:14	41

68:15	44, 67, 105	69	3
68:15–17	77	70:20 LXX	144
68:16	42–4, 92–3, 96	71	103
68:16–19	1, 36, 41, 155	72	33, 103
68:17	27, 42–6, 74, 87, 92–6, 132	72:8	103
		74:2	40
68:17–19	42, 82, 91, 93–4, 97, 115	74:12	62
		75	33
68:18	45–6, 62, 64–6, 87, 92–3, 114	76	33
		76:6	64
68:18–19	46, 65, 74, 82, 92, 96, 120	77:19	39
		78:69	61
68:19	1, 2, 4–5, 7–9, 17–18, 20–1, 24, 26, 30, 36, 42, 45–6, 48–9, 51, 71, 74, 83–7, 91–97, 104, 107, 110–12, 115, 119–23, 125–36, 140–1, 145–53, 155–7	81	33
		84	33
		87:4	68
		89	33–4
		89:9	109
		89:13	43
		93	33
68:19–36	80, 89	95:3	62
68:20	65, 86, 104, 121	95–100	33
68:20–21	74	99:9	109
68:20–33	37	108–110	34
68:20–36	36, 133	110:1	1, 135
68:21	67, 81	111–117	34
68:22	43, 87, 89, 113–15	114	33
68:23	67, 89	116:47	34
68:24	81, 124	117	26, 34
68:25	68, 82, 89	117:22 LXX	26
68:25–26	80	118:15–16	112
68:25–28	105	120–134	34
68:26	88–9, 94	121:1	61
68:26–27	105	138:15	144
68:27	104	138–145	34
68:28	81–2, 89	139:8	145
68:30	44, 46, 67–8, 74, 81–2, 88, 104–5, 127, 132	145	34
		145:11	109
68:31	81–2, 105–6, 116	146–150	34
68:32	88, 132	149	33
68:32–35	63		
68:33	37, 63, 65, 81, 104, 132	Proverbs	
		14:9	114
68:33–36	37, 74, 88, 149	21:22	96
68:34	38, 65, 68, 81, 121, 142		
		Song of Songs	
68:34–35	62–3, 65–6	7:8	95
68:35	65, 104	8:11	95
68:36	37, 81–2, 104, 127, 132, 142		

Isaiah

2:1–4	104
2:2	96
13:13	39
14:15	144
18:4	109
19:1	64
19:6	68
26:19	131
28:16	26
30:7	68
36:6–7	68
40:3	64
40–66	3, 6, 64
51:3	44
51:9	68
57:15	96
59:16–17	131
60:1–2	131
60:11–14	114
60:14	114

Jeremiah

2:6	64
12:7	38
18:17	112
51:5	114
51:21	64

Lamentations

5:3	38

Ezekiel

26:20	144
32:18	144
29:6	68
34:31	75
38:9	109
38:15–16	109
44:30	49

Daniel

7–12	3

Hosea

8:1	38
9:15	38
11:1	38

Joel

2:28–29	120–1
2–3	3

Jonah

3:3	44

Micah

4:1–4	104
5:7	109

Habakkuk

3:3–15	77
3:8	64

Haggai

2:9	132

Zechariah

9–14	3

Malachi

3:22	93

Matthew

27:52–53	120

John

1:17	124
4:21	150
14:15–18	141
20:22	120
20:25	133

Acts

2	100, 121, 147
2:1–12	140
2:33	140–1
13:2	16
19	151
19:1–21	10
19:8	146
19:9–10	15
19:11–19	151
19:27	151
20:17–38	10, 15
28:17	16

Romans

1:7	16
5:14	133
6:17	133

8:9	142	2:11–22	14, 19
8:9–10	141	2:13–18	13
12:1	19	2:18	19
12:6	21–2	2:19–22	128
13:1	16	2:20	26, 28
15:10	17	2:21	25, 28
		2:21–22	24–5, 130, 150
1 Corinthians		2:22	19, 25, 134
1:28–29	16	3:1	19
3:16	26, 150	3:1–21	19
6:19	150	3:2	9, 15, 133, 145, 150
8:6	149	3:2–13	19
10:6	133	3:3	135
10:11	133, 150	3:4	135
12:11	25	3:4–8	13
12:28	14, 21–2, 25	3:5	13
15:20	149	3:9	133, 135, 145, 150
15:26	152	3:10	139, 145
15:45	141	3:19	26
15:54–57	152	3:21	19
		4	91, 127, 146
2 Corinthians		4:1	18–19
1:1	16	4:1–3	18–19
3:17	141	4:1–6	19–21
5:15–21	149	4:1–16	8–9, 18–20, 23
5:17	151	4:2	19
6:2	17	4:2–3	19
6:16	26, 150	4:3	18
		4:3–4	25
Galatians		4:4–6	18–19
1:1	16	4:5	19
3:16	17	4:7	1, 17, 19–22, 24, 133, 157
6:15	151		
		4:7–10	19–21, 23
Ephesians		4:7–11	26, 142
1:1	15, 17	4:7–16	5, 7–8, 13, 18–21, 24, 27–8, 30, 46, 124–5, 127, 129–30, 146–7, 149–50, 155
1:3	142		
1:9	135		
1:10	133, 145, 150		
1:13–14	148		
1:15–16	9, 15	4:8	1, 2, 4–5, 8–9, 17–18, 21, 24, 30, 71, 94, 119–20, 122, 124–5, 128–32, 134–6, 138, 140, 148, 155–8
1:20–22	131, 145		
1:20–23	127		
1:21	131		
1:21–22	150	4:8–10	5, 8, 10, 18, 131, 147–8, 151–2, 157
1:22	26, 146		
1:23	25	4:9	135–44, 147, 157–8
2	127	4:9–10	5, 8–9, 21, 119, 129, 135–41, 143, 145–8, 157
2:2	139, 151		
2:7	141		

4:10	19, 144–5, 147	3:1	19
4:11	19, 21–4, 140	4	14
4:11–13	150	4:13	17
4:11–16	19–24, 28–9, 127–8, 150, 152, 155	**1 Thessalonians**	
4:12	19, 21–4	1:7	133
4:12–13	22	5:12	14
4:12–16	25		
4:13	18–19, 23	**2 Thessalonians**	
4:14	23	3:9	133
4:14–15	23		
4:15	19–20, 23–4, 26, 28	**Titus**	
4:15–16	21, 23	2:7	133
4:16	18–20, 22–4, 28		
4:17	18	**Philemon**	
4:21	15	2	14
5:14	17, 131	3:17	133
5:18	26		
5:32	135	**Hebrews**	
6:10	131	3:7	17
6:11–18	131	10:5	17
6:11	131		
6:12	131	**James**	
6:19	135	4:6	17
Philippians		**1 Peter**	
1:1	14, 16	1:1	16
2:6–11	139, 146	1:11	142
2:9	139	2:5	26
2:10	137, 141–2	5:3	133
2:11	132		
		Strom. 6.15	99
Colossians			
1:9	28	**1 Esdras**	
1:10	28	4:29	135
1:18	27	4:45	25
1:18–20	27	4:51	25
1:19	150		
1:22–23	28	**1 Maccabees**	
1:19	27–8, 30	5:45–54	100
1:20	151		
2:7	28	**2 Maccabees**	
2:8	30	12:27–32	100
2:9	27–8, 150		
2:10	28, 30	**Prayer of Manasseh**	
2:15	131, 150	13	144
2:16	28		
2:16–23	28	**1 Enoch**	
2:18	29–30	6:6	43
2:19	29		

2 Baruch		*Bib. Ant.* 19:10–12	99
4:2–7	97–8		
59:3–11	97–8	Mishnah	
		m. Meg. 3:5	99
Jubilees			
1:1	100	Talmud	
1:2–4	100	b. Bat. 14b	78
1:5	101	b. Bat. 14b–15a	11
6:1	101	b. Šabb 88–89a	92–4
6:1–16	101	b. Meg. 31a	99–101
16:13	101	b. Pesaḥ 68b	99–101
6:17–22	100		
14:10–20	101	Targums	
15:1	100	*Tehillim* 68:15	68
15:1–16	101		
16:13	101	Dead Sea Scrolls	
22:1–2	101	1Q16	105–6, 116
		CD VII, 18–21	110
4 Ezra		1QM I	107–8
3:17–18	39	1QM I–II	107
		1QM III–IX	107–8
Testament of Benjamin		1QM V, 1–2	110
11.2	105	1QM X, 2–5	108
		1QM X–XIV	107–8
Testament of Judah		1QM XI, 6–7	112–13
24.1	105	1QM XII	114
		1QM XII, 1	114
Testament of Dan		1QM XII, 2	115
5.2	125	1QM XII, 7–10	108
		1QM XII, 7–16	106–8, 115
Apocalypse of Elijah		1QM XII, 8–9	110
1:4	121	1QM XII, 10	107, 110–12
		1QM XII, 10–11	110
Josephus		1QM XII, 10–13	109
Ag. Ap. 1.37–42	11	1QM XII, 11	112, 114
Ant. 4.8.48	99	1QM XII, 11–12	113–14
		1QM XII, 12–13	115
Philo		1QM XII, 13–16	111
Somn. 1.36	97	1QM XII, 14	114–15
Mut. 7	97	1QM XII, 14–15	114
Mos. 1.158	97–8	1QM XV–XIX	107–8
Mos. 1.159	98	1QM XVIII, 11	108
QE. 2.27–52	97	1QM XVIII, 12	108
QG. 4.29	97–8	1QM XIX	106, 108
Dec. 9	100	4Q171	106
Dec. 11	100	4Q173	106
		4Q285	109
Pseudo-Philo		4Q492	106
Bib. Ant. 11:15	97–8	11Q5 XXVII, 2–11	106
Bib. Ant. 12:1	98		

Subject Index

atonement 150, 152
Apostles' Creed 5, 136, 137, 157–8

Christology 5, 148–9

David (King) 31–34, 37, 47–8, 76–7, 79–83, 102–4, 106, 116
Descent of Christ 5, 120, 124, 129, 135–48

eschatology 87–9, 106–7, 112–13, 134, 149
Ephesians
  authorship 9–14
  destination 15–17
  gifts to the church 21–2
  Gnosticism 124
Exodus 15
  date 75–8
  as victory song 73–4

Judges 5
  date 78–80
  as victory song 74
  use of Exod 15 83–4

Midrash pesher 123, 124, 127
Moses 37, 42, 47–8, 71, 73, 76–8, 84, 88, 91–101, 118–19, 123–5, 127, 140

Paul's Use of Ps 68
  Eadie 122
  Foord 128
  form of citation 129–130, 134–5
  Gombis 127
  Harris 125
  Lindars 125
  Lunde and Dunne 127
  Patristics 120–2
  prophetic nature 132–4
  Schwindt 126
  Smith, Gary 126
  thematic coherence 130–1

prophecy 2, 4, 77, 86–8, 106, 110, 112–13, 120–3, 130, 134–5, 145, 152
Psalms
  canonical method 33–5
  Gunkel 31–2
  Mowinckel 32–3
Psalm 68
  Baal traditions 62–9
  canonical placement 102–4
  date 80–3
  in Dead Sea Scrolls 105–15
  Exodus 38–9
  gifts 46–9
  Harris, Hall 97–101
  latter days 87–9
  Mosaic interpretation 91–7
  mountains 42–5
  use of Deut 33 64–6
  use of Judg 5 and Exod 15 84–7
  in Septuagint 104–5
  Sinai 45–6
  as victory song 74, 82
pseudepigraphy 10–12, 14

spiritual powers 5, 28, 131, 145, 146, 149, 151

Targum Psalms 38–9, 42, 68, 88–94, 97, 123–5, 140
temple
  Artemis 151–2
  church 28, 149–50, 155
  Colossians 26–30
  Ephesians 24–6
  heavenly 29–30, 127
temple building
  Aramaen texts 59–60
  Assyrian texts 53–5
  Baal Cycle 55–8
  Egyptian texts 52–3
  Enuma Eliš 58–9

typology 156–7

use of the Old Testament
    Christocentricity 4–5
    contextual use 3–4
    testimonia 2–3
    transfer of meaning 6–8

victory songs
    characteristics 71–5, 79, 82–4, 86, 88, 112, 119

War Scroll (1QM)
    literary structure 107–8
    pesher 105–6
    use of Ps 68 106–15

www.ingramcontent.com/pod-product-compliance
Lightning Source LLC
Chambersburg PA
CBHW070639300426
44111CB00013B/2177